VIRGIN MOTHER, MAIDEN QUEEN

Elizabeth I in her coronation robes, c.1559. Artist unknown.
By courtesy of the Trustees of the National Portrait Gallery, London.

Virgin Mother, Maiden Queen

Elizabeth I and the Cult of the Virgin Mary

Helen Hackett
Lecturer in the Department of English
University College London

St. Martin's Press   New York

First published in the United States of America in 1995

Printed in Great Britain

ISBN 0–312–12481–3

Library of Congress Cataloging-in-Publication Data
Hackett, Helen.
Virgin mother, maiden queen : Elizabeth I and the cult of the
Virgin Mary / Helen Hackett.
p. cm.
Includes bibliographical references (p.   ) and index.
ISBN 0–312–12481–3 (hardcover)
1. Elizabeth I, Queen of England, 1533–1603. 2. Virginity–
–Religious aspects—Christianity—History of doctrines—16th
century. 3. Mary, Blessed Virgin, Saint—History of doctrines—16th
century. 4. Great Britain—History—Elizabeth, 1558–1603. 5. Mary,
Blessed Virgin, Saint—Cult—England. 6. England, Church
history—16th century. 7. Queens—Great Britain—Biography.
I. Title.
DA356.H33 1995
942.05′5′092—dc20   94–34701
                                                                CIP

In loving memory of Edward Cobb

Contents

Abbreviations

BCP	*Book of Common Prayer*
BL	British Library
Bod.	Bodleian Library
CSPF 1558–9	*Calendar of State Papers Foreign 1558–9*, ed. Rev. J. Stevenson (London, 1863)
DNB	*The Dictionary of National Biography*, ed. Sidney Lee, 63 vols (London: Smith, Elder, 1885–1900)
ELH	*English Literary History*
ELR	*English Literary Renaissance*
FQ	Edmund Spenser, *The Faerie Queene*, ed. A.C. Hamilton (Harlow: Longman, 1977)
HMC	Historical Manuscripts Commission
HMC Hatfield	*Calendar of the Manuscripts of the Most Hon. the Marquis of Salisbury, K.G., preserved at Hatfield House, Herts.*, 24 vols (London: Historical Manuscripts Commission, 1883–1976)
NCE	*The New Catholic Encyclopedia* (New York: McGraw-Hill, 1967)
OED	*The Oxford English Dictionary*, 2nd edn, eds J.A. Simpson and E.S.C. Weiner, 20 vols (Oxford: Clarendon, 1989)
RES	*Review of English Studies*

Acknowledgements

My first thanks are due to Katherine Duncan-Jones for her invaluable guidance, encouragement and friendship.

I will always be grateful for the teaching of Angela Trueman and Christine Joy, with whom I first studied Renaissance literature and history, and of Anne Hudson, Elizabeth Mackenzie and Nicholas Shrimpton. David Norbrook set me on this particular track and read and commented on my M.Phil. thesis, as did John Carey and Emrys Jones. For reading and discussing either all or part of my D.Phil. thesis, I am grateful to Marie Axton, Jeri McIntosh Cobb, Christopher Haigh, Lorna Hutson, Dennis Kay, John Pitcher, Diane Purkiss, Nigel Smith and Penry Williams. Philippa Berry kindly allowed me to see proofs of her book *On Chastity and Power* at a crucial moment.

I would like to thank audiences at the following venues for their responses to papers: John Carey's research seminar, Blair Worden's research seminar, the Renaissance Studies MA group at Birkbeck College, and the European University Institute in Florence. Special thanks are due to members of the *Women, Text and History* seminar at Oxford in 1988–90, and to members of the London Renaissance Seminar 1990–3.

Much of my work towards this book was supported by a British Academy Studentship, a Jex-Blake Graduate Scholarship and Graduate Bursary from Lady Margaret Hall, and a Junior Research Fellowship at Merton College. I am indebted to Edward Cobb, Joan Cobb and Madeleine Davis for generous gifts of books. I would like to thank the staff of the following libraries: the British Library, the Bodleian Library, Lady Margaret Hall, Merton College, the Oxford English Faculty, the Oxford History Faculty, University College London, the University of London, and Worcester College. The British Library, the Bodleian Library and All Souls College Library have kindly granted permission to quote from manuscripts.

I would like to thank all the students and colleagues in Oxford and London who have shown interest in the writing of this book and have stretched me intellectually. I am especially appreciative of my colleagues in the English Department at UCL for their generosity in friendship, knowledge and ideas. Henry Woudhuysen has

ix

been particularly helpful in suggesting sources to pursue, lending books, and listening to me talk. Keith Walker has also generously lent books, and Kathryn Metzenthin has been patient in sharing her computing skills. Advice on translations was given by Hugh White, and by Laura Lepschy and her colleagues of UCL Italian Department. All remaining errors are, of course, my own.

I am grateful to my editor at Macmillan, Charmian Hearne, for the enthusiastic interest which she has taken in this book, and to her predecessor, Margaret Cannon, for her patience and encouragement in its earlier stages.

I have enjoyed and benefited from conversations with Susan Beardmore, Jacqui Gilliatt, Tricia Kelleher, Pete Tyler and Sue Wiseman. I am deeply thankful to all the friends who have given me interest, support and tolerance.

Steve Hackett has forbidden me to write him a gushing acknowledgement, which is just as well, because no words could be enough.

A Note on the Text

All translations are my own unless otherwise stated.

Dates are given New Style (i.e. I treat each year as beginning on 1 January rather than 25 March).

Where I quote from primary sources, I adhere to original spellings, including unmodified i/j and u/v spellings. Where I am dependent on secondary sources, quotations reproduce spellings given therein, unless otherwise noted.

I have expanded contractions in primary texts, showing inserted letters in italics.

Dates of plays by Shakespeare are taken from *The Oxford Shakespeare: The Complete Works*, eds Stanley Wells and Gary Taylor (Oxford: Oxford University Press, 1986).

The blessed morne fore blessed Maries day,
  On angels wings our Queene to heauen flieth;
To sing a part of that celestiall lay
  Which Alleluiah, Alleluiah crieth.
In heauens chorus so at once are seene
A virgin mother, and a maiden Queene.

I. Bowle, 'Singultientes Lusus', in *Sorrowes Ioy. Or, A Lamentation for our late deceased Soveraigne ELIZABETH, with a triumph for the prosperous succession of our gratious King, IAMES, &c.* [Cambridge: John Legat, 1603], pp. 19–21

Introduction

i. An Elizabethan incident

In the summer of 1578, Elizabeth I made a progress through Suffolk and Norfolk. On her way she stayed at Euston Hall, the home of Edward Rookwood, a Catholic. A vivid account of events during her stay exists in a letter written on 30 August 1578 by Richard Topcliffe, the government agent notorious for his pursuit and persecution of Catholics. Topcliffe was with the royal entourage in East Anglia, and was reporting events to his patron, the Earl of Shrewsbury, keeper of Mary Queen of Scots. He wrote:

> This Rookewoode is a Papyste of kynde newly crept out of his late Wardeshipp. Her Majesty, by some meanes I know not, was lodged at his house, Ewston, farre unmeet for her Highnes, but fitter for the blacke garde; nevertheles (the Gentilman brought into her Majesty's presence by lyke device) her excellent Majesty gave to Rookewoode ordenary thanks for his badd house, and her fayre hand to kysse; after which it was brayved at:[1] But my Lord Chamberlayn, noblye and gravely understandinge that Rookewoode was excommunicated for Papistrie, cawled him before him; demanded of him how he durst presume to attempt her reall presence, he, unfytt to accompany any Chrystyan person; forthewith sayd he was fytter for a payre of stocks; comanded him out of the Coort, and yet to attende her Counsell's pleasure; and at Norwyche he was comytted. And, to dissyffer[2] the Gentleman to the full; a peyce of plaite being missed in the Coorte, and serched for in his hay house, in the hay rycke suche an immaydge of our Lady was ther fownd, as for greatnes, for gayness, and woorkemanshipp, I did never see a matche; and, after a sort of cuntree daunces ended, in her Majesty's sighte the idoll was set behinde the people, who avoyeded: She rather seemed a beast, raysed upon a sudden from Hell by conjewringe, than the Picture for whome it hadd bene so often and longe abused. Her Majesty commanded it to the fyer, which in her sight by the cuntrie folks

1

was quickly done, to her content, and unspeakable joy of every one but some one or two who had sucked of the idoll's poysoned mylke.[3]

Rookwood's estate was eventually confiscated as punishment for his recusancy, and he is heard of again beggared by fines, in the Fleet Prison for debt, in 1619.[4] Topcliffe mentions elsewhere in the letter that eight other gentlemen had also been apprehended and imprisoned during this journey 'for baddness of belyffe'. Rookwood's house, having been commissioned for the enforced hospitality of a royal progress, became no longer his home but 'the Coort', a place which he could be publicly commanded out of by a royal official.

We might wonder why it was that Elizabeth was housed in a place clearly 'farre unmeet' for her, 'fitter for the blacke garde', that is, the scullions and kitchen-servants of the royal entourage (*OED*). The whole scene smacks of a set-up: Rookwood was brought to be received by Elizabeth 'by lyke device', presumably like to the device of housing her at his Hall in the first place. We might well suspect that the icon so conveniently found in the hay house was also planted there 'by lyke device'.[5] If so, what was Elizabeth's part in it all? Was she simply an object manipulated by Topcliffe and his cronies, a symbol as much as the icon, set up to play her part in their scheme to expose and punish papistry? Topcliffe attributes agency to her in the paragraph of the letter where he introduces the incident; he says that:

> her Ma*jes*tie hathe served God with great zeal and comfortable examples; for by her Cownsaille two notorious Papists, young Rookewoode (the Ma*ste*r of Ewston Hall, where her Ma*jes*ty did lye upon Sunday now a fortenight) and one Downes, a Gentle*man* were both comytted . . . for obstynat Papystrie.

One editor of the text modernises 'Cownsaille' as 'Council',[6] but it seems more likely here to mean Elizabeth's own 'counsel'. Of course, though, this is only Topcliffe's version of events, and he had his own reasons for wanting to stress Elizabeth's active participation.

Whether or not Elizabeth was in control of her own deployment in the spectacle, she certainly was deployed as a symbol, especially in the scene of the burning of the icon. The Virgin Mary is set up against the Virgin Queen Elizabeth; the 'false' virgin is destroyed, thereby reinforcing the authority of the 'true' virgin. Elizabeth, Supreme Governor of the Protestant Church of England, who had presided over the condemnation and removal from churches of images of the Virgin and saints as idolatrous, here seems to be used as an idol in much the same way.

This can be interpreted as a 'ritual against ritual' or 'ceremony against ceremony'. It has been suggested that images and practices which were newly banned as corrupt and deceptive had to be defined and run through again before they could be deleted from culture; and ironically, in the process, deletion could itself become a form of reiteration.[7] The very destruction of the icon of the Virgin was an acknowledgement of its power; and the force of the icon, its 'greatnes, gayness, and woorkemanshipp' had to be stressed to make Elizabeth's victory over it as glorious as possible. At the same time, the mode of its destruction was highly ceremonial: a public burning, preceded by country dances, like a folk ritual. A sense of form and of occasion seems to have been necessary to bestow meaning on the event. Protestant iconoclasm could thus, in several senses, be paradoxically idolatrous.

In fact, an absolute iconoclasm, an attempt to purify the world completely of all images, was a virtually impossible position, and held by very few Elizabethan Protestants. Margaret Aston prefers the term 'iconomachy', hostility to religious images.[8] In practice, during the reign of Elizabeth, the use of symbol and ritual tended to pass from the religious sphere to the secular, but did continue there; and, even in the religious sphere, new kinds of image were embraced which were associated with Protestantism, such as emblems, or the Word as symbol. What we see exemplified in the Euston Hall incident, then, is the fact that there was not a complete rejection of imagery, but rather the replacement of old, 'false', Catholic images with new, 'true', Protestant ones: in this case, the Virgin Mary opposed to and destroyed by the Virgin Queen. Elizabeth, as representative of the English Church and the Protestant English nation, is used as a true image of the true faith, whereas the icon of the Virgin is perceived as a falsifying, seductive distraction from the true, direct worship of God.

The opposition between the two virgins is based on similitude as well as difference. Both, obviously, are virgins; both, too, have maternal qualities. Topcliffe writes of 'some one or two who had sucked of the idoll's poysoned mylke', invoking the centuries-old iconography of the Virgin as nursing mother, giving suck to the infant Christ and thereby, symbolically, nurturing the whole of the Church.[9] Elizabeth, too, was often represented as a nursing mother, drawing not only on Marian iconography,[10] but also on a key biblical text for the Protestant reformers, Isaiah 49.23. This verse ran, 'And Kings shalbe thy nourcing fathers, and Quenes shalbe thy nources', and was glossed in the Geneva Bible as 'Meaning, that Kings shalbe conuerted to the Gospel and bestow their power, & autoritie for the preseruation of the Church.'[11] It was stressed by Protestants in support of their doctrine that secular rulers, rather than the hierarchy of the Roman Church, were the proper guardians of the faith. Elizabeth was often eulogised as the nursing mother of the English Church and nation; indeed, on the same progress of 1578, a farewell oration was composed for her departure from Norwich which addressed her as 'the mother and nurse of this whole Common welth, and Countrie', and said of the citizens' distress at her departure, 'How lamentable a thing is it, to pul away sucking babes from the breastes and bosomes of their most louing mothers?'[12]

As a Protestant iconomach, Topcliffe revises the nursing mother image as applied to the Virgin Mary so that her milk is not nutritive, but a source of poison and infection. He draws on the contemporary belief that a child ingested not only nutriment but also character from the milk of its nurse; and perhaps, also, the contemporary knowledge that syphilis could be transmitted to a child through breastfeeding.[13] The place of nurturing is turned to a place of horror: and, interestingly, he uses similar terms later in the letter to speak of the spring at Buxton. He passes on to the Earl of Shrewsbury information, which he says Elizabeth has graciously vouchsafed to him, that a number of Catholics have resorted to Buxton, in the Earl's estates, and that the Earl could win favour by apprehending them. They include 'a detestable Popish Preest' who is 'at the bathe, or lurking in those partts after the Ladyes'. This may be just the usual kind of sexual innuendo associated with a place of resort like a spa, and the common Protestant polemical identification of Catholicism with sexual irregularity; but also, 'going to Buxton' may have been a contemporary euphemism for going to try and see Mary Queen of Scots.[14] Topcliffe advises the Earl to:

> skayle the neste of Papistes . . . for unworthy be they to receve
> any fruite of God's good blessinge under your Lordship's rewle (as
> that bathe is) who will not serve God; and shall in that infected

place poysone others with Papistrie, and disobedience of her Majesty's lawes: God knowes how he and her Majesty would take it.

The Buxton spring is turned by the presence of the Catholics from a place of the 'fruite of God's good blessinge' to an infected place, which rather than being a source of health as it is supposed to be will instead become a source of spiritual poison. The very fact that people flock to it to be cured makes it a dangerous site for the rapid dissemination of spiritual disease. There is a striking congruence between the metaphorical use of the spring and that of the Virgin's breast: both are natural sources of health- and life-giving fluid, places of care, which, when the nutritive fluid is poisoned, become sources of infection and places of danger and horror.

Elizabeth and the Virgin are thus alike in that they are both mothers, but opposites in that the former gives food, the latter, poison. They are both virgins, both queens, but fundamentally opposed in that one represents Protestantism and is therefore 'true', whereas the other represents Catholicism and is therefore 'false'. An opposition has to be grounded in similitudes in order for differences to be clearly delineated. The most difficult term in this formula, though, is sacredness. Is it a ground of difference? – according to many pronouncements by Protestant theologians, it was legitimate to apply high terms of praise to Elizabeth because she was a secular ruler and not a saint, and therefore no idolatry was involved. Praise, and ceremony, however extravagant, were acceptable as long as they did not take place within the walls of a church. On the other hand, though, sacredness would appear to be a ground of likeness.

A striking phrase is used to describe Rookwood's approach to kiss Elizabeth's hand: he is challenged as to 'how he durst presume to attempt her reall presence'. 'Reall' could mean 'royal', as in 'real tennis', but here it carries at least the force of a pun, strongly implying that Elizabeth embodies the spiritual presence of Christ just as it was embodied by the bread and wine of Communion. The Protestant position on the existence and nature of the divine presence in the Eucharist was complex and divided, but many members of the Church of England followed the Lutheran view that although the bread and wine were not physically transformed into the body and blood of Christ, as Catholics maintained, there was a Real or Spiritual Presence of Christ within them.[15] The Elizabethan period also saw a reinforcement of the belief which had developed through the Middle Ages that the anointed monarch was the earthly agent of God; a belief intensified by Elizabeth's role as Supreme Governor of the English Church, and therefore chief guardian of the 'true' faith. Here, then, in Topcliffe's account, she is the earthly instrument of the divine purpose, suggesting implicit parallels with Christ as the Incarnation. He tells the Earl of Shrewsbury that if he apprehends the Catholics at Buxton 'it would not offende the Highest' – meaning Elizabeth, or God? The difference, in this context, is immaterial. The danger of the Catholics is that they will 'poysone others with Papistrie, and disobedience of her Majesty's lawes: God knowes how he and her Majesty would take it'. Offence to God and to the Queen are one and the same thing.

Thus the elevation and celebration of Elizabeth as symbol partly depended on an identification of secular power with sacredness. It also, though, paradoxically, depended on a separation of the secular and the sacred. Note Topcliffe's terms of vilification of the icon of the Virgin: it is such a one as 'for greatnes, for gayness, and woorkemanshipp, I did never see a matche'. He writes as a connoisseur of icons. For a piece of secular art, these would all be terms of unequivocal praise; for a religious image, they are precisely what makes it seem 'a beast, raysed upon a sudden from Hell by conjewringe'. There is no mention by Topcliffe of Elizabeth's presumably magnificent dress on the occasion; nor any direct comment on the reverent attitude towards her maintained by all participants in the episode. For Topcliffe – and it is the prevalent Elizabethan position – there is in this respect a clear demarcation line between the secular and the sacred: what is best in secular art is most dangerous and abhorrent in sacred art; terms of veneration may and indeed should be applied to a secular Protestant monarch, but are idolatrous and detract from the worship of God when applied to holy figures like the Virgin and saints. Thus sacredness is at once a ground of similitude and of difference in the complex opposition between the Virgin and Elizabeth.

ii. A cult of Elizabeth?

I begin with this incident in 1578 because it illustrates the theory that there was a cult of Elizabeth I which replaced the cult of the Virgin Mary, and at the same time illustrates some of the problems attendant upon this theory. The idea of 'the cult of Elizabeth' is

now very familiar from the work of E.C. Wilson, Frances Yates and
Roy Strong, and the widespread use of their pioneering and influential work by other scholars.[16] The word 'cult' is ambiguous; it
could connote merely a cult of personality like that of a modern
celebrity. However, its more controversial religious sense has not
been avoided: the idea has developed that Elizabeth became a sort of
Protestant substitute for the Virgin Mary, filling a post-Reformation
gap in the psyche of the masses, who craved a symbolic virgin-
mother figure. The evidence for this is threefold: the quasi-religious
ceremonies and celebrations which developed around Elizabeth,
like Accession Day;[17] the iconography in literary panegyric of the
Queen; and the iconic quality of her portraits. Yates, for instance,
commenting on the 'Procession' portrait of Elizabeth, says: 'The
bejewelled and painted images of the Virgin Mary had been cast
out of churches and monasteries, but another bejewelled and painted
image was set up at court, and went in progress through the land
for her worshippers to adore.'[18]

Many recent writers have reiterated this idea. Dorothy Connell,
for example, in her book on Sidney, writes of 'the fact that Elizabeth, as the Virgin Queen of Protestantism, came to be identified
symbolically with the Virgin Mary.'[19] Jean Wilson, in *Entertainments
for Elizabeth I*, says that the removal of the Virgin Mary 'from the
English religious scene, left a gap which, as virgin-queen, Elizabeth
was ideally qualified to fill'.[20] Stephen Greenblatt, in *Renaissance
Self-Fashioning*, says that in Elizabeth's 'first address to Parliament . . .
[t]he secular cult of the virgin was born, and it was not long before
the young Elizabeth was portraying herself as a Virgin Mother'.[21]
And Lisa Jardine in *Still Harping on Daughters* contends that 'The
Reformation had terminated the "cult of Mary" in England; to a
significant extent the "cult of Elizabeth" replaced it'.[22] These are just
a few random examples of what has become an assumption in
Renaissance studies.

There are obvious difficulties, though, with the idea that Elizabeth simply filled a vacancy left by the Virgin Mary. How could the
Supreme Governor of a Church which had expelled icons of the
Virgin as idolatrous be herself idolised as a pseudo-Marian icon?
The seminal accounts of Wilson, Yates and Strong are more sensitive to this problem than most of their successors, though they do
not resolve it. For Wilson and Yates, writing within early twentieth-
century attitudes to monarchy, there seems to be an added anxiety
that veneration of a secular monarch as a sacred figure was not

merely idolatrous, but sacrilegious. Wilson asked whether it were possible that Elizabeth's subjects

> unconsciously transferred some of the adoration which by right of strict inheritance was due a far holier virgin? It is a delicate matter. I trespass on sacred ground that cannot be explored with scientific precision. Yet I think the evidence justifies the belief that so it was.[23]

He frequently uses the phrase 'half unconsciously' to describe how Elizabethans could have engaged in this alarming and apparently hypocritical process.[24] Yates picks this up from him, and adds comments on apparent literary comparisons of Elizabeth to the Virgin such as, 'The startling suggestion . . .', 'This staggering remark . . .', and 'it would be, perhaps, extravagant to suggest that, in a Christian country, the worship of the state Virgo was intended to take [the cult of the Virgin Mary's] place'.[25]

Yates's account of the existence of a pseudo-Marian Elizabethan cult is perhaps the one most drawn on by later scholars, but has some limitations. One is that most of the texts she cites are from late in Elizabeth's reign; indeed, several are elegies for Elizabeth, such as one which runs: 'She was, She is (what can there more be said?) / In earth the first, in heaven the second Maid.' Yates comments, 'What more can there be said indeed? Except to add that implications of this kind are not uncommon in Elizabethan literature.' However, it is imprecise to suggest that the terms used under the special circumstances of Elizabeth's death, or indeed towards the end of her 45-year-long reign, are representative of the whole of the reign. Recent work by John King, and by Peter McClure and Robin Headlam Wells, has made headway in introducing chronological sensitivity into study of panegyric of Elizabeth, but more remains to be done to locate texts in relation to contexts.[26]

This contextualisation needs to include considerations of place and class as well as time. Most of the evidence for a cult of Elizabeth is not only from late in the reign, but also from the court, yet it is used to assert the existence of a spontaneous popular cult of Elizabeth. This is to assume that the English nation under Elizabeth was unified in thought and belief. The work of revisionist historians like Christopher Haigh has emphatically shown this not to be the case: many parts of England remained Catholic for many years after Elizabeth's accession, or at least did not fully absorb the teachings of the reformers; what took place was a 'piecemeal Reformation'.[27] Margaret Aston concurs: even in the most active periods of actual iconoclasm (1536–8, 1547–8 and 1559–60), there was not a complete transformation of belief, but rather 'the ground shifted a little and the argument moved forward'. Change was promoted by a small but committed minority, who contended with extreme reluctance from most of the populace.[28] We cannot therefore think in terms of a whole nation abruptly and uniformly ceasing to venerate images of the Virgin Mary in 1558 and looking elsewhere for a symbolic virgin-mother figure.

Another mode of argument employed by Yates is the accumulation of shared terms, the fact that Elizabeth was praised as 'the Rose, . . . the Star, the Moon, the Phoenix, the Ermine, the Pearl', and that all these terms had previously been applied to the Virgin Mary.[29] These were not, though, exclusively Marian images, but had wider associations with femininity and virginity as general qualities. At the same time, several of these images also had specific connotations – such as the rose as Tudor crest, or stellar radiance and the ermine as attributes of the Petrarchan mistress – which afforded other reasons for their association with Elizabeth beyond their Marian significances.

Strong, like Wilson and Yates, also comments on the apparently paradoxical or hypocritical nature of the cult of Elizabeth which he has identified: 'The Anglican position was thus a somewhat peculiar one, for on the one hand the use of religious images was denounced as popish superstition, while on the other, the sacred nature of the royal portrait image was to be maintained.'[30] His work concentrates on the portraits of Elizabeth and on Accession Day and other ceremonies as evidence of a cult. In the process, he briefly indicates that the forces at work may have been not only the spontaneous elevation of Elizabeth by some kind of mass psychology, but also deliberate government policy.[31]

In the work of new historicists this suggestion has been amplified into the idea that a cult of Elizabeth might have been produced by collaboration between the interests of the ruling powers and the desires of the ruled. Louis Montrose, for instance, in his article 'Shaping Fantasies', interprets three diverse texts concerning the Queen in terms of interaction between the centralised promotion of royal iconography and some kind of national psyche or cultural unconscious, describing the object of his inquiry as 'the historical specificity of psychological processes, the politics of the unconscious'.[32] This interest in the political motivations of Elizabethan panegyric is very welcome; the incident at Euston Hall, for example, makes more sense when viewed not merely as the result of spontaneous or half-unconscious popular feeling, but more as a staged event, managed by government officers with a political purpose. However, Montrose and other new historicists perpetuate the assumption that Elizabeth slotted into a psychological gap left by the Virgin Mary: 'a concerted effort was ... made to appropriate the symbolism and the affective power of the suppressed Marian cult in order to foster an Elizabethan cult'.[33] As I have just indicated, this assumption is problematic on several counts.

In the present study, I aim to examine more closely the relations between these two virginal figures. I shall attempt to be precise about whether iconography of Elizabeth which has previously been described as Marian is in fact solely or primarily Marian, or whether there are other reasons for its application to Elizabeth. I shall also look closely at the ways in which indisputably Marian iconography is made use of in relation to Elizabeth. When overt comparisons between Elizabeth and the Virgin are drawn, they most often take the form of typology; that is, the identification of parallels between the two figures which suggest some kind of mystical pattern and divinely-ordained plan underlying the course of Christian history. The identifications of Elizabeth with the Virgin which occur in such typology operate not to supplant Mary, but to use her and her sanctity as a touchstone by which to claim divine endorsement for Elizabeth's own rule.[34]

In fact, as this suggests, when Marian iconography or other sacred iconography is applied to Elizabeth, it may be not so much an effusion of enthusiasm for the Queen as an attempt to enhance her potentially precarious authority. There are many reasons why her hold on the loyalty of her people was in danger at various points in the reign. To mention just a few in summary: she came to the throne amid controversy about female rule; she remained unmarried, contravening Protestant ideology and royal precedent and leaving the succession in doubt; and the later years of her reign were sullied by various political tensions, including economic hardship and weariness of her regime. All these were reasons why a writer seeking royal favour might create images of the Queen which stressed her sanctity and perfection. At the same time, Elizabeth inspired positive feelings of loyalty in so far as she symbolised the Protestant Church and English nation facing combat with foreign adversaries, and this in turn produced celebratory iconography.

All of these are political issues, and the necessarily superficial summary of them here indicates how important it is to provide much more detailed political contextualisation in order to identify some of the purposes of iconography and praise. This book sets out to look beyond the assertion of a uniform national psychological need for a symbolic virgin-mother figure, to situate examples of the magnification of Elizabeth in relation to some specific political circumstances; and to locate changes in those circumstances which produced changes in iconography, bringing it closer to the cult of the Virgin at certain times than others. I have therefore structured the book diachronically, illustrating each historical phase with selected texts. I concentrate on literary evidence of the elevation of Elizabeth as an icon, and inevitably much of my material is courtly panegyric, but I also include ballads, sermons, civic pageants, and other kinds of text.

I aim to be aware of both continuities and diversities. Those who write about the cult of Elizabeth often do so as if praise of a monarch as a sacred figure, and particularly praise of a queen in terms similar to the Virgin Mary, were unprecedented and extraordinary; this disregards ways in which these simply continued established traditions. Iconography of the Virgin Queen can also be seen not as merely a continuation of the cult of the Virgin Mary, but as a perpetuation of a more ancient and enduring veneration of virginity grounded in superstitions about female sexuality and bodily pollution. My study begins with a survey of some of these continuities, looking at iconography of the feminine, the sacred and the regal which already existed before Elizabeth came to the throne.

At the same time, of course, these continuities override disjunctions which one might expect the Reformation to have brought about. For this reason I examine some Elizabethan theological texts which develop theories of representation and praise. Protestantism produced distrust of the image, both in the primary sixteenth-century sense of the word as a sculpted figure, and in its emergent, modern, more abstract senses.[35] The danger of the image lay in its ability to inspire idolatrous worship. At the same time, Protestantism enhanced the spiritual authority of secular rulers, and regarded the Queen as an image to be praised: she was the earthly representative of God, and the symbolic personification of the English Church and nation. Elizabethan theologians grappled with the problem of reconciling these positions, and their books therefore show that Elizabethans were by no means as unconscious in their forms of praise of Elizabeth as so many scholars from Wilson to Montrose have suggested.

I shall continue to use the phrase 'the cult of Elizabeth' because it is the most convenient way of describing the complex of praise, iconography and ritual which grew up around the figure of the Queen. However, I aim to be sensitive to the religious implications of the term 'cult'. As we shall see, Elizabeth's subjects often addressed or described her as a saint or goddess, but when such hyperbole is placed in context it can mean many different things, and not necessarily that they regarded her as literally divine or sacred. Throughout, I want to be attentive to contexts, diversities, ambiguities and complexities.

1

Before Elizabeth

Understanding of how far iconography of Elizabeth appropriated the terms of the cult of the Virgin needs to include some awareness of the previous history of feminine, royal and sacred iconography. This chapter therefore begins by briefly exploring the sources for the cult of the Virgin itself. It then traces the history of appropriations of sacred iconography by secular rulers, and considers how they were reappropriated by the Church. There is a review of the state of the cult of the Virgin in England immediately before the Reformation, and definitions are offered of recognisably Marian iconography. Finally, precedents are examined for the application of Marian iconography to temporal queens, with particular attention to the cases of Elizabeth's mother and sister, Anne Boleyn and Mary I.

i. Pagan origins for the cult of the Virgin

The cult of the Virgin was itself a compendium of iconography from many sources, gathered and enriched over many centuries.[1] In the first place, it appears that it probably adopted iconography from older pagan goddess cults. Some historians have argued that the ancient world was dominated by worship of a Great Goddess or Great Mother, of whom different figures such as Isis, Cybele or Artemis were merely different titles or guises preferred in different geographical locations. The Virgin Mary might then be seen simply as a modernised, Christianised version of this single prior figure.[2] This model whereby different societies across different locations and different centuries have all felt the need for a similar mother-goddess figure would certainly support the idea that Elizabeth was able simply to take over and continue the symbolic role of the Virgin Mary, fulfilling the same universal psychological need.

Other historians, though, have seen the concept of the Great Goddess as reductive, collapsing many different goddess-cults into a single model, and motivated by a modern feminist wish-fulfilling back-projection to find a time when the world was uniformly matriarchal.[3] Any account which is sensitive to difference and complexity seems to be inherently more likely to be accurate; but, nevertheless, there are undoubtedly continuities among the ancient goddess-cults in their concerns with chastity and fertility. There are also strong continuities from particular goddess-cults to the cult of Mary: for instance, her customary pose with her son in her lap echoes that of Isis and Horus, while her association with the moon echoes the iconography of the virgin-goddess Artemis or Diana.[4] The Virgin was sometimes invoked just as they and other goddesses had been as the patron deity of childbirth, making her a sort of fertility goddess.[5]

Many of the early churches of Mary were built on sites previously sacred to pagan goddesses: for example, Santa Maria Maggiore in Rome replaced Cybele's temple on the Esquiline hill, while Santa Maria Aracoeli on the Capitoline hill succeeded a temple of the Phoenician goddess Tanit.[6] Mary took over from pagan goddesses the function of protecting various cities and of presiding over shrines; indeed, much later, this fact was deployed by the author of the Elizabethan Church Homily 'Against Peril of Idolatry' as evidence of the existence of Mariolatry, and of its unChristianity:

> And where one Saint hath images in divers places, the same Saint hath divers names thereof, most like to the Gentiles. When you hear of our Lady of Walsingham, our Lady of Ipswich, our Lady of Wilsdon, and such other, what is it but an imitation of the Gentiles idolaters' Diana Agrotera, Diana Coryphea, Diana Ephesia, &c., Venus Cypria, Venus Paphia, Venus Gnidia?[7]

It was not just earlier pagan goddesses who were assimilated into the cult of the Virgin. There were also prominent female figures in the Hebraic tradition who contributed elements to the developing cult in its early centuries, such as the allegorical figure of Wisdom (Sophia or Sapientia);[8] the female, often virginal, personification of Israel or Zion; the bride of the Songs of Songs; and the Woman Clothed with the Sun of the book of Revelation.

Clearly the cult of the Virgin took at least some of its components from earlier goddess-cults and iconographies of the feminine. Just as with the relation between the cult of the Virgin and iconography of Elizabeth, this could be regarded as evidence of a continuous uniform cultural need for a mother-goddess; or as evidence of a cultural tendency, or necessity, to accommodate new ideas by making use of materials already to hand. Again, this might be regarded as a spontaneous process arising from the masses; or as intentionally imposed by forces of authority, in this case the hierarchy of the early Church, as a means of deploying already familiar and popular forms to appeal to followers and to strengthen its hold over them.

ii. Courtly love as secular source for the cult of the Virgin

Closer to the period with which we are concerned, in the later Middle Ages the cult of the Virgin had borrowed terms from, or shared terms with, the secular poetic convention of courtly love. To a large extent this overlap derived from typological readings of the Song of Songs, interpreting its sensual voicing of desire as an allegory of the love between the Virgin Mary and Christ, whereby the Virgin becomes Christ's bride as well as his mother; or as a representation of the love between the Virgin and humankind.[9] The Antiphon for Vespers on the Feast of the Assumption employed some of the most passionate verses of the Song:

> Tota pulchra es amica mea: et macula non est in te: favus distillans labia tua: mel et lac sub lingua tua: odor unguentorum tuorum super omnia aromata: jam enim hyems transiit: imber abiit et recessit: flores apparuerunt: vinee florentes odorem dederunt: et vox turturis audita est in terra nostra: surge propera amica mea: veni de libano: veni coronaberis.

> (You are all fair, my love: there is no spot in thee: your lips drop as the honeycomb: honey and milk are under your tongue: the smell of your ointments is better than all spices: for now the winter is past: the rain is over and gone: the flowers appear: the flourishing vines give a good smell: and the voice of the turtledove is heard in our land: rise up and hasten, my love: come from Lebanon: come, you shall be crowned.)[10]

This typological tradition opened the way for the Virgin to be addressed in erotic terms similar to those addressed to earthly mistresses.

One fourteenth-century song has the refrain 'Quia amore langueo' ('I languish for love' – Song of Songs 2.5),[11] and is headed in at least one manuscript 'Canticus Amoris' ('Song of Love'). It exists in two versions: in one, Christ woos the human soul; in the other, the

Virgin speaks of how she is sick for the love of her Son, then turns to mankind and urges 'Take me for thy wyfe'.[12]

A fifteenth-century lyric has the refrain 'Veni Coronaberis' ('Come, you shall be crowned' – Song of Songs 4.8),[13] and is a love-song from Christ to the Virgin. It begins:

> Surge mea sponsa,* so swete in syghte,
>   And se thy sone in sete full shene!†
> Thow shalte a-byde with thy babe so brighte
>   And in my glorye be, & be called a qwene.
> Thy mamelles,‡ modur, full well I mene,
>   I hadde to my mete, I myghte not mysse.§
> Aboue all creatures, my modur clene,
>   Veni Coronaberis.[14]

Mary is not only Christ's mother, but also his spouse, giving an erotic as well as maternal charge to the praise of her breasts. She is simultaneously an emblem of purity and an object of desire. In stanza 6, Christ sensuously reminds her of the dew which dropped from their lips when they kissed. Throughout the song there is incantatory repetition of the imperatives 'Veni' and 'Come', giving an insistent sense of love-longing. The use of terms of regal power, representing the Virgin as a queen ascending her throne and receiving her crown, is an important point to which I will return later.

These uses of erotic terms to express spiritual desires and beliefs create close resemblances with love poetry of the troubadour tradition. Some mediaeval lyrics, such as 'Maiden in the mor lay' (early fourteenth century), have left modern critics uncertain as to whether they are secular love songs or allegories of the Virgin.[15] In particular, songs in which the poet expresses his devotion to the Virgin and pleads for her to show him grace parallel the situation and tone of courtly love poetry, in which the writer expresses his desire for an elevated mistress and begs her to yield to him. The Virgin is often addressed as if she were a courtly mistress, as in this thirteenth-century lyric:

---

* Arise my spouse
† fair, bright, beautiful
‡ breasts
§ go lacking

> Nis non maide of thine hewe
> So fair, so shene, so rudy, so bright.
> Swete Levedy, of me thu rewe,
> And have mercy of thine knight.[16]

No other maid 'so derne loviye cunne' (can love so profoundly [? secretly]).

Just as the cult of the Virgin seems to have incorporated pre-Christian goddess cults, it is also possible that aspects of medieval courtly love developed out of pagan goddess-cults and spring festivals.[17] Whatever the relations of these ancient origins, it is evident that late medieval Marian iconography incorporated secular forms of love discourse and representations of femininity. This was more than just one-way traffic: many secular medieval love lyrics address or describe a mistress in terms which could just as easily be applied to the Virgin. Consider these lines from about 1500:

> Most soveren lady, comfort of care,
> A* next† in my hert, most in my minde,
> Right welth and cause of my welefare,
> Gentle trulove, special and kinde,
> Eey‡ pinacle, pight§ with stidfasteness,
> Right tristy,¶ and truth‖ of my salace,**
> Ever well-springinge stillatorye†† of sweteness,
> Tresore full dere, gronded with‡‡ grace.[18]

This praise of the perfection, grace and solace of a lady could easily refer to the Virgin, but in fact it is an acrostic which spells the name 'Margeret' (*sic*). In the early Renaissance, the use of religious language to express love for a mistress was also advanced by Petrarchism and neo-Platonism, movements which regarded chaste and adoring devotion to a beautiful mistress as spiritually ennobling.

There is debate as to how this commerce between secular and

---

*   Always
†   nearest
‡   High
§   fixed fast
¶   trustful, trustworthy
‖   promise (?)
** consolation
†† still (noun)
‡‡ founded in

sacred iconography originated. One theory is that a pre-existent courtly love discourse was appropriated by the Church and incorporated into the cult of the Virgin as a way of attracting and sustaining allegiance, and as a way of making safe a movement which could not be suppressed.[19] Others hold the opposite view, that 'the troubadour convention of courtly love possibly owed more to the cult [of the Virgin] than the cult did to it.'[20] The main point, for our purposes here, is that in pre-Reformation culture there was apparently no blasphemy or idolatry perceived in addressing the Virgin Mary and an earthly beloved in much the same terms. Both were fitted to a somewhat standardised model of feminine beauty and virtue, illustrating again a tendency for symbolic female figures to be overlaid upon one another and to be represented in terms of other already familiar female figures.

iii. The use of sacred iconography by secular rulers

We have seen how the cult of the Virgin borrowed terms from other sources, including secular ones like courtly love. We must now examine the inverse process, whereby secular rulers had over a long period appropriated sacred iconography. This kind of commerce had an extensive history stretching back through early Christian times and into the ancient world; an obvious example would be the uses of ceremonial by Roman emperors, their claims to divinity and their appropriation of prior images of gods as a means of reinforcing their authority.[21] It is not surprising that politics and religion have been entwined across a range of societies in different centuries: both are modes of imposing social structures and systems of representation upon hierarchies of power. It has always been in the interests of secular rulers to try to create cults around themselves.[22]

Among early Christian monarchies, the Byzantine and Carolingian dynasties were of crucial importance in developing an iconography of sacred kingship. In the eighth and ninth centuries, rituals were established of the enthronement, anointing and coronation of new monarchs by priests. These practices derived from Old Testament accounts of the anointing of kings of Israel by priests and prophets; from the New Testament story of the anointing of Christ, marking his union of kingly and priestly functions; and from the numerous scriptural references to the promise of a heavenly crown to believers.[23]

The use of ritual in itself, and the scripturally-endorsed forms which those rituals took, combined to endue the institution of monarchy with an aura of sacredness.[24]

These ceremonies were adopted in England, and were enhanced by a legend which grew up that the oil for the coronation had been given to Thomas à Becket by the Virgin Mary. The legend was promoted during the reign of Henry IV to enforce his claims to legitimacy once he was the anointed king; it then continued in currency and the same oil continued to be used for the coronation until the accession of James I, who objected to it as a popish superstition. Elizabeth, then, was the last monarch to be anointed with the Virgin's oil.[25]

Ideas of the sacredness of monarchy were well advanced by the late Middle Ages.[26] The practice developed of installing a canopy above the head of an enthroned or processing monarch, or over the coffin of a monarch at a funeral; this was a transference of the practice of carrying a canopy over the Host.[27] The King, as an incarnation of holiness, was at once like the Host, like a priest, and, by implication, like Christ himself. In 1501, in civic pageantry staged to welcome Catherine of Aragon to London, Henry VII and his eldest son Arthur, Prince of Wales, were respectively likened to God the Father and Christ the Son.[28]

In particular, the King could exercise Christlike healing powers in the practice of touching those afflicted with scrofula, or the King's Evil. By tradition, this practice began with Edward the Confessor, who possessed healing powers because he was a saint, not because he was a king. There seems to have been a political move, possibly by Henry I, but certainly by Henry II, to attach the tradition of healing to the monarchy and establish the idea of a miracle-working dynasty. The Royal Touch became specifically attributed to the anointing of the monarch as a conferment of holiness. A further development was the blessing by the monarch of cramp-rings, which were supposed to cure epilepsy and muscular pains.[29]

Mary I and Elizabeth, as the first English queens since the Norman Conquest to be anointed monarchs in their own right rather than as wives of kings, were the first women to be attributed with these healing powers.[30] Elizabeth abandoned the blessing of cramp-rings, but continued the practice of the Royal Touch; the last English monarch to practise it was Queen Anne. Elizabeth practised the Touch with the full religious ceremony used by her predecessors, with the only differences that a prayer which mentioned the Virgin and saints was cut out, and the liturgy may have been translated from Latin into English. The Office of Healing foregrounded the sacred nature of the event: while the Queen touched the afflicted, Mark 16.18 was read, the injunction of the risen Christ to the disciples that 'They shall lay their hands on the sick, and they shall recover'; and while Elizabeth placed an angel (a gold coin) round the necks of those touched, the reading was John 1, the passage concerning the incarnation. The Queen also continued to make the sign of the cross over those brought to be healed.[31]

Elizabeth was attacked for her perpetuation of this medieval practice both by Catholics, because she was a heretic, and, after 1570, excommunicate; and by Puritans, who saw it as superstitious. Near the end of her reign, defences of the Touch were written by William Tooker, her chaplain, who published *Charisma sive donum Sanationis* in 1597; and by William Clowes, one of the Queen's surgeons, in 1602. Tooker, like earlier writers, considered that the monarch received the gift of healing at the coronation.[32] For those not occupying Catholic or Puritan positions, Elizabeth's practice of the healing Touch seems to have been seen as a sort of good magic, divinely ordained, contrasted with the bad magic and superstition associated with Catholicism, in an opposition analogous to the one we observed earlier between good images and bad images.

Elizabeth also continued the Maundy Thursday practice of washing the feet of the recipients of alms. Before she started to wash, the Gospel was read of the washing of the disciples' feet by Christ. Elizabeth gave as alms loaves, fishes and red wine.[33]

The Reformation had, if anything, served to enhance the sacred authority of secular rulers by attributing to them the power to protect the true Church and to defend it against papal ambitions. Erasmus had dedicated his Paraphrases on the four Gospels to four monarchs, including Charles V, to whom he had written

> where as no prince is so secular, but that he hath a doe with the profession of the gospell, the Emperours are anoynted sacred for this very purpose, that they may eyther maynteyne or restore, or elles enlarge and spredde abrode the religion of the gospell.[34]

Injunctions made under Edward VI and repeated under Elizabeth laid down that the English translation of these Paraphrases, including the dedicatory prefaces, must be placed in every church in England alongside the English Bible for parishioners to read.

Calvin's *Institutes* further enforced the idea of the spiritual authority of kings. In general, the emphasis of the reformers on the text of the Bible led to a new, enhanced awareness of the scriptural sources for ideas of sacred kingship. For instance, the word 'Gods' in Psalm 82 was generally taken to refer to kings. The Psalm opens, 'God sitteth in the congregation of God, in the middes of the Gods shal he iudge', and goes on, 'I haue sayd, ye are Gods, and children of the most high, all of you' (vv.1, 6). Calvin, in his commentary on the Psalms, interpreted these lines in an admonitory manner, warning rulers not to aggrandise themselves and to be mindful of their spiritual duties. Nevertheless, those duties arose from the fact that they were God's deputies: 'the Prophet calleth the state of Princes by the name of 'Gods' as in whiche a peculier maiestie of God shyneth forth . . . the name of 'gods' is taken for Iudges, in whom God hath imprinted a speciall marke of his glorie.'[35]

A further development of and contribution to the sacred aura of monarchy was the theory of the King's Two Bodies. The idea of the Church as a mystical body, the *corpus ecclesiae mysticum*, had developed into an idea of the state as a mystical body, the *corpus reipublicae mysticum*, or body politic.[36] From this in turn developed the concept that the King himself possessed both a body politic and a body natural, the body politic being the timeless institution and essence of monarchy, whereas the body natural was the private, human, mortal body of the temporary incumbent. The theory, having been current for some time, became established in law early in Elizabeth's reign, in 1561, during a case regarding some leases of land made by Edward VI. The Crown asserted that the leases were invalid because made when Edward was a minor, but the lawyers decided that they were not invalid because Edward was King. Edmund Plowden, the Elizabethan jurist, summed up the verdict thus in his *Reports* of 1571:

the King has in him two Bodies, viz. a Body natural, and a Body politic. His Body natural (if it be considered in itself) is a Body mortal, subject to all Infirmities that come by Nature or Accident, to the Imbecillity of Infancy or old Age, and to the like Defects that happen to the natural Bodies of other People. But his Body politic is a Body that cannot be seen or handled, consisting of Policy and Government, and constituted for the Direction of the People, and the Management of the publick-weal and this Body is utterly void of Infancy, and old Age, and other natural Defects and Imbecilities which the Body natural is subject to.[37]

Marie Axton has shown how widely disseminated this concept was in Elizabethan culture.[38] We shall see later how Elizabeth herself was able to make use of the rhetoric of the King's Two Bodies to overcome her 'infirmity' of femaleness. In general, the theory of the King's Two Bodies could be used to add to the aura of sacredness surrounding the monarchy, in that the individual ruler could claim to be the incarnation of the mystical essence of monarchy, miraculously elevated above all human weaknesses in order to be God's earthly instrument.

iv. The Church and the iconography of rule: originations and reappropriations

As with the relation between devotional and courtly love poetry, the adoption of sacred iconography by secular rulers was by no means a one-way traffic; the Church also appropriated, or reappropriated, emblems of secular power. Again, too, this process can be traced back a very long way. Simon Price, in his study of Roman emperor-cults, reports that in the fourth century the Emperor Julian induced Christians to worship the old pagan gods by placing their images alongside his image. Early Christian sources represent this as a trick, but do not question the legitimacy of doing homage to the Emperor. Price concludes: 'Indeed the imperial image and the ceremony of imperial arrival seem to have had an influence on the growth of adoration of Christian icons and relics.'[39]

As we have already noted, the Bible itself uses motifs such as the heavenly crown and the Kingdom as means of representing the ultimate rewards of belief.[40] It appears that within Hebraic culture the most vivid and accessible means of representing spiritual transcendence were in the potentially problematic terms of temporal supremacy. The careful distinctions made in the New Testament between the pursuit of a corruptible and of an incorruptible crown would not always be so clear in later adaptations of this iconography.

In the specific case of the Virgin Mary, the idea of her as a queen can also be traced back to Scripture. Elizabeth greets Mary as 'The mother of my Lord' (Luke 1.43), and the expression she uses means

queen-mother in the Old Testament.[41] We have already seen also
how identification of the Virgin with the beloved of the Song of
Songs caused the line 'Veni coronaberis' to be applied to her.

The Council of Ephesus in 431 authorised veneration of Mary
as *Theotokos*, 'the Mother of God' or 'God-bearer', a title which enhanced her status and led to increasingly regal representations.[42] It
is striking that this decision, which was greeted with delirious celebrations by the people of Ephesus, should have taken place in the
city famed for many centuries as the site of the temple of Artemis,
one of the Seven Wonders of the World, where the many-breasted
statue of the goddess had presided over a fertility-cult. The temple
may only have been destroyed as recently as c.390, and already by
431 Ephesus had a basilica called the Church of Mary in which the
Council met.[43]

The image of the Virgin as Queen of Heaven was closely bound
to the idea of her Assumption: that after her death, she rose to
heaven to occupy a throne alongside her son, and to be crowned by
him. The figure of Maria Regina was also linked to her role as
personification of the Church. The image of Mary as a heavenly
queen above all temporal kings was used by the papacy in its struggle through the medieval centuries to assert its supremacy over
secular rulers, especially the emperors.[44] This was a struggle which
took on new meaning after England's break with Rome, when earlier conflicts between the papacy and the Empire, and earlier figures
of Christian emperors like Constantine, were recalled in Protestant
iconography of Henry VIII, Edward VI and Elizabeth as protectors
of the Church and vanquishers of popery.[45]

Marina Warner sums up the back-and-forth nature of these appropriations of the iconography of dominion in the later Middle
Ages. The use of the figure of Maria Regina by the Church

> was turned on its head in the later middle ages, when temporal
> kings and queens took back the borrowed symbolism of earthly
> power to enhance their own prestige and give themselves a
> sacred character. The use of the emblems of earthly power for the
> Mother of God did not empty them of their temporal content:
> rather, when kings and queens wore the sceptre and the crown
> they acquired an aura of divinity.[46]

Similarly, Yates shows how Foxe, in the *Book of Martyrs*, associated
Elizabeth with images of Constantine and other Christian Emperors

in a way which depended on emblems of empery having themselves become signifiers of sacredness: 'the politico-religious position which he propounds derives its sanction from the traditions, Christianized it is true, of the worldly empire of Rome.'[47] In Calvin's commentary on Psalm 82, mentioned earlier, even as he explains that in this Psalm the word 'Gods' means 'kings', he simultaneously has recourse to the language of temporal rule to describe God's own supremacy: 'God holdeth still the soueraintie . . . God hath not berefte himselfe of his owne soueraintie, in making you his deputies.'[48]

The long history and complexity of this process of exchange is one reason why it is inadequate to interpret images of Elizabeth crowned and enthroned simply as appropriations of the iconography of the Virgin as Queen of Heaven. Richard Helgerson sees in the figure of Elizabeth enthroned in the frontispiece to Christopher Saxton's atlas of county maps of Britain, 1579, and in the figure of Britain enthroned in the frontispiece to Drayton's *Poly-Olbion*, 1612, 'an image that was . . . an adaptation of the familiar icon of the Virgin Mary'.[49] Similarly, Peter McClure and Robin Headlam Wells draw our attention to representations of Elizabeth as Empress of Heaven and Hell, and their resemblance to Marian iconography.[50] Neither observation is inaccurate, but at the same time it is only half the story. John King notes that among 'traditional Catholic images' which were varied or reconstituted in Tudor royal iconography, the most prominent were 'the figures of Christ the King, the Coronation of the Virgin, and Mary as Queen of Heaven, which had been used in undiluted form to praise late medieval kings and queens'.[51] The fact is that the origins of these Marian icons were themselves adoptions of symbols of monarchical power. One might ask how a monarch is supposed to be represented, if not with such trappings as a crown and a throne. These trappings had taken on sacred connotations through association with Christ and the Virgin, but were not innately Christological or Marian symbols.

Elizabeth might just as well be said to be appropriating the iconography of early Christian emperors and medieval kings.[52] Official images of Elizabeth on seals and coins look directly back to medieval official monarchical images.[53] The lavishly gilded painting of Richard II at Westminster Abbey, in which the King is enthroned, crowned, holding the orb and sceptre, and facing the onlooker full-frontally, gives us all the structural components of the images commented on by Helgerson, as well as other images such as the obverse of Elizabeth's second Great Seal, and the 'Coronation' portrait.[54]

v. The cult of the Virgin in late medieval England

By the early sixteenth century, the cult of the Virgin and the ancillary cult of her mother St Anne, an entirely apocryphal figure, were both well-established and popular in England. New festivals of the Virgin had been recently introduced, and the rosary with its emphasis on the Hail Mary was increasingly popular. The Virgin was a favourite dedicatee for confraternities and was frequently invoked in wills. *The Golden Legend*, a collection of legends of saints including a number concerning the Virgin and her family, had enjoyed excellent sales after its English publication by Caxton in 1483. Henry VII's wife Elizabeth of York, Elizabeth I's grandmother, had hired a girdle of Our Lady to protect herself in pregnancy. Shrines of the Virgin such as Walsingham and Ipswich were flourishing pilgrimage centres, and in 1515 a miracle was reported at Ipswich.[55] It appears that, before England's break with Rome, Marian iconography was both firmly entrenched and widely familiar in culture and society. It is should not therefore be surprising to find elements of Marian iconography surviving or resurfacing in various areas of culture after the official Reformation.

The Virgin was not, technically, worshipped within the pre-Reformation Church: careful distinctions were drawn by theologians between *latria* (adoration), due only to God, Christ and the Holy Spirit; *dulia* (veneration), which was less than adoration or worship, and was due to saints; and *hyperdulia*, an enhanced form of veneration which was due to the Virgin, but was definitely less than the *latria* due to the Holy Trinity.[56] Nonetheless, the sometimes extravagant practices which had developed around the Virgin and saints in the late Middle Ages looked much like adoration or worship to the reformers. The role of intercessor could be seen as laying stress on the humanity of the Virgin, as the medium between humankind and her divine Son; or, it could be seen as an implication of her own divinity, suggesting that she had maternal authority over her Son. John Jewel, one of the architects of the Elizabethan Church Settlement, certainly saw it that way: he wrote in his *Apology of the Church of England* (published in Latin in 1562, in English in 1564) that Catholics 'do not only wickedly, but also shamelessly, call upon the blessed virgin, Christ's mother, to have her remember that she is a mother, and to command her Son, and to use a mother's authority over him'.[57]

Many late medieval lyrics to the Virgin proceeded by piling up epithets, as in this mid-fifteenth-century example:

> Blessed Mary, moder virginal,
> Integrate* maiden, sterre of the see,
> Have remembraunce at the day final
> On thy poore servaunt now praying to thee.
> Mirroure without spot, rede rose of Jerico,
> Close† garden of grace, hope in disparage,‡
> Whan my soule the body parte fro,
> Socoure it frome mine enmies' rage.[58]

Similar rhetorical schemes were used in lyrics to courtly mistresses, and some of the motifs were shared between the Virgin and earthly ladies: both were compared to flowers (especially the rose), stars and pearls.

The use of catalogues of symbolic epithets to address the Virgin was of course the authorised practice of the Church too, where Marian litanies praised her as Mirror of Justice, Seat of Wisdom, Cause of Our Joy, Spiritual Vessel, Mystical Rose, House of Gold, Star of the Morning, Queen of Angels, and so on.[59] One version of the litany of Loreto, in which these titles appear, contained seventy-three different invocations.[60] The medieval Virgin can readily be described in Freudian terms as an 'overdetermined' symbol, a composite figure overlaid with a multiplicity of superimposed meanings because she fulfilled a multiplicity of different desires.[61] This included the accretion of attributes from other iconographies.

vi. The identification of Marian iconography

This is a convenient place to pick some ways through this proliferation of iconography. Before examining the iconography of some temporal queens, and then of Elizabeth, it is necessary to sketch in some guide-lines as to how we might identify and understand iconography as distinctively and significantly Marian, or not.

---

* Perfect
† Closed
‡ despair

Emblems like the rose, the star, the moon, the pearl and the phoenix certainly occurred in litanies and lyrics about the Virgin, but were not solely Marian, having wider associations with pagan goddesses, courtly mistresses, and other idealisations of femininity. They could therefore be applied to other female figures without an echo of Mariology necessarily being implied.

However, three terms stand out in Marian iconography: among the numerous epithets of the litany of Loreto, most were variations on the themes of 'Mother', 'Virgin' and 'Queen'. The combination of these three terms might be described as distinctively Marian. However, if another female figure is herself literally a queen and a mother, or a virgin and a queen, these combinations of terms might be used in her iconography without necessarily invoking the Virgin. Indeed, even metaphorical motherhood, virginity or regality might be produced in iconography by other motivations than a desire to echo Mariology.

An important source for Marian iconography was the Bible. Old Testament figures such as Judith and Esther had been read as typological forebears of Mary.[62] Patristic writings interpreted the Woman Clothed with the Sun of Revelation as a type of the Church and thereby of Mary; this continues to this day in the use of the relevant verses of Revelation in the Roman Catholic Mass for the feast of the Assumption of the Virgin on 15 August.[63] The bride of the Song of Songs had also become traditionally associated with the Virgin, and had given rise to the idea of the Immaculate Conception, from the verse, 'tota pulchra es amica mea et macula non est in te' ('You are all fair, my love, and there is no spot in you').[64] Mary as the Immaculate Conception was believed to have been conceived without lust or sin by her parents, St Joachim and St Anne, and to be therefore exempt from the universal human taint of Original Sin, suitably pure to be in turn the maternal vessel for God's Son. In pre-Reformation England this was a well-developed and widely-known belief, although it had not been ratified by the Church and was not universally accepted.[65]

Representation of a secular female figure as without spot might therefore constitute an appropriation of Marian iconography. On the other hand, it might merely constitute an appropriation of the iconography of the bride of the Song of Songs. An important consideration with post-Reformation typological iconography is that much Protestant theology was precisely about the return to the Word, and rejection of the cults of the Virgin and saints as having no literal scriptural foundation. Typological identification of a female figure with Old Testament heroines or the Woman Clothed with the Sun can therefore be seen as placing her in a direct relation with those biblical figures, bypassing and excluding the Virgin Mary. Classical figures can be seen in a similar way. For instance, Mary took over some attributes of the goddess Diana; if another female figure were then likened to Diana, that need not mean that she was being likened to the Virgin as well. Overall, it is difficult to define as Marian all this iconography which the Virgin herself borrowed and accrued from other prior figures. In a comparison between, say, Elizabeth and the bride of the Song of Songs, an audience may be intended to be aware of unspoken Marian resonances, or not; the Virgin may in effect be present as an assumed third term, or she may be being purposefully deleted. This presents a problem of interpretation, and makes context crucially important.

However, some biblical scenes and roles belong unequivocally to the Virgin, such as the Annunciation, the Nativity, and the role of a Second Eve who reverses the Fall.[66] The use of these terms in panegyric of a secular figure can be justifiably described as an invocation of Mariology. In fact, it represents the direct use of the Virgin herself as a source for typology.

The overall format of the litany of Loreto, in which each invocation is followed by the plea 'Ora' ('Pray for us'), stresses the Virgin's role as intercessor. This is a distinctively Catholic function, though again not confined to the Virgin, since all saints could be invoked as intercessors. The Virgin, however, was the pre-eminent saint and mediatrix; other female saints tended to be modelled on her.[67] This role of loving mediation between the human and divine can therefore be justifiably identified as a Marian transfer when applied to another female figure. In particular, the word 'grace' was distinctively associated with Marian intercession and mercy, arising from the words of the Ave Maria, the prayer to the Virgin in general use since the late twelfth century: 'Ave Maria, gratia plena' ('Hail Mary, full of grace').[68] The prayer was known through the Middle Ages not only in Latin but also in English versions.[69] At the same time, the conception of the Virgin as able to intercede and dispense mercy and grace can be seen, like the iconography of heavenly monarchy, as reflexive of secular social structures of judgement, rule and hierarchical power.

Overall, I suggest that there is a need to restrain a tendency in some previous studies of Elizabethan iconography to seize eagerly on vestigial and indirect resemblances to Mariology. Moreover, where unequivocally Marian iconography is transferred to other female figures, there are different ways in which it can be deployed.

vii. Anne Boleyn's coronation pageants, 1533

Any transfer of Marian iconography to Elizabeth was far from unprecedented. Before the Reformation, it was conventional for regal women to be praised in terms which resembled those addressed to the Virgin Mary. In France, Blanche of Castile, Queen Mother in the late twelfth and early thirteenth centuries, promoted devotion to the Virgin and was herself represented in Marian forms.[70] A poem by the fifteenth-century writer François Villon celebrating the name 'Marie' given to the newborn daughter of the Duke of Orleans praised Marie/Mary as 'Hors le pechié originel' (free of original sin).[71] In England, medieval queens consort could be aptly represented in Marian terms as loving mediators between the King and his subjects, just as the Virgin was believed to intercede between Christ the King and his individual followers. Henry VI's consort for instance, Margaret of Anjou, had been associated with the Virgin in coronation pageants which represented her as an intercessor who would bear a godly royal heir.[72] Unlike Jewel's condemnation of the Virgin Mediatrix as a usurping matriarch, this iconography firmly placed the female intercessor in a subordinate position.

The influence of this medieval tradition can be strongly traced in the coronation pageants for Elizabeth's mother, Anne Boleyn. These civic celebrations combined classical iconography and Latin verses influenced by the new humanist learning with perpetuations of the iconography of medieval queens consort, including the use of Marian terms – even though Anne was the first Protestant Queen of England, and was actively associated with the patronage of Protestant reform.[73]

As she made her way along the route from the Tower to Westminster Abbey on 31 May 1533, the eve of her coronation, Anne stopped at various points to view tableaux and to hear accompanying verses and songs by John Leland and Nicholas Udall.[74] Great stress was laid on her fecundity; she was nearly six months pregnant, and her condition was conspicuous.[75] During the second pageant, at the corner of Gracechurch Street, one of the nine Muses, Urania, sang:

> Imò si retinent fidem,
>   Nec sunt astra nimis falsáque, vanáque,
> Iamdudum Annae vterus tumens,
>   Mox dulcem pariet mox tibi principem.

(Indeed if the stars keep faith, and are neither too false nor vain, already for a long time Anne's womb has been swelling, and soon a sweet prince will appear.)[76]

Marian iconography was most explicit in the pageant at 'Cornehill besides Leaden hall', which made use of the fact that Anne shared her name with the Virgin's mother. This correspondence of names was used typologically, to suggest holy sanction of Anne's coronation. The pageant showed 'the progenie of saint Anne', and was described by one contemporary as follows:

> ... on the said flour sate saynt Anne in the hyest place / on that one syde her progeny with scripture / that is to wete / the thre Marys with their issue / that is to vnderstande: Mary the mother of Christ / Mary Solome the mother of zebedee / with the two chyldren of them / also Mary Cleophe with her husbande Alphee / With their four chyldren on that other syde / With other poetycall verses sayd and songe / with a balade in englische to her great prayse [and] honour / & to al her progeny also.[77]

There was a legend that St Anne had two other daughters besides the Virgin Mary by previous husbands, that their names were also Mary, and that their children were the 'brethren' of Jesus mentioned in the Gospels.[78] The verses spoken made clear the wish for Queen Anne to produce a messianic heir, indeed a holy dynasty:

> For like as from this deuout Saint Anne,
> Issued this holy generacion,
> First Christ, to redeeme the fall of man,
> Then Jams thapostle, and theuangelist Jhon,
> With these others, whiche in suche fascion,
> by teaching and good lif, our faith confirmed,
> That from that tyme yette it hathe not failed,
>
> Right soo dere ladie, our quene moste excellente,
> highly endued with all giftes of grace,

As by your living is well apparente,
Wee the Citizens, by you, in shorte space,
hope suche issue, and descente to purchace,
Whereby the same faith shalbee defended,
And this Citie from all daungers preserued.[79]

The next tableau showed a white falcon, the crest of Anne Boleyn, which descended from a cloud and alighted on a rose bush, the Tudor crest. An angel descended from the same cloud to crown the falcon, accompanied by the line 'it cummeth from God, and not of man'. The audience were to be left in no doubt as to the divine approval of Henry's second marriage. As the Queen moved on past the pageant, a ballad in praise of the falcon was sung: the bird shines brightly, is virtuous beyond mortal praise, is the personification of 'gentilness', and so on. Most strikingly, the song took the following turn:

> In chastitee
> Excedeth she
>   moste like a virgin bright,
> And worthie is
> To liue in blisse
>   Alwayes this Falcon whight.

> But now to take
> And vse hir make
>   Is tyme, as trauthe is plight,
> That she maye bring
> Frute according
>   For suche a Falcon whight.[80]

Anne is praised within a few lines both for her virginal chastity, and for her fruitfulness. This paradox appears to be generated both by mere convention as to the virtues to be praised in a queen, and by a purposeful evocation of the virgin birth.

In an invocation of classical mythology, some verses delivered at the great conduit in Cheapside referred to the Virgilian legend of the return from heaven of the virgin Astraea, patron of justice: the Golden Age had been restored under Queen Anne's auspices.[81] In the circumstances, it seems justifiable to find Marian resonances even in this classical iconography. Since Virgil's Fourth Eclogue referred not only to the return of the virgin Astraea, but also to the birth of a child-saviour, it had been interpreted as a prophecy of the coming of Christ, and Astraea had been interpreted as a type of the Virgin Mary. Astraea/Anne's restoration of the Golden Age is like the Virgin's reversal of the Fall as Second Eve and mother of the Saviour.[82]

As Anne passed through Paul's Gate, three ladies sat in a tableau, each holding tablets with texts. One of these said 'Veni amica coronaberis', 'Come, my love, you shall be crowned', echoing the use of the line 'Veni coronaberis' in medieval hymns to the Virgin, as discussed earlier in this chapter, and therefore invoking the iconography of the Coronation of the Virgin as well as that of the Song of Songs.[83] The pageants concluded with Leland's Latin Acclamation on the Coronation, which described Anne as fairer ('candidior') than the Thames's swans, than milk and than snow. The word used for milk was 'colostrum', a term for the first milk in the breast after giving birth.[84]

The effect of Marian iconography on the audience for these pageants must have been at once familiar and mystical: it assimilated Anne to a well-known and popular model of femininity, while at the same time implying an aura of sacredness and divine endorsement. This was much-needed in the circumstances, with Henry's popular first queen still living, and the refusal of papal sanction for his divorce. In no sense does the Marian imagery set Anne up as a replacement for the Virgin Mary; rather, it is an example of the typological use of Mariology to lay claim to divine approval, for political reasons, in a difficult political situation.

As with previous medieval queens consort, the deployment of Marian imagery defined the Queen's role as primarily that of producing an heir, ensuring a peaceful transition from one king to the next. In the case of Anne Boleyn this role was especially important, since she had attained the throne primarily by virtue of being apparently able to give the King and the nation the male heir which his previous queen had failed to provide. She may have participated in her own Marian iconography as part of her strategy to become the King's wife and not merely his mistress: before Henry's divorce, he and Anne exchanged love-notes in an illuminated Book of Hours which was passed back and forth during morning mass in the royal chapel, and Anne wrote under an illumination of the Annunciation: 'By daily proof you shall me find / To be to you both loving and kind'.[85] 'Kind' at this date could mean 'sexually willing',[86] but Anne was not merely flirting; by attaching this motto to the Annunciation, she was offering the King her safely-virginal and fertile womb for his God-like impregnation, to produce a messianic heir.

The political context of Anne's coronation, in this age when religion and politics were so inextricably entwined, included the need for an heir to secure the 'true' faith, the newly-established Protestant English Church. Retrospective reading of the pageants is ironically coloured by the knowledge that the child in Anne's swelling womb was not a messianic boy-child, but Elizabeth; and that nevertheless Elizabeth would be the heir of Henry VIII who secured the Protestant faith in England. Ironically again, Elizabeth would herself refuse the role of heir-producer so clearly delineated in representations of her mother, and, as we shall see, of her sister, and with such woeful outcomes in their lives.[87] The medieval tradition of using Marian imagery for a mortal queen was in some ways aggrandising and celebratory, comparing her to the Queen of Heaven and Mother of God; but in other ways it was restrictive and depreciatory, defining her as secondary to both her husband and her wished-for son, incapable of independent rule, merely a vessel to be used for the perpetuation of a masculine dynasty.

It notable that Anne, a Protestant queen, was represented in Marian terms with no apparent anxiety concerning idolatry On 1 September 1559, less than a year into Elizabeth's reign, Alexander Ales (or Alesius), an eminent reformist theologian who had been at Henry VIII's court in the 1530s, wrote to her from Leipzig where he was then settled. His letter was an account of her mother's life and death, asserting throughout her active patronage of religious reforms: 'True religion in England had its commencement and its end with your mother.' It was a fairly obvious piece of polemic aimed at influencing Elizabeth to sponsor reform, and possibly to dispense some personal favour to Ales himself. However, even writing from an explicitly Protestant standpoint, Ales used some terms which resembled the cult of the Virgin. He presented his account of Anne Boleyn much like a saint's life from *The Golden Legend*:

> it has often occurred to me that it was a duty which I owed to the Church, to write this history, or tragedy, of the death of your most holy mother, in order to illustrate the glory of God and to afford consolation to the godly . . . I have been admonished from heaven by a vision or dream . . . to make it known to the world.

He recalled how on the day of Anne's execution he visited Cranmer, Archbishop of Canterbury, in the garden of Lambeth Palace, who sadly 'raised his eyes to heaven and said, "She who has been the Queen of England upon earth will to-day become a Queen in heaven."' The doctrine that true believers, especially martyrs for the faith, would be crowned as saints in heaven retained importance in Protestantism; it was only prayers and feast-days to saints which were distrusted as detracting from the worship of God. Godly death is therefore a particular area in which some continuing overlaps between Protestant and Catholic iconography can be traced. This account of Anne Boleyn's death converted iconography of the Assumption and Coronation of the Virgin into a model of godly Protestant death, in a fashion to be recalled decades later by elegies for Anne's daughter. Ales concluded by assuring Elizabeth:

> the fixed decree of God remained unaltered by which you were placed in the room of your most holy mother, whose innocence God has declared by the most indisputable miracles, and proved by the testimonies of all godly men.[88]

In order to stress the divine approbation of Protestant monarchy, Ales mobilised a rhetoric of martyrdom, saintliness and miracle not unlike that whose use by Catholics was condemned by reformist theologians as superstitious and idolatrous.

viii. Ballads for Mary I, 1553–8

The reign of Mary Tudor saw extensive use of Marian iconography in royal panegyric. Again, this was partly a perpetuation of the iconography of medieval queens consort. Mary was the first queen regnant since Matilda's brief and transitory ousting of Stephen from the throne in the twelfth century, and the redeployment of already-familiar imagery was therefore a means of accommodating the aberrant phenomenon of a woman ruling in her own right.[89] At the same time, of course, Marian transfers were given particular impetus by the fact that the Queen had restored Catholicism and shared the Virgin's name. Thus, once more, the use of Marian iconography formed part of the negotiation of potential political problems: female rule, and the reversal of the Henrician Reformation.

A notable example is 'A New Ballade of the Marigolde' by William Forrest, Mary's chaplain. The ballad opened with praise of various flowers, then made clear that this was not just an echo of the imagery of courtly love, but a deliberate appropriation of the abundant floral imagery of many hymns to the Virgin.

> To MARIE our queene, that flowre so sweete,
>> This Marigolde I doo apply ...
> Shee may be calde Marigolde well,
>> Of *Marie* (chiefe) Christes mother deere;
> That as in heaven shee doth excell,
> And *golde* in earth to have no peere,
> So certainly, shee shineth cleere,
>> In grace and honour double folde,
> The like was never earst seene heere –
> Suche is this floure, the Marigolde.[90]

A long ballad of 1554 by Miles Hogarde used the Flight into Egypt as an allegory of the restoration of the banished Catholic faith.[91] His use of typology is made explicit in dedicatory verses to the Queen:

> And because thensample doth serue so well
> howe marye with Christe into egypte fledde
> for fere of herod that Tyraunte fell
> which thynnocent*es* blud most Cruellie shedde
> And yit of his purpose nothing he spedde
> Butt shortlie did die, the scripture is playne
> And then did marie bring Christe home aye*n*ne
>
> This Insample I saie ca*m*me to my mynde
> Seing Christe banyshed oute of theys lande ...
>
>> (f.2v)

The line 'Marie hath brought home, christe agayne' is used in the heading of the ballad itself (f.6r), and runs as a refrain through many of the stanzas. Evidently Herod, the ungodly tyrant, represents Northumberland, while Queen Mary is identified with the Virgin as maternal protector of the true faith.

Hogarde specifically praises the Queen for restoring the doctrine of transubstantiation. He thereby implicitly connects the Eucharist as sacramental with the true monarch as sanctified: just as the

Eucharist is the physical embodiment of Christ, so Mary is the earthly
agent of the divine purpose. He also praises Mary for reversing
Protestant tolerance of the marriage of priests, through both her
policy and her exemplary purity (suggesting that the poem was
probably written before her marriage):

> Where theie we harde did beastlie teache
> That in this lif none could lyve Chaste
> Butt fleshe to fleshe muste nedes be leach
> Suche Beastes marye hath clene defaste
> Grace and vertue sithe she imbraste.

(f.7r)

He frequently refers to Mary as 'hir grace', purposefully blending
Marian and regal connotations.

During Mary's reign was issued John Wayland's *Primer in Latin
and English*, 1555, which contained the last version of the Hail Mary
to be set forth in an official service book of the Church of England:
'Hayle mary full of grace, oure Lorde is with thee. blessed be thou
among women, and blessed be the fruite of thy wombe Jesus.
Amen.'[92] Another ballad of Mary's reign was entitled 'An AVE
MARIA in Commendation of our most Vertuous Queene', and was
full of echoes of the prayer to the Virgin.[93] It opened: 'Haile Quene
of England, of most worthy fame / For vertue, for wisdome, for
mercy & grace.' The Queen's 'grace' was repeatedly stressed through
the stanzas, and she was hailed as 'Marie, the mirrour of merciful-
nesse', and as an intercessor: 'vnto this lande our Lorde, for her
loue, / Hath of his mercy most mercifull bene.' Finally, the wish
was expressed, 'Fruyte of her body God graunte vs to see', again
directly recalling the Ave Maria, with its line, 'blessed be the fruite
of thy wombe'.[94] As in the case of Anne Boleyn, this is a prayer for
the Queen to give birth to a saviour for the nation who will preserve both the Tudor dynasty and the 'true' faith, though in this
case of course that faith was Catholic. When Mary was believed to
be pregnant, religious ceremonies of thanksgiving and prayer made
overt use of texts concerning the Virgin.[95]

The occasion of Mary's death reinforced the analogy with her
namesake. A broadside 'Epitaphe' asserted that 'to praye was her
delight', and she was 'a Mary named right'. She was hailed as 'O
pearle most pure! . . . O mirrour of all woman hed! O Quene of

vertues pure! / O constant MARIE! filde with grace; no age can thee obscure.'[96]

It is perhaps to be expected that a Catholic Queen called Mary should have been compared with the Virgin.[97] The same process occurred in relation to Mary Queen of Scots; for instance, an Italian poem on her death was structured as a gloss on the Ave Maria.[98] It is notable, however, that such identification of a mortal queen with the Blessed Virgin does not seem to have been perceived as sacrilegious by loyal Catholics. It also disrupts the theory that Elizabeth was praised in Marian terms because she filled a psychological gap left when the Virgin was no longer venerated: Mary's subjects were free to venerate the Virgin and her icons, indeed were encouraged to do so, but at the same time appropriated Marian iconography for panegyric of their Queen. In the cases of both Elizabeth's sister and her mother, a counterpoint of purity and fertility was central to queenly iconography, and Marian terms were deployed typologically to lay claim to divine sanction in awkward political circumstances.

2

A New Queen

i. The monstrous regiment of women, 1558

When Elizabeth succeeded to the throne on 17 November 1558, she and her followers urgently needed an effective iconography which would inspire confidence in the new regime. Her sister had left a legacy of political challenges. Mary's burning of Protestants at Smithfield, her marriage to Philip II of Spain, the perceived subjugation of England's foreign policy to his, and the consequent loss of Calais, had all generated hostility not only to Catholicism, but also to female rule. Doubts had been aroused as to the very propriety and legitimacy of government by a woman.

In 1558, before Mary I's death, John Knox published *The First Blast of the Trumpet against the Monstruous Regiment of Women*, a strident attack on the 'regiment' (that is, rule or government) of Mary and the other female Catholic rulers of Europe. Although the book was motivated by religious dissent, Knox formulated his polemic in terms of gender. He wrote that rulers 'oght to be constant, stable, prudent and doing euerie thing with discretion and reason, whiche vertues women can not haue in equalitie with men.'[1] The feminine virtues to which a woman should aspire were fundamentally opposed to the virtues required of a ruler: 'vertues in which [women] excell, they haue not comon with men . . . [woman is] a tendre creature, flexible, soft and pitifull; whiche nature, God hath geuen vnto her, that she may be apt to norishe children' (ff.24r, 25v). In any case, though, female nature was such that a woman was more likely to excel in vice than even feminine virtues:

> Nature, I say, doth paynt [women] furthe to be weake, fraile, impacient, feble and foolishe: and experience hath declared them to be vnconstant, variable, cruell and lacking the spirit of counsel and regiment . . . in the nature of all women, lurketh suche vices, as in good gouernors are not tolerable.
>
> (ff.10r, 25r)

The elevation of a woman to rule was therefore 'monstriferous' (f.33v).

Knox was not alone in his views. He could cite the highest authorities in philosophy and theology, such as Aristotle and St Paul (ff.10r, 12r; 13r, 15r), and he was supported by contemporary texts like Christopher Goodman's *How Superior Powers be Obeyed* and Anthony Gilby's *An Admonition to England and Scotland*. Like Knox's *Blast*, both of these were written in 1558 and were motivated as Calvinist attacks on Mary I. In 1559, after Mary had died and Elizabeth had brought Protestantism to the throne, Knox wrote a series of attemptedly conciliatory letters to Sir William Cecil, her Principal Secretary, and to the Queen herself. However, his persistent argument was that Elizabeth must acknowledge that she was raised by God and not by the laws of man: 'albeit that nature and Godes most perfect ordinaunce repugne to soche regiment . . . the extraordinary dispensation of Godes great mercy maketh that lawfull unto her, which both nature and Godes law denye'. To Elizabeth herself he wrote: 'I cannote denie the writting of a booke against the usurped Authoritie and unjust Regiment of Women; neyther yit am I mynded to retreate or call backe anie principall point, or propositioun of the sam, till truthe and veritie doe farther appear.'[2] Calvin also wrote to Cecil to attempt to reconcile the new regime to the Genevan camp; he said that because female rule 'was a deviation from the primitive and established order of nature, it ought to be held as a judgment on man for his dereliction of his rights, just like slavery.'[3] In other words, he would not oppose female rule, but only because it was to be endured as a divinely imposed penance for human sinfulness, like famine or plague.

Even Knox's attack, however, was a contribution to the iconography of the good female ruler, if only through negativity and contrast. In the *Blast* he contrasted contemporary queens with figures of virtuous female rule from the Old Testament, such as Deborah, Judge of Israel:

> God by his singular priuiledge, fauor, and grace, exempted Debora from the common malediction geuen to women in that behalf: and against nature he made her prudent in counsel, strong in courage, happie in regiment, and a blessed mother and deliuerer to his people.
>
> (ff.41v–42r)

In his letter to Elizabeth, he said that if she would humbly acknowledge that she was raised by God and not man, he would support
her rule 'as the Holie Ghost hath justified the same in Deborah, that
blessed mother in Israel'.[4] Calvin, too, in his letter to Cecil, explained that he had used similar typological figures in remonstra-
tions with Knox: 'I here instanced Huldah and Deborah. I added to
the same effect that God promised by the mouth of Isaiah that
queens should be the nursing mothers of the church, which clearly
distinguished such persons from private women.'[5] Such thinking
prepared the ground for panegyrists of Elizabeth, in searching for
a new Protestant iconography of female rule, to turn to Old Testament figures like Deborah and to Isaiah's metaphor of the nursing
mother. Deborah notably differed from other Old Testament heroines in that she had not been regularly invoked as a type of the
Virgin Mary.[6]

Another strategy used to counter the doubt which had been cast
on female rule was to emphasise the sacredness of monarchy, and
in particular the theory of the King's Two Bodies. In general, according to Plowden, the 'disability of the body naturall is wasshed
away by accesse of the body politicke to it'. In particular, if an
ordinary man had only daughters, the inheritance should be shared
between them, whereas if a king had only daughters, the whole
inheritance passed to the eldest, as if she were a man.[7] Thus, despite the femaleness of her body natural, Elizabeth could lay claim
to the 'masculine' public virtues of rule through her possession of
the body politic. The concept of her two bodies, one private and
feminine, the other public and implicitly 'masculine' in its virtues,
is one element in the well-known proliferation of androgynous iconography around her.

Elizabeth herself deployed the rhetoric of the King's Two Bodies
from the very beginning, in a speech apparently made to her Council shortly after her accession:

> ... considering I am Gods Creature, ordeyned to obey his ap-
> pointment I will thereto Yelde, desiringe from the bottom of my
> harte that I may have assistance of his Graces to bee the minister
> of his Heavenly Will in this office now comytted to me ... I am
> but one Bodye naturallye Considered though by his permission
> a Bodye Politique to Governe.[8]

Elizabeth here allies the idea of her two bodies with the idea that
she is God's instrument. In doing so, she does not counter Knox's

assertion that femaleness and rule are mutually opposed; rather, she suggests that God has chosen to overcome her natural disability of femaleness. Although this rhetoric is not explicitly Mariological, it does proceed along parallel lines to Marian iconography in presenting Elizabeth as an exceptional woman. The Virgin's purity, or Elizabeth's regality, are not taken to prove the potential purity or regality of all women; rather, they emphasise the impurity and unfitness for rule of women in general by stressing how miraculous and unique is the exceptional woman in rising above it, 'alone of all her sex'.[9] Elizabeth asserts her own divine sanction to rule, but does not thereby counter the arguments against female rule in general; indeed if anything, she confirms them.

The images of Deborah, of mother of the nation, and of Elizabeth as God's instrument were all extensively deployed in the iconography surrounding her accession. In surveying some key texts from this period we can see new adaptations of, and departures from, Marian iconography; and, at the same time, we can see Elizabeth herself becoming an image or icon.

ii. Elizabeth's coronation pageants, 1559

Elizabeth made her way along the traditional route from the Tower to Westminster Abbey on the eve of her coronation, 14 January 1559. An account of the procession and the pageants was rushed into print a mere nine days later, entitled *The Quenes Maiesties Passage through the Citie of London to Westminster the Day before her Coronacion*, and almost immediately went into a second edition.[10] The author of the pamphlet, who may well have been Richard Mulcaster,[11] stressed that unlike Mary I's entry in 1553, when the main pageants were staged by the London communities of foreign merchants,[12] on this occasion the city 'without anye forreyne persone, of it selfe beautifyed it selfe' (sig.E2v). We can detect in the description of the spectacle a determined attempt both to refute dissent against rule by a woman, and to reshape traditional iconography in a distinctively nationalistic and Protestant fashion. The pageants are therefore notable for their avoidance of overtly Marian iconography, finding other female icons to whom to compare Elizabeth, or silencing the Marian associations of traditional iconic forms. They also demonstrate an emergent Protestant ideology of 'correct' uses of images.

The first pageant, at the upper end of 'Gracious' or Gracechurch

Street, was entitled 'The vniting of the two houses of Lancastre and Yorke'. An actor represented Henry VII, enclosed in a red rose of Lancaster; next to him was his queen, Elizabeth of York, enclosed in a white rose. Above them were Henry VIII and Anne Boleyn, then a figure representing Elizabeth herself. 'The hole pageant [was] garnished with redde roses and white', but these were decidedly Tudor roses; no connection was drawn with the rose as emblem of the Virgin.

The form of a genealogical tree rising upwards derived from the medieval Marian icon of the Tree of Jesse. This was a representation of the stock of David, deriving from Isaiah 11.1, and showed a line of kings growing from the 'root' of Jesse, culminating in the flower or fruit of either the Virgin Mary or Christ.[13] There were precedents for the use of a genealogical tree in English state pageantry, sometimes using Jesse and other biblical figures, but also sometimes simply using the form to represent an entirely secular dynasty. For instance, the pageants welcoming Charles V to London in 1522 included a tree of descent growing from John of Gaunt and culminating in Charles V and Henry VIII.[14] The pageant of the progeny of St Anne during the coronation procession of Anne Boleyn employed the Marian associations of the form; but the use of the family tree motif for Elizabeth is secularised, entirely centring on the Tudor dynasty, even in its use of the same device of a congruence of names:

> This pageant was grounded vpon the Queenes maiesties name. For like as the long warre betwene the two houses of Yorke and Lancastre then ended, when Elizabeth doughter to Edwarde the fourthe matched in mariage . . . like as Elizabeth was the first occasion of concorde, so she another Elizabeth might maintaine the same among her subiectes, so that vnitie was the ende wherat the whole deuise shotte.
>
> (sigs A4r–B3r)

Elizabeth I is not identified, say, with St Elizabeth, but with her own grandmother Elizabeth of York. Richard Grafton, who was one of the devisers of the pageants[15] and who included an account of them in his *Abridgement of the Chronicles of Englande*, differed from the pamphleteer's entirely secular interpretation, but only to make his own version explicitly Protestant: the pageant 'signified the coniunction and coupling together of our soueraigne Lady with the

Gospell and veritie of Goddes holy woord, for the peaceable gouernement of all her good subiectes'.[16]

The second pageant, at the 'nether end' of Cornhill, showed 'a childe representing her maiesties person, placed in a seate of gouernement, supported by certaine vertues, which . . . did treade their contrarie vices vnder their feete'. These included Pure Religion, who trampled Superstition and Ignorance. To some extent these allegorical figures, who we are told were not only labelled for ease of identification but also aptly dressed, were a perpetuation of the Vice and Virtue personifications of mediaeval morality drama; but, at the same time, the anti-Catholic sentiment of the pageant and the violent treading down of the vices makes for a strikingly and paradoxically iconographic display of iconoclasm. The verses which accompanied the pageant were highly conditional in tone: *if* Elizabeth sustains the virtues and suppresses the vices, *then* the seat of government will stand firm (sigs B3r–C1r). The third pageant, at the great conduit in Cheap, was similarly conditional. It depicted the eight Beatitudes of the Sermon on the Mount, and informed Elizabeth that 'if her grace did continue in her goodnes as she had entred, she shoulde hope for the fruit of these promises' (sig.C2v).

The greatest excitement was generated by the pageant at the little conduit in Cheap. Elizabeth 'espyed' it before she had got to it, 'and incontinent required to know what it might signifye'. She was told that it showed Truth the daughter of Time: 'Tyme? qu*oth* she, and Tyme hath brought me hether', implicitly identifying herself with Truth. When she heard that Truth would present her with an English Bible, 'she thanked the citie for that gift, and sayd that she would oftentimes reade ouer that booke' (sig.C2v).

After she had received a purse from the Recorder of the City, heard his speech, and given a speech in reply, she finally reached the Time/Truth tableau. It showed two hills, one barren, representing a ruined state, and one flourishing, representing a well-ruled nation. Between them was a locked cave, from which Time released Truth after what was said to have been an imprisonment of many years, implying a resemblance to the constraints placed upon Elizabeth during her sister's reign and therefore confirming her earlier identification of Truth with herself. Elizabeth received the English Bible, which had written upon it 'Verbum Veritatis', the word of Truth; she kissed it, held it aloft, laid it upon her breast, and thanked the city, a series of gestures making dramatically clear her commitment to Protestantism (sigs C3v–D1v). The symbolic book recalled the illustration on the title page of the 1539 Great Bible, which showed Henry VIII handing down copies of a book labelled 'Verbum Dei', and which had established a convention of reformist royal iconography.[17] A figure of Veritas holding a book labelled 'Verbum Dei' had appeared in the 1554 entry pageants of Mary and Philip, but only as an incidental figure. In the same pageants, it seems that a book labelled 'Verbum Dei' shown in the hand of a figure of Henry VIII was commanded to be painted out, being 'agaynst the quenes catholicke proceedings' – a striking example of Catholic iconoclasm turned against a Protestant icon.[18] The 1559 tableau as a whole can be seen as an aggressive appropriation of iconography from Mary I, since she had used 'Veritas Filia Temporis' as a personal motto. By the identifying of Elizabeth with Truth, Mary's truth is implied to have been deceit.

A Latin oration outside St Paul's School associated Elizabeth with the return of the Golden Age (sigs D1v–2v); then a pageant at the conduit in Fleet Street showed 'Debora the iudge and restorer of the house of Israel'. The representation of Deborah clearly identified her with Elizabeth: she was 'a semelie and mete personage richlie apparelled in parliament robes, with a sceptre in her hand, as a Quene, crowned with an open crowne'.[19] She was flanked by three pairs of personages representing the three estates – the nobility, the clergy and the commons. Both the pamphleteer and Grafton interpret this not only as a proof that women can rule, when aided by God, but also that rulers should consult and take advice from the estates (sigs D3r–4r).[20]

The need for proofs and precedents of successful female rule, and the implication that a queen will be unusually dependent on the support of God and her advisers, bespeak underlying anxiety about Elizabeth's ability to govern. This is confirmed by the verses summing up the pageants, which were displayed on tablets at Temple Bar, and which were directly didactic towards the Queen (sig.E1v); and by the farewell verses spoken by a child dressed as a poet. Just as several of the verses which we have already looked at were conditional in tone, so these are provisional, anxiously hopeful rather than confident:

This citie sendeth thee firme hope and earnest praier.,

For all men hope in thee, that all vertues shall reygne,

For all men hope that thou, none errour wilt support,
For all men hope that thou wilt trueth restore agayne . . .

(sig.E2r)

This not only speaks of the uncertainty of the political outlook in January 1559; it also initiates what was to become an important strain in Protestant panegyric. Praise of a monarch could be regarded as justified and not idolatrous if it was implicitly didactic, setting up an ideal to which the monarch should aspire, a template of future perfection for her to fulfil.

Throughout the pamphlet account the Queen's loving demeanour is highlighted, and its conclusion is headed: 'Certain notes of the quenes maiesties great mercie, clemencie, and wisdom vsed in this passage' (sigs E3r–4v). Here several incidents centring on Elizabeth are noted and commented upon. She was seen to smile when she overheard someone say 'Remember old king Henry theight', and this is interpreted as evidence that she will restore the supposed golden days of his reign (sig.E3r). The pamphleter also recounts:

How many nosegaies did her grace receiue at poore womens handes? how ofttimes staied she her chariot, when she saw any simple body offer to speake to her grace? A branche of Rosemarie giuen to her grace with a supplication by a poore woman about fleetebridge, was sene in her chariot till her grace came to westminster.

(sig.E3v)

This antecedent of the modern royal walkabout is given as evidence of the Queen's concern for the poor. In the detailed narrating of such episodes, her expressions, gestures and words are all scrutinised and interpreted. Elizabeth herself is treated as a text to be read, an image of the ideal female ruler. Anne Boleyn, in her coronation pageants, had been described as 'pudicitiae splendida imago' (splendid image of chastity), a use of the term 'imago' which strikingly verges on the modern figurative sense of the word 'image'.[21] It is easy to feel that in the account of Elizabeth's pageants she is not only being compared with images of ideal female rule, but is herself being turned into a symbol, a collection of signifiers which bear meaning.

In particular, Elizabeth's demeanour is interpreted as a sign of her godliness. As monarch she is the image of God, but at the same time she is to be read for confirmatory signs that she is a true godly ruler, and not an ungodly ruler sent as a punishment. She is therefore scrutinised much as a Protestant might examine his or her own behaviour and internal states as evidence of having been saved. The pamphleteer notes 'two principall sygnes' that Elizabeth is a truly godly ruler: her prayer as she set off from the Tower, and her manner of receiving the English Bible (sig.E4r). In the prayer, Elizabeth compared herself to Daniel in the lion's den, preserved and released by God, implying that her survival of her troubles under her sister's rule was miraculous. This mythologisation of her early years became a popular means of suggesting divine sanction for her rule. Grafton, for instance, who quotes the full speech from the pamphlet in his account of the procession, affirms that God sent Elizabeth in response to the prayers of the people, 'whome the same Almyghty God had (by speciall miracle) preserued in her innocencie from the malice, spoyle and daunger, of her extreame enemies'.[22] The assertion that both Elizabeth and the people of England had suffered under Mary I and come through created a sense of a special bond between them, a shared relief and cause for joy when Elizabeth succeeded.

The latter example of her godliness, her reception of the Bible, is a vivid instance of the dramatic qualities not only of the pageants themselves, but of Elizabeth's participation in them. Near the beginning of the pamphlet the author comments,

> if a man should say well, he could not better tearme the citie of London that time, then a stage wherin was shewed the wonderfull spectacle, of a noble hearted princesse toward her most louing people.
>
> (sig.A2v)

Elizabeth not only showed herself as a spectacle, but was shown to herself as a spectacle: she saw direct representations of herself in the first and second pageants, those of the uniting of the houses of Lancaster and York, and of the virtues supporting the seat of governance; and in the later pageants the modes of representation of Deborah and of Truth closely associated them with the Queen. Already this mirroring effect set up a reverberation between image and reality; and the line between image and reality, stage and audience, was crossed by Elizabeth's reception of the Bible and her dramatic display of pleasure in the gift. It was this traversal of the imaginary line which provided the most exciting, impressive and memorable moment for the audience; indeed, the audience themselves, whose cries and movements are described by the pamphleteer, were incorporated in the spectacle to fulfil the role of a dramatic chorus. It was a potent blurring of image and reality which set a precedent for many other public occasions of Elizabeth's reign.

Alongside these dramatic and iconographic qualities of the pageants, we should note the large quantity of writing which they employed. As in previous pageants, figures were labelled with their names and significances, and explanatory verses were both spoken and pinned up to be read next to the tableaux to which they applied. On this occasion, though, this textual content was more prolific than ever before. In most of the pageant descriptions, the pamphleteer remarks that 'euery voide place in the pageant was furnished with sentences touching the matter and ground of the said pageant' (sigs C3r, 4r). The labelling is often duplicated and elaborated, as in the description of Truth:

> directlye ouer her head was set her name and tytle in latin and Englyshe, *Temporis filia*, the daughter of Tyme ... And on her brest was written her propre name, whiche was *Veritas*. Trueth who helde a booke in her hande vpon the which was written, *Verbum veritatis*, the woorde of trueth.
>
> (sig.C4r–v)

On top of all this, a child spoke verses of explanation. There is almost a sense of verbalisation run wild. The pageants demonstrate the Protestant emphasis upon not only the Word, but words in general, as a repositories of Truth, as against visual images, which were felt to be falsifying and diversionary. It appears that a visual image could be legitimated by its incorporation of words and texts, and by its strong allegorical and didactic content. In both these qualities the pageants point forward to the emblem books which in subsequent decades were an acceptable and indeed popular form of visual imagery for Protestants.[23]

The pageants can therefore be said to be attempting to forge a new Protestant form of state iconography. The need for forms to represent political and spiritual power made inevitable some continuity from pre-Reformation precedents, such as in the use of typology. But typology in itself is not necessarily Marian, and it is striking how this typology bypasses Marian iconography. Elizabeth is compared to Deborah, but it is a comparison which is merely analogous to the interpretation of Old Testament figures as types of the Virgin, rather than a deployment of a figure with overt Marian associations. The pageant of the houses of York and Lancaster could have been given a Marian slant, but is kept decidedly secular; and the pageant of Truth is aggressively Protestant, taking over and cancelling out an iconography used by Mary I. Resemblances to the cult of the Virgin are in structure more than content: as with Mariology, the need to praise a female figure produces a proliferation of representations, suggesting that, at root, the pre-eminence of a woman generates anxiety.

The motivations behind this praise of Elizabeth can be seen partly in terms of mass psychology, a general relief at the end of Mary I's reign and therefore a spontaneous and popular outpouring of devotion to the new Queen. However, at the same time the tentative and conditional nature of many of the pageant verses suggests that, far from longing for a new symbolic virgin-mother figure, the citizens of London were deeply worried about female rule. They were working out an iconography which would both enable them to feel more comfortable with a female ruler, and set out clear guidelines for that ruler of what they wanted of her.

It is important to examine who was involved in the making of the pageants. A letter of 3 January 1559 from the Queen to Sir Thomas Cawarden, Master of the Revels, and other documents of the Revels Office, record the loan of costumes by the Crown for the pageants.[24] This strongly implies that Elizabeth gave her patronage and approval to the pageants while they were in preparation. Her anticipation of the Time/Truth tableau, and her quick-fire aphoristic response, suggest that she knew what was coming, either because she had been briefed in advance, or possibly even because she had had some influence in the content of the pageants. Undoubtedly the principal devisers of the pageants were representatives of the City,[25] and one need not suggest that a celebratory tone was imposed on reluctant citizens from above; but the performance of the love between the Queen and her people was less spontaneous than the pamphleteer pretended. To this extent, the Queen, the pageant-devisers and the pamphleteer can be seen as colluding in an act of propaganda. In its very purporting to be merely a record of a spontaneous upwelling of love between the Queen and her subjects, the pamphlet performs a political function.

In 1559 there was strong motivation to create a new iconography of Protestant female rule, but it was a mixed motivation from various groups: the Queen herself; her immediate supporters who hoped for a prominent role in her government; writers seeking patronage; and, on a more spiritual level, the Protestants of London, who hoped for a new godly regime. This hardly constitutes a populace bereft of the Virgin Mary and yearning for a replacement; and this is reflected in the resolutely non-Marian quality of the iconography of the coronation pageants.

iii. Faint praise of female rule

John Aylmer was a Protestant exile during Mary I's reign who returned to become Bishop of London under Elizabeth. In April 1559 he wrote a reply to Knox, entitled *An Harborowe for faithfull and trewe svbiectes*, which was intended both to reconcile Elizabeth to the Calvinist camp and to encourage Protestant loyalty to the new Queen. It is somewhat half-hearted as a defence of female monarchy. One of Aylmer's main lines of argument is to take Knox to task for the extremity of his terms: female rule was not 'vnnaturall', though of course no one could deny that it was 'not so continent, so profitable, or mete'.[26] He also echoes the coronation tableau of Deborah seeking advice from the three estates. He argues that the government of England is a combination of monarchy, oligarchy and democracy; therefore, 'it is not in England so daungerous a matter, to haue a woman ruler, as men take it to be. For . . . it is not she that ruleth but the lawes' (sigs H2v–3v) – and the officers who implement the laws are all men. As in the coronation pageants, there is a perceptible underlying nervousness about female rule.

However, Aylmer's *Harborowe* also participates in forging a new Protestant iconography of female rule. Aylmer expounds the doctrine that God's choice of a weak instrument such as a woman is evidence of his own miraculous strength:

> Placeth he a woman weake in nature, feable in bodie, softe in courage, vnskilfull in practise, not terrible to the enemy, no Shilde to the frynde, wel, 'Virtus mea' (saith he) 'In infirmitate perficitur' My strengthe is most perfight when you be moste weake, if he ioyne to his strengthe: she can not be weake. If he put to his hande she can not be feable, if he be with her who can stande against her? . . . It is as easy for him to saue by fewe as by many, by weake as by strong, by a woman as by a man.
> (sigs B2v–3r)

Here again is evidence of the 'exceptional woman' motif, whereby Elizabeth's miraculous gift of rule actually denies the ability of women in general. Aylmer uses Deborah and Judith here as examples of just such divine use of weak instruments (sig.B3v), and elsewhere as exemplary women rulers (sigs D2v, O4r), participating in the use of Old Testament typology to endorse the new Protestant Queen.

Another rhetorical device of Aylmer's is to accommodate Elizabeth to the familiar role of queen as prompt producer of an heir, and securer of the male dynasty: her subjects should pray for God,

> to guide hir harte in the choise of hir husbande, and to make hir frutefull, and the mother of manye chyldren, that thys Realme maye haue the graftes of so goodly a tree, That oure chyldren and posterite maye see hirs occupying hir throne, with honour, ioye, & quietnes.
>
> (sig.I2r–v)

Not only is she is to be a mother to her own physical offspring, but also, it becomes clear, a metaphorical mother to the whole nation. Throughout, Elizabeth's maternal clemency is stressed: 'She commeth in lyke a lambe, and not lyke a Lyon, lyke a mother, and not lyke a stepdam'; she is 'a louing Quene and mother to raigne ouer vs' (sigs N4v, Q3v). The figure of the mother, at once authoritative and caring, can be assimilated by Aylmer to a model of good rule, unlike Knox's categorical definition of the virtues of rule as exclusively masculine. At the same time, Aylmer is picking up on Knox's and Calvin's suggestions that if such an unlikely thing as a good female ruler existed, she would be a mother to the Church.

This is of course an allusion to the nursing mother metaphor in Isaiah, but Aylmer also perhaps alludes to the iconography of the Virgin as mother of the Church. His contrast between Mary I and Elizabeth as unnatural and natural mothers produces an echo of Marian iconography:

> as for thys losse we haue nowe, I doubte not, but as the olde fathers are wonte to saye, that as by a woman came death: so by a woman was broughte fourthe life. In like manner as bi a womans (whether negligence, or misfortune, I wote not) we haue taken this wound, so bi a nothers diligence and felicitie, we shal haue it againe healed.
>
> (sig.L3r–v)[27]

Just as the Fall was both caused by a woman and reversed by a woman, so the loss of Calais and the general injury to the nation by Mary I can be just as easily redeemed by a woman, associating Elizabeth with the role of the Virgin as Second Eve. Unusually for the iconography of these early years, Aylmer uses the Virgin directly as a source of typology, but even so does so only fleetingly, avoiding naming her, and with little elaboration.

Aylmer's text has a strongly nationalistic thrust: a passage on how God will defend the Protestant English state against its infidel enemies carries the marginal note 'God is English' (sig.P4v). Again drawing on Old Testament typology, England is represented as the new Israel, God's chosen though beleaguered nation. The national and maternal strains combine in the book's ending, where 'Mother England' describes a vision of peace and urges her children to be obedient to Elizabeth. This conventional representation of the nation as feminine, following on as it does from the incidental use of maternal imagery through the text, has the effect of identifying Elizabeth with the nation.

Mother England converts maternity from a Marian, Catholic attribute into a symbol of the progress of Protestantism, by claiming to have given birth to the Reformation: '. . . . out of my wombe . . . [came] Ihon Wyclefe, who begate Husse, who begat Luther, who begat truth. What greter honor could you or I haue, then that it pleased Christ as it were in a second birth to be borne again of me among you?' (sig.R1v) The placing of Truth at the end of this line of descent recalls the coronation pageants, but here Truth is identified not with Elizabeth but with Christ, implying a role for Elizabeth as nurturer of the faith.

Mother England speaks of her cornucopian bounty to her children: England here is not the people of England, who are placed in the dependent role of children or subjects, but the land and the timeless concept of the nation. This detachment of the concept of nation from the people facilitates the identification of England with Elizabeth. Love of England and obedience to Elizabeth are one and the same: England says, 'Obey your mistres and mine which God hath made lady ouer vs, bothe by nature and lawe. You can not be my children, if you be not her subiectes: I wyll none of you, if you will none of hir' (sig.R2r). If the people 'obey [Elizabeth], honour hir, and loue hir', the duties owed to a mother, then England will reward them with the 'good frutes' of a mother: 'I wyll fill your bosomes and your mouthes, your wyues, and your children, with plentie' (sigs R1v–2r). Simultaneously Elizabeth's own maternal tenderness continues to be stressed, as 'that care and loue whiche she beareth toward you' (sig.R2v), so that the figures of Mother England and Elizabeth overlap closely with each other.

As in the pageants, Aylmer's vision of a peaceful nation is utopian, hopeful and idealistic rather than confident. As a Protestant churchman, Aylmer badly wants Elizabeth to be a successful monarch, but in 1559 this looks far from certain. Figures like Deborah, Judith and Mother England are identified with Elizabeth, but only to the extent that it is hoped she might grow into these identities. Much maternal imagery is used to naturalise female rule, but Aylmer avoids explicit or extended allusion to Mariology.

iv. The question of marriage

According to Aylmer, Elizabeth's role of mother to the nation included a duty to be a physical mother, to produce an heir of her body and ideally several spares as well. The immediate precedent to Elizabeth, Mary I, had evidently seen her first duty as Queen in this way. Elizabeth was different, though, and her reluctance to marry seems to have been more than mere avoidance of her sister's sad and unpopular example. Princess Elizabeth had already made clear her aversion to matrimony before she became Queen. When Sir Thomas Pope was sent by Mary to discover Elizabeth's response to a proposal from a foreign prince, the Princess reminded him that when Edward VI was King, she had asked permission 'to remayne in that estate I was, which of all others best lyked me or pleased me . . . I am even at this present of the same minde . . . I so well like this estate, as I perswade myselfe ther is not anie kynde of liffe comparable unto it'. Pope suggested that she would accept an offer if it were sanctioned by Mary; this suitor had breached royal etiquette by approaching Elizabeth directly.

> Wherunto her Grace answered, what I shall do hereafter I knowe not; but I assure you upon my truthe and fidelitie, and as God be mercifull unto me, I am not at this tyme otherways mynded, than I have declared unto you; no, though I were offered the greatest Prince in all Europe.[28]

Despite the unpopularity of Mary I's Spanish marriage, Elizabeth's subjects seem to have persisted in the assumption that the first duty of a Queen was to marry and produce a male heir. One of the first deeds of Elizabeth's first Parliament, in February 1559, was to petition the 25-year-old Queen to marry. Her reply echoed and amplified her statement to Pope:

> I may saye vnto yow, that from my yeares of vnderstanding syth I first had consideracion of my self to be borne a servitor of almightie god I happelie chose this kynde of life, in which I yet lyve which I assure yow for myne owne parte, hath hitherto best contented my self and I trust hath bene moost acceptable to god.[29]

She went on to refer to her rejections of offers of marriage during her sister's reign, despite pressures on her to accept them, and declared:

> But constant have [I] allwayes contynued in this determinacion although my youth and wordes may seme to some hardlie to agree together; yet is it moost true, that at this daie I stand free from anie other meaninge that either I have had in tymes paste, or have at this present with which trade of life I am so throughlie acquainted, that I truste, God who hath hitherto therin preserued me, and led me by the hand, will not nowe of his goodnes suffer me to goe alone.

She assured them that if she did marry, it would be to someone who had as much care for them as herself – no doubt a strategic inducement of a shudder at the memory of Philip of Spain. She argued that just as God had brought her to the throne, he would provide an heir by his own means when necessary; besides, 'yet may my issue growe out of kynde, and become perhappes vngracious'. She declared, 'And in the end this shalbe for me sufficient that a marble stone shall declare that a Queene, hauing reygned suche a tyme, lyued and dyed a virgin.'[30] She ended by thanking Parliament 'more yet for your zeale, good will & good meanyng then for your message and peticion'. Although she was careful to leave the door to matrimony slightly ajar, she clearly wished the subject to be closed.

The reasons for Elizabeth's reluctance to marry are open to speculation. Perhaps it was the result of the childhood trauma of her mother's execution by her father; or the adolescent trauma of the Thomas Seymour scandal; or her reluctance to surrender absolute political autonomy; or the fact that all the various candidates at

various times carried liabilities of one kind or another; or that inter-
minable marriage negotiations were a useful tool in foreign policy;
or a combination of all of these factors. Whatever is true, her reluctance was clear; the letters of Cecil from the early years of the reign
refer repeatedly and with increasing desperation to the fact that
'her Majestie cannot be induced, whereof we have cause to sorrow,
to allow of any marriadg with any manner of person.'[31]

This reluctance was out of step not only with political thinking,
but also with Protestant theology. The Protestant line was that celibacy was impossible to fallen human beings; that the imposition of
celibacy on Catholic priests and nuns had produced secret fornication and perversion; and that it was less hypocritical to aspire to
virtuous matrimony.[32] This thinking was endorsed in such early
Elizabethan texts as Thomas Becon's *Booke of Matrimony*, 1560, in
which he repeatedly praised matrimony over virginity.[33] He explained that marriage is necessary because chastity is so difficult;
chastity is 'the greate and singulare benefite of God (whiche is so
rare a gifte, that it chaunceth to fewe) . . . the Wyseman sayth: I
knowe, that I can not lyue chaste, except God geueth me the gifte.'[34]

It becomes clear from such expositions that the Protestant recom-
mendation of virtuous matrimony is actually predicated upon an
even more elevated view of virginity: virginity is so special that it
can only be attained by a tiny number of the exceptionally sinless,
aided by God, and therefore remains the highest goal to which to
aspire.[35] This is confirmed by Becon's *Catechisme* of the same year,
where he categorises the 'greate nomber of godlye persons' who
'lyued before the coming of Christ' as 'Patriarches, Judges, Kinges,
Priestes, Leuites, Prophetes, Matrones, Virgins. &c.'[36] Becon's terms
for female virtue include virginity as well as motherhood. It is incidentally striking that virtuous women come last on his list, and
that he has no terms for them *other than* matrons and virgins.

It seems that virginity, and in particular female virginity, continued to carry a powerful mystique after the Reformation. The idea
persisted that the female body needed purification after menstrua-
tion or childbirth; and the intact female body continued to be seen
as charmed in the lore of folk-magic.[37] There are many examples of
the persistence of veneration of female virginity through Elizabeth's
reign and beyond: one might cite Donne's *Anniversaries*; or Milton's
Comus, where the Lady is said to be 'clad in complete steel' because
'No goblin, or swart faëry of the mine / Hath hurtful power o'er
true virginity.'[38] The fact that the boundaries of the virginal female

body had not been transgressed led it to be seen as a symbol of purity, wholeness and perfection. At the same time the virgin's resistance to the weaknesses of the flesh was seen as a spiritual transcendence and a triumph over the Fall.[39]

Belief in the holy or magical qualities of the intact female body had of course been a central component of the cult of the Virgin, and of the attendant cults of virgin saints and martyrs.[40] What is striking about Elizabeth's 1559 speech to Parliament is the way in which, in swimming against the pro-matrimonial tides of both politics and religion, she takes advantage of this more ancient and primal belief. She strongly implies that her virginity has been a form of dedication to God, and has directly brought about God's special protection of her. Her trust that 'God who hath hitherto therin preserued me, and led me by the hand, will not nowe of his goodnes suffer me to goe alone', is functionally ambiguous: will God keep her from being alone by providing a spouse? Or is he himself fulfilling the role of that spouse, as he leads her by the hand?

The role of 'bride of Christ' was familiar from Marian iconography and from the complementary iconography of female saints and of nuns. We have already seen how medieval lyrics represented the Virgin as bride of Christ, through typological reading of the Song of Songs which identified the bride of the Song with the Church, and thereby with the Virgin. Protestant typology erased the Marian application, but sustained the identification of the bride with the Church, as in the 'Argument' heading the Song of Songs in the Geneva Bible, which explained that the Song was an allegory of Christ's love for 'the faithful soule or his Church'.[41] This reading was confirmed by other scriptural texts: there is the figure of the bride of the Lamb in the Book of Revelation (21.9), of which the Geneva commentary says 'Meaning the Church, which is maried to Christ by faith';[42] and Ephesians 6.23–7 explicitly speaks of the Church as the spotless bride of Christ.

Elizabeth, then, was partly continuing the Catholic iconography of virginity, but also invoking scriptural texts which for Protestants too used the figure of the virginal bride of Christ for the Church. This opened the way for the subsequent proliferation of iconography identifying Elizabeth with the Protestant Church and nation. The picture is complicated, though, by other iconography which represented the nation as the entity to which Elizabeth was symbolically espoused.

v. Bride of the nation

We know from the portrait and the miniature of Elizabeth in her coronation robes that Elizabeth wore her hair long and flowing for her coronation.[43] This denoted the status of virgin and bride, and therefore implied that the coronation was also Elizabeth's marriage to the nation. There were precedents for this in Elizabeth of York and Anne Boleyn, each of whom wore their hair loose for their coronation.[44] In their cases, as queens consort, this presumably signified that their earlier private wedding to the king was now to be publicly consolidated by marriage to the kingdom.

At the same time, the theory of the King's Two Bodies implied that the monarch him- or herself was the spouse of the kingdom, as an analogue to the priest's, or Christ's, marriage to the mystical body of the Church. This marriage metaphor was used in France in the early sixteenth century at the courts of Francis I and Henry II.[45] The little we know of the iconography surrounding the coronation of Mary I, the first crowned and unmarried queen regnant of England since the Conquest, does not include bridal imagery;[46] but the pageants for the entry to London of Philip and Mary after their wedding in 1554 did include a female figure of England lovingly welcoming the new King.[47]

It seems that the idea of the monarch as the nation's spouse reached its fullest expression in England with Elizabeth.[48] It is the basis of a popular ballad from 1558–9 by William Birch, 'A songe betwene the Quenes majestie and Englande'. The speakers, 'E' and 'B', are England and Bessy (that is, Elizabeth):

> E   Come over the born bessy,
>   come over the born bessy
>   Swete bessy come over to me
>   And I shall the take,
>   and my dere lady make
>   Before all other that ever I see.

> B   My thinke I hear a voice,
>   at whom I do rejoyce
>   and aunswer the now I shall
>   Tel me I say,
>   what art thou that biddes me com away
>   and so earnestly doost me call.

E   I am thy lover faire,
      hath chose the to mine heir
            and my name is mery Englande
      Therefore come away,
      and make no more delaye
            Swete bessie give me thy hande.

B   Here is my hand,
      my dere lover Englande
            I am thine both with minde and hart
      For ever to endure,
      thou maiest be sure
            Untill death us two depart.[49]

This song is a secularised version of the Marian hymns with the refrain from the Song of Songs, 'Veni coronaberis'; here, 'Come, you shall be crowned' is reworked as 'Come over the born'. 'Bourn', to give it its modern spelling, means either a brook or a boundary; the idea is that Elizabeth has been in metaphorical or spiritual exile. Just as medieval lyrics used the form of a courtship dialogue and a tone of desire to represent the union of Christ and the Virgin (or the Church), so here the same form and tone are used to represent the union of the nation and the Queen.

The song also echoes sacred precedents in deploying a sort of hagiography from stanza 6 onwards, narrating Elizabeth's martyr-like sufferings during Mary's reign.

B   ... my lover England,
      ye shall understand
            How Fortune on me did lowre
      I was tombled and tost,
      from piller to post
            and prisoner in the Towre ...

      Then was I caried to wodstock,
      and kept close under lock
            That no man mighte with me speake
      And against all reason,
      they accused me of treason
            And tirably thei did me threate.

Bessy goes on with the story of the perils inflicted upon her. We have already seen the incipient mythologisation of Elizabeth's sufferings before her accession in the coronation pageants. This continued through her reign and afterwards, with increasing stress on her miraculous survival of dangers, in such texts as Foxe's *Book of Martyrs* (1563), William Alabaster's *Elisaeis* (c.1588–91), and Thomas Heywood's *If you know not me, you know no bodie* (1605) and *England's Elizabeth* (1631).[50] As in Ales's narration of Anne Boleyn's life to Elizabeth, the resources of Catholic hagiography were redeployed to create an aura of sanctification and divine destiny around a Protestant heroine. This hagiographical treatment of Elizabeth's life *before* her accession also served to create a sense that it was not only her anointment as monarch which had raised her to a sanctified level, but that she had an innate personal holiness which destined her for that anointment.

Also as in the account of the coronation pageants, the memory of Elizabeth's father is invoked. England exclaims in outrage: 'why dere Lady I trow, / those mad men did not knowe / That ye were doughter unto Kinge Hary.' Again, a tradition of iconography was being established: Elizabeth herself in the following years would frequently invoke her father in her speeches. In 1566, for instance, in a furious rebuke to Parliament's attempts to make her settle the succession, she said: 'though I be a woman, yet I have as good a courage, answerable to my place, as ever my father had.'[51] This rhetoric was not only a means of laying claim by inheritance to the masculine qualities considered necessary to a ruler, but also a way of refuting doubts cast on Elizabeth's legitimacy. It is notable that in the song England refers to Bessy several times as his 'heir', conflating the role of lover with that of father, as if Henry VIII is speaking as the spirit of the nation.

The ballad ends on a strongly Marian note:

> E   Oh swete virgin pure,
>   longe may ye endure
>   To reigne over us in this lande
>   For your workes do accord,
>   ye are the handmaid of the lord
>   For he hath blessed you with his hand.
>
> B   My swete realme be obedient
>   To gods holy commaundement

> and my procedinges embrace
> And for that that is abused,
> shalbe better used
> and that within shorte space.

The relation between England and Bessy is more complex than it might at first appear. In one sense, the song simply reapplies to Elizabeth the iconography of queens consort as brides of the nation. A queen like Anne Boleyn married the nation through marrying the king, implying an identification of king and nation. This also implied that the nation was the masculine partner in the marriage, running counter to the more usual metaphorical gendering of the nation as feminine. In the case of Elizabeth, the assignation of the masculine gender to England accommodates her to this iconography of queens consort. The invocation of Henry VIII makes up for the absence of a husband for Elizabeth: he is identified with the nation, and he is the male ruler whose dynasty it is the Queen's duty to perpetuate. Contemporary doctrine maintained that the wife was the 'weaker vessel' in the marriage partnership: the official Homily on matrimony declared that 'the woman is a weak creature, not endued with like strength and constancy of mind', and therefore needed husbandly tolerance and guidance.[52] Thus the alliance of conjugal iconography with England's description of Bessy as his heir implicitly make Elizabeth subordinate to the nation, its handmaid rather than its master, and conform her to a normative queenly role.

On the other hand, Elizabeth is after all monarch in her own right, invoking the metaphor of the king himself as spouse of the nation. The theory of the King's Two Bodies was based on the priest's, or Christ's, marriage to the Church; medieval lyrics like 'Veni Coronaberis' represented Christ's union with the Church as Virgin. In so far as these were precedents for the metaphor of marriage between the monarch and nation, they supposed a union of a male ruler with a feminine nation: it was the more abstract, collective entity in the coupling which was represented as feminine. In Birch's song, though, it is the masculine wooer, England, who is the collective entity, apparently inverting the iconographic tradition.

Thinking again, though, since Elizabeth's accession meant the restoration of Protestantism, Elizabeth can be seen here as representing the Protestant Church, whose return has been long awaited by England. This is at once a perpetuation of the Marian tradition of the bride as Church, and a new Protestant application of it. It makes Elizabeth herself a collective symbol, and this was increasingly the trend in panegyric: the image of Elizabeth as bride of the Protestant nation was popular, but so was the direct identification of Elizabeth with the Protestant nation. The unusual gendering of England as masculine in Birch's song shows how the Marian bridal metaphor was in the background of Elizabethan iconography, but had to be fissured to fit Elizabeth as female ruler.

Philippa Berry, in her book *Of Chastity and Power*, suggests that because *respublica* and *ecclesia* were gendered feminine, 'Elizabeth performed a double symbolic marriage with both these feminine domains . . . In this respect, Elizabeth's rule figured *the feminine in a mystical or symbolic relationship with itself*'.[53] Berry here confuses marriage with identification. Evidence like Birch's song suggests that when Elizabethans used the marriage metaphor for Elizabeth's rule, they did not think in terms of a union of the female with the feminine, but regendered the nation as masculine. In her old age, Elizabeth told Sir John Harington's wife that her people were 'all my husbands'.[54] She herself could even be represented as the masculine partner, as by Anthony Munday in 1584: 'her Highnesse is the most louing Mother and Nurse of all her good Subiectes, and is lykewise the husband of the common weale, maried to the Realme, and the same by ceremony of Ring as solemnly signified, as any other mariage.'[55] When the focus is on England as feminine, as in Aylmer's *Harborowe*, she is identified with Elizabeth rather than presented as her spouse. As Berry indeed states, the nation was more usually gendered feminine, and 'this similarity of gender . . . led Elizabeth to be more closely identified with both state and church than any male Renaissance monarch'.[56] Elizabeth's gender seems to have promoted the rapid transformation of her after her accession into an iconic personification of England and Protestantism.

vi. Marian iconography in popular ballads

Birch's song is not only a secularisation of Marian hymns, but also a popularisation: the implied identification of Elizabeth with the Virgin is moderated by the use of the humble epithet 'Bessy', very unlike the later elaborate and inflated representations of Elizabeth which are more renowned. Even the ballad's most blatant invocation of Marian terminology, 'ye are the handmaid of the lord', emphasises the Virgin in her aspect of humility and dedication to her role as God's instrument, rather than her aspect as Queen of Heaven.

The popular tone of Birch's song is confirmed by its many analogues. It closely resembles not only the fifteenth-century lyric 'Veni coronaberis', but also a song between Christ and the soul from about 1500:

> Com home againe!
> Com home againe!
> Mine owene swet hart, com home againe!
> Ye are gone astray
> Out of youer way,
> Therefore, com home againe!

A modern editor comments, 'The burden of this carol is quite probably secular'; it is likely 'that this religious poem was sung to a well-known secular tune, Christ complaining to the erring soul with the same music as a lover to his wandering sweetheart.'[57]

After Birch had used the format for his song of Elizabeth, it turns up again in William Wager's play *The longer thou livest, the more foole thou art*, 1569 (?), as an example of an idle popular love-song. The decadent Moros (meaning Fool) sings snatches of dittles, including: 'Com ouer the Boorne Besse, / My little pretie Besse, / Com ouer the Boorne besse to me.' Moros describes how he learned these songs: 'A fond [i.e. foolish] woman to my Mother, / As I war wont in her lappe to sit, / She taught me these and many other.'[58] It crops up yet again in *King Lear*, where, on the heath, one of the snatches of song sung by Edgar as Poor Tom is 'Come o'er the bourn, Bessy, to me'.[59] There are numerous other examples of popular ballads, some of them risqué, in which a lover woos a mistress called Bessy or Betty.[60] These may derive from 'Come over the born bessy', or Birch's song may itself draw on an older tradition not only of songs of the Virgin and Christ, but also of erotic Bessy-ballads.

The different versions of this song therefore illustrate the transferability of iconography within popular culture. The form of the dialogue inviting a mistress to come nearer originates in the late medieval climate of interchange between secular and sacred verse. It is then applied to Elizabeth's accession as a familiar iconography which comes readily to hand, part of a continuing history of representation of a queen's coronation in terms of the Coronation of the

Virgin and the Song of Songs. The ballad then passes easily back
into secular popular culture, losing its sacred and regal connotations and becoming simply a song of courtship and seduction. No
doubt this process was aided by its having a good tune.

Another ballad from the early years of the reign makes relatively
explicit use of Marian iconography. It was printed under an engraving of Elizabeth, and began:

> Loe here the pearle,
> whom God and man doth loue:
> Loe here on earth,
> the onely starre of light.

The metaphors of the pearl and the star echo Mariology, though of
course they could equally be emblems of the courtly mistress. But
the second stanza opens:

> Loe here the heart,
> that so hath honord God:
> That for her loue,
> we feele not of his rod.[61]

Elizabeth is represented in distinctively Marian terms as an intercessor, for whose sake the nation is spared by God.

This overtly religious iconography marks a distinct difference
from the courtier verse of Elizabeth's first decade, which, as Steven
May has noted, 'all but ignores the important issue of religion,
whether as a matter of national policy or the expression of an author's personal beliefs.' May suggests that this inhibition arose from
uncertainty and tension: 'The issues were of the utmost seriousness,
and only gradually did it become clear that the new regime would
be able to cope with them.'[62] It was only later in the reign that
courtly writers gradually applied explicitly religious, and then
overtly Marian iconography to Elizabeth.

The authors of such popular ballads need not be assumed to have
been making Elizabeth fulfil the role of the absent Virgin because
they felt psychologically bereft. It seems more likely that they were
simply making use of material which came readily to hand and was
liked and familiar, as the case of 'Come over the born bessy' would
suggest. Elizabeth was the anointed monarch and represented England and its Church, providing plenty of partisan motivation to

assert her sanctity; and when seeking a means of doing so, not all of her subjects necessarily appreciated the theological arguments for the avoidance of Marian iconography at all costs.

vii. Laying down laws on images

A central part of the Elizabethan Church Settlement was the laying down of official policy on the use of religious images. This process entailed both likening and differentiating between religious images and civil images, and was therefore an important framework for the development of Protestant royal panegyric; and a significant context for the transfer of apparently Marian iconography to Elizabeth.

The official policy on religious images was set out in the Articles of Inquiry and the Royal Injunctions issued for the church visitations of late summer and early autumn 1559. It was imperative to try to eliminate images which could be used in Catholic forms of worship; when Mary I had made her entry to London on her accession, images of the Virgin and saints had immediately reappeared to be displayed in people's windows, having presumably been hoarded in cellars and attics.[63] The rooting out and destruction of 'images . . . or other monuments of feigned or false miracles, pilgrimages, idolatry or superstition . . . especially as have been set up in churches, chapels, or oratories' was a gesture demonstrating that Protestantism had come to stay.[64]

The Articles of Inquiry were based on those issued by Cranmer under Edward VI in 1548, but with a few alterations. Likewise, the 1559 Injunctions were based on the 1547 Edwardian Injunctions, but were modified so as to place the emphasis on the destruction of images which had specifically been abused. This sought to restrain the elimination of all and any images, as had taken place during Edward's reign; nevertheless, many of the Visitors of 1559 were zealous reformists and chose to interpret the Injunctions as a licence for wholesale destruction. The Injunctions were more than just a temporary instruction; they had to be subscribed to by all the clergy, they were reprinted many times during Elizabeth's reign, and they had to be read in every parish church once a quarter.[65]

The twenty-second of the thirty-nine Articles of Religion condemned the 'Romish Doctrine' of 'Worshipping and Adoration, as well of Images as of Reliques, and also invocation of Saints', because it was 'grounded upon no warranty of Scripture, but rather

repugnant to the Word of God'.[66] The formulation neatly sums up
the reformist binary opposition between the pictorial as false and
the verbal as true. The official Homily 'Against Peril of Idolatry',
c.1560, possibly by John Jewel, declared that:

> the images of God, our Saviour Christ, the blessed Virgin Mary,
> the Apostles, Martyrs, and other of notable holiness, are of all
> other images most dangerous for the peril of idolatry; and there-
> fore greatest heed to be taken that none of them be suffered to
> stand publicly in churches and temples.[67]

There is evidence that Elizabeth moderated the Homily 'Against
Idolatry' before approving it.[68] Throughout the religious debates of
these early years of her reign her role seems to have been one of
making clear her commitment to Protestantism, but at the same
time restraining extremism and encouraging compromise.[69] It is not
clear whether this stance derived from a personal attachment to the
externals of Catholic worship, or from political pragmatism. Certainly her education had been rigorously Protestant, under instruc-
tions passed on by her mother to Matthew Parker before she died,[70]
and then in the household of Catherine Parr, a centre of reformist
thinking. A Book of Devotions which is a collection of prayers for
use by Elizabeth is devoutly and orthodoxly Protestant, and may
have been composed by the Queen herself.[71]

Perhaps she was aware of the potential political dangers of widespread religious iconoclasm. During her father's reign, Stephen
Gardiner had expressed fears that contempt for religious images
would engender contempt for images of secular power:

> If this opinion should proceed, when the King's Majesty hereafter
> should show his person, his lively image, the honour due by
> God's law among such might continue; but as for the King's
> standards, his banners, his arms, [they] should hardly continue in
> their due reverence.[72]

The monarch's own body was itself an image, the living image of
the monarchy. The apparatus of state power depended upon much
the same use of symbolism and ceremony as did the Church; indeed, a recent analysis has suggested that ritual and spectacle are
not merely transient means of enhancing power, but are of the very
essence of power.[73] Unbridled iconoclasm clearly held dangers for
the Crown.

Some of the more zealous iconoclasts destroyed funerary monuments and statues of notable persons, and the argument shifted rapidly from whether it was wrong to worship images, to whether all images and all art were wrong.[74] In 1560 a proclamation was issued forbidding anyone to destroy merely commemorative monuments, or 'to break any image of kings, princes, or noble estates of this realm'.[75] The subtext of this was that there was a resemblance between religious and civil images, sufficient for them to be mistakenly categorised together, but that this was indeed a mistake; that civil images did not present any danger of idolatry.

Only the following year, however, 1561, official orders for church maintenance commanded that the rood statues of Christ crucified, the Virgin and St John should be replaced with 'some convenient crest', which, in practice, meant the royal arms. The separation of religious and civil images, then, was closely followed by the use of a state emblem in the place of a religious image. The substitution of the royal arms for the rood statues had been initiated in the reign of Edward VI, and in 1585 was used by the recusant polemicist Nicholas Sander as an accusation that the Church of England was guilty of idolatry: it 'was like a declaration on their part that they were worshippers, not of our Lord, whose image they had comtemptuously [sic] thrown aside, but of an earthly king, whose armorial bearings they had substituted for it'.[76] The visual and institutional apparatus of state power had always been intertwined with religious structures; after the establishment of the Church of England, with the Queen as its Supreme Governor, this became an even closer relationship.

viii. The theology of representation

To preach iconomachy in the Church while simultaneously sustaining the use of images of the secular Governor of that Church required delicate manoeuvring, as is evident in early Elizabethan theological texts like Becon's 1560 New Catechisme.[77] At one point Becon maintains that it is wrong to make images of the sun, moon and stars, of men, and of all creatures, as well as of God (f.331v). He then goes to great lengths, though, to moderate this extreme iconoclastic position by drawing a careful distinction between civil and sacred images. The catechism is a dialogue between father and son: 'Father. Is it then lawfull in polityke, ciuile, & worldly matters to haue Images? Sonne. It is not forbidden' (f.333r). The son proceeds to give scriptural precedents, such as the image of Caesar on the coins which Christ instructs to be rendered unto Caesar and distinguishes from what is to be rendered unto God, in Matthew 22. The son continues:

> All these thinges declare manifestlye, that in polityke, ciuile, prophane and worldly thinges the vse of images is not vnlawful. *Father*. If in politike and worldlye matters, why not also in diuine and holye thinges? *Sonne*. In the one, is no pearill, in the other, great daunger, as we haue learned to much by experience.
>
> (f.333v)

Here is a clear distinction between religious and civil images. However, in writing of civil 'Magistrates . . . Superiours and gouernours', Becon says that God commands them to be 'honoured, reuerenced and obeyed' (f.346v). In another text published in the same volume, his *Booke of Matrimony*, Becon also stated that: '[the] Magistrate is the seruaunt and officer of God . . . The Magistrate also . . . representeth the most worthy person of God, and for that cause he is called in the holy scripture, God, because hee ruleth as God among the people of God' (f.560r). Thus Becon's approval of images of secular rulers depends upon a rigid separation of secular and sacred images; but at the same time his exhortation to honour and reverence those rulers depends upon a belief that they are themselves the images of God.

Ten years on, in 1570, another catechism was published by Alexander Nowell, Dean of St Paul's.[78] This became a standard textbook in Elizabethan schools, and was one of the most widely-read books in England in the late sixteenth and seventeenth centuries. Thomas Norton's preface describes Elizabeth as the instrument of God to advance true religion (sig.A3r). The text then proceeds as a dialogue between a 'Maister' and a 'Scholar':

> *Ma*. What is idolatry, or to haue strange Gods?
> *Sch*. It is in the place of the one only true God . . . to set other persons or thinges, and of them to frame and make to our selues as it were certayne Gods, to worship them as Gods, and to set and repose our trust in them.
>
> (f.7r)

This sounds not too distant from the kind of praise of Elizabeth as an iconic figure which had developed in the early years of the reign. The Scholar asserts, though, that we must 'geue vnto his Maiestie the soueraigne honor', by whom he means God, continuing the tradition of using the iconography of regal power to represent the divine.

On the making of images, the Scholar explains that 'the lawfull vse of making portraitures, and of painting, is not forbidden'; it is only forbidden to make images of God and to worship them (f.8r–v). The Master adds that 'it is very perilous to set any images or pictures in churches' (f.8v). The authority of parents is said to come from 'the lawes of God . . . bicause by these it hath pleased God to rule and gouerne the world.' (ff.13v–14r). A crime against the magistrate is more heinous than a crime against a parent, because traitors turn 'against their countrey the most auncient, sacred, and common mother of us all . . . and against the prince the father of the countrey it selfe and parent of the commonweale' (f.15r–v).

Later, the dialogue turns to images in their wider sense of signs and symbols; the water of baptism, for instance:

Ma. Thou semest to make the water but a certaine figure of diuine thynges.
Sch. It is a figure in dede, but not empty or deceitefull, but such as hath the truth of the things themselues ioyned and knit vnto it. For as in Baptisme God truly deliuereth vs forgeuenesse of sinnes and newnesse of lyfe, so do we certainely receiue them. For God forbid that we should thinke that God mocketh and deceiueth vs with vayne figures.

(f.71v)

Later, the Master explains that the Eucharist delivers 'not an onley figure but the truth it selfe, of the benefites, that thou hast rehearsed' (f.74r). The Scholar concurs: 'sithe Christ is the truth it selfe, it is no doubt but that the thing which he testifieth in wordes and representeth in signes, he performeth also in deede and deliuereth it vnto vs' (f.74v). In this Nowell confirms the teaching of the twenty-fifth Article on the Sacraments: they 'be not only badges or tokens of Christian men's profession, but rather they be certain sure witnesses, and effectual signs of grace, and God's good will towards us'.[79]

Here, then, in these early years of Elizabethan Protestantism, rather than all images being rejected as false, distinctions are being drawn between different kinds of images. A religious image is dangerous, but a civil image is safe. Even among religious images, not all are

dangerous or false: the true image is ordained by God; it is intrin-
sically bound to its own meaning; and it is effectual in bringing
about salvation. Such true images are a legitimate part of Protestant
worship. Words can also serve as true images: Becon recounts how
God gave his Word to the Israelites, commanding them 'to wryte it
vpon the gates & postes of theyr houses, that it might be alwayes
before their eyes' (ff.328r–9r). A world without any form of visual
representation would clearly have been impossible. At the same
time, iconoclasm was itself predicated on a profound belief in the
power of images; in a curious way, it was itself a form of idolatry.
The result was an ongoing process of distinction between false and
true images, a distinction which was complex, shifting, and undergoing continual redefinition and refinement.[80]

Within this process, early Elizabethan theologians made it clear
that their attack was not upon the holiness of the Virgin and saints,
but only upon images of them. Even so, the goal of directing all
worship solely to God inevitably involved an apparent demotion of
the Virgin. Jewel in his *Apology* stressed the humanity of the Virgin:
'We believe that Jesus Christ . . . did take of that blessed and pure
Virgin both flesh and all the nature of man . . .'[81] In the Church
Homilies, the two main mentions of the Virgin cite her as a model
of civil obedience, for her unquestioning submission to Caesar's
order to go to Bethlehem for the census.[82] As with the raising of the
royal arms in churches and the diatribe against treason in Nowell's
catechism, this seems a clear example of a religious medium being
exploited for the enforcement of state authority. Nowell's catechism
itself mentioned the Virgin merely as the pure vessel for the incarnation of Christ, and in doing so, rather than following the pre-
Reformation line of praising Mary's Immaculate Conception, he
transposed the iconography of the Immaculate Conception onto
Christ himself: 'Christ therfore that most pure lambe, was begotten
and borne by the holy Ghost and the conception of the virgin without sinne, that he might cleanse, wash, and put away our spottes'.
Christ was 'fashioned in the wombe of the most chast and pure
virgin, and of her substance, that he should not be defiled with the
common stayne and infection of mankinde' (f.31v).

ix. Sexual iconography

However, even if the Virgin herself tended to drop from view,
female sexual purity continued to carry symbolic force in the

iconography of theological writing. It became a commonplace to describe idolatry as spiritual whoredom: it was spiritual adultery (being infidelity to the loving God) and spiritual lechery (being an attachment to material, carnal things). This metaphor arose from biblical exegesis, including that of St Augustine,[83] and was closely entwined with Protestant identification of the Church of Rome with the Whore of Babylon in Revelation. The application of Revelation to contemporary events had begun in the Middle Ages with interpretation of particular bad popes as Antichrist. Luther had then established the idea of using recent history to read Revelation, and of the whole institution of the papacy as Antichrist.[84] English Protestant interpretation began with John Bale's *The Image of Both Churches*, c.1545, which set up an opposition between the Whore of Babylon as the 'proude paynted churche of the pope', and the Woman Clothed with the Sun, also a figure from Revelation, as the 'poore persecuted churche of Christe, or immaculate spowse of the lambe'.[85] Elizabethan theologians developed this line of typology: Becon wrote that those who defend the use of images are 'still infected with the dyrtye dregges of that whore of Babilon' the Roman Church, and that idolatry was 'whorehunting from god' (ff.327v, 328v, 336v–7r). Foxe cited Dante, and Jewel cited Petrarch, as authorities who identified the Pope with the Babylonian Whore.[86] In the 1560 Geneva Bible, the description of the woman who was 'araied in purple & skarlat, & guilded with golde, & precious stones, and pearles, and had a cup of golde in her hand, ful of abominations, and filthines of her fornication', was glossed, 'This woman is the Antichrist, that is, the Pope with the whole bodie of his filthie creatures . . . whose beautie onely standeth in outwarde pompe & impudencie and craft like a strumpet.'[87]

This line of rhetoric quickly shifted from a castigation of the spiritual whoremongering of the idolater to a vituperation of the whorishness of that which tempted him. A vivid example of this is the Homily 'Against Idolatry':

> the idolatrous Church . . . being indeed not only an harlot (as the Scripture calleth her) but also a foul, filthy, old, withered harlot, (for she is indeed of ancient years,) and understanding her lack of natural and true beauty, and great loathsomeness which of herself she hath, doth (after the custom of such harlots) paint herself, and deck and tire herself with gold, pearl, stone, and all kind of precious jewels.

This is to entice lovers to:

> spiritual fornication with her: who, if they saw her, I will not say
> naked, but in simple apparel, would abhor her as the foulest and
> filthiest harlot that ever was seen . . . Whereas, on the contrary
> part, the true Church of God, as a chaste matron, [is] *espoused* (as
> the Scripture teacheth) *to one husband, our Saviour Jesus Christ,*
> whom alone she is content only to please and serve.[88]

With benefit of hindsight, it might strike the modern reader that
the colourful descriptions of a woman painting, bedecking and
bejewelling herself in order to disguise her actual withered agedness
ironically resembles Elizabeth herself in later life. At this date,
though, Elizabeth's public image was that of the godly and studi-
ous Protestant princess, including emphasis on the modesty and
sobriety of her apparel, as in Aylmer's *Harborowe* where these qualities in her were contrasted with the 'superfluous ruffes, furres,
fringes, and such other trinkettes' of less virtuous ladies (sigs N1r,
P1r). Since the 1540s, figures like Anne Askew, Lady Jane Grey and
Princess Elizabeth herself had been used to develop a model of the
godly Protestant heroine who was identified with the bride of the
Song of Songs and the Woman Clothed with the Sun, the direct
opponent of the Babylonian whore.[89]

At the beginning of Elizabeth's reign there was already in place
a structure of sexualised iconography which was available to be
superimposed on the Queen as conventions of panegyric developed. It was already established that the opposition between Protestant and Catholic, true and false, could be forcefully represented
by a polarisation of the female into virginity or whorishness. Female sexuality was a focus of anxiety, and was therefore able to
carry many meanings. It is hardly surprising, then, that as Elizabeth's reign progressed a ruler who was female and unmarried,
who was the anointed monarch, restorer of Protestantism and Supreme Governor of the Church, should have been turned into an
iconic figure of virginity onto which many symbolic meanings were
projected.

We have seen that the early years of Elizabeth's reign saw the
forging of a new Protestant iconography of female rule. Some of the
new iconography strategically avoided overtly Marian terms,

although it almost inevitably paralleled some of the typological sources and structures of Mariology. Other examples of panegyric, especially of a more popular kind, borrowed Marian terms fairly openly, though often with some revision. However, the two main things which the emergent iconography of Elizabeth had in common with the cult of the Virgin at this time were not particular borrowed emblems, but were more fundamental and structural. First, there was the practice of representing the Queen in terms of other, already familiar female figures, a process which was not unlike the origins and growth of the cult of the Virgin, and which suggests, at base, over-compensation for anxiety about the pre-eminence of a female figure. Secondly, discourses which included Elizabeth's own rhetoric for avoiding marriage, and the invective of churchmen against idolatry, perpetuated belief in the mystique of female virginity, and its counterpart, belief in the depravity of female sexuality. This belief-structure was continuous from the cult of the Virgin. However, at this early stage in the reign, Elizabeth seems to have applied the iconography of sanctified virginity to herself with more seriousness than did her subjects, as we shall see in the next chapter.

3

1560–78:
The Meanings of Virginity

i. Marriage, or not?

Through the 1560s and early 1570s, Elizabeth's public attitude to matrimony continued to be a marked reluctance qualified by a professed acquiescence to duty if her marriage appeared to be in the best interests of the country. Robert Dudley, Earl of Leicester, with whom she was publicly flirtatious in the first two years of her reign, was an impolitic choice as husband after the death of his wife in dubious circumstances in September 1560.[1] As for the marriage negotiations with foreign powers, the letters of her ministers through the 1560s continued to express increasing exasperation with her prevarications.[2] At a masque in July 1564 Elizabeth told the Spanish Ambassador of her predilection for black and white, saying 'These are my colours',[3] a profession borne out by the many portraits in which she wears black and white; since black signified constancy and white virginity, their combination signified eternal virginity, and Elizabeth was thus giving a strong signal of her inclination to remain perpetually unmarried. However, in a written reply to a petition by the 1563 Parliament regarding the succession, the Queen told them they were mistaken if they thought her vowed to celibacy, 'For though I can think it best for a private woman, yet do I strive with myself to think it not meet for a Prince. And if I can bend my liking to your need, I will not resist such a mind.'[4] Again, at the 1566 Parliament, she declared: 'And therefore I say again, I will marry as soon as I can conveniently, if God take not him away with whom I mind to marry, or myself, or else some other great let happen.'[5]

At least one foreign ambassador seems to have found it unthinkable that Elizabeth might never marry, and therefore took her professions of preference for virginity as disingenuous. Baron Pollweiler, an imperial negotiator for the marriage of Elizabeth to the Archduke Charles, wrote to the Emperor Ferdinand in 1559:

... in the natural course of events the Queen is of an age where she should in reason and as is woman's way, be eager to marry and be provided for. It would also be best for her Kingdom ... The natural and necessary inference from all this is, either that she has married secretly, or that she has already made up her mind to marry someone in England or out of it, and ... is postponing matters under the cloak of Your Imperial Majesty's son, my gracious master. For that she should wish to remain a maid and never marry is inconceivable.[6]

Pollweiler may be correct that at this date Elizabeth's evasiveness was strategic; nevertheless, his conviction that Elizabeth could not possibly genuinely wish to remain single is striking. Her subjects seem to have found her reluctance to marry similarly perplexing, and to have been unequivocally convinced that her marriage was what the nation needed. At the opening of the 1563 Parliament, Alexander Nowell gave a sermon which ended by remarking that Elizabeth's lack of issue 'is for our sins to be a plague unto us'.[7] In the same year, Sir Nicholas Bacon wrote wheedlingly to the Queen: 'If your Highness could conceive or imagine the comfort, surety and delight that should happen to yourself by beholding an imp of your own ...'.[8] The tone of the parliamentary petitions to the Queen to marry illustrates the contradiction between attitudes to her as an icon and as a woman: her subjects idealised her in panegyric as a wonder and a marvel, but when it came to petitioning her on this subject, Members of Parliament could become remarkably patronising.[9]

In 1572, in a letter to Sir Francis Walsingham, one of her chief agents in foreign marriage negotiations, Elizabeth wrote of 'the importunacy of our own subjects of all estates to have us marry'.[10] It appears that until around the mid-1570s Elizabeth was viewed by her subjects as a Virgin Queen not in the sense of perpetual virginity on the model of the Virgin Mary, but in the sense of being nubile, in a state preparatory to and ripe for matrimony. This is reflected in entertainments provided on her progresses. The biblical heroines with whom she was most often compared in these early years, Deborah, Judith and Esther, were either married women or widows, and were somewhat matronly figures.[11] When she passed through Coventry in 1565, the Recorder of Coventry's Oration expressed the wish that her metaphorical motherhood of the nation might be made literal:

like as you are a mother to your kingdom, and to the subjects of
the same, by justice and motherly care and clemency, so you
may, by God's goodness and justice, be a natural mother, and,
having blest issue of your princely body, may live to see your
children, unto the third and fourth generation.[12]

In some cases such wishes seem to have been loyally voiced on the
assumption that they would be received by Elizabeth as compliments; in others, they have an undertone of criticism. In any case,
Elizabeth returned clear signals of what she preferred to hear: when,
in Cambridge in 1564, the Public Orator made a speech in praise
of virginity, she responded, 'God's blessing of thyne heart; there
continue.'[13]

As the 1570s progressed, one senses that Elizabeth's subjects began
to accept that she might never marry. This made the succession no
less a matter of public concern, but at the same time gave added
impetus to conventional wishes for the Queen's long life. Sir Thomas
Smith wrote anxiously in March 1572, 'God preserve her Majesty
long to reign over us by some unlooked-for miracle, for I cannot see
by natural reason that her Highness goeth about to provide for it.'[14]
Sir Christopher Hatton, a favourite of the Queen's, wrote to her
flirtatiously in 1573: 'Live for ever, most excellent creature; and love
some man, to shew yourself thankful for God's high labour in
you ... Pardon me; I will leave these matters, because I think you
mislike them.'[15]

At the 1576 Parliament, Elizabeth again made clear her private
preference: 'if I were a milkmaid with a pail on my arm, whereby
my private person might be little set by, I would not forsake that
poor and single state to match with the greatest monarch.'[16] She
was now 42, and her subjects were becoming accustomed to the
idea that her virginity might be more than just a passing phase.

ii. Antichrist's whore

Meanwhile, a series of significant politico-religious events hard-
ened the division between Catholic and Protestant, and the representation of that division in terms of extremes of female sexuality.

The north of England continued to be prevalently Catholic, and
the year 1569 saw the outbreak of the Northern Rebellion, led by
the Catholic Earls of Northumberland and Westmorland. The rising
was violently quashed: some 600 men who had been sent by their

villages to fight were hanged.[17] A Protestant ballad on the occasion, 'An Aunswere to the Proclamation of the Rebels in the North', summed up the opposition between the two Churches as chaste bride of Christ and degenerate whore, good mother and bad mother:

> The mother Church you will defende.
> What children call ye these,
> When trayterously themselues they bende
> their Mother to disease?
> But like it is, the Mother that
> ye meane to prop with power,
> The spouse of Christ that she is not,
> but Antichristes whoore.[18]

The excommunication of Elizabeth by Pope Pius V in 1570, and the St. Bartholomew's Day Massacre in Paris in 1572, further intensified the animosity between Catholic and Protestant and the demonisation of each side by the other.

Catholicism was seen as at once a foreign threat, and an enemy within. On several occasions in the 1570s when mass was said at the London houses of foreign ambassadors or other visitors it was broken up by officials who reported that native English subjects were also among the congregation.[19] Catholic practices were consistently and specifically vilified as idolatrous: John Aylmer, now Bishop of London, wrote of one such mass to William Cecil, now Lord Burghley, in 1573: 'Sundry he [the sheriff of London] found there ready to worship the calfe . . . There was found the altar prepared, the chalice, and their bread god'.[20] Another of Burghley's correspondents, one William Fletewood, recounted how a Catholic named Nicholas Mounslowe had stabbed himself to death, and added: 'The idol that he took for his God I have sent here unto your Lordshipp. It loketh rather like the figure of a divell, than a saynt.'[21] This letter is dated 1578, the same year as the incident at Euston Hall discussed in my Introduction; Fletewood's description of the image as resembling a devil is strikingly similar to Topcliffe's description of the icon of the Virgin, as though such remarks had become formulaic among seekers-out of recusancy. Besides these incidents in and around London, Catholicism was entrenched in more far-flung regions: a report on North Wales in about 1580 found that the population 'maintain the absurdist points of popish heresy'.[22]

At the same time, religious and political stability was threatened from another side by the growth of Puritanism. Burghley heard from the Bishop of Peterborough in 1573 that the Puritans 'neglect, if they do not abhorre, the divine service sette oute by public authoritie'. Instead they perform it 'contrarie to forme prescribed by the publique order of the realme . . . I wolde not thus trouble you, my good Lorde, if this matter touched not as muche the peace and quietnes of the laietie, as it doth the regiment of the spiritualtie.'[23] Such reactions to Puritanism illustrate the political interdependence of Church and State, and the shared concern of their hierarchies with uniformity and obedience.

In iconographic terms, however, the peril of Catholicism offered more imaginative stimulus. We have already seen in the last chapter how, by the beginning of Elizabeth's reign, the opposition between the two Churches was conventionally represented as the opposition of the Woman Clothed with the Sun to the Whore of Babylon.[24] This feminine iconography took on new force not only from the identification of the Protestant cause with Elizabeth, but also from the identification of the Catholic cause with Mary Queen of Scots. As Elizabeth's cousin, Mary Stuart was a leading claimant to the English throne, and from 1559 she quartered her coat-of-arms with that of England.[25] In 1561 she returned from France to take the throne of Scotland. Her marriage to Lord Darnley in 1565 was followed by the murder of her rumoured lover David Rizzio in 1566, then in 1567 the murder of Darnley, her immediate marriage to his suspected murderer the Earl of Bothwell, and her abdication. She fled to England in 1568, where she spent the rest of her life in custody. The longer Elizabeth remained childless, the greater Mary's claim to be named her heir, and the greater the incitement to Catholics to plot to supplant Elizabeth with her, producing the Ridolfi Plot of 1570–72, the Throckmorton Plot of 1582–3, and finally the Babington Plot of 1586.

The religious opposition between the two queens produced a flood of sexually polarised feminine iconography.[26] The personification of the Catholic Church as the Whore of Babylon was readily transposed to Mary in the light of her scandalous history. Thomas Wilson, in *Actio contra Mariam*, 1571, wrote: 'May we commit our safety to her, whom never shame restrained from unchastity, womankind from cruelty, nor religion from impiety?'[27] In Parliament in 1572, in the wake of the Ridolfi Plot, MPs attacked Mary not only on the point at issue, as an accused traitor, but also as an adulteress;

even Francis Alford, who argued against her condemnation and execution, acknowledged 'I think her to be as vile and as naughty a creature as ever the earth bare, and am ... thoroughly persuaded of her lewd demeanours.'[28] Peter Wentworth, the Puritan, called before a parliamentary committee in 1576, called Mary 'Jezebel', and 'the most notorious whore in all the world'.[29]

This polarised rhetoric could easily be turned on its head by the other side. There were precedents for such inversion: during Mary Tudor's reign, while Protestants had vituperated her as 'Jezebel' and had identified Protestant women like Anne Askew and Princess Elizabeth with biblical heroines, John Proctor, author of *The waie home to Christ and truth*, 1554, praised the Catholic Queen as virginal and maternal, and attacked Protestants for turning 'from a lovinge mother to a flatteryng harlote'.[30] Likewise in the late 1560s and early 1570s, defences were penned of Mary Stuart's purity, virtue, and innocent incapability of the crimes of which she was accused,[31] and rumours were circulated of Elizabeth's promiscuity and sexual deviancy with favourites like Leicester and Hatton.[32]

iii. Elizabeth as mother

Refutation of such scandal was one motive for representation of Elizabeth as a chaste and loving matron, dedicated to the care of her nation. During the 1560s and 70s the image of Elizabeth as mother and nurse of the Church and nation became a commonplace.[33]

On the one hand, the figure of the mother was a figure of authority; the Fifth Commandment not only instructed the godly to honour their fathers and mothers, but was interpreted in such places as Nowell's catechism as an exhortation to obey one's parents, and beyond that, to obey magistrates, the parents of the nation.[34] State and family were seen as homologous hierarchical structures, such that the metaphor of motherhood for Elizabeth was a means of asserting her power, and the unnaturalness of those 'children' who resisted it.

At the same time, the figure of the mother also signified tender loving care, and as such could be used by subjects to lay claims to rights and privileges. During the heated succession debates of the 1566 Parliament, a petition to the Queen was composed, though never delivered, asserting the rights of Parliament to liberty of speech. It concluded with a wish to be 'your faithful, lowly subjects, honouring and obeying you, like children, for duty, reverence, and love, without the burden of any unnecessary, unaccustomed, or undeserved yoke of commandment'.[35] A speech probably at the same Parliament proposing the nomination of an heir and a bill of succession said that if Elizabeth would remove the peril to her people of an unsettled succession, 'then doth she declare herself to be a deare mother and tender nource over them'; but if not, she 'will (without the assistance of God's grace) coole the heate of love in any, how fervent so ever it be'.[36] Here the mother-child relationship was being used for a sort of metaphorical emotional blackmail: if Elizabeth really loved her people as she repeatedly declared, she should be tolerant of their desire for a degree of autonomy, while acting in accordance with their needs as they saw them.

As Elizabeth's reign proceeded towards its third decade, it was increasingly acknowledged that female rule brought with it some benefits, in the supposedly greater inclination of a female monarch towards peace and mercy. Speaker Bell, in his end of session oration at the 1576 Parliament, 'showed what a punishment it was to a nation to have a tyrannical king, and thereby what a blessing to have a virtuous, mild, and merciful princess.'[37] A letter from an unnamed MP to a Privy Councillor on the eve of the 1581 Parliament described how the people's disposition 'to love her Majesty, being so good a one, doth so far exceed the fear of her, being a woman and so merciful, that her lovingest means doth make them most obsequious.'[38] The figure of the mother was therefore a popular means of representing female rule since the archetypal maternal virtues of mercy and loving care could be claimed as advantages to subjects in a monarch.

So, the popularity of the mother-image in this period can be seen not so much as an attempt to replace the Virgin Mary, but rather as a means of constructing a virtuous image of Elizabeth as figurehead of the Protestant Church, and a positive image of female rule; and as a means for subjects to put forward claims to degrees of autonomy and free speech under monarchy.

iv. Elizabeth as a sacred figure

During the 1570s, the discourse of courtly love increasingly permeated the English court. The Earl of Oxford and Sir Edward Dyer developed a new poetry of love influenced by Petrarch and the French Pléiade.[39] Elizabeth's relation with such leading courtiers as Leicester and Hatton was often highly flirtatious, and they responded with language which echoed the medieval, Petrarchan and neo-Platonic traditions of love-discourse. As in those traditions, religious language was frequently used as a metaphor for erotic feeling, so that we increasingly find Elizabeth addressed as a saint or goddess. Consequently, a double layer of metaphor is built up: religious devotion to the Queen is a metaphor for erotic desire for her, which in turn is a metaphor for political loyalty to her.

Some of the most striking expressions of this multi-layered devotion and passion are in the correspondence of the royal favourite Sir Christopher Hatton. In 1573, after an illness, he wrote to the Queen to say that the kindness of her letters gives him cause 'to thank you on my knees', and that his absence from her has been an agony: 'Bear with me, my most dear sweet Lady. Passion overcometh me. I can write no more. Love me, for I love you. God, I beseech thee witness the same on behalf of this poor servant. Live for ever.'[40] Later the same year he wrote in a similar vein, probably from Spain: 'I pray God, you may believe my faith . . . I love yourself. I cannot lack you. I am taught to prove it by the wish and desire I find to be with you . . . God bless you for ever . . .'[41]

A few years later, in a letter to Sir Thomas Heneage clearly intended to be passed on or reported to the Queen, Hatton spoke of his love for her, and sent a 'ring, which hath the virtue to expel infectious airs, and is, as is telled to me, to be wearen betwixt the sweet dugs, – the chaste nest of most pure constancy'. He was undertaking a 'solitary pilgrimage', 'to view my house of Kirby, which I never yet surveyed; leaving my other shrine, I mean Holdenby, still unseen until that holy saint may sit in it, to whom it is dedicated.'[42] Holdenby in Northamptonshire was a vast and ornate mansion which he had built solely for the purpose of entertaining Elizabeth on progress. Burghley stayed there in 1579, and wrote to Hatton of their shared devotion to 'her Majesty, to whom it appeareth this godly, perfect, though not perfected work is consecrated'. He himself had built a 'prodigy house' in which to host the Queen at Theobalds: 'God send us both long life to enjoy Her, for whom we both meant to exceed our purses in these.'[43]

The combination of intimacy and religious awe in the Hatton correspondence is remarkable. Description of Elizabeth as a saint or goddess had more to it than just a courtly-love metaphor: it also comprehended belief in the sacredness of monarchy. The biblical texts favoured by Protestant commentators which described princes as gods[44] were frequently quoted or alluded to in the letters of ministers and courtiers;[45] for example, Aylmer writing to Hatton in 1578 in an attempt to overcome royal displeasure with him made a somewhat extraordinary statement for a bishop: 'I trust not of God, but of my Sovereign, which is God's lieutenant, and so another God unto me – for of such it is said *Vos estis dii*' (You shall be gods).[46] Elizabeth was addressed as 'Dea' and 'Diva' (Goddess) in some Latin verses for New Year 1570 by Dr Thomas Wilson.[47] The Mayor of Salisbury noted that her visit to the city in 1574 was attended by strange portents such as fire in the sky.[48]

In many cases the attribution of quasi-divinity to Elizabeth went beyond the titles of saint or goddess to compare her with Christ himself. She presented herself as a messianic saviour in reply to the 1563 parliamentary petition regarding the succession: 'I trust you likewise do not forget that by me you were delivered whilst you were hanging on the bough ready to fall into the mud, yea to be drowned in the dung'.[49] In the same year, the decorated initial C which opened Foxe's *Actes and Monuments* showed Elizabeth enthroned receiving the homage of three kneeling bearded men, recalling the Adoration of the Magi such as to make Elizabeth Christ-child and Virgin Mother in one.[50] In a more private context, in 1582 Sir Thomas Heneage conveyed to Sir Christopher Hatton Elizabeth's assurance that he, nicknamed her 'Mutton', had nothing to fear from 'Water', or Sir Walter Ralegh, who had become his rival as favourite. She said:

> that if Princes were like Gods, (as they should be,) they would suffer no element so to abound as to breed confusion . . . And, for better assurance unto you that you should fear no drowning, she hath sent you a bird, that (together with the rainbow) brought the good tidings and the covenant that there should be no more destruction by water. And further she willed me to send you word, with her commendations, that you should remember she was a Shepherd, and then you might think how dear her Sheep was unto her.[51]

In the early 1570s Nicholas Hilliard executed a pair of nearly-symmetrical portraits of the Queen, one showing her wearing a jewel in the shape of a pelican, the other, a phoenix.[52] According to legend, the pelican fed its young with blood from its own breast; as an image of self-sacrifice, it was therefore primarily associated with Christ, while as an image of self-denying maternal care it could also be associated with the Virgin.[53] At the same time it had a clear application to Elizabeth, sacrificing the private happiness of marriage in order to devote her whole care to sustaining the nation from her own person alone.[54]

As for the phoenix, its primary characteristics were that only one was alive at any time, and that it lived for several centuries, then mysteriously and asexually renewed itself from its own ashes. As such it had been associated with Christ's resurrection, and with the chastity and uniqueness of the Virgin;[55] it could also be used in praise of any mistress for exceptional beauty and virtue.[56] Its connotations of virginity and singularity made it highly applicable to Elizabeth; it may also have denoted Elizabeth's triumphant emergence from the ashes of her mother's disgrace and death and her own years in disfavour as a princess.[57] Sir Nicholas Bacon, in his opening oration to the 1571 Parliament, described the Queen as the phoenix, that 'blessed bird'.[58] It went on to become one of the most popular emblems for the Queen, especially in conjunction with the motto she adopted, 'Semper Eadem' ('Always one and the same' – my translation).[59] Both the phoenix and the pelican, then, were images which had associations with both Christ and the Virgin, but which also had precise personal applications to Elizabeth which encouraged their use in iconography.

Another favourite image for Elizabeth in this period was the sun. This too had multiple significances which went far beyond the patristic interpretation of the Woman Clothed with the Sun as a type of the Virgin Mary. As we saw earlier, before Elizabeth came to the throne the Woman was already established as a figure of the Protestant Church and of the godly Protestant heroine.[60] Moreover, the Sun/Son was a favourite punning emblem for Christ, and therefore had messianic overtones which made it highly applicable to Elizabeth as the supposed saviour of the nation, restorer of the faith, and dutiful heir to her father. It represented Elizabeth as militant Protestant evangelist: Becon, for instance, wrote that 'her hyghnes is to this Realme, that the sonne is to the earth after many stormy, cloudy and tempestuous dayes'.[61] The sun was also a traditional image of monarchy; the author of an account of the Queen's visit to Norwich in 1578 wrote in his dedicatory epistle that he had seen 'the Maiestie of my Prince, which beautifieth her kyngdome, as the bright shinyng beames of beautifull *Phoebus* decketh forth the earth'.[62] In addition, the sun could connote the inspiring radiance of the Petrarchan mistress, as when Hatton wrote to Elizabeth that she was 'the brightness of that Sun that giveth light unto my sense and soul.'[63] All these resonances combined in some verses published with the account of the Norwich visit, 'To the Sunne couered with cloudes, vpon Monday, being the .18. of August. 1578', which compared Elizabeth with the sun on grounds of beauty and radiance, both physical and spiritual, dispelling the clouds and darkness of 'Poprye'.[64]

A more specifically Marian epithet which came to be frequently applied to Elizabeth was that of 'handmaid of God'. She described herself thus in a speech to the 1576 Parliament,[65] and she was also so described in several prayer-books associated with her personal devotional use, such as Richard Day's *Christian Prayers and Meditations*, 1569, also known as 'Queen Elizabeth's Prayer Book';[66] Day's *A Booke of Christian Prayers*, 1578;[67] and the manuscript Book of Devotions.[68] The epithet was consistently used to denote Elizabeth's humble submission to her destiny as God's instrument to advance the true faith, and was therefore again a distinctly Protestant appropriation of a Marian title.

In these prayer-books, there appears to be some recuperation of pre-Reformation iconography of the Virgin. In the French Prayer of the *Book of Devotions*, Elizabeth is given the sentiment that for God's 'grande misericorde envers moy ta tres humble servante' (great mercy toward me, thy servant), keeping her from the abyss of ignorance and superstition in which many other princes dwell, 'ie te loueray en magnifiant ta nom, o mon Pere' (I will praise thee, O my Father, magnifying thy name), by singing many psalms to Him.[69] This is a conflation of the Magnificat, a hymn associated with the Virgin, with the tenor of many of the Psalms, which were favourite texts with Protestants.

Day's prayer-books of 1569 and 1578 carried woodcut frontispieces and borders which included such distinctively Marian iconography as a tree of Jesse with the Virgin and child at its top, and St Anne giving birth to the Virgin. All the woodcut borders, however, had the distinctively Protestant component of scriptural texts, and several were explicitly anti-Catholic. The text 'He shall breake downe their altars, he shal destroy their images' was illustrated with one picture of the golden calf, and one of three men kneeling to a statue of the Virgin and child. Another border showed a female figure of Love of God trampling such implements of Catholic worship as a rosary, a chalice and a candle, with the message 'Idolatry, is Spirituall adultery'. Between these borders, the main text of the book included such overt Protestantism as an anti-Catholic prayer by Foxe.[70] Here, then, some traditional images of the Virgin were being incorporated in iconography which was otherwise characteristically Protestant in its use of moralising texts and its anti-idolatrous message.

v. Accession Day

It was against this background, in the 1570s, that Elizabeth's Accession Day became a national holiday. Historians have speculated that the development of the festival might have been a popular loyal Protestant response to the suppression of the Northern Rebellion in 1569 and to the papal excommunication of Elizabeth in 1570; and, simultaneously, compensation for the diminution in the number of saints' day celebrations.[71] It is in fact unclear exactly how Accession Day started, and how far it was a spontaneous popular thanksgiving, how far organised by the government. However, the official institution of a national festival designed to promote political and religious unity was not unthought of: back in Henry VIII's reign, during Cromwell's reforms, an annual celebration of the break from Rome had been proposed as a means of reinforcing the hold of Protestantism.[72]

Much of our information as to the origins of the Elizabethan celebration comes from the less than objective source of Thomas Holland, a loyal servant of the established Church, Regius Professor of Divinity at Oxford, and Rector of Exeter College, a post he gained by Elizabeth's influence.[73] He published 'The Apologie or Defence of the Church and Common-wealth of England for their annuall celebration of Q.Elizabeths Coronation Day [sic] the 17. of Novemb.' as an appendix to his 1599 Accession Day sermon. Holland writes as an encomiast of Elizabeth, and is therefore at pains to stress the voluntary nature of the celebrations. Even so, he describes their inception in around 1570 as follows: 'the first publike celebrity of it was instituted in *Oxford* (by *Dr Cooper* being then there Vicechauncelour after Bishop Of *Lincolne*, and by remoue from thence Bishop of *Winchester*) from whence this institution flowed by a voluntary current over all this Realme.'[74] Even if Holland's account is correct, it looks as if this was not so much a spontaneous show of popular allegiance as a well-organised and effective career-move by Dr Cooper.[75]

From the early 1570s onwards the local officials of provincial

towns and parishes organised the marking of Accession Day with
bell-ringing, bonfires, and various other festivities, and ballads and
verses for the occasion began to be published.[76] It was added to the
Church's calendar of Holy Days, and in 1576 there appeared, under
royal authority, *A fourme of Prayer, with thankes geuyng, to be vsed
euery yeere, the .17. of Nouember, beyng the day of the Queenes Maiesties
entrie to her raigne.*[77] Both the title page and the final page of this
official service-book carried an emblem of a pelican feeding her
young. The first lesson was a choice of Old Testament passages
concerning godly kings who opposed idolatry and were rewarded
with divine favour; the second was Romans 13, with its sonorous
opening pronouncement:

> Let euery soule be subiect vnto the higher powers: for there is no
> power but of God: and the powers that be, are ordeyned of God.
> Whosoeuer therfore resisteth the power, resisteth the ordinance
> of God: and they that resist, shal receiue to themselues iudgement.[78]

The psalms used in the service concerned godly rulers, and the
relation between God and Israel, expressing a sense of national
isolation and beleaguerment from which God listens to the prayers
of his chosen people and raises them to victory. The Epistle was 1
Peter 2.11–18, which is about obedience to rulers; the Gospel was
Matthew 22.16–23, the story of the tribute money, with its moral of
rendering to Caesar the civic duty which is rightfully his. In total,
then, the service used the authority of Scripture to promote a combination of national self-righteousness and a sense of the sinfulness
of political disobedience.

This service book was reissued in a slightly expanded form in
1578.[79] In 1585, Edmund Bunny compiled an alternative order of
service for Accession Day which was also published under royal
authority.[80] Bunny included a dedication to the new Archbishop of
Canterbury, Whitgift, urging 'that order should be taken for the
continuance of the exercise begunne in your Graces Predecessors
time' of a thanksgiving on 17 November; and explaining that he
had compiled his service book 'for the better accomplishment
whereof, especially in these partes where I am resident' (sig.A2r–v).
The dedication was dated from York, where Bunny, an itinerant
preacher, held a clerical post. The implication is that Accession
Day was not celebrated with the same enthusiasm in all parts of

Elizabeth's realm, and in some places was in danger of dying out by the mid-1580s.

There is a difference in tenor between the 1576/78 text and Bunny's book. In 1576/78, the prayers generally ask God to aid Elizabeth and her subjects to live up to an as-yet-unfulfilled Protestant ideal:

> most hartily we beseech thee with thy fauour to behold our most gracious soueraigne Ladie Queene Elizabeth, and to replenish her with the grace of thy holy spirit, that she may alway encline to thy wil, and walke in thy way . . . so rule the heart of thy chosen seruant Elizabeth our Queene and gouernour, that she (knowing whose minister she is) may aboue al thinges seeke thy honour and glory, and that we her subiectes (duely consydering whose authoritie she hath) may faythfully serue, honour, and humbly obey her, in thee, and for thee, according to thy blessed woorde & ordinance.[81]

Bunny's text gives more of a sense that Elizabeth is already the completely perfect Protestant ruler, and that the purpose of the service is simply to give thanks to God for sending her:

> O Most high and eternall God, we are not able to expresse in word, or in heart to conceiue, how infinitely we are beholding to thee, for giuing vs so gracious a Princesse, sent laden vnto vs with so many and so speciall giftes and blessings . . .
> (sigs D4v–E1r)

He includes a table setting out the reasons for celebrating Accession Day, which lists Elizabeth's graces and gifts and England's benefits from God (between sigs E2v and E3r).

Bunny's service veers towards what might be called worship of Elizabeth, whereas the compilers of the 1576/78 service appear to have been conscious of the danger of incurring charges of idolatry. They keep carefully to Protestant theological limits by asking God's aid in Elizabeth's endeavour to approach an image of divine perfection in a ruler which may never be fully realisable in this fallen world, just as the individual believer is engaged in an effort to be as holy as possible but is limited by the bounds of humanity. Bunny does not acknowledge this implied gap between Elizabeth and the image of the ideal ruler; in his prayers, she *is* that ideal. The reasons for his more adulatory tone may lie partly in the fact that he was writing for still largely Catholic northern areas, and therefore had an aggressive polemical purpose which required a presentation of Elizabeth which allowed no room for question. He also includes a prayer which stridently refutes various Catholic doctrines (sig.D4r–v). Reasons may also lie in the later date of his text, as representations of Elizabeth became increasingly reverential. However, the 1578 text seems to have remained the official service-book for general use, and was reissued in almost identical form in 1590.[82]

Accession Day was marked at court by a tournament, possibly instituted as early as 1570 by Sir Henry Lee, who offered himself as the Queen's champion.[83] In 1577 Philip Sidney made his first appearance at the tiltyard, and wrote two songs for the occasion which play on the fact that in that year 17 November fell on a Sunday, and so was in two senses a 'sabbath'. One song stressed the popularity and universality of the thanksgiving: '. . . great and small, rich, poor, and each degree / Yield faith, love, joy, and prove what in them be'. The other celebrated the occasion as a holy-day and therefore explicitly addressed Elizabeth as a saint:

> Sing, neighbours, sing; hear you not say
>   This Sabbath day
>   A Sabbath is reputed
>   Of such a royal saint
>   As all saints else confuted
>   Is love without constraint?

The refrain incorporated the response 'Good Lord, deliver us' from the Prayer Book litany:

> Let such a saint be praised
>   Which so her worth hath raised:
>   From him that would not thus
>   Good Lord, deliver us.[84]

The tone of Sidney's songs probably lies somewhere between the conceitful wit of courtly compliment and a serious profession of loyalty to the Protestant regime. This is the kind of panegyric whose extravagant terms may seem to us to verge on idolatry or blasphemy, but whose context was a by-now-conventional view of Elizabeth as God's instrument and as a personification of Protestant

England. Like Bunny, Sidney is eulogising Elizabeth as symbol rather than as a person.

There is evidence that at least a few of Elizabeth's subjects objected to Accession Day as idolatrous. In 1581 Mr Barwick, a parson, got into an argument at Lord Rich's house with Robert Wright, Lord Rich's chaplain, and Richard Riche over a sermon which he had preached about the observance of Accession Day. Wright and Riche alleged that Barwick had called Accession Day a 'holy day', and had compared it to the celebrations of the birthdays of Romulus, Alexander and Lycurgus, who were objects of idolatrous worship. Barwick claimed that he had only used the term 'solemn day', but that he would willingly defend the term 'holy day'. Wright and Riche found themselves thrown into prison.[85]

It seems fair to conclude that Accession Day was a centrally authorised and promoted festival, combining courtly celebrations with dissemination through the provinces by means of the official Church services and the efforts of local officials eager to show their loyalty. Bunny's dedication and the Wright case are evidence that it provoked different kinds of controversy. In general, though, at this stage in the reign Accession Day does not seem to have aroused much religious anxiety or political resistance; it was in later years that defences like Holland's began to be felt necessary.

The general acceptance of the festival probably rested on a combination of factors. First, the official church service avoided charges of idolatry by concentrating on prayers for the Queen to be godly, rather than worship of her divinity. Secondly, even the more overtly idolatrous practices and forms surrounding the occasion were in step with the prevalent belief in the holiness of the Queen, or at least in what she represented as a symbol of the Protestant Church and nation. Thirdly, the ritual itself inculcated the belief that the regime was sanctified, and that dissent was therefore sinful. Finally, we should not of course discount the popular enjoyment of a day of national celebration. However, it was not so much a spontaneous popular upwelling of a substitute saint's day, as a meeting half-way of the interests of government and people, and a further example of the close conjunction of the Elizabethan Church and State.

vi. The use of classical goddesses in panegyric

Although biblical heroines like Deborah and Judith dominated early Elizabethan royal iconography, there was a parallel tradition of the use of classical goddesses. One favourite mythological motif was that of the Judgement of Paris, which was used in Anne Boleyn's coronation pageants,[86] and again in a portrait of 1569 of *Queen Elizabeth and the Three Goddesses*, which depicts Pallas, Juno and Venus overwhelmed as Elizabeth advances towards them carrying the royal orb.[87] The idea is that the three goddesses (more usually Diana, Juno and Venus) resign the contended prize of the golden apple to the Queen, who combines and surpasses all their allegorical virtues of chastity, majesty and beauty in one person. It was especially appropriate to Elizabeth as a sole female ruler, who was required to combine contradictory virtues of 'masculine' authority and 'feminine' beauty and chastity.

In court entertainments of the 1560s, the issue of the succession was obliquely addressed in debates between marriage and chastity, personified as Juno or Venus versus Diana or Pallas.[88] From the mid-1570s on the use of these figures increases, probably partly because of a growing uncertainty as to whether to represent Elizabeth as marriageable or as ever-virgin. The appearance in the same masque of goddesses of love and marriage and virgin-goddesses as different aspects of the Queen was a means of coping iconographically with this unresolved question.

At the same time, classical figures were extremely useful to the panegyrist in the latitude which they allowed in speaking of the 'divinity' of the Queen. Encomiasts could have it both ways, describing Elizabeth as a goddess in such a way as simultaneously to imply the sacredness of Christian Protestant monarchy, while deflecting charges of idolatry or blasphemy because of the context of classical mythography, in which 'divinity' was understood as a literary convention distinct from the true divinity of the Christian God.

vii. Entertainments at Kenilworth and Woodstock, 1575

Two entertainments by George Gascoigne from Elizabeth's progress of 1575 exemplify some of these iconographic trends. For the magnificent pageants laid on over several days by the Earl of Leicester at Kenilworth, Gascoigne composed a masque concerning the quest of the goddess Diana for one of her nymphs, Zabeta, clearly a persona for Elizabeth. Although the masque was not in the event performed, it was published in the *The Princely Pleasures at the Courte at Kenilworth*, Gascoigne's account of the festivities. It exemplifies the increasing use of classical goddesses and of Petrarchan religious metaphor as a means of speaking of Elizabeth's divinity while remaining within the safe boundaries of literary convention. As Diana seeks Zabeta she says: 'It cannot be that such a Saint to see / Can long in shrine her seemely selfe to shroude'.[89]

The representation of Elizabeth as a nymph of Diana implied a positive evaluation of her virginity as a divine quality. As the masque continued, though, Iris appeared and urged Elizabeth to follow not Diana but Juno; in other words, to choose marriage rather than celibacy:

> How necessarie were
>   for worthy Queenes to wed,
> That know you wel, whose life alwaies
>   in learning hath been led.
> The country craves consent,
>   your virtues vaunt themselfe,
> And Jove in Heaven would smile to see
>   Diana set on shelfe ...
> ... where you now in princely port
>   have past one pleasant day,
> A world of wealth at wil,
>   you henceforth shall enjoy;
> In weded state ...[90]

On the surface this looks like a last-ditch attempt by Leicester to advance his own suit as potential king consort; even though he had fathered a son the previous year by Douglass Sheffield, who may or may not have been secretly married to him; and even though he may already have begun his liaison with Lettice Devereux, Countess of Essex, whom he was to marry in 1578.[91] Alternatively, perhaps marriage was here a metaphor for political favour, just as love-language was deployed in Hatton's letters of the same period; perhaps Leicester was 'wooing' Elizabeth simply to confirm him as chief favourite at a time when both personal and political circumstances made him vulnerable.[92] Whichever is true, the text of the entertainments as a whole seems confused between these exhortations to marry and, elsewhere, acceptance or even affirmation of Elizabeth's virginity.

Also at Kenilworth, the character of Sibylla informed Elizabeth 'You shall be called the Prince of Peace', a title which conveniently

combined Christological connotations, the respectably feminine virtues of conciliation and tranquillity, and the respectably monarchical virtue of achieving national stability.[93]

Most striking for our interests is a dialogue between a Savage
Man and an Echo, in which the Echo explains that the people
are rejoicing for a Queen, and the Savage Man replies:

> Queene? what, the Queene of Heaven?
> They knew hir long agone!
> No, sure, some Queene on earth,
> whose like was never none.[94]

The description of the Queen of Heaven as known 'long agone' is
ambiguous in a fashion useful for Protestant panegyric, potentially
scorning the Virgin Mary as old-fashioned while avoiding overt
disrespect by simultaneously implying a continuing familiarity in
which her high status can be assumed. At the same time, the use of
the title 'Queen of Heaven' enables the presence of a perfect Queen
on earth to be presented as a miraculous and sacred phenomenon.
The iconography of queenship is taken back from the Virgin as the
natural appellation for an earthly female monarch, while continuing to trail the connotations of sacredness which it had acquired in
its association with the Virgin.

From Kenilworth Elizabeth went on to Woodstock, the estate of
Sir Henry Lee, where the entertainment included a dramatised tale
of a hermit, again provided by Gascoigne. Elizabeth performed the
Christlike act of restoring the hermit's sight. The developing combination of an ideology of the sacredness of monarchy with the
neo-Platonic and Petrarchan traditions of the courtly mistress as
divine inspiration was made explicit in the epilogue: 'If God wolde
deigne to make a Petrark's heire of me, / The coomlyest Quene that
ever was my Lawra nedes must be'.[95]

viii. *The Lady of May*, 1578

In the spring of 1578 Elizabeth stayed at the Earl of Leicester's
house at Wanstead in Essex and saw Sidney's masque of *The Lady
of May*.[96] As was now conventional for such royal entertainments,
Elizabeth was required to cross the boundary between stage and
audience and make a quasi-divine intervention in the dramatic

action: in this case, to choose between the two suitors of the May Lady, the forceful forester Therion and the mild shepherd Espilus. The latter was her choice. Some critics have taken the view that the pageant was a political allegory, with Therion representing Leicester and his aggressive view of foreign policy, and that Elizabeth's choice was contrary to the author's intentions.[97] It is unlikely by now that Leicester was literally pursuing the Queen's hand in marriage, since he married Lettice Devereux nee Knollys the following September. Other critics have preferred alternative, often more complex readings.[98] However, two things about the masque are of particular relevance to our interests here: its invocation of ancient traditions of spring festivals; and references to Catholicism in the closing speech.

Spring festivals, and particularly May festivals, celebrating fertility and marked by songs, dancing and flowers, have a history which stretches back to pagan goddess-cults. The nymph Maia after whom the month of May was named was associated with fecundity by the Romans, and their *Ludi Floreales* from 23 April to 3 May were a riotous celebration of the goddess Flora which included pelting one another with flowers. Since the Middle Ages, May Day has been popularly marked throughout Europe by the crowning of the Queen of the May; while the mediaeval aristocracy customarily celebrated on 1 May with jousting and poetry. The Virgin Mary, as a figure of maidenhood and fertility, became associated with the figure of the Queen of the May, but this was not firmly established until the eighteenth century, when May was designated as Mary's month.[99]

The use of the figure of the May-Lady in Sidney's masque, then, and the theme of wooing-choices which implicitly associated Elizabeth with the May-Lady, drew to the figure of the Queen ancient traditions of the celebration of maidenhood and regeneration. At this point, in early 1578, it must have looked highly unlikely that the Queen would ever marry; the Anjou courtship did not begin to look serious until later in the year. Sidney's masque may then be seen as an early example of the dominant iconography of the later years of the reign, when, paradoxically, representation of Elizabeth as a goddess of love and fertility was amplified even though, or perhaps precisely because, her singleness and childlessness had become certain.

The Lady of May ends with a curious speech by a character named Rombus, a pedantic schoolmaster. He presented Elizabeth with 'a

chain of round agates something like beads', then explained that
Leicester 'is foully commaculated with the papistical enormity' and
'is a huge *catholicam*'. He went on: 'I have found *unum par*, a pair,
papisticorum bedorus, of Papistian beads, *cum quis*, with the which,
omnium dierum, every day, next after his *pater noster* he *semper* suits
"and Elizabeth", as many lines as there be beads on this string'.[100]
Leicester seems to refer jokingly to this speech in a letter to Hatton
which apparently concerns a visit to a spa for his health while
Elizabeth visited Wanstead in his absence: 'God grant I may hear
that her Majesty doth both well rest, and find all things else there
to her good contentment; and that the good man Robert, she last
heard of there, were found at his beads, with all his *aves*, in his
solitary walk.'[101]

The representation of Leicester as a Catholic can hardly be other
than ironic, in the light of his extensive patronage of the more radical of Protestants and of anti-Catholic propaganda.[102] The use of the
figure of the beadsman bears relation to the use of the figure of the
hermit at Woodstock in 1575: in both cases, contemplative religious
figures were used to represent single-minded devotion to and adoration of Elizabeth. This was part of the Petrarchan tradition of
using religious language to figure erotic devotion; a trope which
itself, as we have seen, came to be a metaphor in Elizabethan panegyric for loyal political service. What is especially striking about
Rombus's speech is the use of the specifically Catholic practice of
telling the rosary as a figure for this political-religious-erotic devotion. This use of identifiably Catholic terms in Elizabethan courtly
love discourse is a point I will return to.

We can discern several different factors at work in resemblances
between iconography of Elizabeth and Marian iconography in the
period 1560–78. The identification of Elizabeth with the Protestant
Church and State resulted in aggressive Protestant appropriations
of scriptural types like the Woman Clothed with the Sun. The celebration of Accession Day in the style of a saint's day was also a
mark of the political and religious values projected onto Elizabeth
as symbol, and of the efforts of the government to use this glamorous symbol as a focus for religious and political uniformity. Meanwhile, it was beginning to be realised that Elizabeth was likely to
be a virgin in perpetuity, and a mother only in the symbolic sense
of mother to the nation.

Resemblances to Marian iconography, then, were produced by

particular shifting political circumstances, rather than by a mass psychological desire to find a Virgin-substitute. The next such shift was the Anjou courtship of 1578–82, which marked Elizabeth's conclusive transition into perpetual virginity.

4

1578–82:
Into Perpetual Virginity

i. The Anjou Courtship

Negotiations for a marriage between Elizabeth and Francis, Duke
of Anjou, youngest son of Catherine de Medici, had rumbled along
intermittently through the 1570s, but in 1578 they took a serious
turn.[1] They were an unlikely couple: Anjou was 23 years old and
disfigured by pock-marks;[2] Elizabeth was 44. Anjou's interest in the
marriage was to add force to his military ambitions in the Netherlands, while the advantage for the English side lay mainly in pre-
venting France and Spain from combining against England. Other
pros and cons for England were clearly set out by the Earl of Sussex
in a letter to Elizabeth of 28 August 1578. She would gain strength
in her defence of the Protestant rebels in the Netherlands and would
secure the succession (assuming, that is, that Elizabeth was still
capable of child-bearing). In addition, 'you shall have a husband as
a servant and defender of all your causes present'. Disadvantages
included 'Your own mislike to marriage,' now generally understood as a given fact, 'which might breed a discontented life hereafter', and 'The general mislike which Englishmen have to be
governed by a stranger.'[3]

Walsingham, Elizabeth's chief minister of foreign policy and therefore a man much employed in her foreign marriage negotiations,
clearly felt weary of the whole business: he wrote to Sir Christopher
Hatton in October 1578, 'I would to God her Majesty would forbear
the entertaining any longer the marriage matter. No one thing hath
procured her so much hatred abroad as these wooing matters, for
that it is conceived she dallieth therein.'[4] Nevertheless, the courtship intensified in 1579, first with the arrival at the English court in
January of Anjou's envoy Simier, who flirted elaborately with the
Queen; then with the secret arrival in August of the Duke himself
for a thirteen-day romantic visit.

At last Elizabeth appeared to have a firm intent to marry, and this reversal in turn produced a reversal in the attitude of her subjects. Having become accustomed to the rule of a single woman, disliking the French, and still rankling at the memory of Mary I's marriage to a foreign prince, they now opposed her marriage. Their 'general mislike' for it was vehemently expressed, not least by John Stubbs, who in September 1579 published *The discovery of a gaping gulf, wherein England is like to be swallowed by another French marriage, if the Lord forbid not the banns by letting her Majesty see the sin and punishment thereof*. At Elizabeth's command the book was banned, and Stubbs and his publisher had their right hands chopped off with a cleaver. John Aylmer summed up the popular realisation that a Virgin Queen with no heir of her body might be preferable to a queen married to foreigner: 'so long as their eye is fixed upon her, they find themselves as it were ravished: but looking aside at the stranger . . . they are like them that by long looking on the sun, their eyes are become so dazzled that they judge everything else to be monstrous.'[5]

In October and early November the Privy Council debated the marriage. A majority of councillors opposed it, but they decided to inform the Queen that they would advise her neither for nor against. From this point on the marriage effectively ceased to be a realistic prospect: Elizabeth would not go against a divided and reluctant Council as well as a hostile populace. The negotiations dragged on for another two years, and Elizabeth continued to pen intimate letters to her 'Frog', as she playfully called him,[6] like this one from around June 1581: 'Monsieur, my dearest, grant pardon to the poor old woman who honours you (I dare say it) as much as any young wench that you will ever find.'[7] By this time, though, the courtship was mainly a means of making use of Anjou in the Netherlands conflict, and by 1582 even the pretence of courtship was over. Anjou died in 1584.

From an iconographic point of view, the Anjou courtship is important because it marks some important changes: the realisation by Elizabeth's subjects that a Virgin Queen might be preferable to a married Queen; and, simultaneously, the end of any prospect that Elizabeth might produce an heir of her body. From now on she would be unequivocally celebrated as ever-virgin. Texts from the period 1578–82 are especially interesting because they show this transition in progress by combining contradictory or even confused attitudes to the virginity or matrimony of the Queen. At the same time, they illustrate developments in the practice of panegyric, and in representations of Elizabeth as divine.

ii. The Norwich entertainments, 1578

Elizabeth's progress of 1578 took her through Suffolk and Norfolk; it was on this journey that the incident at Euston Hall discussed in my Introduction took place. The entertainment of the Queen in Norwich is recorded in two complementary accounts, one by a Master Garter and one by Thomas Churchyard.[8] In his prefatory epistles, Churchyard declares the panegyrical and didactic motives of his text: 'I meane to make it a mirror and shining glasse, that al the whole land may loke into, or vse it for an example in all places (where the Prince commeth) to our posteritie heereafter for euer' (sig.A2v). He amplifies: 'I will boldly hold on my matter which I have penned, for those people that dwell farre off the Court, that they may see with what maiestie a Prince raigneth, and with what obedience and loue good Subiectes do receiue hir' (sig.B1v). Loyal pageants celebrating the Queen are to be communicated through the power of print and the attractiveness of news, in order to instruct the general populace in the proper veneration of their monarch. The panegyrics performed at Norwich are thus given double force, impressing both an immediate audience and readers distanced by place and time.

The entertainments display much uncertainty as to whether Elizabeth would be pleased by praise of marriage or of chastity, and make much use of classical goddesses as means of negotiating the issue. Churchyard describes a masque for the Tuesday of the visit in which Venus and Cupid were suppressed by Chastity, who then made a presentation:

> bycause (sayd *Chastitie*) that the Quéene had chosen the best life, she gaue the Quéene CVPIDS bow, to learne to shoote at whome she pleased, since none coulde wounde hir highnesse hart, it was méete (said *Chastitie*) that she should do with CVPIDS bow and arrows what she pleased.
>
> (sig.D1r)

This elegantly contrives simultaneously to praise Elizabeth's virginity, while commending any choice of husband which she might make. However, the masque proceeded with speeches in praise of chastity (sig.D2v) and in dispraise of Cupid and Venus as pagan gods (sigs D3r–E1r).

Garter tells us that on the Thursday evening there was a masque of gods and goddesses, during which Mercury explained: 'Onely HIMINEVS [god of marriage] denyeth his goodwil, eyther in presence, or in person: notwithstanding, DIANA hath so countrechecked him therefore, as he shall euer hereafter be at your commaundement' (sig.E1v). Again, a courteous ambiguity was sustained as to whether Elizabeth's virginity or potential marriage is the object of praise. Elizabeth was endued with the contradictory qualities of various goddesses: Venus declared the Queen to be 'an'other VENUS', but the virgin goddess Pallas also identified herself with her, and Diana hailed her as 'Virgin Queene' (sigs E2r–3r). Finally, in an echo of Churchyard's masque for the Tuesday, Cupid presented Elizabeth with a golden arrow, saying: 'Shoote but this shafte at King or Caesar: He, / And he is thine, and if thou wilt allowe' (sig.E3v). Once more, praise of Elizabeth as virgin is tempered by a continuing possibility of marriage. The very gift of the arrow is two-sided, in one sense associating Elizabeth with love, by giving her an attribute of Cupid which connotes desire, but in another sense arming her in a fashion reminiscent of Diana, whose weapons denote chastity and independence.

However, some extra verses printed at the end of Garter's text laid the emphasis firmly on virginity: Elizabeth is 'Vnspoused *Pallas*', 'Vnarmed *Pallas*', and 'a Virgine pure, which is, and euer was' (sig.G2r). In Churchyard's account of the Tuesday masque, Chastity's maids, Modesty, Temperance, Good exercise and Shamefastness, performed a song in praise of chastity:

> Chast life a pretious pearle,
> doth shine as bright as Sunne,
> The fayre houre glasse of dayes and yeares,
> that never out will runne.

(sigs E1v–2r)

There is an implication here that sexual purity brings longevity or even immortality, a double triumph over the flesh. This was to become a prominent theme of panegyric in the later years of the reign when Elizabeth's virginity became absolute. Wishes for the Queen's immortality occur at several points in the Norwich pageants:

'Most happy England were, if thou shouldst never die' (Garter, sigs B3r–v); 'You can not die, Loue here hath made your lease' (Garter, sig.E2v).

In accordance with this increasing emphasis on Elizabeth's virginity as perpetual, her motherhood is represented as a symbolic property more than as a biological probability. Garter prints a farewell oration by a Mr Lambert (not in fact spoken, because of a delay, but a copy was presented to the Queen). He described the townspeople's grief at Elizabeth's departure in the following terms: 'How lamentable a thing is it, to pul away sucking babes from the breastes and bosomes of their most louing mothers? That sonnes and fathers, through some miserable misfortune, shoulde be sundered?' But the subjects' love and goodwill to Elizabeth is greater than that between parent and child or vice versa, because she is 'the mother and nurse of this whole Common welth, and Countrie' (sigs F3v–4r).[9] The motivation for maternal imagery here is not to echo Mariology, but to naturalise obedience to the Crown.

Churchyard follows his account of the Norwich festivities with a description of the houses where Elizabeth stayed as the progress continued, including the sentence 'from thence to *Rockwood Hall*, but howe the trayne was there entertayned, I am ignorant of' (sig.H1r). This may perhaps be a reference to Euston Hall, seat of Edward Rookwood, the house at which the incident described in my Introduction took place. It is possible to read deeper implications into Churchyard's profession of ignorance: either as knowledge of the inadequacy of Euston to house the royal train, and therefore surprise at its use as a place to stay; or as a desire to distance himself from the dramatic events which took place there.

Overall, the Norwich pageants bespeak an uncertainty as to whether Elizabeth should be addressed as potential bride or perpetual virgin; and an increasing confidence in praising her as a goddess, though Garter qualifies this: 'This Lady mayst thou Goddesse call, for she deserues the same: / Although she will not vndertake, a title of such fame' (sig.G2r).

iii. Puttenham's *Partheniades*, January 1579

At New Year 1579, George Puttenham presented Elizabeth with the gift of a sequence of poems entitled *Partheniades*, or 'virgin-songs'.[10] The verses are set out as speeches by each of the Muses. Two aspects of them are of interest to us in this discussion: their treatment of the question of Elizabeth's marriage; and their articulation and practice of theories of panegyric, in relation to which they offer depictions of Elizabeth as divine.

The third Partheniad is headed 'That her Ma*jes*tie (twoo thinges except) hath all the partes that iustly make to be sayd a most happy creature in this world'. Elizabeth's gifts are catalogued, beginning with 'Youthfull bewtye, in body well disposed' – in other words, her nubility. It is concluded that she is 'a Princelye paragon' –

> But had shee, oh the twoo ioys shee doth misse
> A Cesar to her husband, a kinge to her soone
> What lackt her highnes then to all erthly blisse.

> (f.169v)

This is an unusually explicit statement of a wish for Elizabeth to marry.

Partheniad 7 is also strikingly explicit; it is a blazon which is surprising in its specificity, eroticism and voyeurism:

> Her bosome sleeke as Paris plaster
> Held vpp twoo bowles of Alabaster.
> Ech byas was a little cherrye
> Or as I thinke a strawberrye.
> A slender greve swifter then Roe
> A pretye foote to trippe and goe
> But of a solemne pace perdye
> And marchinge with a maiestye
> Her body shapte as strayghte as shafte,
> Disclosed eche limbe withouten craft
> Saue shadowed all as I could gesse
> Vnder a vayle of silke Cypresse.

> (f.171v)

This seems to emphasise Elizabeth's nubility and fertility; yet Puttenham goes on to describe her resistance to love. Although she attracts suitors with the magnetic power of adamant, her heart is impenetrable:

> Her hart was hidd none might yt see
> Marble or flinte folke weene yt bee

> Not flint I trowe, I am a lyer
> But Syderite* that feeles noe fier.

(f.172r)

Her erotic attractions are retrospectively revised by this statement: instead of being signs of her ripeness for love, they designate by contrast her extraordinary power to move while remaining unmoved. Puttenham elaborates:

> Kinges and kinges peeres who haue soughte farre and nye
> But all in vayne to bee her paramoures
> Since twoo Capetts,[11] three Cezairnes[12] assayde
> And bidd repulse of the great Briton Mayde.

(f.172v)

At this point, then, her combination of desirability and unsusceptibility to love becomes an emblem of qualities of pride, steadfastness and unassailability which are national as well as personal.

However, this is immediately followed by 'A verye strange: and rufull vision presented to the authoure, the interpretation wherof was left to her Ma*jes*tie till by the purpose discovered' (f.172v). It is an emblem of a plant with three buds:

> Twoo blossoms falne, the thirde began to fade
> So as with in the compas of an houre
> Sore withered was this noble deintye flowre
> That noe soyle bredd, nor lande shall loose the like
> Ne no seazon or soone or sokinge showre
> Can reare agayne for prayer ne for meede.
> Woe and alas, the people crye and shrike
> Why fades this flower, and leaues noe fruit nor seede.

(ff.172v–173r)

This undoubtedly represents the Tudor dynasty, of which two blossoms, Edward and Mary, have already fallen without issue, and a

---

* syderite, i.e. loadstone, magnetic stone

third, Elizabeth, stands in danger of doing so, and in fact is ominously shown as already fading. The emblem resembles the dynastic rose-tree which appears on the title page of John Stow's *Chronicles of England, from Brute unto this present yeare of Christ 1580*, of which John King comments: 'Interpretation of the Stow title page is ambiguous . . . . Would Elizabeth be the last bud upon the rose arbor? Or, flanked by sterile offshoots, Edward VI and Mary I, is she still capable of perpetuating her line?'[13] Yet there is no ambiguity as regards Puttenham's apparent desire at this point for Elizabeth to marry: the next Partheniad is 'Another vision happned to the same authoure as Comfortable & recreatyve as the former was dolorous'. He describes a royal ship sailing smoothly:

> None but a kinge, or more maye her abourde
> O gallant peece, well will the lillye afoorde
> Thow strike mizzen and anker in his porte.

(f.173r)

The lily clearly refers to Anjou, and his royal French crest of the fleur-de-lys.

However, Puttenham continues to oscillate back and forth in his attitude to the Queen's virginity or matrimony. Partheniad 12 speculates on 'What causes, mooved so many Forreinge Princes to bee sutours to her Majestie for mariage, and what by coniecture hath hitherto mooved her to refuse them all' (f.174r). Here he reverts to praise of Elizabeth for her capacity 'To conquer all, an be conquerd by none' (f.175r). The final Partheniad, a hymn to Elizabeth as Pallas, states: 'we suppose thou hast forswore / To matche with man for evermore' (f.178r).

Thus Puttenham veers between advocating the possible French match, and praising Elizabeth for a virginity which sets her above other women, indeed above all mere mortals, and makes her a goddess-like figure. This implicitly invokes the Christian tradition of virginity as a sanctified attribute, although it is classical virgin-goddesses who are explicitly invoked as analogues to Elizabeth. It is Elizabeth's virginity which renders her an 'exceptional woman', and therefore provides most of the grounds for panegyric: Partheniad 12, for instance, defends 'her Majesties honoure and constancye for not enclininge her courage (after the example of other ordinarye Weemen) nor yet to the appetite of most great greate [*sic*] Princes eyther in the affayre of her Marriage or of her manner of regyment' (f.175r). Her virginity is increasingly becoming a keystone of panegyric.

The *Partheniades* begin by overtly announcing themselves as panegyric. Ancient and modern poets are listed who were inspired to write in praise of rulers, heroes and lovers, but the author prefers his subject of Elizabeth above any other. Her femininity and her chastity determine the manner and genre in which he composes: 'in chast style . . . To blazon foorthe the briton mayden Queene' (f.169v). From this point on, Puttenham tends towards adoration of Elizabeth as a divinity. He states at various points that she is 'a thinge verye admirable in nature' (f.170r); 'not to be reputed an humane, but rather admire perfection' (f.170r); 'mayde Minerue thine ydoll true' (f.170v); and 'a goddesse and noe Queene / Fitter to rule a worlde then a realme' (f.172v).

Puttenham's attitude towards the potential idolatrous dangers of panegyric seems to be one of unconcern. Opposition to Puritanism is apparently expressed in Partheniad 13, although this is a poem which presents some difficulties to the reader. It is headed 'What thinges in nature common reason and cyvill pollicye goe so faste linked together as they maye not easilye bee soonedred without preiudice to the politike bodye whatsoever evill or absurditye seeme in them' (f.175r). Puttenham then goes on to list some linked entities which his diction implies, in contradiction to that subheading, *should* be sundered:

> Remove misterye from religion
> From godly feare all superstition
> Idolatrye from deepe devotion
> Vulgare worshippe from worldes promotion.

> (f.175v)

Terms like 'superstition', 'idolatry' and 'vulgar worship' are strongly pejorative. Yet as this catalogue of pairs goes on, Puttenham's sense seems to turn around again, and he appears to be criticising their division:

> Take pompe from prelates, and maiestie from kinges
> Solemne circumstance from all these wordly [sic] thinges

We walke awrye and wander without lighte
Confoundinge all to make a Chaos quite.

(f.175v)

Behind the incoherence his general gist seems to be that civil disorder is liable to be provoked by the suppression of ceremony in both the religious and the secular sphere. A note gives the 'Purpose' of this Partheniad as 'an invective agaynste the puritants with singular commendacion of her Majesties consyderate iudgment & manner of proceedinge in the cause of religion. The daunger of innovations in a commonwelth . . .' (f.175v).

This strain continues into Partheniad 14, headed: 'That amonge men many thinges be allowed of necessitye, many for ornament which cannot be misliked nor well spared without blemishe to the cyvile lif.' (ff.175v–176r) Here Puttenham argues more lucidly that it is wrong to take away authority from rulers, ceremony from public occasions, mirth from banquets, rich clothes from ladies, and so on, drawing equivalences between all kinds of ornament and festivity in all spheres of life. Ornament and festivity are presented as natural human pleasures:

From worldlye thinges take vanitee
Sleit, semblant, course order and degree
Princesse yt ys as if one take awaye
Greene wooddes from forrests, and sunne shine fro the daye.

(f.176r)

Puttenham seems to equate all kinds of religious and civic ceremony and artifice with one another, and to justify them on grounds that they preserve order, that they are natural, and simply that they give pleasure.

Partheniad 16 consists of a series of comparisons, such as:

As britest noone to darkest nighte
As amerike is farre from easte . . .
So farre my princes prayse doth passe
The famoust Queene that ever was.

(f.176v)

Puttenham gives an explanation, again somewhat incoherent, that this is a strategic panegyrical device: it is 'prayse by resemblance', which is 'voyde of offence', 'tempringe the excesse' of other kinds of praise which, 'be it never soe true', possibly 'favoureth a certayne grosse adulation' which is 'to her Ma*jes*ties naturall modestye nothinge agreeable' (ff.176v–7r).

However, having performed this exercise in restrained panegyric, Puttenham then launches into a final section which is far from moderate, 'An hymne or divine prayse vnder the title of the goddesse Pallas settinge foorthe hir ma*jes*tie commendac*io*n for hir wisedome & glorious governement in the single lief.' (f.177r) Again, note that it is Elizabeth's celibacy which is the basis for praise here. The poem opens with praise of Pallas for being 'a true virgin all thy life', for martial courage and for learning (f.177r). It is then revealed that Elizabeth and the goddess Pallas are one and the same,

> But O now twentye yeare agon
> Forsakinge Greece for Albion
> Where thow alone dost rule and raigne
> Emperesse and Queene of great brittayne.

> (f.177r)

She has 'conquerd the god of love / And skapte his mother suttle gynne'*; her earthly name is 'ELIZABET', the 'Britton Minerve' (f.178r).

Puttenham lets rip in a remarkable final crescendo:

> Whye build we not thye temples hye
> Steples and towers to touch the skye
> Bestrewe thine altars with flowers thicke
> Sence them *with* odours arrabicque.
> Perfuminge all the revestries
> *With* muske, Cyvett, and Ambergries
> In thy feast dayes to singe and dawnce
> *With* lively leps, and countenance
> And twise stoope downe at everye leape
> To kisse the shadow of thy foot stepe
> Thy lyvinge Ymage to adore

---

* escaped his mother's subtle trap

> Yealding the all Eartly [sic] honore
> Not earthly no. but all divyne
> Takinge for one thys hymne of myne.

(f.178r)

Here is no restraint, no anxiety about the possibility of committing idolatry or blasphemy in adulating a secular ruler, no attempt even to forge an iconography of Elizabeth which would be distinctively Protestant and avoid Catholic resonances. Puttenham revels in the possibility of raising altars, burning incense and genuflecting to her just as if she were a pre-Reformation saint's image. Plainly and simply, she is to be 'adore[d]' because she is 'all divyne'.

The extravagance of Puttenham's panegyric prefigures developments later in the reign, but in the 1570s he stands out as something of an eccentric case. His twentieth-century editors, Willcock and Walker, supply biographical evidence of his religious views: for instance, he was accused of conspiring to murder the Calvinistic Bishop Grindal in 1569, and another Bishop condemned him as a man of 'evil life' and a 'notorious enemye to God's Truthe'. They conclude that these facts confirm the impression given by the *Partheniades* of 'a man who hated puritanism, desired a state religion which was aesthetically satisfying and conducive to political and social harmony, and in his heart inclined to a roomy deism incompatible with strict Christian orthodoxy'.[14] His main religious feeling seems to be an attachment to tradition and an aesthetic, even sensuous delight in ceremony and splendour. He therefore relishes the opportunity to lavish ornament and magnificence upon the figure of Elizabeth in his poetry. Several passages in his *Arte of English Poesie* also eulogise Elizabeth, and he states that he also wrote *Triumphals* and *Minerva* in her honour, although these are not extant.[15] Puttenham thus provides an example of an uninhibited worshipper of Elizabeth; and, at the same time, in his *Partheniades*, exhibits the continuing uncertainty as to whether she should be praised for an impending marriage, or for superhuman perpetual virginity.

iv. Spenser's 'Aprill' Eclogue, 1579

Edmund Spenser's *Shepheardes Calender* was completed and licensed in December 1579, at the height of the Anjou marriage controversy.

Its eclogue for 'Aprill' presents one of the most notable and influential encomiastic icons of Elizabeth, setting a trend for the pastoral praise of Elizabeth as 'Queene of shepheardes all' (1.34).[16] Spenser had associated himself with Leicester and Sidney, both of whom vigorously opposed the French match; we might therefore expect the Eclogue to celebrate Elizabeth as perpetual virgin, rather than as nubile maiden. To a degree, this is the case: she is 'The flowre of Virgins' (1.48), 'a mayden Queene' (1.57), statically enthroned in a timeless and monumental form. Yet the place where she is enthroned is 'upon the grassie greene', and her crown is made of flowers:

> Upon her head a Cremosin coronet,
> With Damaske roses and Daffadillies set:
> Bayleaves betweene,
> And Primroses greene
> Embellish the sweete Violet.

> (ll.59–63)

In fact, the poem is full of flowers and emblems of natural growth and fertility.

This is partly a product of Spenser's choice of the pastoral genre, rendering Elisa as a 'Bellibone' or rustic country lass (1.92, n.92). The placing of the praise of Elizabeth in April, like the setting of Sidney's *Lady of May*, associates her with spring festivals and ancient celebrations of seasonal regeneration presided over by fertility goddesses. Spenser seems also, like the authors of the Norwich pageants, and Puttenham, to be keeping open the possibility of the Queen's marriage, whether to Anjou or someone else. One of the floral stanzas could be read as a compliment to her on her apparently imminent nuptials:

> The pretie Pawnce,*
> And the Chevisaunce,†
> Shall match with the fayre flowre Delice

> (ll.142–4)

---

* pansy
† flower-name invented by Spenser

– the fleur de lys, the regal crest of France.

The verse on Cynthia also seems to express a desire to keep open the possibility of the Queen's future motherhood:

> ... I will not match her with *Latonaes* seede,
> Such follie great sorow to *Niobe* did breede.
> Now she is a stone,
> And makes dayly mone,
> Warning all other to take heede.

(ll.86–90)

In the notes by 'E.K.' which were printed with the *Shepheardes Calender*, it is explained that Niobe's pride in her numerous children caused her to scorn Latona, in revenge for which Latona's offspring Apollo and Diana slew Niobe's sons and daughters. Niobe's grief caused her 'to be turned into a stone upon the sepulchre of her children. For which cause the shepheard sayth, he will not compare her to them, for feare of like mysfortune' (n.86–7); that is, he wishes to avoid incurring a curse of childlessness and sterility upon Elizabeth.

This combination throughout of virginity and fertility in the figure of Elisa is a paradox which invites comparison with the iconography of the Virgin Mary as both virgin and courtly mistress, patron saint of procreation as well as purity. What is striking, however, is how scrupulously Spenser avoids any blatant Marian analogy. Elisa's cheeks contain 'The Redde rose medled with the Whyte yfere' (l.69), but these are not Marian roses, but dynastic ones; as with the 'flowre Delice', these flowers have precise political allegorical significance. As in the 1559 coronation pageants, they symbolise Tudor peace and unity: 'By the mingling of the Redde rose and the White, is meant the uniting of the two principall houses of Lancaster and of Yorke ...' (E.K., n.68).[17] Elisa's robes too are scarlet and white (ll.57–8), colours suggesting the combination of majesty and maidenliness appropriate to 'a mayden Queene' (l.57), but markedly not the blue and white robes of the Virgin.

Instead of the Virgin Mary, Spenser invokes a classical precedent of the combination of love and chastity: the figure of Venus Virgo. The Eclogue ends with the 'Embleme', '*O quam te memorem virgo? ... O dea certe*' (ll.162–5) (Oh how am I to address a maiden like you? ... Surely you must be a goddess). E.K. explains: 'This

Poesye is taken out of Virgile, and there of him used in the person of AEneas to his mother Venus, appearing to him in likenesse of one of Dianaes damosells: being there most divinely set forth'. The reference is to the *Aeneid*, I.325–30. Like Venus disguised as Diana, Elizabeth combines in one person perfect love and perfect chastity; she is divine, but her true divinity is veiled from mere mortals unless revelation is granted. The allusion to a classical goddess allows Spenser to imply Elizabeth's holiness while avoiding potentially idolatrous or blasphemous comparisons.[18]

Spenser was not alone in representing Elizabeth as Venus Virgo at this period: the manuscript frontispiece to *Regina Fortunata*, by Henry Howard, Earl of Northampton, written around 1576–80, shows Elizabeth enthroned, with a scroll at her feet inscribed, '[O quam te] memore[m] uirgo. O Dea digna deo' (Oh how am I to address a maiden like you. Oh goddess worthy of a god). However, Howard also opts for a direct Marian allusion: a book on the Queen's lap carries the inscription 'Pax tibi ancilla mea' (Peace be with you, my handmaid).[19] Even this, though, can be understood as part of the tradition established by now of representing Elizabeth as handmaid of God in her dissemination and preservation of the true Protestant faith.

Spenser's foregrounding of classical rather than Marian iconography continues in the suggestions in the Eclogue that Elizabeth might have been blessed with some form of Immaculate Conception. The bride of the Song of Songs, who is 'sine macula' (without spot), is clearly alluded to when Spenser writes of Elisa,

> ... shee is *Syrinx* daughter without spotte,
> Which *Pan* the shepheards God of her begot:
> So sprong her grace
> Of heavenly race,
> No mortall blemishe may her blotte.

> (ll.50–4)

Marian allusion appears to be strong here, but again it is contained by classical, pagan iconography. Elisa's asexual conception is narrated as an Ovidian metamorphosis; as in Ovid, sexual desire is sublimated into a higher creativity. E.K.'s gloss explains the several levels of allegory:

... here by Pan and Syrinx is not to bee thoughte, that the shephearde simplye meante those Poetical Gods: but rather supposing (as seemeth) her graces progenie to be divine and immortall ... by Pan is here meant the most famous and victorious King, her highnesse Father, late of worthy memorye K. Henry the eyght. And by the name, oftymes (as hereafter appeareth) be noted kings and mighty Potentates: And in some place Christ himselfe, who is the verye Pan and god of Shepheardes.

(n.50)

One effect of this is to elevate the union of Henry VIII and Anne Boleyn above Catholic charges of adultery: Elizabeth is purified of the taint of being a bastard child of a licentious coupling. At the same time, her father is not only Henry VIII as nostalgically-recalled ideal king; she is also allegorically represented as fathered by Christ, or the Christian God. Her conception therefore resembles not so much that of the Virgin Mary by St Joachim and St Anne, as that of Christ himself, the impregnation of the Virgin's womb by the breath of God.

A sense that it might be appropriate to look for messianic associations here is reinforced by the fact that the panegyric of the Queen falls in the fourth eclogue of Spenser's *Calender*. Spenser takes Virgil as a poetic model in the *Calender*, and Virgil's Fourth Eclogue prophesied the return to earth of Astraea, banished goddess of justice, to restore the Golden Age, and the birth of a child to rule over this new age of peace and plenty. As I have mentioned before, this had been interpreted by Christians from the time of the Emperor Constantine as a prophecy of the birth of Christ, identifying Astraea with the Virgin Mary.[20] The central figure of Spenser's fourth eclogue might therefore be associated with the holy virgin, or with the newly-born Messiah – or perhaps even with both. Messianic associations would be appropriate to Elizabeth in so far as she was the anointed monarch incarnating God on earth, and the saviour and advancer of the true Protestant faith. Spenser can be seen as juggling virginal and messianic symbolism in his comparisons of Elisa with both Phoebus and Phoebe, the masculine sun as well as the feminine moon.

Of course the description of Elisa as 'without spotte' (1.50) could direct us not to the Virgin as the Immaculate Conception, but straight back to the source of that belief, the immaculate bride of the Song of Songs, traditionally interpreted as a figure of the Church. This provides another way of understanding Spenser's stress on fertility and nubility in the Eclogue. Elisa is being decked as a bride, but the marriage for which she is being prepared might be the symbolic one of the true Protestant Church to Christ, following allegorical readings of the Song of Songs; or the marriage of the true Church to the nation of England, represented by the homage-paying shepherd Colin. It is not so much Elizabeth's potential for marriage to a human spouse like Anjou which is being celebrated, as her marriage as a symbol, metaphor of both the realisation of true religion in England and the harmonious union of monarch and people.

The simultaneous chastity and nubility of Spenser's Elisa is represented by her attendants. The poet instructs,

> Let none come there, but that Virgins bene,
>   to adorne her grace. . . .
>   Binde your fillets faste,
> And gird in your waste . . .

> (ll.129, 133–4)

And yet, in only the previous stanza, he has told us that she is served by nymphs, whose name 'in Greeke signifieth Well water, or otherwise a Spouse or Bryde' (n.120). Their leader is Chloris, whose name 'signifieth greenesse, of whome is sayd, that Zephyrus the Westerne wind being in love with her, and coveting her to wyfe, gave her for a dowrie, the chiefedome and soveraintye of al flowres and greene herbes, growing on earth' (n.122).

From one angle, Spenser's eclogue might seem to stand at the end of a period of celebration of the Virgin Queen for her youth and nubility. Back in the first year of her reign, on 10 July 1559, Colin's floral lay was anticipated by an entertainment for the new young monarch:

> now therefore was set up in Greenwich Park a goodly banqueting-house for her Grace, made with fir poles, and decked with birch branches, and all manner of flowers, both of the field and garden, as roses, julyflowers, lavendar, marygols, and all manner of strewing herbs and rushes.[21]

1579, when Elizabeth was 45, might seem to be nearly the last possible date on which such youthful springtime adornment would be deemed appropriate to the Queen. Yet the reverse is the case: the

'Aprill' Eclogue produced a torrent of imitations in the genre of pastoral panegyric, continuing long into Elizabeth's old age. As late as 1601, in the madrigal collection *The Triumphs of Oriana*, pastoral and floral imagery prevail. Elizabeth/Oriana is 'the beautiest of beauties'; in Thomas Morley's contribution, which is especially reminiscent of 'Aprill', she is dressed in 'gaudy green', and her path is strewn with roses.[22]

The 'Aprill' Eclogue served to establish an iconographic convention whereby virginity and fertility were seen not as opposites, but as complementary properties in the figure of Elizabeth. As she passed from an age when her marriage and motherhood existed as potentials, in anticipation, to an age where marriage was unlikely and physical motherhood an impossibility, symbolic nubility and fertility came all the further to the fore, and came to represent a triumph over time, a myth of perpetual youth and beauty. It was as if she were eternally frozen in a bridal moment of virginal purity on the brink of conjugal amorousness and maternal fruitfulness. At the same time, her combination in one person of virginity and symbolic fertility was a mystical paradox, figuring divine wholeness and self-sufficiency. The 'Aprill' Eclogue, perhaps more than any of the other panegyrics from this transitional period of the Anjou courtship, marks a turning point after which representations of the Queen became increasingly symbolic and unconnected from her real physical state.

This process gave additional force to the representation of Elizabeth as an icon which had been practised ever since the coronation pageants. On that occasion, an audience had watched Elizabeth in turn performing the role of audience to symbolic and idealised figurations of herself; Queen and image faced one another as if in a mirror.[23] Similarly, in the 'Aprill' Eclogue, Spenser/Colin the poet separates 'Elisa', his poetic creation, from 'Eliza', to whom she is presented and from whom he hopes for reward: 'Now ryse up *Elisa*, decked as thou art, in royall aray / . . . Let dame *Eliza* thanke you for her song' (ll.145–50). Just as the coronation pageants contained an element of prescription, so this may be seen as enacting a theory of non-idolatrous Protestant panegyric: the perfect image created by the panegyrist may represent not the living reality of his subject, but a superhuman ideal for her and others to aspire to.

The Marian resonances of the 'Aprill' Eclogue can be seen in at least two different ways. On the one hand, Spenser might be seen as employing Marian iconography consciously but surreptitiously, dressing it in terms of the classical mythography of Ovidian meta-morphosis, Virgilian prophecy, and the figure of Venus Virgo. He is thus able to deploy deep-seated Marian traditions of the Immaculate Conception and the holy virgin-bride-mother figure while avoiding the appearance of quasi-Catholicism. Alternatively, he can be seen as not adopting Marian iconography, but reappropriating the myth of the holy virgin-bride-mother for Protestantism, tracing it directly to its roots, especially the Song of Songs, and purifying it of Marian and Catholic connotations. In the Geneva Bible, verse 4.7 of the Song of Songs, 'Thou art all faire, my love, and there is no spot in thee', carries no gloss, erasing interpretation of this as a figure of the Virgin Mary as Immaculate Conception. However, the 'Argument' prefaced by the Geneva commentators to the Song as a whole explains that it

> ... by moste swete and comfortable allegories and parables describeth the perfite loue of Iesus Christ, the true Salomon and King of peace, and the faithful soule or his Church, which he hathe sanctified and appointed to be his spouse, holy, chast and without reprehension.[24]

Throughout the Geneva commentary, the bride is frequently and consistently referred to as the Church. Spenser perhaps aims to participate in the same iconoclastic process of deletion of the Virgin Mary from the allegorical reading of the spotless bride, and the establishment of an emphatically Protestant allegory in its place.

v. Lyly, *Euphues and His England*, 1580

In 1580 John Lyly published *Euphues and his England*, the sequel to *Euphues: The Anatomy of Wit*. The new book included a section headed 'Euphues Glasse for Europe', in which Euphues describes England as a perfect, virtuous nation which sets an example to all others.[25] At the centre of this looking-glass stands Elizabeth, the ultimate image of perfection for all rulers and ladies to emulate.

Rather than presenting a confidently delineated icon of Elisa as Spenser does, Lyly chooses to magnify the Queen's perfection by asserting that it is beyond human representation: 'I know not when to begin, nor where to ende: for the more I go about to expresse the brightnes, the more I finde mine eyes bleared, the neerer I desire to come to it, the farther I seme from it' (p.204). This is partly a metaphor of the sun, simultaneously an emblem of majesty, of Christ, and of the Woman of Revelation. However, the theme of unrepresentability also enables Lyly to build up an intense sense of Elizabeth's miraculousness as exceeding the iconic, lying beyond human perception and understanding, in the sphere of the divine. There is an obvious neo-Platonic subtext to this: Elizabeth is the perfect metaphysical Idea, who can only be imperfectly shadowed by mere mortals. This is at once a highly effective form of panegyric in its elevation of Elizabeth; and perhaps an acceptably Protestant one, avoiding the verbal depiction and erection of an icon which might be perceived as idolatrous.

Euphues does invite us to think of panegyric in terms of the verbal creation of a visual icon, through the use of metaphors of portraiture. However, he consistently protests the inaccuracy and inadequacy of any attempt to create an image of the Queen's glorious reality. He will 'frame a table for *Elizabeth*, though he presume not to paynt hir'; he will prove 'his good will to grinde his coulours: hee that whetteth the tooles is not to bee misliked, though hee can-not carue the Image' (pp.204–5). As his encomium proceeds, it is punctuated by this emphasis on unrepresentability: at one point he professes that the best he can do is to paint the Queen's back, and 'leaue you gasing vntill she turne hir face' (p.212). Near the end, he tells us that her virtues are so many that, 'being in this Laborinth, I may sooner loose my selfe, then finde the ende' (p.215).

This text continues and contributes to many conventions of Elizabethan royal panegyric. Lyly participates in the hagiographical mythologisation of Elizabeth's sufferings before her accession (p.206). He also emphasises the Queen's virtues of clemency and of the preservation of peace (p.207), virtues which associate her with Christ; later, several paragraphs discourse on the theme that peace is distinctively a blessing of Christ (pp.210–11). However, at the same time these are also virtues which are comfortingly feminine, and which might implicitly associate Elizabeth with the tender-hearted Virgin Mother as intercessor. Lyly specifically mentions an incident

when hir maiestie was for hir recreation in her Barge vpon the Thames . . . a Gun . . . was shotte off though of the partie vnwittingly, yet to hir noble person daungerously, which fact she most graciously pardoned, accepting a iust excuse before a great amends, taking more griefe for hir poore Bargeman that was a

little hurt, then for care for hir selfe that stoode in greatest hasarde:
O rare example of pittie, O singuler spectacle of pietie.

(p.207)

The same incident had been the subject of 'A newe Ballade, declaryng
the daungerous shootyng of the Gunne at the Courte', 1578.[26] According to the ballad, the shooter of the gun, Thomas Appletree,
was brought to the gallows, where, although the firing had been
entirely accidental, he nobly resigned himself to death for the danger into which he had brought the Queen. Elizabeth, seeing his
readiness for 'sacrifice', was moved to 'pittie' and pardoned him.
The words 'pittie' and 'piteous' are constantly reiterated through
the ballad, with Elizabeth represented as an intercessor with God
for her people; there is praise of '. . . the mercie of her grace, her
subjects lives to save, / By whom these xx yeres in peace, suche
quiet lives wee have'. Everyone was moved to tears – the refrain of
the ballad is 'Weepe, weepe' – and they knelt 'And saied a praier
for her grace': 'praie to God that rules the skies, her highnesse to
defende, / To raigne with him perpetually when her highnes life
shall ende'. Lyly's reference to the incident invokes the same
resonances, presumably by now established in popular report, of
the Queen's behaviour on this occasion as embodying mercy
and compassion like those of a female saint or of the Virgin
herself.

Lyly also endues Elizabeth with symbolic fruitfulness: she has
gifts 'in chiefest glorye, to bring forth chiefest grace, in abundance
of all earthly pompe, to manifest aboundance of all heauenlye pietie'
(p.208). As in Spenser, analogies with the Virgin are unspoken, with
preference given to classical comparisons, including again the figure of Venus Virgo:

she [is] adourned with singuler beautie and chastitie, excelling in
the one *Venus*, in the other *Vesta*.[27] Who knoweth not how rare a
thing it is (Ladies) to match virginitie with beautie, a chast minde
with an amiable face, diuine cogitations with a comleye coun-
tenaunce? But suche is the grace bestowed vppon this earthlye
Goddesse, that hauing the beautie that myght allure all Princes,
she hath the chastitie also to refuse all, accounting it no less praise
to be called a Uirgin, then to be esteemed a *Venus* . . .

(p.209)

This strength to refuse all princely suitors becomes, as in Puttenham, a badge of national pride. Lyly mentions various famous virgins from classical myth, but declares:

> If Uirginitie haue such force, then what hath this chast Uirgin *Elizabeth* don, who by the space of twenty and odde yeares with continuall peace against all policies, with sundry myracles, contrary to all hope, hath gouerned that noble Island. Against whome neyther forren force, nor ciuill fraude, neyther discorde at home, nor conspirices abroad, could preuaile. What greater meruaile hath happened since the beginning of the world, then for a young and tender maiden, to gouern strong and valiaunt menne, then for a Uirgin to make the whole worlde, if not to stand in awe of hir, yet to honour hir, yea and to liue in spight of all those that spight hir, with hir sword in the sheth, with hir armour in the Tower, with hir souldiers in their gownes . . .
>
> (p.209)

Elizabeth's virginal rule is represented here as miraculous on several counts. First, it is an emblem of strength in weakness, of God choosing a weak vessel to be his instrument in order the greater to demonstrate his power. Secondly, the success of a woman in ruling over men, by peaceful rather than warlike means, becomes a mystical paradox, extending the dualism of the figure of Venus Virgo to other rhetorical dichotomies. In this respect Lyly is closely echoed by Philip Sidney in his description of Queen Helen of Corinth, usually identified as a figure of Elizabeth, in the *New Arcadia*, which he wrote within a few years of Lyly's book. Queen Helen, too, miraculously 'made her people by peace, warlike; her courtiers by sports, learned; her ladies by love, chaste . . . it seemed that court to have been the marriage-place of love and virtue, and that herself was a Diana apparelled in the garments of Venus'.[28]

The passage from Lyly also stresses containment: the bodily restraint which Elizabeth practises seems to be suffused through the whole nation, such that swords are not unsheathed, armour is not unpacked, soldiers are in their gowns, enjoying holiday pursuits of rest or love-making. The whole nation might be seen as effeminised,[29] and the intactness of the Queen's virgin body seems increasingly to be identified with the intactness of the peaceful and independent nation. In the Norwich entertainments, England's miraculous twenty-years' immunity from invasion or civil war had been attributed to

Elizabeth, implying that she was somehow charmed.[30] Now Lyly wrote:

> Now is the Temple of *Ianus* remoued from *Rome* to *England*, whose dore hath not bene opened this twentie yeares . . . This is the onelye myracle that virginitie euer wrought, for a little Island enuironed round about with warres, to stande in peace, for the walles of *Fraunce* to burne, and the houses of *England* to freese, for all other nations eyther with ciuile sworde to bee deuided, or with forren foes to be inuaded, and that countrey neyther to be molested with broyles in their owne bosomes, nor threatned with blasts of other borderers . . .
>
> (pp.209–10)

Lyly has mentioned various virgins of classical mythology to whom lesser miracles were attributed; Elizabeth's success is therefore the 'onelye myracle' of virginity by comparison with them. The only biblical heroine he mentions as a comparison is Deborah. However, the very absence of reference to the Virgin Mary or any virgin saints could be seen as implicitly discounting all their supposed miracles. Lyly presents Elizabeth as the only virgin whose power to work miracles is a historical truth.

The 'little Island' described in this passage, apparently weak and vulnerable but miraculously made strong, may be identified with the 'young and tender maiden' who rules it. The coldness of the houses of England parallels the cool chastity of its Queen; the description of civil war as broils of the bosom, and of invasion as blasts of borderers, suggests that the impregnability of the Queen's body to either inner turmoils of love or outer assaults by suitors is one and the same as the proud self-determination of the nation. The Queen's virginity is a magic charm which keeps the nation in God's favour and therefore safe; moreover, the orderly and unconquered nation state is symbolised by the intact body of its monarch.

The anthropologist Mary Douglas has written of somatic symbolism:

> The body is a model which can stand for any bounded system. Its boundaries can represent any boundaries which are threatened or precarious. The body is a complex structure. The functions of its different parts and their relation afford a source of symbols for other complex structures . . . we [must be] prepared

to see in the body a symbol of society, and to see the powers and dangers credited to social structure reproduced in small on the human body.[31]

In particular, she describes the preoccupation of isolated or persecuted social groups with bodily purity and wholeness. In the Levitican laws of the early Jews, 'the . . . idea that emerges is of the Holy as wholeness and completeness . . . the idea of holiness was given an external, physical expression in the wholeness of the body seen as a perfect container' (pp.51–2). For the Israelites, 'The threatened boundaries of their body politic would be well mirrored in their care for the integrity, unity and purity of the physical body' (p.124). Similarly, for early Christians,

> The idea that virginity had a special positive value was bound to fall on good soil in a small minority group. For . . . these social conditions lend themselves to beliefs which symbolise the body as an imperfect container which will only be made perfect if it can be made impermeable.
>
> (p.158)

Marina Warner uses Mary Douglas's theories to interpret the cult of the Virgin as a continuation of ancient beliefs regarding the body and sexuality. She writes that the Christian religion inherited from the classical world an assumption 'that virginity was powerful magic and conferred strength and ritual purity'; 'the image of the virgin body was the supreme image of wholeness, and wholeness was equated with holiness'.[32] All of this enables us to understand the emphasis on Elizabeth's virginity not so much as a simple appropriation of the cult of Mary, as a similar phenomenon occurring for complex reasons at a precise historical moment. The continuity is in the unfading deep-rooted belief that virginity is holy and charmed, a belief of which the cult of the Virgin and the iconography of Elizabeth are each separate expressions at different historical junctures.

In 1580, England felt isolated and beleaguered as a Protestant nation surrounded by daunting foreign and Catholic enemies. Many panegyrists, including Lyly, represented England as a new Israel, a persecuted but godly nation chosen to receive God's special favour: Lyly writes, 'So tender a care hath he alwaies had of that *England*, as of a new *Israel*, his chosen and peculier people' (p.205).[33] Not unlike the ancient Israelites and the early Christians, the Elizabethan English were preoccupied with the maintaining of boundaries, with the preservation of their spiritual and national purity against outside contamination. This, combined with a diversity of opinion at home which meant that civil unrest was a constant danger, meant that there was strong motivation for panegyrists to celebrate the virginity of their Queen as an emblem of the defiant impregnability of the body politic. The reasons for this celebration of virginity bear some analogy to the reasons why the Virgin Mary had been used as an emblem of the Church, but many more forces were at work than just a desire to compensate for the loss of the Catholic Virgin.[34]

Even so, Lyly's text contains a further parallel to the figure of the Virgin in that the result of Elizabeth's bodily intactness is a fruitfulness which exceeds any mere progeneration of the individual human body. Instead, the whole nation is made fruitful and abundant: 'Their fields haue beene sowne with corne . . . they haue their men reaping their haruest . . . their barnes [are] full . . .' (pp.209–11). Elizabeth's inviolability is a magic charm which even guarantees the sexual safety of her subjects' womenfolk: 'their wiues [are] without daunger, when others are defamed, their daughters chast, when others are defloured' (p.211).

At this point, Euphues moves on from praise of Elizabeth's public achievements to her private person. He describes how, when he beheld the wonder of Elizabeth, he wished:

> that as she hath liued fortie yeares a virgin in great maiestie, so she may lyue fourescore yeares a mother, with great ioye, that as with hir we haue long time hadde peace and plentie, so by hir we may euer haue quietnesse and aboundance, wishing this euen from the bottome of a heart that wisheth well to *England*.
>
> (p.212)

At first the reader might think he simply means that Elizabeth will be a symbolic mother to all her people. However, it becomes clear that, in spite of all the foregoing veneration of Elizabeth's virginity, Euphues is indeed expressing a wish for her to bear a physical heir, because of the uncertainty as to what will befall England otherwise. He:

> . . . feareth ill, that either the world may ende before she dye, or she lyue to see hir childrens children in the world: otherwise, how tickle their state is that now triumph, vpon what a twist they

hang that now are in honour, they that liue shal see which I to thinke on, sigh.

Lyly thus keeps open a possibility of welcoming any future marriage by the Queen, while at the same time rendering the wish for it somewhat equivocal. He does this firstly by framing the whole of this passage with the past tense – it is what Euphues thought when he beheld Elizabeth, on some past occasion in his travels, and may not apply in quite the same way any more. Secondly, he blurs wishes for Elizabeth's late fruitfulness with wishes for her own long life and sole survival. He hopes that God will grant England:

> the Prince they haue without any other chaunge, that the longer she liueth the sweeter she may smell . . . that she maye be . . . fruitfull in hir age lyke the Uyne . . . so that there be no ende of hir praise, vntill the ende of all flesh.
>
> (p.212)

Among his praise of her various virtues, Euphues lists her preservation of true religion, which again he describes through sexual metaphors of purity and pollution: 'the perswasions of Papists, (which are Honny to the mouth)' could not 'allure hir, to violate the holy league contracted with Christ, or to maculate the blood of the auncient Lambe, which is Christ' (p.214). As he goes on he turns increasingly towards representation of her as a symbolic rather than biological mother: in 'the loue shee beareth to hir subiectes', she shows herself 'a mother to the afflicted'; 'This is that good Pelican that to feede hir people spareth not to rend hir owne personne' (p.215).

Euphues and His England is thus another text of this period which hovers between wishing for Elizabeth's marriage and accepting that her virginity is perpetual; but here, the balance is tipping towards perpetual virginity, symbolic motherhood, and a metaphoric identification of Elizabeth's intact body with the integrity of the nation state. At the same time, the theme of unrepresentability provides one solution to the problem of how to write panegyric without committing idolatry.

vi. Blenerhasset, *A Revelation of the True Minerva*, 1582

Thomas Blenerhasset's *Revelation* confirms the prevalence of certain motifs in panegyric at this point in the reign. Like Puttenham, he

identifies Elizabeth with the classical virgin-goddesses Pallas and
Minerva, here conceived as sisters rather than different names for
the same deity; Minerva is lost, but Pallas finds her anew in Elizabeth. The latter part of his poem illustrates the literary influence of
the 'Aprill' Eclogue, which it echoes in its metrical form, verbal
detail, and floral decoration.[35]
  At an early stage, Blenerhasset presents a magnificent icon of
Elizabeth enthroned:

> The seat wherein this courtly Queene did sit
> was Rubie rare, none seene for sice so great,
> a golden globe was vnder both her feete,
> a comely cloude did compasse all the seate,
> the sea in vayne the cloude and globe did beate
> With foming froth, about her heauenly heade
> *Pallas* persaude* a posie, which shee reade.

The posy reads: 'Not such a godesse againe in *Asia, Europ,* or *Affricke,*
/ for vertue, great degree, for her magnanimitie . . .' (sig.A4v).
  It might appear hard to claim that Blenerhasset is anything other
than idolatrous here. It might consequently further appear that his
praise of Elizabeth as a champion of iconoclasm is fraught with
unintentional irony. Mercury tells Elizabeth that Saturn and the
other Roman gods sent him to find her:

> The Queene replide, I knowe no God but one
> And hee of heauen, who guides mee by his grace:
> The Heathen had their Gods which nowe bee gone,
> Whose Idols I by Gods spell did deface.

                                              (sig.B3v)

  However, Blenerhasset is at pains throughout to stress that the
exaltation of Elizabeth is justifued because based on her godliness.
Minerva is the goddess of 'heauenly wisedome' ('The Printer to the
Reader'); 'For heauenly wisedome shee exceld eche one'; the new
Minerva will restore 'diuinitie' and 'true knowledge' (sig.A2r). High
praise of Elizabeth is therefore legitimate in that she represents the
establishment and advancement of true religion. In that first iconic

---

* perceived

vision of her, the golden globe under her feet and the cosmic imagery allude to the Woman Clothed with the Sun, identifying the Queen with the true Church; and the fact that a 'posie' or motto surrounds her head turns her into an emblem, with a spiritually improving meaning explained in a text.

Blenerhasset is concerned to explain that the classical gods who people his poem are not pagan idols but allegorical personifications of the virtues of a Christian ruler:

> . . . *Saturne* doth signifie
> good gouernement: *Neptune* and *Mars* of might
> By Sea and land in warre haught valiancie,
> *Apollo* how diuinely to indight,
> *Pallas* wisdome to rule and raigne aright.
>
> (sig.B4r)

When they pledge service to Elizabeth, she proclaims them 'my seruants? no, my saints, / Copertiners of my crowne and dignitie' (sig.B4v). Blenerhasset is thus careful to make clear the Christian and Protestant legitimacy of his panegyric. To praise Elizabeth in high terms as a classical goddess is not to erect a false idol, but to recognise the Queen's true sanctity as a chosen earthly agent of God and a figure of exceptional virtue destined for a heavenly crown.

Although published as late as 1582, Blenerhasset's poem still seems to keep open the possibility of royal matrimony. Minerva/Elizabeth sits on top of the wheel of fortune, 'A glorious seat by which but one did sit, / and hee not knowne' (sig.C1v, p.viii). Yet this unknown partner does not appear to be Anjou; when a garland is made to deck the Queen, 'The Flower deluce' is rejected because 'It representes trouble and cruell thrall' (sig.D2v).

Overall, more stress is laid on Elizabeth's achievement of immortality. Mercury praises 'Her heauenly hewe, her more then mortall grace, / (For vertue may mortall immortall make,)' (sig.B4v). The wish for the Queen's immortality can be seen, as in Lyly, as the product of anxiety as to what the future holds for England, unprovided of a direct heir. However, Blenerhasset is vague as to whether Elizabeth's immortality is to be achieved physically on earth, or in terms of earthly fame beyond death, or in heaven. The gods declare that if, as they expect, they find that Elizabeth is the most beloved and loyal follower of God on earth,

> Then her we may and will immortall make...
> All men that liue her grace they shall adore
> Both at this present time, and euermore.

(sig.D1r)

After they have determined that her 'due desert' makes her 'a goddesse great', Pallas announces:

> The *Britttain* [sic] Queene shalbe that Phoenix rare,
> Whom death to touch with dart shall neuer dare:
> Thou shalt on earth eternally remaine.

(sig.E4v)

As Elizabeth passed beyond child-bearing age, the phoenix became an increasingly apt image of her singularity, sexual purity and self-perpetuation by spiritual rather than physical means.

The gods crown her, and 'of mortall her immortall make' – perhaps an unspoken reminiscence of the Coronation of the Virgin. Elizabeth speaks, 'with more then mortall grace', in interpretation of her own immortality:

> The life (quoth shee) of euery liuing thing
> Must perish quite, for death will it deface
> But death to death by due desert to bring
> Such death on earth is life euerlasting.

(sig.F1r)

This seems to return us to the more familiar notion of immortality as granted in heaven, not on earth.

The poem ends:

> Thus shee who once was but a mortall Queene,
> And subiect sate on fortunes turning wheele,
> The greatest goddesse nowe on earth is seene:
> Whose hie estate can neither roule nor reele,
> Not fortunes force shall neuer hurt her heele:
> For vertue did and due desart aduaunce
> Her grace, and not the force of changing chance,

Shee is not nowe as other princes bee,
Who liue on earth to euery tempest thrall,
Desert hath crownde her with eternitie,
Her godly zeale in seate sempiternal
Hath set her nowe, from thence shee can not fall:
But liuely liue on earth eternally:
And haue in heauen heauenly felicitie.

(sig.G1r–v)

Elizabeth's immortality here seems to signify three things: an invulnerability to time and chance; eternal earthly fame; and eternal life in heaven. At the same time, Blenerhasset allows the impression to stand, astounding though it seems, that the Queen might miraculously achieve immortality on earth, thereby securing England's future.

This concern with the Queen's triumph over mutability was to become the prevalent theme of panegyric from now on, as we shall see in later chapters. It was often associated with the figure of the moon-goddess Cynthia, and even this is prefigured by Blenerhasset at this early stage: Elizabeth's 'life is like dame *Sinthias* siluer rayse' (sig.F1v). Thus, although Blenerhasset's poem falls within the transitional period when it was still just possible that Elizabeth might marry, that period was very nearly over, and the emphasis of panegyric was beginning to fall more upon the longevity of the Queen as sole and ageing ruler. From now on interest would grow in the mythologisation of Elizabeth's triumph over the flesh as a triumph over time.

vii. Bentley's *Monument of Matrons*, 1582

The same year saw the publication of Thomas Bentley's *The Monument of Matrones: conteining seuen seuerall Lamps of Virginitie*, a collection of holy writings by and for women, including a translation which Elizabeth had made when she was eleven of *The Mirror of a Sinful Soul* by Margaret of Navarre. Bentley presents his compilation of exemplary feminine devotional texts as a mirror for Elizabeth, 'the cause of a virgine to a Virgine, the works of Queenes to a Queene; your owne praiers to your selfe.'[36] He eulogises Elizabeth as a perpetual virgin in a fashion not found in earlier years. Furthermore, the text illustrates how final certainty of her virginity as a permanent state encouraged representation of the Queen as holy and sanctified.

In his dedication to the Queen, Bentley describes his compilation as 'seuen Lamps of your perpetuall virginitie'. Elizabeth is 'the most naturall mother and noble nursse' of the Church; 'Iesus Christ' is 'your sweet spouse', formulae which echo Mariology, but without explicitly invoking the Virgin.[37] Like Spenser in the 'Aprill' Eclogue, Bentley can be seen as surreptitiously exploiting Marian resonances, or as enacting a purposeful Protestant reclamation of the scriptural sources of Isaiah and the Song of Songs. Although the Virgin is included in a list of godly women, as an example of 'motherlie and carefull affection towards their children',[38] direct comparison by name between her and Elizabeth is noticeably avoided.

The Third Lamp contains prayers for Accession Day, and includes a dialogue between God and Elizabeth, wherein God declares his benediction upon Elizabeth's rule:

> ELIZABETH, thou Virgin mine, the KINGS Daughter, and fairest among women; most full of beautie and maiestie: attend a little to my Heast, and marke what I shall say. Thou art my daughter in deede, this daie haue I begotten thee, and espoused thee to thy king CHRIST, my Sonne; crowned thee with my gifts, and appointed thee QVEENE, to reigne vpon my holie mount Sion.[39]

However, rather like the official Accession Day prayers introduced in 1576 and 1578,[40] this promotion of Elizabeth's rule as divinely-endorsed is combined with provisional hopes that Elizabeth will in the future fulfil an as-yet-unrealised goal of perfect godly rule. Bentley's God 'describeth vnto hir Grace, the woorthie properties that are required to bee in euerie godlie Prince', 'exhorteth hir Maiestie to the faithfull discharge of hir office and dutie in his feare and seruice', and promises to defend and bless her 'vpon this condition: if finallie she perseuere in the perfect loue and due obedience of hir spirituall spouse Christ Iesus'.[41]

E.C. Wilson sees *The Monument of Matrons* as suggesting that 'patriotic Englishmen unconsciously half shifted their affection for a sacred Virgin to a profane'.[42] McClure and Headlam Wells's interpretation of the above passage from the Third Lamp is that 'Elizabeth is a Protestant simulacrum of the Virgin Mary-qua-Holy Church'.[43] It is certainly true that Bentley's figuration of Elizabeth more closely resembles Mariology than did earlier panegyric. The end of the Anjou courtship marked a watershed, giving new force to representations of Elizabeth as bride of Christ, and establishing her as an immutable icon of sanctified virginity. A movement was beginning towards using the Virgin herself as a source for typological comparisons with Elizabeth; but at this stage, writers continued to avoid naming the Virgin and making these comparisons explicit.

viii. Sidney's *Defence of Poesy* and Protestant panegyric

I have mentioned Sir Philip Sidney at a couple of points as a participant in panegyric of Elizabeth. This might seem surprising in the light of his opposition to certain of Elizabeth's policies, including notably the proposed Anjou marriage,[44] and the fact that he seems not to have enjoyed much favour from the Queen. His apparent encomium of Queen Helen in the *New Arcadia* can be read as strategically ambiguous, voicing criticism under the cover of praise. Perhaps Sidney, who favoured a more aggressive foreign policy in support of Protestants abroad, and who longed to distinguish himself in military service, intended the reader to be disquieted by the statement that Queen Helen 'made her people by peace, warlike . . . For by continual martial exercises without blood, she made them perfect in that bloody art'.[45] What, after all, is the point of honing martial skills by perpetual ornamental tournaments at court if those skills are never to be employed on the battlefield?

However, before he set about revising the *Arcadia*, Sidney wrote his *Defence of Poesy*, completed some time in 1582.[46] His discussion of the truth and value of poetry – or, as we might roughly translate into modern English, fiction – can also be read as delineating some of the principles of Protestant panegyric. Neo-Platonism is an important ingredient: the belief that the poet's task is to supply edifying glimpses of the metaphysical truths which lie beyond the material world. The poet does not simply imitate nature, but:

> doth grow in effect another nature, in making things either better than nature bringeth forth, or, quite anew, forms such as never were in nature, as the Heroes, Demigods, Cyclops, Chimeras, Furies, and such like . . . [Nature's] world is brazen, the poets only deliver a golden.[47]

Nature has not brought forth 'so right a prince as Xenophon's Cyrus', but the poet's delivering forth of the *idea* of a Cyrus 'worketh, not only to make a Cyrus, which had been but a particular excellency as nature might have done, but to bestow a Cyrus upon the world to make many Cyruses, if they will learn aright why and how that maker made him' (p.79). Such idealised images can improve the reader, by inspiring emulation, as in heroical poetry, 'For as the image of each action stirreth and instructeth the mind, so the lofty image of such worthies most inflameth the mind with desire to be worthy, and informs with counsel how to be worthy' (p.98).

Even when such an idealised poetic image bears the name of a real person, this is not necessarily an accurate depiction of that person:

> [Poet's] naming of men is but to make their picture the more lively, and not to build any history; painting men, they cannot leave men nameless . . . The poet nameth Cyrus or Aeneas no other way than to show what men of their fames, fortunes and estates should do.
>
> (p.103)

Thus, if a poet represents Elizabeth as glorious, perfect and divine, this does not necessarily mean that the poet believes that in her living person she is perfect and divine. She can be used as an ideal of virtue to inspire readers to emulation; and, more specifically, as a model of the ideal godly ruler, for other rulers to emulate. Most specifically of all, an idealised figure of 'Elizabeth' could be set up as a model of the perfect godly ruler for the real Elizabeth herself to aspire to and to be instructed by. As Ben Jonson would later put it, 'I have . . . praised some names too much, / But 'twas with purpose to have made them such'.[48] Hence it would not be idolatrous or blasphemous to represent 'Elizabeth', especially when given a poetic pseudonym like Elisa or Minerva, as a goddess inspiring adoration: the symbol 'Elizabeth', rather than the person Elizabeth, would be the object of praise. Roy Strong comes to a similar conclusion in his discussion of Italian theorists of state portraiture of the period: 'In short, for the Renaissance Platonist the portrait painter was concerned with the ruler, not as an individual, but as the embodiment of the "Idea" of kingship'.[49]

As we have seen, the period 1578–82 marked a crucial transition between the years when Elizabeth might potentially marry and produce an heir, and the years when it was certain that she would not do so. Consequently, panegyric from this period is often some-what self-contradictory, leaving an opening for praise of her future spouse, but at the same time increasingly celebrating her perpetual virginity. This virginity, now becoming a static monumental state rather than a preparatory phase, becomes increasingly symbolic. Elizabeth's bodily intactness can be used to figure the inviolability of the English nation state. Anxiety as to the future beyond her death also begins to produce loyal assertions that her triumph over the flesh in sexual terms will accomplish a triumph over time and death.

The terms of praise over this period become more lofty: Elizabeth is increasingly addressed and described as a 'goddess', and the emphasis on her holiness, or even divinity, is closely allied to her transition to perpetual virginity. Her transcendence of the flesh and of human weakness encourages representation of her as an elevated spiritual figure on a supernatural plane.

At the same time, we see Protestant writers like Spenser and Sidney thinking out acceptable Protestant modes of panegyric, in which the iconic figure erected by the poet is understood as an exemplary ideal. There are undoubted parallels to Marian iconography in representations of Elizabeth as the Immaculate Conception (as in the 'Aprill' Eclogue), as intact symbol of the unity of the devout nation (as in Lyly), and as a mortal granted a heavenly crown of immortality (as in Blenerhasset). However, Marian ana-logues are not explicitly emphasised; instead, classical iconography is preferred. This can be seen either as a surreptitious deployment of Marian connotations by other means; or, as an attempt to appro-priate virginity-symbolism for Protestantism, deleting Marian asso-ciations in the process.

5

1583–93:
Patronage, Prayers and
Pilgrimages

i. Patronage

Representations of the Queen as quasi-divine were reinforced by the fact that she stood at the pinnacle of a hierarchical structure of government. We have already seen how medieval queens consort were readily compared to the Virgin Mary because of their role as loving intercessor between the people and their king, just as the Virgin and the other saints were intercessors between believers and Christ.[1] This pattern of mediation within a hierarchical structure is another way in which the medieval Church and medieval monarchies had emulated one another's models of power. It has been suggested that a religion based on numerous saints and supernatural intercessors particularly thrived in a highly stratified society which was heavily based on patronage.[2] The Elizabethan court, too, was a hierarchical society in which advancement depended upon gaining the favour of a patron and ascending up the ladder of status, with the ultimate goal of furthering one's cause with the supreme power, Elizabeth.

There are many examples of letters to Elizabeth and to her ministers which read remarkably like prayers.[3] The Countess of Derby, for instance, wrote to the Queen in 1580 pleading to be restored to favour: 'I lie most humbly at your gracious feet, and pray to God that shortly my heavy and dry sorrows may be quenched with the sweet dew and moisture of your Majesty's abundant grace and virtue.'[4] More commonly, suitors wrote to ministers begging them to act as saint-like intercessors and present their cases to the Queen. As Steven May has written, even at court very few people had direct access to the Queen; she spent most of her time in the Privy Chamber, where she received only an inner circle of officials and friends. 'These persons alone held a status that linked them directly to their sovereign; their rank enabled them, for example, to prefer suits to their fellow courtiers and to Elizabeth herself.'[5] Those without such access, or even intimates in disfavour, sued to those who were admitted to the inner sanctum to intercede on their behalf with Elizabeth. The system produced conceptualisation of the Queen as on another plane, above and beyond.

Thus Sir Walter Mildmay wrote to Hatton in 1582, in hope that Elizabeth would show favour to a Mr Yelverton,[6] 'I trust her Majesty will be his gracious Lady'.[7] John Stubbs, the author of *The discovery of a gaping gulf* which opposed Elizabeth's proposed marriage to the Duke of Anjou, wrote to Hatton from prison, after his hand had been cut off, to protest his loyalty and seek Hatton's intercession in restoring him to Elizabeth's favour:

I love that most honourable, profitable, and necessary ordinance of God, wherein we are commanded to obey our sovereign magistrates, especially the government of the Queen of England, by whom the Lord hath dispensed such benefits to our country, both bodily and spiritually, as five hundred years past cannot speak of.[8]

In Stubbs's letter Elizabeth resembles the Virgin Mary as mediatrix and dispenser of God's graces. Such suing letters often represent Elizabeth in terms similar to Mariology, stressing her pity, mercy and grace towards the humble. An unknown correspondent wrote to the Queen,

May it please your most excellent Majesty to vouchsafe with your gracious and pitiful eyes the reading of these few lines . . . [I write] calling to mind how ready your sacred hands have been to receive the supplications of the poor, and how rightly noble your princely heart hath ever showed itself in pitying the state of the miserable . . .[9]

Many motivations for such language can be adduced, over and above any desire to create a substitute for the Virgin Mary. In the first place, grace and pity were useful to panegyrists and courtiers as virtues which were at once regal and safely feminine, avoiding the danger that praise of Elizabeth for monarchical virtues could render her image disturbingly masculine. Indeed, remembering the precedents of medieval queens consort, stress on Elizabeth's intercessive role could be a way of locating her comfortingly in a secondary position of power, subject to the ultimate authority of a masculine God. At the same time, such language was generated by the political context of patronage and hierarchy within which all were to some degree insecure dependants. It has been remarked that the illuminated capital C in Foxe's *Book of Martyrs* which shows three male figures kneeling before the Queen 'links the representation of authority in the realm of politics and religion . . . with the ability to appeal for preferment and reward'.[10] It has also been commented that 'The Queen was the source of her subjects' social sustenance, the fount of all preferments.'[11] In this respect, iconographic emphasis on Elizabeth's virginity could be seen as figuring an absence of preference for any one 'suitor', any one individual or faction; it combined with her metaphorical motherhood to figure her supposed availability and generosity to all.

ii. Catholic iconographical onslaughts

Meanwhile, Catholic polemic against Elizabeth intensified through the 1580s. In place of Protestant celebration of Elizabeth's metaphorical motherhood, Catholic attacks increasingly concentrated on Elizabeth's own parentage, not only in order to assert the dubiousness of her claim to the throne, but also because of the potential for colourful sexual allegations which the topic entailed. Nicholas Sander's hugely influential *Rise and Growth of the Anglican Schism*, written some time before 1581, was first published in 1585. This text alleged that Elizabeth was not only a bastard but also the product of an incestuous union, since Anne Boleyn was Henry VIII's own daughter. Moreover, Anne was said to have been physically deformed: she 'had a projecting tooth under the upper lip, and on her right hand six fingers. There was a large wen under her chin, and therefore to hide its ugliness she wore a high dress covering her throat.' Sander acknowledged that Anne had charms, but represented them as the attractions of a Circean seductress: 'She was handsome to look at, with a pretty mouth, amusing in her ways, playing well on the lute, and was a good dancer'. Behind this beguiling demeanour 'she was full of pride, ambition, envy and impurity'. Sander reported that before coming to Henry's attention she had committed fornication with her father's butler and chaplain and with the nobles and King of France.[12]

Sander implied that, as a result of the scandalously immoral nature of the union between Henry and Anne, Elizabeth herself was not only a bastard but a monster of sinfulness. He directly set himself against recent Protestant texts which acclaimed Elizabeth as a messianic figure presiding over England as the new Israel; he quotes a typical one in which,

> speaking of the marriage of Henry and Anne Boleyn, [the author] says, 'Oh, truly blessed and providential wedlock! birth and child divine, by which the country was rescued and delivered out of slavery and darkness worse than those of Egypt, and brought to the true worship of Christ.'

Sander retorts:

> Oh, the infinite goodness of God! He would not suffer these heresies of yours to come forth in any other way than through this incestuous marriage, thereby showing them to be the fruits of darkness, and that they could not be had but by deeds of darkness. The child must sin with the father, the sister with the brother – for Anne Boleyn sinned with her brother, as we shall soon see[13] – in order to give birth to that evil thing which banished out of the land, and declared unworthy of life and the light of day, the Carthusian fathers and others, who, following the counsel of Christ, had made themselves eunuchs in order to gain the kingdom of heaven.[14]

'That evil thing' had also supplanted the apostolic Catholic Church with a furtive and barbaric sect, without priesthood or sacrifice. A sinful union produces a sinful child; and that child, 'that evil thing', is simultaneously the English Reformation, and Elizabeth herself, blurrily identified with one another here, in a striking variation upon the identification of Elizabeth with the English Protestant Church made by her loyal panegyrists.

Published with Sander's tract in 1585 was a continuation by Edward Rishton. This places a similarly striking twist on the Protestant celebration of and symbolic investment in Elizabeth's virginity. Just as Protestants argued that the supposed celibacy of Catholic religious orders was merely a hypocritical mask for sexual promiscuity and deviancy, so Rishton takes a cyncial view of Elizabeth's supposed virginity. Both Houses of Parliament, when they begged Elizabeth to marry, for the sake of the succession and the safety of the realm . . . were either satisfied or mocked by her assertion that she was resolved to live and die a virgin; nor will I speak of the great scandal which she gave not only to Catholics, but to the people of her own sect, by this pretence of a single life, which was the ruin of the state.[15]

Rishton implies that Elizabeth's unmarried state is only a mask for sexual profligacy. At the same time, in opposition to loyalists' metaphors of Elizabeth's motherhood, both Sander and Rishton stress her lack of children, and see the sterility of the Tudor line as divine retribution upon Henry VIII:

It was the will of God that Henry VIII., for his sins and for the schism, should be thus severely punished: for though when he died he left three children living – Edward, Mary, and Elizabeth – yet of none of them might a child be born and reared.[16]

Physical sterility is here construed as a punishment for spiritual sterility.

Sander also significantly developed the iconography of Mary Queen of Scots, representing her not merely as naive and innocent, as most previous Catholic writers had done, but as a saintly martyr for her religion. In fact, as early as 1572 he had included the sufferings of Mary in England in a Catholic martyrology.[17] Subsequently, the sentencing of Mary for treason at the end of 1586 and her execution in February 1587 provoked a tide of Catholic polemic reviling Elizabeth as a monster of depravity. This included the republication in 1587 of the *Rise and Growth of the Anglican Schism*; and the repeating and embroidering of Sander's stories about Elizabeth's parentage in such texts as Adam Blackwood's *Martyre de la Royne d'Escosse*. Numerous ballads and poems dubbed Elizabeth a Jezebel and a she-wolf. Some *Vers Funèbres* attributed to Cardinal du Perron described the English Queen as 'this monster, conceived in adultery and incest, her fangs bared for murder, who befouls and despoils the sacred right of sceptres, and vomits her choler and gall at heaven'. Obscene poems alleged that Elizabeth had had illegitimate children by Leicester and other members of the Privy Council, and that she had deliberately avoided marriage in order to indulge her carnal appetites to the full.[18]

iii. God as Englishman

Meanwhile, for loyal English Protestants, the course of political events both at home and abroad provided manifest proof that the prophecies of the Book of Revelation were being fulfilled in daily life. Topical interpretation of Revelation, especially the identification of the papacy with Antichrist and with the Whore of Babylon, continued in such texts as *The Revelation of S.Ihon reueled* by Giacopo Brocardo, translated into English in 1582.[19] This commentary precisely interpreted particular verses of Revelation as prophecies of contemporary events like the Protestant rising in the Netherlands and the St Bartholomew's Day Massacre. It explained that the Whore of Babylon was the corrupt Church of Rome, 'which boasteth that shee is the mother, and mistresse of other Churches: and which draweth all men to Idolatry, & wickednesse' (sigs Pp2v–4r); while the Woman Clothed with the Sun represented the true Church, clothed in Christ (sigs Hh4v–Ii1r). Christ himself was described in a strikingly maternal fashion, adopting a kind of iconography previously associated with his mother: he 'fed [the Apostles] with the milke of his Gosple. Christ Iesus yeelded the mylke of the Gosple out of his heart' (sig.I4v). The opposing images of good mother and bad mother, virgin and whore, were by now well-confirmed as means of representing the opposition between the two Churches.

Elizabeth herself was frequently identified with the Woman Clothed with the Sun, dispelling the clouds of popery. A ballad of 1587 by Maurice Kyffin, 'The Blessednes of Brytaine', declared:

> As Shyning Sunne recleeres the darkned Skye,
> And foorth recalles eche thing, from shiv'ring Shrowds,
> So hath our Second Sunne, both farre and nye,
> by brightning Beames, outcleerd erronious Clouds;
>   A pow'rfull Prop of Christes Euangell pure,
>   One* whose Support, it rests Reposed sure.[20]

John Lyly, in 'Euphues' Glass for Europe', had rejoiced in England's felicity: 'O blessed peace, oh happy Prince, O fortunate people: The lyuing God is onely the Englysh God'.[21] Job Throckmorton, speaking at the 1586–7 Parliament after the discovery of the Babington

---

* on

Plot which brought Mary's downfall, called attention to Elizabeth's miraculous survival of Catholic threats:

> sure, we that have lived in the eyes of all men, so choked, as it were, with blessings of God beyond desert, we that have lived to see her Majesty's life, so dear unto us, pulled out, as it were, even out of the lion's jaws in despite of Hell and Satan, may truly – not in any pride, but in humbleness of soul to our comforts – confess that indeed the Lord hath vowed himself to be English . . . It is an argument unanswerable, to prove the Pope to be that man described in the Apocalypse – I mean that man of sin, that beast with the mark in his forehead – to prove him, I say, to be Antichrist.[22]

This sense that God was an Englishman was intensified by the Armada victory of 1588. Celebrations of the defeat of the Spanish did not lay claim to superior English nautical skill as one might expect, but instead frankly laid stress on luck and the weather: the fact that these had been on England's side must mean that God Himself had been fighting for England. A song attributed to Elizabeth herself, and probably performed during her procession to the thanksgiving ceremony at St Paul's, developed the themes of benign meteorology, of England as the new Israel,[23] and of its Queen as bride of Christ:

> he made the wynds and waters rise
> To scatter all myne enemyes.
>
> This Josephs Lorde and Israells god
> the fyry piller and dayes clowde
> That saved his Sainctes from wicked men
> And drenshet the honor of the proude
> And hathe preserved in tender love
> The Spirit of his Turtle dove.[24]

A ballad of similar date deplored how the 'pagon pope that filthy sort of Roome / the devill doth legat send', but rejoiced that:

> The spannish spite which made the papiste boast
> hath done them little good
> god dealt with them as with king Pharoes host
> who were drowned in the flood

> *Elizabeth to saue.*
> The lord him selfe with streached arme
> did quell ther rage that sought our harme
> ther threatning bragges the lord did charme . . .
> . . . *Elizabeth so braue*
> did not in strength of navie trust
> nor yet in steell that is but rust
> but in her Lord who is most Iust.

Elizabeth is presented as an intercessor: her virtues are extolled, and it is explained that:

> for her it is god doth vs spare
> one her he hath a fervent care . . .
> . . . his mercies great which he hath showne
> all for her sake not for our owne.

As in earlier popular ballads, there is an absence of inhibition about using strongly Marian iconography:

> *Elizabeth so braue:,*
> Doth never tread from vertues trace
> her hart and mind are full of grace
> from pittie she tournes not her face.[25]

In 1589 Edward Hellwis published *A Marvell Deciphered*, a commentary on Chapter 12 of Revelation, the chapter concerning the Woman Clothed with the Sun. Hellwis avoids directly naming Elizabeth in his commentary – he says that 'I dare not to name any person, either presume to confesse any exposition, of so rare, and secrete mistery of God.'[26] However, his allusions to Catholic conspiracies and the Armada clearly indicate that he regards Revelation 12 as a prophecy of recent and impending events, in which the Woman is both the Church of England (sig.A4r–v), and the Queen who is the Church's guardian. This is confirmed by a series of side-headings opening with the formula 'Not to be doubted . . .', of which the first, for instance, runs, 'Not to be doubted what woman before all the kings or persons whatsoeuer vpon earth from the first publishing of this prophesie vnto this day hath beene most apparantly clothed with the son namely Iesus Christ' (p.1).

The Antichrist and the dragon are of course the Pope and the Roman Church, cast down with 'all his drosse of superstition, idolatrie, and all his other filthines' (p.6). The child born of the Woman/Elizabeth is 'the Lorde Iesus which is his sacred worde' (p.3). This typological reading functions to extend the well-established image of Elizabeth as nursing mother of the Church and nation: her promotion of the Protestant faith is now represented as an act of giving birth, recalling Aylmer's representation of Mother England as giving birth to the Reformation.[27] This in turn prompts the drawing of an analogy between Elizabeth and the Virgin Mary:

> And as the Virgin Marie, iustlie and rightlie reioiced for that by election, she before all women naturally did bring forth, the Lord and Sauiour of the worlde: euen so that woman, which aboue all women, hath to this daie since the first publication of this prophesie, beene adopted by Gods mercie, to reuiue his honour and glorie: and thereby doth accept to saie to be hir Sonne; in hir portion hath iust cause to saie; *Magnificat anima mea Deus.*
>
> (p.5)

This suggests that, in the late 1580s, earlier inhibitions about directly naming the Virgin in typological comparison to Elizabeth were fading. Even so, it is striking that Hellwis does not perpetuate or revive the pre-Reformation identification of the Virgin with the Woman Clothed with the Sun. It seems that for Protestants at this time the Woman was unequivocally regarded as a symbol of their Church and of Elizabeth as protector of the Church. The Virgin Mary is merely brought in incidentally to reinforce by analogy the representation of Elizabeth's metaphorical motherhood.

Thus the dramatic political events of the late 1580s served both to rigidify and to amplify the binary oppositions which governed the iconographic combat between Catholic and Protestant. To a Protestant, Mary Stuart was a treacherous whore, and Elizabeth was a holy paragon; to a Catholic, Elizabeth was a whore of wolvish cruelty, and Mary Queen of Scots was a saintly martyr.

iv. Henry Constable

Henry Constable is of interest in this context as an English convert to Catholicism who resisted such rigid polarities. Until around 1590 he was a Protestant and a loyal servant of the Elizabethan regime, travelling abroad on missions for Walsingham. In 1589–90 he seems to have been in England at court, and was said to have been a favourite of the Queen's. One of three sonnets which he wrote in praise of Elizabeth may date from this time, and is titled 'To the Queene touching the cruell effects of her perfections'.[28] It was conventional for the Petrarchan lover to lament the cruelty of his mistress in the sense of her impregnable chastity, but the cruelty which is deprecated in this sonnet is of a different order, producing a poem strikingly fraught with negative undertones and simmering anxieties within the outward conventions of panegyric. The poet ostensibly praises Elizabeth as an angel, while lamenting in strong terms the effect of her perfections on both followers and enemies:

> Most sacred prince why should I thee thus prayse
> Which both of sin and sorrow cause hast beene
> Proude hast thou made thy land of such a Queene
> Thy neighboures enviouse of thy happie dayes [. . .]
>
> Thus sin thow causd envye I meane and pride
> Thus fire and darknesse doe proceed from thee
> The very paynes which men in hell abide . . .

(p.138)

It seems likely that this poem is close in date to Constable's conversion to Catholicism, which took place some time in 1589–90 (p.33). Constable remained patriotic, writing letters from Paris to the Earl of Essex through the 1590s to protest his national allegiance: 'Though I am passionately affectionated to my Religion, yet am I not in the nomber of those which wish the restitution thereof with the seruitude of my country to a forrein Tyranny'.[29] The sonnet therefore seems to express the developing divided loyalties of a loyal servant of the English Crown who was finding himself drawn towards a Church which branded the English Queen a Jezebel and she-wolf.

Although renowned among his contemporaries as an author of secular sonnets, it seems that Constable wrote no more of these after his conversion, turning instead to spiritual sonnets (pp.33, 59). However, he followed the Italian tradition in continuing to employ the language of erotic desire in his spiritual poetry; and went further than this to integrate the type of diction characteristic of secular panegyric. A sonnet 'To our blessed Lady' opens:

> Sovereigne of Queenes: If vayne Ambition move
> my hart to seeke an earthly prynces grace:
> shewe me thy sonne in his imperiall place,
> whose servants reigne, our kynges & queenes above.

It concludes:

> . . . love, my hart to chaste desyres shall brynge,
> when fayrest Queene lookes on me from her throne
> and jealous byddes me love but her alone.

(p.189)

Constable seems to allude to his own career as a courtier in his frank acknowledgment of his susceptibility to ambition; then goes on to represent the Virgin as Queen and mistress in terms highly reminiscent of encomia of Elizabeth.

Another poem on the same subject posits the heavenly queen and earthly queen as direct alternatives, opening by asking the Virgin, 'Why should I any love O queene but thee?' This might be read as a reply to the earlier poem in which Elizabeth was challengingly asked, 'Most sacred prince why should I thee thus prayse[?]'. Constable goes on to employ maternal imagery which implies a rejection of Elizabeth, whose image as mother of the nation was now a commonplace, in favour of the nurturing figure of Mary, to whom he says: 'thy wombe dyd beare, thy brest my saviour feede; / and thow dyddest never cease to succoure me'. He proceeds through questions and answers which express the continuing dangerous attraction he feels to earthly ambition:

> If Love doe followe worth and dignitye?
> thou all in [thy] perfections doth exceede:
> if Love be ledd by hope of future meede?
> what pleasure more then thee in heaven to see?

(p.190)

Again, love and ambition are identified with one another, as in so much court panegyric; this is the language of patronage, but Constable has replaced Elizabeth as the pinnacle of the patronage hierarchy with the figure of the Virgin.

These poems by Constable illustrate a continuing cross-fertilisation of secular and religious verse, within the context of an emergent Counter-Reformation aesthetic. Just as mediaeval poets had used much the same terms to praise the Virgin Mary, an earthly queen, or an earthly mistress, so Constable praises the Virgin as queen and mistress, but now with accreted overtones of comparison with the earthly Virgin Queen, Elizabeth. The erotic/religious/political devotion of the Elizabethan courtier to his Queen provides Constable with a language for re-conversion to service of the heavenly Queen.

v. The 1590 *Faerie Queene*

Edmund Spenser, on the other hand, seems to have held Protestant beliefs which tended towards the radical; and in his national epic emphatically placed Elizabeth at the summit of the patronage structure which he sought to climb. Books I, II and III of his *Faerie Queene* were published in 1590, and make fruitful use of the iconographic combat of preceding years.

Among the numerous figures which represent facets of Elizabeth is the presiding regal icon of Gloriana, whom Spenser invests with the sun-like brightness of both majesty and the Woman of Revelation:

> In widest Ocean she her throne does reare,
> That ouer all the earth it may be seene;
> As morning Sunne her beames dispredden cleare.

> (II.ii.40)[30]

As we have seen, the Woman Clothed with the Sun had already been adopted before Elizabeth's accession as an emblem of the Protestant Church and Protestant heroines, and the evangelical anti-Catholic force of solar imagery had been reinforced in its applications to Elizabeth through the 1570s and '80s.[31] What we have here, then, is less an echo of the iconography of the Virgin Mary as the Woman Clothed with the Sun than continuation of an established Protestant iconographical tradition. Other figures of Elizabeth in Books I to III share in this solar imagery. In the case of Belphoebe, her radiant eyes are at once sun-like and star-like, incorporating a conventional attribute of the Petrarchan mistress:

> In her faire eyes two liuing lampes did flame,
> Kindled aboue at th'heauenly makers light,
> And darted fyrie beames out of the same.

(II.iii.23)

Una too, at her betrothal, reveals 'The blazing brightnesse of her beauties beame, / And glorious light of her sunshyny face' (I.xii.23).

Una in particular is deployed as one side of a binary opposition with Duessa, in which Spenser perpetuates and elaborates upon the use of female sexuality as an iconography of religious truth which we have already observed developing since the earliest years of the reign.[32] In Spenser's multi-layered allegory, Una, as a virgin, stands at once for truth, for Elizabeth, and for Protestantism; her adversary, Duessa, stands for deceit, for Mary Queen of Scots and for the Catholic Church, and is, of course, a whore. She is described through close biblical allusion to the Whore of Babylon; she is:

> A goodly Lady clad in scarlot red,
> Purfled with gold and pearle of rich assay,
> And like a *Persian* mitre on her hed
> She wore, with crownes and owches* garnished,
> The which her lauish louers to her gaue.

(I.ii.13)

The Geneva Bible, as we have seen, glossed the source text in Revelation, 'This woman is the Antichrist, that is, the Pope with the whole bodie of his filthie creatures . . .'.[33] Spenser invokes this interpretation while sustaining the femaleness of the Whore, enabling him to deploy misogynistic disgust at the female body as a means of vividly conveying her moral turpitude. Duessa is stripped, exposing the hideous deformity of her genitals:

> . . . her misshaped parts did them appall,
> A loathly, wrinckled hag, ill fauoured, old,
> Whose secret filth good manners biddeth not be told . . .

---

* jewels

Her neather parts, the shame of all her kind,
My chaster Muse for shame doth blush to write . . .

(I.viii.46–8)

When, therefore, Spenser describes Una's betrothal garment as
'All lilly white, withoutten spot, or pride' (I.xii.22), the point is not
to turn Elizabeth into a substitute for the Immaculate Virgin Mary,
but to participate in the by-now-commonplace use of binary oppositions of virgin and whore to represent the political and religious
opposition between England and its enemies. The spotlessness of
the bride of the Song of Songs – glossed in the Geneva Bible as a
personification of the Church – is being appropriated to denote the
sanctity, purity and truthfulness of Una/Elizabeth/the English Protestant Church in opposition to the duplicity, immorality and excess
of Duessa/Mary Queen of Scots/the Catholic Church.

Spenser's Belphoebe, another figure of Elizabeth, is similarly
spotless: her face is 'Cleare as the skie, withouten blame or blot'
(II.iii.22). In description of this character Spenser comes closest to
echoes of Mariology, giving an account of her conception and birth
which, like that of Elisa in the 'Aprill' Eclogue, draws on the idea
of the Immaculate Conception. Her mother, Chrysogonee, fell asleep
on a grassy bank after bathing, whereupon:

> The sunne-beames bright vpon her body playd,
> Being through former bathing mollifide,
> And pierst into her wombe, where they embayd
> With so sweet sence and secret power vnspide,
> That in her pregnant flesh they shortly fructifide.

(III.vi.7)

Because she conceived without lust, Chrysogonee gave birth without pain, just as the apocrypha asserted of Mary: 'She bore withouten
paine, that she conceiued / Withouten pleasure' (III.vi.27). A further
consequence of her sinless conception is that her twin daughters
Belphoebe and Amoret are born free from sin, 'Pure and vnspotted
from all loathly crime, / That is ingenerate in fleshly slime' (III.vi.3).

Just as the 'Aprill' Eclogue can be understood as a defence of
Elizabeth against slurs of bastardy, so here Spenser's appropriation
of the iconography of the Immaculate Conception can be interpreted

as a direct response to the recent Catholic polemic which alleged Elizabeth to be the child of an incestuous, monstrous, carnal union, and therefore an insatiable sexual deviant herself. Spenser's rejoinder has an opposing logic of cause and effect: Elizabeth was conceived without sin, and is therefore herself a model of sexual purity – a sexual purity which in turn symbolises political and religious truth and uprightness.

There are two other resemblances between this episode and the 'Aprill' Eclogue. One is that, again, the Catholic iconography of the Immaculate Conception is contained by the classical literary convention of Ovidian metamorphosis. The second is that, as in the earlier poem, the conception and birth of a figure of Elizabeth resembles not only the Immaculate Conception of the Virgin Mary, but the parthenogenesis of Christ himself. In fact, one phrase used by Spenser to introduce the account of Belphoebe's birth, 'Her berth was of the wombe of Morning dew' (III.vi.3), is almost a literal translation of the Prayer Book version of Psalm 110:3, 'The dew of thy birth is of the womb of the morning'[34] – a verse generally regarded as referring to the begetting or Incarnation of Christ and, by extension, to the formation of the Church.[35] As we have seen before, Elizabeth is being associated not just with female figures like the bride of the Song of Songs, but with Christ himself. The idea of Elizabeth as a messianic figure of divine ancestry is sustained by incidental remarks throughout the text: Belphoebe, at her first appearance, before the narration of her birth, is described as 'borne of heauenly birth' (II.iii.21); Gloriana 'is heauenly borne, and heauen may iustly vaunt' (I.x.59).

Spenser's celebration of Elizabeth as divine in *Faerie Queene* I–III may seem at times to verge on the idolatrous, and to be difficult to reconcile with the poet's Protestant beliefs. Sir Guyon says of Gloriana,

> . . . men beholding so great excellence,
> And rare perfection in mortalitie,
> Do her adore with sacred reuerence,
> As th'Idole of her makers great magnificence.

> (II.ii.41)

'Adore', 'Idol' – these are strong words for a Protestant to use. However, there are several ways of understanding Spenser's employment of them. On the one hand, Elizabeth is an 'idol' in the sense that God has made her in his own image to be his instrument on earth; she therefore justifies adoration, as a personification of God's will and of the advancement of the true faith. This interpretation is one which stresses the sacred aspects of Elizabeth as Protestant monarch.

On the other hand, we may pursue the idea of a Protestant panegyric which held up an idealised perfect image to its subject not as an act of flattery, but as an exhortation to match up to that image.[36] Panegyric was therefore not incompatible with full awareness of the human flaws of one's subject, and, to a lesser or greater degree, could have a critical, rather than celebratory, motivation. Such a reading of Spenser's Gloriana is supported by the Red Cross Knight's vision of the New Jerusalem in I.x. Cleopolis, the seat of the Faerie Queene, and therefore a version of London, is said to be the nearest an earthly city can approximate to the heavenly citadel: it is 'for earthly frame / The fairest peece, that eye beholden can' (I.x.59). Yet Red Cross's first response to the New Jerusalem is of how far it excels Cleopolis: 'this great Citie that does far surpas, / And this bright Angels towre quite dims that towre of glas' (I.x.58). Spenser seems to be asserting that although the English Protestant nation is the closest yet achieved to the fulfilment of God's will on earth there is still a long way to go to build or reach the New Jerusalem. Red Cross and Una, the English nation and the true Church, are only betrothed within the time-frame of the poem; their full union lies in the uncertain future. Similarly, by implication, the 'heauenly borne' Gloriana is the closest thing on earth to a Messiah, but has not yet fulfilled her godly mission of establishing the true faith in full accordance with God's will. At the same time, Gloriana can be thought of as standing in the same relation to Elizabeth as the New Jerusalem does to England: an image of perfection, attainable, but requiring to be striven for.

These alternative readings can coexist in Book I of the *Faerie Queene*: we can see Spenser as celebrating the perfect icon Gloriana, insofar as she symbolises the English Church and nation, while simultaneously critically implying the need for Elizabeth to strive harder to become identical with Gloriana, and Una and Belphoebe. In Spenser's later works overt celebration and implied criticism are less harmoniously intertwined, as we shall see. However, the main point to make here is this: many of the figures of Elizabeth which occur in the three books of the 1590 *Faerie Queene* do have elements which resemble aspects of Mariology; but such figures are most fully understood not as evidence of a need for a Virgin Mary substitute, but as strategic adaptations or reappropriations from biblical sources, always motivated by the requirements of a distinctive and polemical Protestant iconography.

vi. *'Vivat Eliza* for an *Ave Mari'*

1590 also saw the first performance of a song repeatedly quoted by those who argue that Elizabeth was directly substituted for the Virgin Mary. The lines usually quoted are:

> When others sings [*sic*] *Venite exultemus,*
> Stand by and turne to *Noli aemulari;*
> For *quare fremuerunt* use *Oremus,*
> *Vivat Eliza* for an *Ave Mari.*[37]

E.C. Wilson remarks that these are 'verses that suggest an actual substitution of the English virgin for the Catholic in the hearts of ardent Protestant knights'.[38] Yates quotes the lines as evidence that Elizabethans did not flinch from a direct comparison of Elizabeth with Mary: ' "Long live Eliza!" instead of "Hail Mary!" . . . [a] startling suggestion.'[39] Allison Heisch considers that the lines 'cheerfully acknowledged' that 'the Virgin Elizabeth either rivalled or replaced the Virgin Mary . . . Long live Eliza instead of Hail Mary.'[40] And Robin Headlam Wells quotes the song as evidence of 'the tendency for Protestant Elizabethans to see the adulation of their Virgin Queen as a precise and proper substitute for the cult of the Virgin Mary.'[41]

All these writers interpret the lines as if they were a popular slogan or rabble-rousing chant, urging the erection of shrines to Elizabeth and veneration of her as a cult-image in exact imitation of the pre-Reformation cult of the Virgin. In fact their context is rather different from this: they are drawn from a courtly song, composed for a particular occasion. The song, 'Times eldest sonne, olde age, the heyre of ease', forms a pair with another, 'My golden locks time hath to silver turnd'. 'My golden locks' is recorded as having been sung by the royal lutenist Robert Hales on 17 November 1590 at the Tilt Yard, when Sir Henry Lee resigned his title of Queen's Champion. The occasion is described by George Peele in *Polyhymnia* (1590) and by William Segar in *Honour Military and Civil* (1602), both of whom print the words of the song.[42] 'Times eldest sonne' may well also have been composed for the same occasion; in one manuscript, it is headed 'In yeeldinge vp his Tilt staff: sayd:', and closes 'quod Sir Henry Leigh'.[43]

When the lines are replaced in this very probable context, it becomes clear that they can be read in at least three different ways. In the first place, '*Vivat Eliza* for an *Ave Mari*' can be read simply as lines referring to retirement: Lee will now pray for Elizabeth instead of fighting for her. In the second place, both songs can be interpreted as part of the general usage of religious, and specifically Catholic language as a trope for courtly love, which in turn is a trope for political allegiance. And thirdly, and most controversially, the lines can be read as implying that Lee will indeed not merely pray *for* Elizabeth in his retirement, but pray *to* Elizabeth as a religious icon – a stance justified for Elizabethan Protestants by belief in her truth as image and agent of God.

To illustrate the first reading, recognising the theme of retirement, it is helpful to quote both 'My golden locks' and 'Times eldest sonne' in full. 'My golden locks' runs as follows:

My golden locks time hath to silver turnd,
    (Oh time too swift, and swiftnes never ceasing)
My youth gainst age, and age at youth hath spurnd.
    But spurnd in vaine: youth waineth by encreasing.
Beauty, strength, and youth, flowers fading beene,
Duety, faith, and loue, are rootes and ever greene.

My Helmet now shall make an hive for Bees,
    And lovers songs shall turne to holy Psalmes:
A man at Armes must now sit on his knees,
    And feed on pray'rs, that are old ages almes.
And so from Court to Cottage I depart,
My Saint is sure of mine unspotted hart.

And when I sadly sit in homely Cell,
    I'le teach my Swaines this Carrol for a song,
Blest be the hearts that thinke my Sovereigne well,
    Curs'd be the soules that thinke to do her wrong.
Goddesse, vouchsafe this aged man his right,
To be your Beadsman now, that was your Knight.[44]

The stanzas of the song follow a sequence: the first establishes the theme of age; the second describes the retired soldier's transition from martial exploits to the contemplative life; and the song ends with the conventional courtly love trope of the mistress/monarch as her servant's goddess or saint. Running throughout is a theme of substitution: age instead of youth, prayers instead of deeds of arms. 'Times eldest sonne' develops the same themes, stanza by stanza:

> Times eldest sonne, olde age, the heyre of ease,
>   Strengths foe, loves woe, and foster to devotion,
> Bids gallant youthes in martial prowes please,
>   As for himselfe hee hath no earthly motion,
> But thinks sighes, teares, vowes, praiers and sacrifices
> As good as shewes, maskes, justes or tilt devises.
>
> Then sit thee downe, and say thy *Nunc demittis*,
>   With *De profundis*, *Credo*, and *Te Deum*,
> Chant *Miserere*, for what now so fit is
>   As that, or this, *Paratum est cor meum*?
> O that thy Saint would take in worth thy hart,
> Thou canst not please hir with a better part.
>
> When others sings *Venite exultemus*,
>   Stand by and turne to *Noli aemulari*;
> For *quare fremuerunt* use *Oremus*,
>   *Vivat Eliza* for an *Ave Mari*;
> And teach those swains that lives [*sic*] about thy cell
> To say *Amen* when thou dost pray so well.[45]

Lee is to become a hermit, or, as the other song had put it, a beadsman. The term 'beadsman' could imply one who counts the beads of the rosary as he prays, but literally meant simply one who 'bids', or prays, for a benefactor, and was therefore close in sense to 'hermit'. Both hermit and beadsman were courtly love figures already used in entertainments for Elizabeth, such as the depiction of Leicester as a beadsman in Rombus's speech at the end of the Lady of May, and the pageant at Lee's own estate of Woodstock in 1575 which had concerned a hermit and Lee as 'Loricus'.[46] However, they were also common figures for retirement from public office. Elizabeth, for instance, wrote an affectionately bantering letter to Burghley in 1591 to dissuade him from retiring, in which she called him 'Sir Eremite', and teased him for having 'possessed yourself of Theobalds with her sweet rosary', presumably a punning reference to his rose-garden.[47] Now these 1590 songs represent Lee as taking on the persona of a hermit, a role which he seems to have firmly embraced and continued to make great play of in the years after 1590: in 1591 he wrote to Sir Thomas Heneage, asking him to excuse him to the Queen for leaving her entourage on progress, on the grounds that 'I am old, and come now evil away with the inconveniences of progress . . . All these things considered hath made me return, with my more ease, to my poor home, where I am much more fit to pray for her Majesty than now to wrestle with the humours of Court.'[48]

The primary substitution with which both songs are concerned is that of age for youth, contemplation for action, private life for public life; and the substitution of '*Vivat Eliza*' for '*Ave Mari*' must be understood within this context. To this end, it is worth looking in detail at all the Latin phrases used in 'Times eldest sonne', and attempting to establish what might have been their meanings and connotations for an English audience in 1590.[49] All these Latin phrases are snatches of the liturgy. The fact that they are in Latin is not necessarily an allusion to Catholic forms of worship; all the phrases denote prayers or psalms which were in continued use in the Church of England, and which continued to be given these Latin headings in the Book of Common Prayer.[50]

Lee, the retiring knight, will say his '*Nunc d[i]mittis*': this is the Song of Simeon, the old man who was able to die content having seen the infant Messiah (Luke 2.29). Its opening words are 'Lord now lettest thou thy seruant depart in peace', and it was used in the Church of England at the daily service of Evening Prayer.[51] '*De profundis*' is Psalm 130, 'Out of the deep haue I called vnto thee', a penitential psalm associated with mourning, and used once a month at Evening Prayer.[52] '*Credo*' is of course the Creed; '*Te Deum*', 'We prayse thee, O God', is a hymn of praise and thanksgiving used at daily Morning Prayer.[53] '*Miserere*', 'Haue mercy vpon me, O God', is Psalm 51, another penitential psalm.[54] '*Paratum [est] cor meum*' is Psalm 108, 'O God, my heart is ready', a hymn of victory, used monthly at Evening Prayer, and on the evening of Ascension Day.[55] This tag is neatly woven into the song by the next line, 'O that thy Saint would take in worth thy heart . . .'. Overall, the hymns and prayers recommended in the second stanza of the song are associated with thanksgiving, with penitence, or with evening prayer, making them highly appropriate to an ageing knight retiring as the Queen's champion.

In the third stanza the question of what these Latin phrases denote becomes more significant, because it is here that we get the substitutions of one prayer for another culminating in *'Vivat Eliza* for an *Ave Mari'*. Lee is not to sing with others *'Venite exultemus'*, Psalm 95, 'O Come, let vs sing vnto the Lord', a song used at daily Morning Prayer.[56] Instead, he should sing *'Noli aemulari'*, Psalm 37, 'Fret not thy selfe, because of the ungodly'. This psalm speaks at length of how the ungodly will be vanquished ('Wicked doers shalbe rooted out: and they that patiently abide the Lord, those shal inherit the land', v.9). Its emphasis is upon how God himself will take action, without the need for human aid; it contains the verse 'I haue bene yong and now am olde' (v.25), and was used monthly at Evening Prayer.[57] The knight should not use *'quare fremuerunt'*, Psalm 2, 'Why doe the heathen so furiously rage together', a belligerent psalm of admonition to ungodly monarchs, used on the morning of Easter Day, and monthly at Morning Prayer.[58] Instead, he should simply say *'Oremus'*, 'Let us pray'. The force of these substitutions appears to be that Lee is to abandon the battle-cries of the godly warrior in place of the self-abnegating prayers of the hermit who leaves punishment of the heathen to God.

It is at the culmination of all of this that Lee is urged to pray *'Vivat Eliza'* instead of *'Ave Mari'*. In the context of the theme of retirement, this denotes not so much that he is aggressively to depose the Virgin in favour of Elizabeth, but that his service to Elizabeth should now take the form of prayers and contemplation, resembling the prayer of the rosary. The point is not that he should pray to Elizabeth as if she were a new Virgin Mary, but that he should pray for her rather than fighting for her. The author of the song is careful not merely to transpose the idolatrous religious acclamation 'Hail Mary' to Elizabeth, but to substitute for it an acclamation expressive of secular loyalty, 'Long live the Queen'. It is further in keeping with the general theme of age that Lee's prayer should be for the Queen's long life.

As I have said, the use of Latin liturgical phrases in 'Times eldest sonne' does not necessarily carry Catholic connotations, since these Latin headings continued to be used in the Book of Common Prayer.[59] Nevertheless the allusion to the Ave Maria at this point does invoke distinctively Catholic devotional practice. This might denote the fact that Lee is elderly, and so can recall the old days of

Catholicism. He was born in 1533 (the same year as Elizabeth),[60] and was therefore one of the older generation well able to remember a time when the Ave Maria was still current. Allusion to Catholic prayers was given just this sense some years later, in John Savile's 'Salutatorie Poeme' to greet James I in 1603: he asserted that old people of ninety wished they were nineteen again to enjoy the full benefits of James's reign, and described the old as '. . . the whitest heads/That liu'd in Antique tyme, and praid on beades'.[61]

The implication of '*Vivat Eliza* for an *Ave Mari*' might also be that saying Ave Marias or prayers like them is what goes on in the country, a recognition of the fact that, although the court and London were resolutely Protestant, Catholicism had proved resilient in some rural areas. Lee was a Justice of the Peace in Oxfordshire; as such one of his main duties was to keep a watch upon recusants and their activities, and there is evidence that some residents of his area of jurisdiction were Catholics.[62] His substitution of '*Vivat Eliza*' for '*Ave Mari*' might represent the taking of modern metropolitan practices to backward rural areas. Allusion to the Ave Maria thus contributes to the theme of retirement by connoting both archaism, and the rusticity of a pastoral retreat.

'*Vivat Eliza* for an *Ave Mari*' can be read as uncontroversially asserting that Lee will pray not *to* Elizabeth, as others pray to Mary, but merely *for* her. This reading is supported by the companion song, 'My golden locks', in which the example given of Lee's prayers is 'Blest be the hearts that thinke my Sovereigne well, /Curs'd be the soules that thinke to do her wrong.' Peele's versified account of the retirement tilts in *Polyhymnia* also confirms this: Lee resigns his champion's armour and lance,

> Protesting to her princely Majesty,
> In sight of heaven and all her lovely lords,
> He would betake him to his orisons,
> And spend the remnant of his waning age,
> Unfit for wars and martial exploits,
> In prayers for her eternal happiness.[63]

However, both 'Times eldest sonne' and 'My golden locks' also refer to Eliza as Lee's saint and goddess. Scandalised commentators like Yates respond to the line '*Vivat Eliza* for an *Ave Mari*' on the assumption that Elizabeth is to be prayed *to*, as a sanctified image for veneration. This is an ambiguity inherent to the line which should not be overlooked. Again, it is supported by elements of the occasion of Lee's retirement. As both Peele and Segar record, the backdrop for his resignation of his arms was a pavilion arrayed as a temple of Vesta. As Segar describes it,

> This Temple seemed to consist upon pillars of Pourferry, arched like unto a Church, within it were many Lampes burning. Also, on the one side there stood an Altar covered with cloth of gold, and thereupon two waxe candles burning in rich candlesticks, upon the Altar also were layd certaine Princely presents, which after by three Virgins were presented unto her Majestie.

At the door of the temple was a crowned pillar, on which was written a Latin prayer for Elizabeth. It was at the foot of this pillar that Lee offered up his armour.[64]

Although the altar and candles suggest Catholic trappings, it is notable how carefully the deviser of the pageant negotiates possible dangers of idolatry. It is not a temple dedicated to Elizabeth, but to Vesta; and even if Vesta is assumed to be being implicitly identified with Elizabeth, the invocation of a classical goddess, as in the panegyrics of Spenser and others already discussed, circumscribes implications of sacredness within a permissible secular, literary setting. However, even the ideas of a shrine dedicated to Elizabeth, and of prayers *to* the Queen rather than merely for her, become somewhat less startling suggestions if we recognise that in both 'Times eldest sonne' and 'My golden locks', as in other courtly poetry of the period, religious language is a trope operating on several levels.

As we have seen, the tradition of courtly love, stretching back through the Middle Ages, deployed religious imagery to denote erotic devotion;[65] and the continued use of such language by Elizabethan courtiers added a further layer of metaphor, whereby religious imagery stood for erotic devotion which in turn stood for political allegiance. The hermit or beadsman, in particular, could be used as figures for the courtly servant.[66] Such a reading of the two songs already considered is supported by a third song associated with Lee, 'Farre from triumphing Court'. This has words attributed to Lee, and continues the style and theme of 'My golden locks' and 'Times eldest sonne', but appears to belong to the period after Elizabeth's death (although born in the same year as Elizabeth, Lee lived until 1611, when he died just short of his seventy-eighth birthday).

The speaker professes his willingness to transfer his service to the new Queen, Anne of Denmark: although 'That Goddesse whom hee servde to heau'n is gone', a new 'Saint' has been revealed to him.[67] Clearly here professed dedication to a 'saint' equates with the pursuit of political patronage.

It is notable that specifically Catholic terminology became increasingly popular in the Elizabethan discourse of courtly love. We have seen how at the end of *The Lady of May* Leicester was represented as 'a huge *catholicam*' saying prayers for (or to?) Elizabeth on his 'Papistian beads'. By the 1590s, incense, pilgrimages, the veneration of images and of saints at shrines, were all becoming conventional emblems of erotic desire. Sir Arthur Gorges, in a sonnet of c.1584, said that a place from which his mistress was absent was 'as a shryne wher no Saynte is att all'.[68] B. Griffin, in his sonnet-sequence *Fidessa*, 1596, also addressed his mistress as a saint, and described his mounting desire as like rising clouds of incense.[69] The term 'idolatry' itself was used relatively unpejoratively in a secular sense to describe utter devotion of body and soul, as in *Romeo and Juliet* (1594–5), where Juliet says, 'swear by thy gracious self, / Which is the god of my idolatry'.[70] It seems plausible that one resonance of '*Vivat Eliza* for an *Ave Mari*' is participation in this fashionable association of specifically Catholic language with courtly love.

An especially striking example of such secular, or indeed profane, use of distinctively Catholic imagery is Ode 3 of Barnabe Barnes's *Parthenophil and Parthenophe* (1593), a sonnet-sequence which recounts the pursuit of a 'Virgin' (Parthenophe) by a 'Virgin-lover' (Parthenophil). Ode 3 reads as follows:

> Vpon an holy Saintes eue
> (As I tooke my pilgrimadge)
> Wandring through the forest warye
> (Blest be that holy sainte)
> I mette the louely Virgine *Marye*
> And kneeled with long trauell fainte
> Performing my dew homage,
> My teares fore told mine hart did greeue
> Yet *Mary* would not me releeue.
>
> Her I did promise euery yeare,
> The firstling foemale of my flocke
> That in my loue she would me furder.

I curst the dayes of my first loue,
My comfortes spoiles, my pleasures murther:
She, she alas did me reproue,
My suites (as to a stonie rocke)
Were made, for she would not giue eare.
Ah loue, deare loue, loue bought to deare!

Mary, my sainte chast, and milde
Pittie, ah pittie my suite;
Thou art a virgine, pittie me:
Shine eyes, though pittie wanting
That she by them my greefe may see
And looke on mine hart panting:
But her deefe eares, and tonge mute
Shewes her hard hart vnreconcil'de,
Hard hart, from all remorse exil'de.[71]

As throughout the *Parthenophil* sequence, Barnes is being calculatedly risqué here. The speaker's unyielding mistress called Mary is metaphorised as a stone statue such as might be found at a forest shrine; pleading with a mistress for sexual satisfaction is implied to be equivalent to praying to the Virgin for spiritual succour. The speaker's preoccupation with deflowering is suggested by his offering to his Virgin as homage not merely 'a milkwhite Lamb', as Spenser's Colin does,[72] but 'the firstling foemale of my flocke'. Barnes is describing no metaphysical neo-Platonic devotion, but the pursuit of a virgin which ends in consummation and ravishment. This prayer to Mary is followed by a prayer to Bacchus for tumescence, which is at the very least a cheeky juxtaposition.

Barnes was the son of a Church of England bishop, and author of *A Divine Centurie of Spirituall Sonnets*, 1595. These strike a theological and aesthetic line which is resolutely Protestant. Although Mary Magdalen, the Saints Michael and George, and the Virgin are mentioned incidentally, there are no sonnets directly addressed to or in praise of such personages.[73] Instead, all the sonnets invoke or extol Christ or God the Father, and stress their absolute power of salvation. We might then think of Ode 3 of *Parthenophil* as deliberately satirising 'idolatrous' Catholic practices and hymns to the Virgin, emptying their terms of spiritual significance in an act of secularisation and even verbal iconoclasm.

On one level, the line '*Vivat Eliza* for an *Ave Mari*' can be thought of as participating in this kind of secularisation of distinctively Catholic language and forms of worship. The implication that Elizabeth should be prayed to as others pray to Mary could mean merely that Elizabeth will occupy the role of an archetypal mistress and object of courtly devotion, which in turn figures political allegiance.

However, I would suggest that the song is more complex than this. It seems to participate in this kind of emptying out of spiritual significance from Catholic discourse, while simultaneously and paradoxically deploying religious language as a medium of spiritual fullness to imply Elizabeth's quasi-divine status. I have written before of how many Elizabethan theologians and aesthetic theorists asserted the legitimacy of reverential images of the Queen through elaborate manoeuvres simultaneously separating and drawing together the spiritual and secular spheres. Glorious images were legitimate so long as they were outside the Church (this was the separation of spiritual and secular); but eulogistic images of Elizabeth were legitimate in any case since she represented a spiritual truth, as Protestant symbol and chosen agent of God (this was the drawing together of spiritual and secular). 'Times eldest sonne' is a good example of this simultaneous distinction and conjunction of the secular and sacred: Elizabeth is praised in religious and Catholic terms which could be read as merely denoting courtly love, and/ or as elevating her to a spiritual status previously and erroneously occupied by the Virgin Mary.

The iconography of the 1590 retirement tilts was reprised two years later, in entertainments provided for Elizabeth's visit to Lee's home at Ditchley. On the second day, a chaplain narrated how an old knight, Loricus (using the same title for Lee as at Woodstock in 1575), was 'now a newe religious Hermite: who, as heretofore he professed the obedience of his youthe, by constant seruice of the worldes best Creature, so at this present presentethe the deuotion of his yeares by continuall seruing of the worldes onlie Cre[a]tor'. In all his endeavours, Loricus had made 'solemne sacrifices to the Idoll of his harte'. The chaplain described how one day Loricus ranged abroad in his meditations, and, coming across the chaplain's cell, asked him:

> where lyes the highe-waie I pray you. Marry here, gentell Knight (sayde I) looking on my booke with mine eyes, & poyntyng up to heauen with my finger; it is the very Kinges hie-waye. You say true in deede (quoth he) the verie Queenes hie-waye.

Loricus resolved to 'become an Heremite, I should be his Chaplaine, & both ioyntlie ioyne in prayers for one prince, & the prayses of one god,' and for this purpose they built a lodging called the Crown Oratory. Afterwards, Loricus fell into a mortal sickness; but the Queen now entered the oratory, and miraculously cured him by her presence. When he blessed the Queen for curing him, 'Hereat Stellatus, his Chappelaine, besought him to blesse God onelie, for it was Gods spirite who recouered his spirites. Truthe (quoth he again) yet whosoeuer blesseth her, blesseth God in her: and euer blessed be God for her'.[74]

Throughout this entertainment, quasi-religious veneration of Elizabeth was justified on the grounds that she was the instrument of God and the true earthly image of the divine purpose. This was underwritten not only by patriotic Protestantism but also by neo-Platonism: on the first day of the Ditchley entertainment, an old knight (almost certainly Lee)[75] hailed Elizabeth as 'O mortall substance of immortall glorie! / To whom all creatures ells are shaddowes deemed'.[76] In these terms, praying to her as an icon in the way that idolaters prayed to the Virgin would be wholly legitimate, in the same way that the destruction of the icon of Mary at Euston Hall in the sight of the resplendent Virgin Queen was seen as legitimate:[77] the Virgin represented false distraction from the true worship of God, whereas Elizabeth was a true earthly image of the divine, such that homage paid to her was homage paid directly to God.

Thus 'Vivat Eliza for an Ave Mari' expresses far more than just mass compensation for the psychological loss of a symbolic virgin-mother figure. Those who read it in this way fail to do justice to the song's wit, finesse and playfulness. On one level, it simply represents Elizabeth as a leader now to be prayed for rather than fought for by her retiring champion. On a second level it represents Elizabeth as a fit object for prayer in the sense that the terms 'saint' and 'goddess' represent a courtly love mistress, which in turn denotes Elizabeth as an object of political allegiance. On a third level, the line represents Elizabeth as a fit object for prayer in that she is a true agent and earthly image of God. I would argue that all these meanings are present in this deft and elegant song, interacting and resonating against one another, legitimating veneration of the Queen while simultaneously rebuffing potential charges of idolatry, and thus representing in capsule form the complex attitude to royal iconography sustained by the Elizabethan court.

vii. Ralegh's 'Walsingham'

Sir Walter Ralegh also made use of Catholic terminology to represent his desire for, and in turn his political service to, the Queen. In a poem beginning 'Our Passions are most like to Floods and streames', he wrote of how:

> ... I sue to serue
> A Saint of such Perfection,
> As all desire, but none deserue,
> A place in her Affection.[78]

Much of his poetry is highly charged, and bespeaks an intensity of feeling such that it seems inadequate to describe him as using courtly love as a metaphor for political allegiance. Rather, in the poetry which he wrote about his relationship with Elizabeth, love and power seem to be inextricably intertwined; his laments for his lapses from her favour suggest a tormenting disturbance of his sense of selfhood and the disappointment of a desire in which the erotic and the ambitious cannot be separated.

His poem 'Walsingham' uses specifically Marian associations to represent some of these feelings generated by the figure of Elizabeth. The piece was composed some time before 5 March 1593, when it was entered in the Stationers' Register. It alludes to the shrine of Our Lady of Walsingham, the popular pilgrimage centre, which had been dismantled by Crown commissioners in 1538.[79] The poem uses ballad form, and opens:

> As you came from the holy land
> of Walsinghame
> Mett you not with my true loue
> by the way as you came –

The first four lines in the manuscript replace the following four deleted lines:

> As you went to Walsingam
> To that holy lande
> Met you not with my true loue
> By the waye as you went:

The text continues:

> How shall I know your trew loue
> That haue mett many one
> As I went to the holy lande
> That haue come that haue gone
> She is neyther whyte nor browne
> Butt as the heauens fayre
> There is none hathe a form so deuine
> In the earth or the ayre
> Such a*n* one did I meet good *Sir*
> Suche an Angelyke face
> Who lyke a queene lyke a nymph did appere
> by her gate by her grace . . .[80]

The speaker goes on to lament his abandonment by this mistress, presumably Elizabeth. Like Ralegh's longer poem about his relationship with the Queen, *The Ocean to Scinthia*,[81] the piece veers between wondering adoration of the figure of the angelic queen, vilification of her as a typically fickle woman whose love is 'a trustless ioye', and meditation upon mutability.

Ralegh's use of the ballad-form bespeaks the survival of Catholic refrains in popular, orally transmitted forms. Many scholars have reasonably assumed that his poem makes use of an established ballad dating from the years when the shrine was still in operation.[82] Pilgrimages were a popular subject for ballads and songs, apparently both before and after the Reformation. A madrigal published in 1609 includes in its nonsense-refrain allusion to another pilgrimage-centre, the shrine of Thomas à Becket at Canterbury:

> Heave and ho,
> Rumbelo.
> Hey trolo, troly lo!
>
> My lady's gone to Canterbury,
>   Saint Thomas, be her boot!
> She met with Kate of Malmesbury,
>   Why weep'st thou, maple root?[83]

There are some specific ballad-analogues for Ralegh's 'Walsingham',[84] but since recorded examples date from after his version, difficulty lies in establishing whether these ballads pre-existed Ralegh's poem, or whether both these ballads and his poem derive from earlier sources, or whether these ballads themselves derive from his poem. Such a conversion of a courtly poem into a popular ballad would not have been unprecedented: in 1587 Ralegh wrote a poem to the Queen beginning 'Fortune hath taken thee away my Love', to which she wrote a verse-reply, and the exchange was combined with an existing ballad to produce the popular 'Fortune my foe, why doest thou frowne on me'.[85]

There is a ballad which was copied into a manuscript miscellany between 1600 and 1603 from some earlier printed source which opens:

> As I went to *Walsingham*,
>   to the shrine, with speede,
> Mett I with a Jollye palmer,*
>   in a pilgrim's weede.
> Nowe, God saue yow, iolly Palmer!
>   *Fran* Welcome, Ladye gaye!
> Oft haue I su'de to thee for love.
>   *Besse* Oft haue I sayd yow naye.[86]

With this introduction of different speakers, the ballad turns into a mini-drama in four acts, telling how Bess, a farmer's wife, eludes the adulterous designs of Francis, the palmer, by substituting herself with his own wife at a nocturnal assignation. The story resembles both Chaucerian fabliau and Shakespearian bed-trick; and the song is another example of the frequency of Bess or Bessy as a name for a ballad-heroine who is the object of a wooer.[87] This is not to suggest that Bess here stands in some sort of direct parodic relation to Ralegh's regal mistress, but rather that this 'Jolly palmer' ballad provides evidence of cross-currents between courtly poetry and popular song, and of the survival of the pilgrimage-motif. This ballad may have been in existence for some years, and may be the source on which Ralegh drew. However, it seems more likely that the 'Jolly palmer' ballad is a derivative of either Ralegh's or another song, since it carries the instruction 'To the tune of *Walsingham*'.

Another ballad somewhat surprisingly combines echoes of Ralegh with a bawdy theme: this is 'The contented cuckold', a black letter

---

* pilgrim

broadside ballad from about 1625. It is a dialogue between a New-
castle man whose wife has left him, and a seaman, of whom he
enquires:

> And metest thou not my true Loue
>   by the way as you came
> How should I know your true Loue,
>   that haue met many a one,
> She is neyther whit nor black
>   but as the heauens faire
> Her lookes are very beautifull,
>   none may with her compare.[88]

The verbal echoes continue, but unlike Ralegh's angelic nymph this
mistress has put on a gay gown and petticoat and taken a coal-ship
to London in search of pleasure. In a second part of the song, which
is devoid of echoes of Ralegh, the husband takes ship with the
sailor, pursues his wife to London and brings her home. This song
also resembles an Elizabethan ballad, 'Came you not from New-
castle', and so may represent a conflation of two or more popular
songs.[89]

A tune known as 'Walsingham' certainly existed by the mid-
1590s, when it appears in several virginals books, variously titled as
'Walsingham', 'Have with you to Walsingham' or 'As I went to
Walsingham'.[90] In *Have with you to Saffron Walden*, 1596, Nashe
mockingly lists Gabriel Harvey's favourite works of literature as
various ballads, including 'As I went to Walsingham'.[91] A number
of other late sixteenth-century and seventeenth-century authors refer
to 'Walsingham' as a popular song, often with the implication that
it is a foolish love-ditty.[92]

The fact that Ralegh's poem is either the source of this popular
song, or that it derives from this popular song which pre-existed it,
is attested to by two other literary sources. One of the snatches of
song which drifts to the surface of Ophelia's disordered mind is
'How should I your true love know / From another one?', although
she goes on to present her pilgrim as a wayfarer to the shrine of St
James at Compostela rather than Walsingham: 'By his cockle hat
and staff /And his sandal shoon'.[93] In *The Knight of the Burning
Pestle*, published 1613, among the snatches of ballads sung by Old
Merrythought is:

> As you came from *Walsingham*,
>   From that holy land,
> There met you not with my tru-love
>   By the way as you came?[94]

It is thus hard to establish the relation between Ralegh's 'Walsingham' and 'Walsingham' as popular love-song. What is clear, however, is that references to particular pilgrimage centres continued as a motif in folk-songs, especially amorous ones, long after the practice of pilgrimage had died out in England. In Ralegh's poem, the journey to Walsingham has become a lover's quest which is timeless and archetypal.

At the same time, Ralegh's preoccupation with mutability echoes another kind of 'Walsingham' ballad which certainly existed before his poem, and which may be the source of the tune called 'Walsingham'. This is the recusant lament for the destruction of the shrine, which must surely have been composed not long after the event in 1538, although its enduring currency is manifested in its inclusion in a manuscript collection from about 1600.[95] It begins:

> In the wrackes* of walsingam
>   Whom should I chuse,
> But the Queene of walsingam,
>   to be guide to my muse.

The metre is similar to that of Ralegh's poem and the other 'Walsingham' love-ballads, but the mistress who presides over this lament is the Virgin Mary.

The speaker goes on to grieve:

> Such were the workes of walsingam:
>   while she did stand
> Such are the wrackes as now do shewe
>   of that holy land,
> Levell Levell with the ground
>   the towres do lye
> Which with their golden glitteringe tops
>   Pearsed once to the skye,

---

* destruction, devastation, ruin

> Wher weare gates no gates ar nowe,
> the waies unknowen
> Wher the presse of peares* did passe
> While her fame far was blowen . . .[96]

Although he uses images of nature rather than fallen buildings, and although his grief is for his personal loss rather than loss of a shrine, the speaker of Ralegh's poem strikes a very similar note:

> She hath lefte me here all alone
> All allone as vnknowne . . .
> . . . I haue loude her all my youth
> Butt no[w] ould as you see
> Loue lykes not the fallyng frute
> From the wythered tree . . .

The two poems share the theme of the transience of earthly joy; and the 'unknowen', unfrequented condition of the 'waies' of Walsingham is echoed not only by Ralegh's complaint here of being 'All allone as vnknowne', but also by another of his poems, known as 'Farewell to the Court', published in 1593, in which he lamented that 'My lost delights now cleane from sight of land, / Haue left me all alone in vnknowne waies'.[97]

Ralegh's laments for the loss of his mistress's affection are inextricably intertwined with regret for falling from political favour. It is concomitant upon this that mutability, the transience of worldly joy, is a prevalent concern of much of his poetry; and since it seems that pilgrimage-ballads, and specifically Walsingham-ballads, were associated with both forsaken love and worldly mutability, it is easy to see why the form appealed to him. Finally, though, Ralegh's 'Walsingham' mainly provides evidence of how Catholic terminology persisted in currency in popular culture through the entire course of Elizabeth's reign; and of how it could be used uncontroversially to evoke the plangency and timelessness of folk-song rather than any direct identification of Elizabeth with the Virgin.

viii. A secular Catholic revival

Ralegh's 'Walsingham', and the other songs and courtly poems from this period which make use of Catholic terminology, indicate a

---

* peers

survival of knowledge of Catholic devotional practices. The private use of some of these, including the saying of the Ave Maria and the use of the rosary, had no doubt continued uninterrupted in Catholic families and those parts of the country where the old faith still had a strong hold. Other more public practices, such as pilgrimages and the use of shrines, had ceased, but evidently persisted in people's memories. Whereas the early years of the regime were marked by insecurity, tentativeness, and concern to forge a new and distinctive Protestant iconography, confidence and the passage of time appear to have brought relaxation as regards more open use of Catholic iconography.

This is evident from the extension of the 1590 Accession Day tilts beyond 17 November to encompass 19 November. This was formerly the feast day of St Elizabeth, but had been one of the thirty-eight feasts omitted from the reformed breviary in 1568. The appropriation of the former saint's day seems to have been conscious: Sir Richard Brakenbury wrote to Lord Talbot on 20 November: 'Thene the 19 day, beynge *Saynt Elyzabeth's daye*, th'Erle of Comberland, th'Erle of Essex, and my Lord Burge, dyd chaleng all comers, sex courses apeace, whiche was very honorably performed.'[98]

The resurgence of such open allusion to Catholic practices in court culture of the latter years of Elizabeth's reign might be thought of almost in fashion terms as a secularised Catholic revival: a long enough period had passed for these terms to have nostalgic appeal for the older generation and novelty value for the younger. It might also be connected to the general medieval revivalism of the court in the later years of the reign, with the enthusiasm for jousting and chivalric legend: hermits and beadsmen decoratively peopled the same kinds of landscapes as green knights, wild men, fairy queens and other such favourite characters of romance and pageant. Catholic terminology was apparently perceived as secularised, even pagan, and therefore available in much the same way as classical mythography for literary and artistic use.

Another factor inducing the use of Catholic terminology was the increasing extravagance of panegyric of the Queen. Just as the Accession Day celebrations expanded to fill several days rather than just one, so panegyric of Elizabeth became increasingly prolific and voluminous into the 1590s. This seems to have resulted in some rivalry between writers to produce more and more attention-catching and inventive works. Thomas Churchyard, in some verses presented to the Queen in 1592, endearingly describes the predicament of the second-rate poet: he says that there are

> a multitude of people . . . running & preasing apace . . . some with rare inuentions & some with deep deuices to the honouring of your Maiestie. I feare . . . that ther is left no deuice, nor matter to study on, such is the bounty of our time, & forwardnes of their wittes which are learned, that all fine inuentions are smoothly reaped from my reach, & cunningly raked away from my vse or commoditie.[99]

As panegyric became increasingly exuberant and fanciful, writers seem to have been willing to look to a wide range of sources, and this included a diminishing of inhibitions towards adopting Catholic iconography.

6

The 1590s:
The Literature of
Disillusionment

The theory that Elizabeth became a replacement for the Virgin Mary
is often supported by quotations from texts which appear to praise
the Queen as a perfect, sacred icon. By the 1590s, as we have seen,
such praise was a well-established convention, and was supported
by arguments in Protestant theology and aesthetic theory. Something which can reasonably be called a 'cult of Elizabeth' had come
into existence. However, we should be cautious about reading
idealisations of the Queen at face value; especially because, alongside the mounting hyperbole of panegyric, some writers began to
question Elizabeth's supposed perfection and sacredness and to
challenge her iconic status. The very years which provide the strong-
est evidence of a cult at its zenith also produced reactions of negativity and even iconoclasm towards the Queen.

i. Mirrors more than one

The extravagance of 1590s panegyric includes not just the invention
of many different personae for Elizabeth by different competing
poets, as described by Churchyard, but also the creation of multiple
personae for Elizabeth within individual works. In the 1590 *Faerie
Queene* Spenser described himself as showing the Queen her image
'In mirrours more then one' (III proem 5): she was Gloriana, Una,
Belphoebe, Britomart, with more personae to come in the 1596 in-
stalment. A single short lyric by Ralegh named her as 'Cynthia,
Phoebe Flora / Diana, and Aurora'.[1] By 1599 we find the Prologue
to Dekker's *Old Fortunatus* presenting the following dialogue between two old men:

1. Are you then trauelling to the temple of *Eliza*?
2. Euen to her temple are my feeble limmes trauelling. Some cal

her *Pandora;* some *Gloriana,* some *Cynthia:* some *Belphoebe,* some *Astraea:* all by seuerall names to expresse seuerall loues: Yet all those names make but one celestiall body, as all those loues meete to create but one soule.
1. I am one of her owne countrie, and we adore her by the name of *Eliza.*[2]

This perception of the Queen as possessing diverse aspects requiring a plurality of titles provides a formal resemblance to both the cult of the Virgin and the cults of pagan goddesses, whose multiple personae, we might recall, were condemned in the official Church Homily 'Against Peril of Idolatry'.[3] This is not to say that the proliferation of personae of Elizabeth was a direct imitation of these older cults. Rather, it can be seen as arising from somewhat similar causes: the Virgin Mary acquired different aspects across the centuries as she was required to meet various symbolic needs, both spiritual and political; Elizabeth acquired different aspects as she was required to fulfil various symbolic needs, not only through time, but synchronically, because of her anomalousness as an unmarried and autonomous woman ruler.

Especially after it became clear that she would never marry, Elizabeth was an unprecedented and potentially disturbing figure. The iconography of panegyric had to do a lot of work of justification and naturalisation. As a woman ruler, Elizabeth needed to be perceived as being no less decisive, martial, just and eloquent than a male ruler. At the same time, she needed to exercise these stereotypically masculine virtues without being regarded as unnaturally mannish or Amazonian.[4] As a prominent woman, she needed to be perceived as a paragon of femininity and beauty. At the same time, she had to negotiate alternative models of feminine perfection: the virtue of her virginity had to be emphasised, but without representing her as unnaturally sterile, and this gave rise to parallel images of her as mistress or metaphorical mother.

As I have already mentioned, the introduction of classical goddesses into royal panegyric in the 1560s and 70s provided one means of accommodating contradictory aspects of the Queen as symbol: several goddesses could be used in a single text to represent her different qualities.[5] Some panegyrists brought together all her multiple aspects under the one title of Pandora (that is, 'the all-gifted one').[6] Other panegyric made much use of dualism: the potential contradictions in the figure of the Queen were not suppressed but foregrounded, to represent her as bringing binary oppositions into a mystical and miraculous union. The popular image of the queen as Venus Virgo is an example of this, personifying her fusion of desirability and chastity.

Many texts accentuated Elizabeth's combination of masculine and feminine qualities, such as James Aske's *Elizabetha Triumphans*, 1588, a celebration of the Armada victory, in which she is 'A Maiden Queene, and yet of courage stout', with the effect that her followers 'did joyntly joy and feare'.[7] Similarly, in the figure of Britomart Spenser provided Elizabeth with a mythical ancestor who was a warrior-woman, but softened any implications of excessive masculinity. At crises in martial combat her helmet is removed or displaced, revealing a cascade of golden hair (III.ix.20, IV.vi.20). The purpose of her quest is to find her destined husband, and its outcome will be that she is called from arms by her 'wombes burden' (III.iii.28). In any case, her arms are to a large degree a metaphor for her chastity. Again, antithesis predominates: '. . . she was full of amiable grace, / And manly terrour mixed therewithall' (III.i.46).

The idea of the King's Two Bodies provided another foundation for dualistic royal iconography. This conception of the Queen as possessing both a body politic and a body natural seems to underly the explanatory letter from Spenser to Ralegh which was published with the *Faerie Queene*:

> In that Faery Queene I meane glory in my generall intention, but in my particular I conceiue the most excellent and glorious person of our soueraine the Queene, and her kingdome in Faery land. And yet in some places els, I doe otherwise shadow her. For considering she beareth two persons, the one of a most royall Queene or Empresse, the other of a most vertuous and beautifull Lady, this latter part in some places I doe express in Belphoebe.[8]

Such iconography is double-sided in another sense than simply its obvious emphasis on dualism. It can be read either as celebrating oneness, the union of diverse qualities in the sole person of the Queen; or as acknowledging and even accentuating division. The alternative facets of Elizabeth, as Queen and woman, quasi-divine symbol and fallible mortal, can be set against each other to introduce a note of criticism, as in Ralegh's 'Walsingham', where veneration of Elizabeth as heavenly, divine, angelic Queen is succeeded by bitter resentment of her fickleness as typically feminine: 'Of women kynde suche indeed is the loue'.[9] Similarly, panegyrics which create a multiplicity of personae for the Queen can be seen either as praising her fusion of so many diverse virtues in one person, or as celebrating her superabundance of gifts, or as representing through fragmentation the absurdity of the fiction that all these contradictory qualities could be combined in one person.[10] 1590s panegyric becomes progressively divided between increasingly extravagant professions of devotion to the Queen, and oblique expressions of dissent and disillusionment, which in turn make iconographic use of the incipient fractures between the diverse aspects of Elizabeth as Queen and woman.

ii. Fulke Greville

By now it was conventional to celebrate the Queen as a sacred figure. However, alongside this there existed other currents of Elizabethan political thought which stressed the humanity of monarchs in general, which regarded monarchs who aspired to place themselves above earthly law as tyrants, and which questioned the use of visual splendour and extravagant praise in the support of temporal power.[11] Views of this sort were held by Fulke Greville, who wrote in his play *Alaham*, c.1599–1600:[12]

> People are superstitious, caught with showes:
> To power why doe they else their freedome giue,
> But that in others pompe these *shadowes* liue? [13]

Here he recognises the political force of visual show, but suggests that this makes it dangerous; and that it exploits the same human weaknesses as heathenish or popish idolatry.

Some of Greville's earlier work even seems to imply republican sympathies: 'No People, No. Question these Thrones of Tyrants; / Reuiue your old equalities of Nature'.[14] However, while condemning tyranny, in his *Treatise of Monarchy* (c.1599–1604) he also took a critical view of democracy as tending towards anarchy. Relatively speaking, monarchy is preferable; he supports

> Formes establisht, which must be obay'd
> As levells for the world to guide her owne,
> Foundations against Anarchie well layd,
> Whose beinge is but beings overthrowne:

Where Thrones (as mortall shrynes) with mortall feare
Must be ador'd, and worshipt everie where.[15]

Monarchy is the least bad form of government, provided that the
individual occupying the throne does not abuse it:

... who well observes a monarchie,
Shall finde disorder there a fatall thinge,
The head beinge both of unprosperitie,
Good fortune, fame, or infamie the springe.[16]

This is to imply that monarchs are fallible, rather than perfect images of God.

During Elizabeth's reign Greville was often critical of the Crown
and its policy. Much of his sonnet-sequence *Caelica* was written
before the Queen's death, and contains negative attitudes towards
monarchy.[17] In Sonnet 90, he compares the dictatorship of the Turk-
ish Sultan with the so-called 'Christian freedome' of English law,
which in fact 'proues ... crooked as power lists to draw, / The rage
or grace that lurkes in Princes brests'.[18] In 92, he wryly comments,
'place a Coronet on whom you will, / You straight see all great in
him, but his *Ill*'. Even so, the sequence contains an iconic and ad-
miring depiction of Elizabeth, in Sonnet 81:[19]

Vnder a Throne I saw a Virgin sit,
The red, and white Rose quarter'd in her face;
Starre of the North, and for true guards to it,
Princes, Church, States, all pointing out her Grace.
The homage done her was not borne of Wit,
Wisdome admir'd, Zeale tooke Ambitions place,
State in her eyes taught Order how to fit,
And fixe Confusions vnobseruing race.
    Fortune can here claime nothing truly great,
    But that this Princely Creature is her seat.

This poem contains vaguely Marian resonances in its use of the
emblems of rose and star, although, as I have said before, these
were by no means exclusively Marian epithets. The idea of the rose
being 'quarter'd' in this virgin's face, explicitly linking the blazon
of a courtly mistress with the heraldic blazon, identifies it as the
Tudor crest. Perhaps the most striking iconographic feature of the

poem is the way it sets Elizabeth up as a static and monumental figure at the centre of a tableau, with all orders of society looking to her as the focal point of the cosmos. The line 'The homage done her was not borne of Wit' is problematic and sounds a note of unease, at first sight perhaps implying criticism of admiration of the Queen as unthinking, but this is quickly effaced by the succeeding lines which suggest that higher qualities than mere Wit, namely Wisdom, Zeal, State, Order, and Fortune, are all in her service. Elizabeth is erected by Greville as an emblem of judicious rule. Even as a shrewd critic of civil idolatry, he was evidently not averse to a display of respectful esteem towards the Queen as symbol.

After her death, he wrote again about Elizabeth in his biography of Sidney (c.1610–11), where his picture of her seems to be coloured by a nostalgic glow. Even here, though, his praise of the Queen is consistent with his earlier thinking, in that he depicts her as no tyrant, with a proper sense of her own subjection to human law. He writes: 'how sovereign soever she were by throne, birth, education, and nature, yet was she content to cast her own affections into the same moulds her subjects did, and govern all her rights by their laws.'[20] For Greville, in this retrospective portrait of Elizabeth, her perfection lay in her knowledge of her own imperfection.

iii. Peace, grace and mercy

The iconic quality of Greville's virgin in *Caelica* 81, and the way in which she is surrounded by allegorical figures, both strongly resemble Spenser's figure of Mercilla, who appears in Book V of *The Faerie Queene*, one of the three Books first published in 1596. She stands both for Elizabeth and for 'peace and clemencie / With which high God had blest her happie land' (V.ix.30).

The figure of Mercilla extends an already well-established tradition of identifying Elizabeth with mercy and grace. I have written previously of how, from a fairly early stage in the reign, Elizabeth's subjects embraced the idea of her as mild and tender mother of the nation; this could be taken to imply her liberality towards them, in contrast to the horrors of tyrannical rule.[21] I have also described how, in a variety of texts, she appears as a sort of mediatrix, a channel for divine grace.[22] These aspects of her iconography do have Marian resonances, but they were largely produced by enduring traditions of the 'safe' representation of female power. Mercy and grace were virtues which could comfortably be identified with a female monarch without suggesting either that she was inadequate as a ruler, or that she was unnaturally mannish.

Thus, for the visit to Norwich on the progress of 1578, an oration was composed to be given in front of the hospital for the poor which praised Elizabeth for her mercifulness, presenting it as a godlike and princely virtue.[23] Some Accession Day verses of 1587 praised in one breath Elizabeth's 'Princely giftes, her Iustice mylde, her Peacefull lasting dayes'.[24] The ballad on the Armada with the refrain *'Elizabeth lord save'* declared:

> For Iustice Iust for grace and pittie both
> no Realme hath had her like.
> She pardons them full oft that would be loth
> to hold if they durst strike.

The point of the Armada victory is that *'Elizabeth so braue* / The lord did quite from tirant swaye'.[25] Part of the picture of Gloriana as the perfect monarch, along with her greatness and her lofty throne, is that 'in her face faire peace, and mercy doth appeare' (II.ii.40).

Invocation of Elizabeth's feminine compassion could also be a means of distancing her from some of the more unpleasantly brutal business of government. In James Aske's poem in celebration of the Armada victory, *Elizabetha Triumphans*, 1588, he prefaces the description of the victory over Spain with an account of the English intervention against the French in Scotland in 1560. He presents the military campaign as a massacre of England's enemies, describing with grisly relish the carnage and the howling of women and children. Then comes an abrupt shift of tone:

> Our gracious Queene, who never thurst for blood,
> (When thus the Frenchman once had felt her force)
> Did use a meane which nearer was to peace.[26]

Cecil was sent north to make the Treaty of Edinburgh. Aske has it both ways: his poem caters to jingoism and bloodthirstiness in its depiction of England's aggression, but then the taint of barbarity is effaced by accentuating the pity and mercifulness of England's Queen. The feminine delicacy and tenderness of the Queen could be invoked to cosmeticise actions by her government which, though politically necessary, might appear distasteful; and, simultaneously, to absolve her of personal responsibility for such actions.

As some of these examples show, in catalogues of Elizabeth's virtues and accomplishments the terms mercy and grace are often accompanied by peace. Peace was a quality particularly able to bridge gender-definitions, especially when applied to Elizabeth, as it often was, in the epithet 'Prince of Peace'. In the proem to Book IV of *The Faerie Queene*, Elizabeth is 'The Queene of loue, and Prince of peace from heauen blest' (IV proem 4).[27] The term 'prince' was not necessarily masculine in the sixteenth century, meaning simply 'ruler'. However, while mercy and grace were traditionally associated with the Virgin Mary, the phrase 'Prince of Peace' invoked Christological associations, being drawn from the prophecy of the Messiah in Isaiah 9.6.

Despite this, conventional images of war as masculine and peace as feminine persisted through Elizabeth's reign. In the 'Aprill' Eclogue, Elisa is crowned with olives as a fit garland for a *princess*, which unlike 'prince' was a specifically gendered term:

> Olives bene for peace,
> When wars doe surcease:
> Such for a Princesse bene principall.

> (ll.124–6)

In the 'October' Eclogue, when Cuddie laments the decay of poetry through the lack of fit subjects and of patronage, Piers advises him:

> . . . sing of bloody Mars, of wars, of giusts.
> Turne thee to those, that weld the awful crowne,
> To doubted Knights, whose woundlesse armour rusts,
> And helmes unbruzed wexen dayly browne.

> There may thy Muse display her fluttryng wing,
> And stretch her self at large from East to West:
> Whither thou list in fayre *Elisa* rest,
> Or if thee please in bigger notes to sing,
> Advaunce the worthy whome shee loveth best,
> That first the white beare to the stake did bring.

> And when the stubborne stroke of stronger stounds,
> Has somewhat slackt the tenor of thy string:
> Of love and lustihead tho mayst thou sing,

And carrol lowde, and lead the Myllers rownde,
All were *Elisa* one of thilke same ring.

(ll.39–53)

Here Elisa, already presented in 'Aprill' as the fruit of the union of
Pan and Syrinx and therefore the personification of pastoral poetry,
is identified with the song of peace and holiday, while Leicester,
'the worthy whome shee loveth best', whose crest was a white bear
tied to a stake, is associated with the 'bigger notes' of war. E.K.
glosses 'woundlesse armour' as 'unwounded in warre, doe rust
through long peace'. Thus a somewhat intractable problem under-
lies Piers's advice: an epic poet needs heroic martial feats to write
about, yet Elizabeth's England has apparently abjured war.

In my discussion of Lyly's *Euphues and his England* and of Sidney's
Arcadia, I suggested that their representations of Elizabeth's paci-
fism, in which both use paradoxes, can be taken as superficially
acclaiming her achievements as miraculous, while implicitly criticising her reluctance to go to war as rendering the whole nation
idle and effeminised.[28] I want now to suggest that, as seen in
Spenser's figure of Mercilla, the other 'feminine' regal qualities of
mercy and grace could also be used to create a surface appearance
of panegyric while subtly communicating dissent. Like the arms of
war in the 'October' Eclogue, *Euphues and his England* and the *Arcadia*,
Mercilla's sword of justice is rusted: 'at her feet her sword was
likewise layde, / Whose long rest rusted the bright steely brand'.
Spenser reassures us that 'when as foes enforst, or friends sought
ayde, / She could it sternely draw, that all the world dismayde'
(V.ix.30). Nevertheless, the line between praising the Queen's restraint and criticising her inaction is acutely fine. In Spenser's *View
of the Present State of Ireland*, a dialogue, one of the speakers, Irenius,
declares that Ireland can only be reformed 'by the sworde', and 'by
the sworde I meante the Royall power of the Prince which oughte
to stretche it selfe forthe in her Chiefe strengthe'.[29] This text was
written in 1596, but was not published in Elizabeth's lifetime, probably because in it Spenser voiced his dissent from her regime more
candidly than in most of his published poetry.

Mercilla appears in Book V of *The Faerie Queene* as the judge
presiding at the trial of Duessa. Whereas in Book I Duessa was a
plurally allegorical figure of Deceit, the Roman Catholic Church,
and Mary Queen of Scots, she is now more closely identified with

the latter individual, with the trial scene fictionalising Mary Stuart's trial.[30] Through the 1580s, Elizabeth's supposed 'feminine' mercifulness had been much stressed in relation to the problem of the Queen of Scots. In the 1584–5 Parliament the Bill for the Queen's Safety was blocked by Elizabeth, and in his summing up Speaker Puckering sought to assuage the frustration of MPs by attributing her obstructiveness to 'her clement and pitiful nature'.[31] Elizabeth too, despite her sound political reluctance to set a precedent of execution of a fellow-monarch, also foregrounded her supposed feminine delicacy as a rhetorical means of strengthening her case: 'What will [my enemies] not now say, when it shall be spread that, for the safety of her life, a maiden queen could be content to spill the blood even of her own kinswoman?'[32] After the execution, W. Kempe, the author of *A Dutiful Invective, Against the moste haynous Treasons of Ballard and Babington*, 1587, retrospectively stressed Elizabeth's feminine scruples regarding the death sentence: 'Whereto our Queene with wonted grace and mercie beinge moued / Was lothe to yealde consent thereto, for that shee well her loued'. She confirmed the sentence 'with a fainting breath'.[33]

Just before the scene of Duessa's trial, Spenser suggests in canto vii of his Book of Justice that a feminine quality of mercy should have precedence over masculine justice. Britomart has a vision at the Temple of Isis of a crocodile under the feet of the goddess's statue. The vision is interpreted thus:

> . . . that same Crocodile *Osyris* is,
> That vnder *Isis* feete doth sleepe for euer:
> To shew that clemence oft in things amis,
> Restraines those sterne behests, and cruell doomes of his.

(V.vii.22)

The crocodile is also identified with Artegall, the Knight of Justice; so that, in this idealised icon, harsh justice is shown as being restrained and ameliorated by feminine clemency.

However, this is an abstract emblem; the trial of Duessa depicts justice and mercy in action. The allegorical figure of Zeal leads the prosecution of Duessa, and brings as witnesses the Kingdom's care, Authority, the law of Nations, Religion, the Commons, and Justice. Pleading in her defence are figures of Pity, Regard of womanhood, Danger, Nobility of birth, and Grief. Then, though, the case against her is made conclusive by the calling of yet more prosecution witnesses: Ate (i.e. strife), Murder, Sedition, Incontinence, Adultery and Impiety (V.ix.43–8). Clearly the charges against her outweigh the claims in her favour; but Mercilla's response is as follows:

> But she, whose Princely breast was touched nere
> With piteous ruth of her so wretched plight,
> Though plaine she saw by all, that she did heare,
> That she of death was guiltie found by right,
> Yet would not let iust vengeance on her light;
> But rather let in stead thereof to fall
> Few perling drops from her faire lampes of light;
> The which she couering with her purple pall
> Would haue the passion hid, and vp arose withall.
>
> (V.ix.50)

Spenser ends the canto here, suspending the action at a point when it looks as if Mercilla's clemency might induce her to pardon Duessa, an outcome which the depiction of the trial has led us to regard as wrong. Mercilla's tears of compassion may be beautiful, but they are also superfluous, and possibly even obstructive of 'iust vengeance'.

At the opening of the next canto the reader is held in suspense to hear Mercilla's verdict while Spenser spends two stanzas praising mercy, and one praising Mercilla. Mercy is celebrated as a divine attribute:

> ... in th'Almighties euerlasting seat
> She first was bred, and borne of heauenly race;
> From thence pour'd down on men, by influence of grace.
>
> (V.x.1)

However, it is also defined as a virtue which seeks to reform and save, but 'neuer doth from doome of right depart' (V.x.2). After this hiatus, the fourth stanza somewhat hastily informs us that Mercilla did condemn Duessa, when

> ... strong constraint did her thereto enforce.
> And yet euen then ruing her wilfull fall,
> With more then needfull naturall remorse.
>
> (V.x.4)

Several things are going on here. In the first place, as in Aske's presentation of the Scottish campaign in *Elizabetha Triumphans,* the forceful action of Elizabeth's government is shown to be politically essential, while she personally, through emphasis on her feminine virtues, is elevated above controversial events and exonerated from blame. The additional effect of the episode, however, is to cast the Queen's compassion in an ambiguous light. A disjunction is implied between mercy in the abstract, as a divine ideal, and the pragmatic needs of earthly life and human politics. When we first encounter Mercilla on her throne, she is a static icon, like Greville's virgin sitting under a throne. Although her identity as personification of mercy could associate her with the Virgin Mary as mediatrix, Spenser chooses instead to echo biblical texts concerning God on his mercy-seat or throne of justice.[34] In the divine sphere, mercy is masculine, iconic, timeless. In the human sphere, however, excessive mercy can be effeminate, inexpedient, inappropriate.[35] The depiction of Mercilla thus registers some unease with Elizabeth as sacred icon and as paragon of feminine virtues.

iv. Lunar imagery

One of the most common images of Elizabeth in the last fifteen years or so of her reign was that of the moon-goddess, Cynthia or Diana. Diana had been used in varying ways as a representative of virginity in masques performed for Elizabeth since the earliest years of the reign; and in texts like the 'Aprill' Eclogue, 1579, Elizabeth's beauty had been compared with that of the moon-goddess. An early example of the use of Cynthia as a persona for the Queen was John Lyly's *Endimion* (published 1591, but possibly written in 1585).[36] However, it was in the 1590s that the use of this figure really flourished, producing such notable works as Ralegh's *Ocean to Scinthia* (1592? – see below), George Peele's *The Honour of the Garter* (1593), George Chapman's *The Shadow of Night* (1594), and Ben Jonson's *Cynthia's Revels* (1600).

The moon was an established motif in iconography of the Virgin Mary.[37] Origen, Ambrose and Augustine had all seen the partnership of the sun and moon, in which the moon reflects the sun's light, as an emblem of the relationship between Christ and his Church. The identification of Mary with the Church in the Middle Ages meant that the lunar imagery was transposed onto her.[38] It was reinforced by the iconography of the Woman Clothed with the

Sun, who has the moon under her feet and a crown of stars (Revelation 12.1). From the late fifteenth century, the Virgin standing on the moon became a standard icon of the Immaculate Conception.[39] Because the moon was also associated with the cycles of women's bodies, pagan moon-goddesses like Diana and Isis had been regarded as patronesses of fertility and childbirth. Unsurprisingly, in view of the fact that one of her primary attributes was maternality, Mary also inherited this role from them.[40]

However, far more was involved in application of the motif to Elizabeth than mere appropriation of a Marian attribute. For one thing, Ralegh seems to have been instrumental in popularising the name of Cynthia for the Queen, and had personal reasons for doing so: Elizabeth's nick-name for him was 'Water',[41] so there was a particular aptness in his representing himself as in the thrall of the moon, drawn in and out of her favour like the movement of the tides. Spenser told him that he named 'Belphoebe, fashioning her name according to your owne excellent conceipt of Cynthia, (Phoebe and Cynthia being both names of Diana.)'[42] This statement was dated 1589, indicating that Ralegh had already written Cynthia-poems by that date (either early drafts of *The Ocean to Scinthia*, or other poems now lost). Indeed, in a portrait of Ralegh from 1588, dressed in the Queen's colours of black and white, a tiny crescent moon looks down from the top left-hand corner.[43]

Some reasons why the image should have gained general popularity are illustrated by the incidental appearance of Elizabeth as moon-goddess in Shakespeare's *Midsummer Night's Dream* (1594/5):

> That very time I saw, but thou couldst not,
> Flying between the cold moon and the earth
> Cupid, all arm'd; a certain aim he took
> At a fair vestal, throned by the west,
> And loos'd his love-shaft smartly from his bow,
> As it should pierce a hundred thousand hearts;
> But I might see young Cupid's fiery shaft
> Quench'd in the chaste beams of the wat'ry moon;
> And the imperiall votaress passed on
> In maiden meditation, fancy-free.[44]

The simple fact that the moon is a heavenly body invokes qualities of radiance, ethereality, mysticism and other-worldliness. At the same time, the classical tradition identifies the moon with virginity and female power. The Virgin Mary had herself taken over these associations from pagan sources; thus no direct identification with Mary is necessarily implied.

Other factors contributed to the distinctive aptness of the lunar image to Elizabeth. Like Diana/Cynthia, the Queen enjoyed hunting as her favourite pastime. The association of the moon with water and the oceans could be used to assert English claims to imperial power, as at the Queen's visit to Elvetham in 1591: an elaborate pool was constructed upon which water-pageants took place to entertain 'Faire Cinthia the wide Ocean's Empresse'.[45] It is therefore inadequate to view images of Elizabeth as moon-goddess merely as appropriations of Marian iconography. Representations of Elizabeth developed significances of the moon which had not formed part of the cult of the Virgin. At the same time, some attributes which the Virgin Mary had inherited from pagan moon-goddesses were not appropriated to Elizabeth, especially their responsibility for fertility and for soothing women's birth-pangs.[46]

However, lunar imagery is worth dwelling on at length in this study, for two reasons. First, the use of the lunar image to represent Elizabeth's supposed immortality and immutability perpetuates certain attitudes towards the female body and sexuality which were also present in the mediaeval cults of the Virgin and female saints. Secondly, the moon was a dualistic image, with a dark side as well as a bright side, which enabled apparent celebration of Elizabeth as a quasi-divine icon to incorporate negative undertones of criticism.

v. Immutability

The moon could be associated with power over time and with immutability, since it goes through a cycle of perpetual self-renewal. This accorded with a trend in panegyric to celebrate the Queen's longevity, and even to profess belief in her immortality.

A number of different cultural currents combined to produce this claim. In the first place, prayers for the Queen's long life were a well-established feature of all displays of loyalty and patriotism.[47] It had also become a convention, of which the entertainments at Kenilworth in 1575 provide an early example, to assert that time stood still for the duration of a visit by the Queen; in other words, time was in her thrall.[48] I have mentioned in previous chapters that the transition in the late 1570s and early 1580s towards certainty of the Queen's virginity as never-ending was naturally accompanied

by increased interest in her longevity, as in the Norwich entertainments and Blenerhasset's *Revelation*. Furthermore, there was
evidence that God had miraculously preserved the Queen from
numerous mortal dangers, such as the threats to her safety during
her sister's reign, the various Catholic plots, and the Armada. Add
all of this together, plus the very fact of the Queen's advanced
years, and the result was expressions of hope and even belief that
she would live forever.

Thomas Kyd, in *Soliman and Perseda*, c.1588, gave the following
speech to Death, associating Elizabeth with the moon-goddess
Cynthia, another guise of Diana:

> I, now will *Death*, in his most haughtie pride,
> Fetch his imperiall Carre from deepest hell,
> And ride in triumph through the wicked world;
> Sparing none but sacred *Cynthias* friend,
> Whom *Death* did feare before her life began:
> For holy fates haue grauen it in their tables
> That *Death* shall die, if he attempt her end,
> Whose life is heauens delight, and *Cynthias* friend.[49]

An epilogue from 1599, possibly by Shakespeare, expressed a wish:

> that the babe which now is yong
> & hathe yet no vse of tongue
> many a shrouetyde here may bow
> to that empresse I doe now
> that the children of these lordes
> sitting at your counsell bourdes
> maye be graue & aeged seene
> of her that was ther father Quene
> once I wishe this wishe again
> heauen subscribe yt with amen.[50]

The fiction developed that as well as being immune to death,
Elizabeth was also immune to the ravages of age and time. A 'Her-
mit's Oration' presented during the entertainments for Elizabeth at
Theobalds in 1594 asserted that:

> with theis same eyes doe I behold you the self-same Queene, in
> the same esteate of person, strength and beautie, in which soe

many yeares past I beheld yow, finding noe alteration but in admiration, in soe much as I am perswaded, when I looke aboute me on your trayne, that Time, which catcheth everye body, leaves only you untouched.[51]

The Queen's portrait image became a 'mask of youth', as seen in numerous Hilliard miniatures and the Rainbow Portrait at Hatfield House.[52] She was shown with the flowing hair and uncovered bosom of a virgin, and the unlined face and skin of youth, implying that her sexual intactness had brought with it resistance to bodily decay. At Norwich in 1578 and in Blenerhasset's *Revelation*, 1582, it had already been implied that Elizabeth had earned immortality by means of her sexual purity.[53] Sir Arthur Gorges also wrote in the 1580s that 'hir bewtyfull lymmes triumphant over tyme / Are banyshte sweete delights through Devyne chastytie'.[54] Triumph over sexuality was interpreted as triumph over the Fall, in turn enabling triumph over the penalty for the Fall, mortality. Elizabeth's motto, 'Semper Eadem', 'Always one and the same', came to signify not simply constancy, integrity and singularity, but also a miraculous physical purity and immutability.

This provides a point of resemblance with the cult of the Virgin. It was widely held in the medieval Church, supported by many apocryphal legends, that Mary's body had not suffered dissolution in death, and that this was a direct consequence of the fact that she had resisted sexual contamination of the body in life. One such text has Jesus saying to Mary in her sepulchre, 'Rise up my love and my kinswoman: thou that didst not suffer corruption by union of the flesh, shalt not suffer dissolution of the body . . .'. As Marina Warner comments, although the Virgin was not accorded all the divine attributes, 'agelessness and immortality are hers'; and this tradition was founded in a deep-seated and enduring association in Christian symbolism between sex, sin and death.[55] The legends of numerous female martyrs were grounded in the same belief that the virgin body was pure and holy, and that chastity, asceticism and the endurance of torture – in sum, the denial of the body – could achieve spiritual purity and some form of reversal of the penalties for the Fall.[56] Just such an identification of different kinds of bodily purity seems to have become attached to Elizabeth, such that praise of her virginity developed into praise of her triumph over time, age and death.

Examples of the use of lunar imagery to represent the Queen's supposed powers of self-renewal include George Chapman's 'Hymnus in Cynthiam' in *The Shadow of Night*:

> Ascend thy chariot, and make earth admire
> Thy old swift changes, made a yong fixt prime,
> O let thy beautie scorch the wings of time.[57]

Similarly, a song praising Elizabeth published in Dowland's *Third Book of Songs*, 1603, stresses the fact that Cynthia's monthly cycle is part of a larger perpetuity:

> See the moon
> That ever in one change doth grow
> Yet still the same; and she is so;
> So, so, so, and only so.[58]

Some 'Verses sung to Queene *Elizabeth* by a Mairmead as shee past upon the Thames to Sir Arthur Gorges house at Chelsey', probably from November 1599, ran:

> Seas, yeares, and beawties ever ebb and flow
> But shee still fixt doth shine
> When all things dyed; her Raigne begins to growe
> To prove shee is devyne.
> Soe those in whose chast harts virtue survyves
> Finish their fading yeares, but not their lives.[59]

In this latter case there is an implication that, although Elizabeth has achieved longevity on earth, her reward of immortality remains to be gained in heaven. After all, it seems unlikely that her subjects believed in her literal immortality; especially as there was evidence before them that she was far from immune to the ravages of time. In the last decade of her reign the Queen was in her sixties. There are records of her dancing, hunting and continuing to undertake progresses on horseback during these last years,[60] and some foreign observers reported her amazing youthfulness, like that of a sixteen- or twenty-year-old.[61] Perhaps her use of wigs and make-up did produce a remarkably ageless public image, especially when seen from a distance.[62] However, other foreigners commented on the artificiality of these wigs, and on her wrinkles and her black, yellow or missing teeth.[63]

It is highly likely that the increasing hyperbole of panegyric was matched by deterioration in Elizabeth's physical state, producing a widening gulf between image and reality. Elizabeth's immortality and divinity was all the more loudly proclaimed as her mortality and humanity became more evident. This may not be unconnected to the fact that contemplation of her approaching death entailed considerable uncertainty about the future. Although it became increasingly evident that James VI of Scotland would succeed Elizabeth, she never formally named an heir.[64] By the 1590s only the old could remember a time when Elizabeth was not Queen, and the prospect of having a new monarch must have been both exciting and disturbing.

The preoccupation with age, time and death can be regarded as produced by anxiety about change as the reign was felt to be drawing to a close. Indeed, Chapman, in his 'Hymnus in Cynthiam', even as he celebrates Cynthia's triumph over time, writes of the earth's jealous desire to reclaim her, and of the fear that she 'Should yeeld to change, Eclips, or heauinesse'.[65] Wishes for the Queen's immortality were in effect wishes for the infinity of the Elizabethan era. We have seen how her virginity had become an emblem of the prosperity and proud independence of the English nation. Chapman, again, pairs celebration of the intactness of her body with thanksgiving that '[our] dores thou guardst against Imperious fate / Keeping our peacefull households safe from sack'.[66] Similarly, claims of her resistance to age were implicit wishes for the nation to continue in its relatively peaceful and successful state. Such wishes were perhaps consolatory to writer and audience, perhaps merely formally complimentary to the Queen. Either way, the more her immortality was asserted, the more the actual imminence of her death was the latent focus of concern and anticipation. A mingling of excitement and trepidation at the end of the old era and the beginning of the new is evident in the fact that the last ten years of the reign were fraught with rumours of the Queen's illness and death.[67]

vi. Doubts and discontents

The 1590s were also marked by a good deal of economic hardship, caused by such factors as war taxation, inflation, the exploitation of trade monopolies by the nobility, and the failures of harvests. Dissatisfaction often took the form of revived doubts as to the efficacy and validity of female rule. An Essex labourer, in 1591, said that people should pray for a King, because 'the Queen is but a woman and ruled by noblemen, and the noblemen and gentlemen are all one, and the gentlemen and farmers will hold together so that the poor get nothing'.[68] The French ambassador in 1597 observed that 'if by chance she should die, it is certain that the English would never again submit to the rule of a woman'.[69] Bishop Goodman, looking back on the Elizabethan era, said that towards its end 'the Court was very much neglected, and in effect the people were very generally weary of an old woman's government'.[70]

Faced with such rumbling discontent, and with the attempts of courtiers like the Earl of Essex to impose their policies upon her, Elizabeth cultivated a protective aura of transcendence and mystique. It was more in her interests than ever to sustain a public image of quasi-divinity. Anthony Bacon, in a letter to Essex of 1599, wrote of 'that deep and inscrutable center of the Courte (which is her Majesties minde)'.[71] Sir John Harington later recalled that 'Hir wisest men and beste counsellors were often sore troublede to knowe her wyll in matters of state: so covertly did she pass hir judgemente.'[72] Poems like Chapman's *Shadow of Night* celebrated her in lunar imagery as an enigmatic and occult divinity, 'Enchantresse-like, deckt in disparent lawne, / Circkled with charmes and incantations'.[73]

However, the obverse of this was a tendency to regard her dismissively as a 'typically' unpredictable, wilful and irrational woman. The Earl of Essex gradually became the loudest among the voices of dissent. In 1597 he told the French ambassador that 'they laboured under two things at this Court, delay and inconstancy, which proceeded chiefly from the sex of the Queen.'[74] In 1598, after the incident in which he turned his back on the Queen and she boxed his ears, he replied thus to the Lord Keeper's urgings that he should sue for forgiveness:

> What, cannot princes err? Cannot subjects receive wrong? Is an earthly power or authority infinite? Pardon me, pardon me, my good Lord, I can never subscribe to these principles . . . let them acknowledge an infinite absoluteness on earth, that do not believe in an absolute infiniteness in heaven.[75]

There is evidence that Essex made rather too clear his sense that the courtly-love discourse which dominated Elizabeth's relations with her favourites was merely hypocritical play-acting: Francis Bacon had advised him to flatter her more 'familiarly', as Leicester and Hatton had done, since at present 'a man may read formality in your countenance'.[76] The letter to the Lord Keeper frankly reveals that he regarded quasi-religious veneration of Elizabeth in the same light, as empty rhetoric.

vii. The moon as negative image

The moon as symbol had a dark side which was admirably suited to such expressions of disillusionment. For one thing, the moon as a source of light was dependent upon and secondary to the sun; it was therefore often used as an image of female inferiority.[77] It was also associated with the troubling changeability of the female body: Richard Mulcaster, in his educational treatise *Positions*, 1581, explained that girls' bodies were weaker, 'as of a moonish influence'.[78] Other negative connotations of the moon included brainsickness (that is, lunacy), strange behaviour in nature, darkness and night, the occult, sinister female powers, and female licentiousness.[79]

The moon as symbol was therefore an effective vehicle for challenging the Queen as icon. 'A Poem made on the Earle of Essex (being in disgrace with Queene Elizabeth): by mr henry Cuffe his Secretary' is an evocative expression of the distemper which discoloured the 1590s. The poem opens 'It was a time when sillie Bees could speake'; the Queen is figured as a flower around which bees swarm. Motifs associated with Elizabeth, including the moon, are turned to images of sickness and decay:

> I worke on weedes when moone is in the waine,
> 　　Whilst all the swarme in suneshine tast the Rose;
> On blacke roote fearne I sitt, and sucke my baine,
> 　　Whilst on the Eglentine the rest repose;
> 　　　　Havinge too much they still repine for more,
> 　　　　And cloide with sweetness surfit on the store.[80]

This poem makes metaphoric capital of the fact that the moon wanes. Despite what I have said about its use as an emblem of immutability, the principal negative property of the moon was its changefulness. Thus Juliet tells Romeo,

> O, swear not by the moon, th'inconstant moon,
> That monthly changes in her circled orb,
> Lest that thy love prove likewise variable.[81]

Some 'Verses on the Order of the Garter' stated that: 'Lyke to the Moone, that Moonthly chaungeth newe, / I maie compare a fleeting fickle mynde'.[82] In Elizabeth's old age, the moon as symbol of mutability and fickleness became an apt means of representing both her decline towards mortality, and her perceived 'womanish' irrationality and unpredictability. The exceptional usefulness of the lunar image was its duality: these negative undertones could be implied, while ostensibly praising the Queen by associating her with the positive qualities of the moon.

In fact this began to occur as early as 1585, if we accept this date for John Lyly's *Endimion, The Man in the Moone*.[83] Endimion, devoted lover of Cynthia the moon-goddess, delivers a long speech in the first scene which is riddled with contradictions: he declares that Cynthia is unchanging; but that inconstancy is a virtue, and she is inconstant; but that through her inconstancy she achieves constant youth (I.i.30–56). Cynthia's paradoxical nature is summed up in a later scene: she is *'shee whose figure of all is the perfectest, and neuer to bee measured – alwaies one, yet neuer the same – still inconstant, yet neuer wauering'* (III.iv.155–7). These self-contradictions and paradoxes are equivocal, able to be read either as celebrating the Queen as a divine mystery beyond human comprehension, or as exposing the absurdity of the fiction of the Queen's immutability.

In that first scene, Endimion becomes excited at the thought of Cynthia's beauty which inspires a desire to ravish her, and of her periodic descents into earthly form. His companion Eumenides interrupts him: 'Stay there *Endimion*, thou that committest Idolatry, wilt straight blaspheme, if thou be suffered' (I.i.61–2). These religious terms intertwine the discourse of courtly love and that of reverence for monarchy. Endimion's love is 'Idolatry', the obsessive passion of a devoted courtly lover, implying a secularisation and eroticisation of the term; but to attempt too familiar an intimacy with Cynthia/Elizabeth is blasphemy, suggesting that in some sense she does indeed partake of the divine.

Later, Endimion is seen in debate with Tellus, whose name means Earth, a temptress who tries to lure him away from Cynthia. She has been variously interpreted as Mary Queen of Scots, or as Elizabeth's own earthly side, her body natural as opposed to her body politic.[84] Endimion admonishes her,

Endimion: You know *Tellus*, that of the Gods we are forbidden to dispute, because theyr dieties [*sic*] come not within

the compasse of our reasons; and of *Cynthia* we are
allowed not to talke but to wonder, because her vertues
are not within the reach of our capacities.

Tellus:	Why, she is but a woman.
End.:	No more was *Venus*.
Tel.:	Shee is but a virgin.
End.:	No more was *Vesta*.
Tel.:	Shee shall haue an ende.
End.:	So shall the world.
Tel.:	Is not her beautie subiect to time?
End.:	No more then time is to standing still.
Tel.:	Wilt thou make her immortall?
End.:	No, but incomparable.

(II.i.75–88)

Rhetorical equivalences cancel each other out here: either Cynthia's
beauty is subject to time (she is ageing), just as time is subject to
standing still (she is not ageing); or, her beauty is not subject to time
(she is not subject to ageing), just as time is not subject to standing
still (she is ageing). Lyly makes gestures of belief in the Queen's
divine immutability while at the same time opening possibilities for
ambiguity and doubt.

The ambivalence of lunar imagery also provides much of the
force of Ralegh's dark and enigmatic long poem *The 21th: and last
booke of the Ocean to Scinthia*. This may have been composed when
Ralegh was in the Tower after Elizabeth's death, accused of treason,
but seems more likely to date from his earlier stay in the Tower in
1592, a punishment for his liaison with Elizabeth Throckmorton,
one of Elizabeth's Maids of Honour.[85] In the earlier stages of the
poem, he participates in veneration of her immutability: ' "such force
her angellike aparance had/" to master distance, tyme, or crueltye'.[86]
She is ' "A vestall fier that burnes, but never wasteth/" that looseth
nought by gevinge light to all' (ll.189–90). Her virginity mystically
makes her at once self-renewing and an endless source of maternal
nurture and abundance. Elizabeth herself used this conceit in her
last address to Parliament, the 'Golden Speech' of 1601: 'I haue . . .
bene content to be a taper of trewe virgin waxe that I might giue
light and comfort to those that liue vnder me'.[87]

However, Ralegh moves gradually from celebration of her eternal beauty to grief that it is the source of eternal woe: 'that as her
bewties would our woes should dure/thes be th'effects of pourfull

emperye' (ll.199–200). There ensues a *volte-face*: ' "Yet have thes wounders want which want cumpassion, /" yet hath her minde some markes of humayne race' (ll.201–2). This goddess is human after all; but her humanity, though it entails compassion, is not necessarily a positive quality: ' "yet will shee bee a wooman for a fashion/" so douth shee pleas her vertues to deface' (ll.203–4). This is an abrupt transition from woman as divine mistress, to the opposite extreme of woman as wayward, irrational and incomprehensible. Ralegh elaborates:

"so hath perfection which begatt her minde
"added therto a change of fantasye
"and left her the affections of her kynde.

(ll.209–11)

Cynthia is infected with the fickleness and shallowness in love which characterise women in general.[88]
Now Cynthia is identified with change and uncertainty: 'in love thos things that weare no more may bee' (l.219). Rather like Ralegh's 'Walsingham', the poem becomes a melancholy reflection on a mutability which is both universal, and centred on the figure of the poet's mistress:

when shee that from the soonn reves poure and light
did but decline her beames as discontented
convertinge sweetest dayes to saddest night
all droopes, all dyes, all troden under dust
the person, place, and passages forgotten
the hardest steele eaten with softest ruste
the firme and sollide tree both rent and rotten.

(ll.250–6)

Ralegh's Cynthia presides over not a golden age, but a post-lapsarian world infected with mutability. Her love is now cynically painted as 'Unlastinge passion, soune outworne consayte/wheron I built, and onn so dureless trust' (ll.295–6). Roles are reversed: the spurned lover becomes the figure of constancy, and the timeless qualities previously attributed to Cynthia are transferred to him:

> my love is not of tyme, or bound to date . . .
> my bound respect was not confinde to dayes
> my vowed fayth not sett to ended houres.

(ll.301, 304–5)

Ralegh's preoccupation with mutability arises not only from a sense of the Queen's mortality and of living through the end of an era, but also from the generic insecurity of the Elizabethan courtier. This was especially intense for someone like Ralegh who did not have aristocratic rank to fall back on. He was the Queen's 'creature', as he describes himself (l.319); his whole identity was dependent on her favour. The effectiveness of imagery of the moon, the mysterious ruler of the seas and tides, as a means of expression of this insecurity, was another reason for its popularity in the 1590s. In Spenser's *Colin Clouts Come Home Againe* (publ. 1595, written 1591), Cynthia/Elizabeth presides over the uncertain and insecure realms of both the ocean and the court.

Ralegh's poem builds up an intense atmosphere of bitterness and frustrated desire, expressed in cryptic, disjointed language. This finally breaks down into outright self-contradiction and incoherence: 'Shee is gonn, Shee is lost, shee is found, shee is ever faire!' (l.493). Elizabeth is lost to Ralegh; yet her image, her allure, endures. This phantasmagoric poem opens up fractures between the Queen's divinity and humanity: she is a changeless, idealised, dreamlike vision, but she is also a changeable, blameworthy woman. In general, lunar imagery was found to have great potency in the 1590s, not as a means of echoing the cult of the Virgin Mary, but as a means of subtly destabilising iconic representations of the Virgin Queen.

viii. The Queen as image

Throughout the reign Elizabeth had been presented with fictional images of herself, as in the coronation pageants, and the 'Aprill' Eclogue of 1579 which presents Elisa to Eliza. Many entertainments included playful transgression of the line between performance and audience, including Peele's *Arraygnement of Paris* (1583/4), in which Diana reached out from the stage to give the golden apple to the Queen;[89] and Gascoigne's unperformed masque for Kenilworth in 1575, in which the Queen was 'spotted' in the audience and hailed by her mythical counterpart.[90] The complimentary import of such mirroring- or recognition-scenes was that Elizabeth was even more perfect than her magnificent fictional image.

The mirroring device continued to be used in masques in the later years of the reign. In the 'Prologue at Court' to Dekker's *Old Fortunatus*, 1599, the two old men say:

2. See howe gloriously the Moone shines vpon vs.
1. Peace, foole: tremble, and kneele: The Moone saist thou? Our eyes are dazled by *Elizaes* beames. [*Both kneele.*[91]]

In Jonson's *Cynthia's Revels*, 1600, Cynthia recognises the Queen in the audience:

O front! O face! O all celestiall sure,
And more than mortal! Arete, behold
Another Cynthia, and another queen.[92]

These scenes look out from the fiction of the stage to the real physical presence of the Queen. It has often been observed, however, that even the real figure of the Queen was itself of the nature of an image, a symbol, or a theatrical performance.[93] In 1586 Elizabeth told a parliamentary deputation that 'we Princes, I tell you, are set on stages, in the sight and view of all the world duly observed'.[94] As we saw earlier, the author of the account of the coronation pageants described London as 'a stage wherin was shewed the wonderfull spectacle, of a noble hearted princesse toward her most louing people'.[95] Her public appearances were all performances in which she provided the spectacle of monarchy and played the role of the loving queen.

Often mirroring-scenes include professions of the inadequacy of dramatic representation in the face of the dazzling real presence of the Queen. This makes them similar to the emphasis on the unrepresentability of Elizabeth which we observed in Lyly's *Euphues and his England*.[96] Lyly was by no means the only panegyrist to use this compliment in the form of an assertion that the Queen's excellences were beyond human depiction: other examples include an entertainment at Bisham in 1592 whose author explained that 'some thought your Pourtraiture might be drawen, other saide impossible: some thought your vertues might be numbred, most saide they were infinite: Infinite and impossible, of that side was I.'[97] Richard

Barnfield disclaimed any intention to describe the Queen's beauty, because:

> No pen can paint thy commendation due:
>   Saue only that pen, which no pen can be,
>   An Angels quill, to make a pen for thee.[98]

However, such statements of the failure of art often generated a proliferation of art. Lyly's expatiation on the Queen's unrepresentability in *Euphues and his England* is followed by many pages of description of her. Spenser tells Elizabeth that her perfect chastity is such that

> . . . liuing art may not least part expresse,
>   Nor life-resembling pencill it can paint . . .
>   Ne Poets wit, that passeth Painter farre
>   In picturing the parts of beautie daint,
>   So hard a workmanship aduenture darre,
> For fear through want of words her excellence to marre.

> (*FQ* III proem 2)

However, the fear of 'want of words', the professed reluctance to 'darre', produces not silence, but a profusion of words. Spenser goes on:

> But O dred Soueraine
> Thus farre forth pardon, sith that choicest wit
> Cannot your glorious pourtraict figure plaine
> That I in colourd showes may shadow it.

> (III proem 3)

The impossibility of true representation generates a plethora of 'colourd showes', of fictive invention.

In examples like these, compliment is effected through the assertion of a metaphysical essence beyond the textual or dramatic image. The real Elizabeth is implied to exist as a transcendent, mysterious presence which the panegyrist can never hope to represent fully or accurately. This appears to set up a contrast between image and reality; yet this 'real Elizabeth' is herself a textual construct. It is these very texts which, by their professions of inadequacy, create the image of Elizabeth as existing somewhere above and beyond. Their disclaimer of ability to represent is itself a form of representation. Similarly, in the mirroring-scenes, not two, but three images are present: first, the actor playing the Queen-persona of, say, Cynthia or Diana; secondly, the physical presence of the Queen in the audience; and thirdly, the conception of the Queen as perfect, radiant and divine which is constructed in the speech of the actor, and which invests her real presence with value.

There is evidence that at least some Elizabethan writers were aware of the Queen's dependence upon them to create her perfect public image. In particular, she was dependent upon them to render her immortal. Although, as we have seen, many panegyrists suggested that she would live forever, some texts contain the more realistic implication that her triumph over death will be achieved not in the flesh, but through fame. Theirs is the power to create images which will endure beyond the grave. In about 1584 Sir Arthur Gorges described Elizabeth's immortality as the work of poets through the ages: 'The voices off our dayes the trompetts of her fame / And all posterityes as Eccoes to the same.'[99] Sir John Davies wrote in *Hymnes of Astraea*, 1599:

> The pompe of Coronation
> Hath not such power her fame to spread,
> As this my admiration.[100]

Spenser seems to have been especially conscious of the dependence of the Queen upon the poet to make her divine and immortal. In *The Teares of the Muses* (published 1591), he at first seems to be issuing the conventional wish for the Queen's immortality, then converts this into a claim for the immortalising power of art:

> Liue she for ever, and her royall P'laces
> Be fild with praises of divinest wits,
> That her eternize with their heavenlie writs.[101]

Just as sonneteers asserted their power to eternise their mistresses, so Elizabeth is dependent on the powers of the poet to immortalise her. A further likeness to Petrarchan sonneteering is that the poet's achievement is not only to eternise his subject, but to eternise himself through the displays of artistic skill which the creation of her

image affords him. They are thus bound together by a mutual dependence, almost a contractual agreement. This is made clear in
Colin Clouts Come Home Againe, when Colin/Spenser speaks of the
divinity and unrepresentability of Cynthia/Elizabeth:

> . . . vaine it is to thinke by paragone
> Of earthly things, to judges of things divine:
> Her power, her mercy, and her wisedome, none
> Can deeme, but who the Godhead can define.
> Why then do I base shepheard bold and blind,
> Presume the things so sacred to prophane?
> More fit it is t'adore with humble mind,
> The image of the heavens in shape humane.
> With that *Alexis* broke his tale asunder,
> Saying, By wondring at thy *Cynthiaes* praise,
> *Colin*, thy selfe thou mak'st us more to wonder,
> And her upraising, doest thy self upraise.[102]

There is evidence in the later books of *The Faerie Queene* that
Spenser was coming to feel some weariness of his task of creating
perfect images of the Queen, such as the note of criticism in the
story of Timias and Belphoebe in Book IV; the digression from
Gloriana's court in Book VI; the precedence accorded the poet's
mistress over the Queen in the vision on Mount Acidale in canto x
of that Book. This is accompanied by an increasing anxiety about
change and time. In *Faerie Queene* III.vi, the description of the Garden of Adonis, mortality and mutability are depicted as part of a
positive natural cycle of renewal, a pattern of continuity through
change, rendering the world 'eterne in mutabilitie' (III.vi.47). In
Book V, however, the contrary view is expressed, that 'All change
is perillous, and all chaunce vnsound' (V.ii.36), a view echoed in
the *View of the Present State of Ireland.*[103]

As I have said, in *Colin Clouts Come Home Againe* Cynthia/Eliza-
beth is identified with the troubling insecurities of court life. Her
poets 'do their *Cynthia* immortall make', but the truth is that Queen
and poets are alike mortal:

> And when as death these vitall bands shall breake,
> Her name recorded I will leave for ever . . .
> And long while after I am dead and rotten:
> Amongst the shepheards daughters dancing rownd,

My layes made of her shall not be forgotten,
But sung by them with flowry gyrlonds crownd.
And ye, who so ye be, that shall survive:
When as ye heare her memory renewed,
Be witnesse of her bountie here alive,
Which she to *Colin* her poore shepheard shewed.[104]

The lines look forward to a time when both Queen and poet will be dead and rotten and will contend with encroaching oblivion. Perhaps in their joint creation of the regal icon they can defeat time, but not in their physical selves.

ix. The *Mutabilitie Cantos*

The *Mutabilitie Cantos* continue the practice we have observed of using lunar imagery not to echo Marian iconography, but on the contrary to question the elevation of Elizabeth as a goddess and sacred icon. They contain Spenser's most negative representation of the Queen, and once again use the figure of Cynthia/Diana as a means of expressing unease and disillusionment. This negativity is partly generated by dissent from Elizabeth's Irish policy, but also, as with other uses of the moon-goddess persona, entails reflection upon time, change and mortality. In Spenser's case, having made panegyric of Elizabeth the substance of so much of his major work throughout his career, this involves meditation upon not only the Queen's mortality, but also his own.

The fact that the Cantos were not published until 1609, six years after Elizabeth's death, suggests that contemporaries regarded them as dangerously critical of the Queen. The date of composition is uncertain, but it seems likely that they were late, perhaps even Spenser's last work before his death in January 1599.[105] The two closing stanzas certainly have an air of finality and leave-taking. It is ambiguous whether the speaker 'loath[es] this state of life so tickle', or is 'loath [to leave] this state of life so tickle' (VII.viii.1.6); whether the culminating note of the poem is one of despairing rejection of the world, or of consolatory resignation.[106] This matches the ambivalence of the whole poem towards mutability. At the beginning of the Cantos the poet bewails the 'pittious worke of MVTABILITIE' (VII.vi.6), but in canto vii she is shown to be responsible for the vibrant and entrancing pageant of the months and seasons. However, whatever tone we impute to it, the final canto

certainly describes a relinquishing of this changeable world and a
hopeful gaze to heaven: the poet yearns for 'that same time when
no more *Change* shall be' (VII.viii.2.2), with God in eternity.

The world of mutability from which the poet withdraws is a
significant context for his representation of Elizabeth. Her naming
in the Cantos as Cynthia and Diana immediately alerts us that she
is being shown in her most changeable aspect. Other details imply
her mortality: Cynthia's gates are guarded by Tyme, 'an hory /
Old aged Sire, with hower-glasse in hand', suggesting that her time is
waning (VII.vi.8). Her page is Vesper, suggesting that she is in the
evening of her life (VII.vi.9). The eclipse brought about by
Mutabilitie's attempt to thrust her from her throne seems to presage the confusion consequent upon Elizabeth's death. The lower
world is 'darkned quite', and everyone

> . . . wondred at that sight;
> Fearing least *Chaos* broken had his chaine,
> And brought againe on them eternall night.

> (VII.vi.14)

Mutabilitie's challenge is essentially a challenge to the distinction
between the heavens and the earth, the superlunary and sublunary
regions.[107] At Nature's court she says 'heauen and earth I both
alike do deeme' (VII.vii.15). The heavens, in this instance, are not
the eternal home of the Christian God, but the region between
the empyrean and the earth, occupied by the heavenly bodies.
Mutabilitie demonstrates that the earth is ruled by processes of
time and change; she then seeks to show that the heavens are no
different. She challenges Jove, 'what if I can proue, that euen yee /
Your selues are likewise chang'd, and subiect vnto mee?' (VII.vii.49).
For Nature's reply to constitute a triumph over Mutabilitie, she
ought to uphold the distinction, showing that the heavenly bodies
are immune to change; but this she does not do. She merely argues
that change is ruled by the creatures of Nature, and not vice versa.
But this is presumably true in the heavens as much as on earth, and
change has therefore been conceded to exist in the heavens.

Within this, Mutabilitie specifically challenges the convention of
praising Elizabeth as a quasi-divine icon. After all, the starting point
of the whole problem is Mutabilitie's iconoclastic attempt to oust
Cynthia from her throne; and when, at Nature's court, Mutabilitie

sets out to prove the mutability of the heavenly bodies, Cynthia is her prime example. At this point Spenser makes his most bold statement of Cynthia/Elizabeth's variability:

> ... her face and countenance euery day
> We changed see, and sundry forms partake,
> Now hornd, now round, now bright, now brown and gray:
> So that *as changefull as the Moone* men vse to say.

> (VII.vii.50)

The allusion to proverbial wisdom, to what 'men vse to say', brings into play traditional folk-beliefs associating Cynthia with madness and 'feminine' instability.

The question as to the power of change centres on the question of whether Cynthia/Elizabeth is subject to change. In turn, the question of whether Elizabeth is immutable or mortal is part of the larger question of her divinity and/or humanity. We have seen that the monarch was held to have a dual nature, as both the eternal, spiritual, body politic and a human, fallible body natural; and that Spenser had already divided Elizabeth into 'Queene' and 'Lady', choosing Belphoebe, a lunar name, to signify her human, feminine aspect. The moon was a dualistic symbol not only in that it was both changeful and perpetually self-renewing, but also in that it was supposed to stand on the border of the earthly region and the heavens. This is stated in the *Mutabilitie Cantos*, where Cynthia is said to have her seat on 'heauens coast' (VII.vi.12). The moon partakes of both regions, without being wholly part of either; she is both earthly and heavenly, both human and divine, just as Elizabeth was supposed to be. But as Elizabeth aged, her symbolic, divine, immortal role was becoming ever more obviously far-removed from her actual ageing, fallible state; the two sides of her nature were becoming opposed rather than complementary.

Some panegyrists followed a strategy of stressing the mutability of the realm under the moon while implicitly placing the moon on the side of immutability. Ralegh, in a poem opening 'Praisd be Dianas fair and harmles light', asserted that 'Mortalitie belowe hir orbe is plaste'.[108] Jonson used the same conceit in *Cynthia's Revels*: 'Years are beneath the spheres: and time makes weak /Things under heaven, not powers which govern heaven'.[109] However, there was a more equivocal exploration of the relation between the sublunary

and superlunary spheres in a song presented by the Earl of
Cumberland on May Day 1600:

> Th'Ancient Readers of Heauens Booke,
> Which with curious eye did looke
>   Into Natures story;
> All things vnder *Cynthia* tooke
>   To bee transitory.

> This the learned onely knew,
> But now all men finde it true,
>   *Cynthia* is descended;
> With bright beames, and heauenly hew,
>   And lesser starres attended.

> Landes and seas shee rules below,
> Where things change, and ebbe, and flowe,
>   Spring, waxe olde, and perish;
> Only Time which all doth mowe,
>   Her alone doth cherish.

> Times yong howres attend her still,
> And her Eyes and Cheekes do fill,
>   With fresh youth and beautie:
> All her louers olde do grow,
> But their hartes, they do not so
>   In their Loue and duty.[110]

Although Cynthia is said to be immune to time, she has 'descended'
and become earthly; and stress is laid upon the transience of the
realm of this earthly Cynthia, and the ageing of her followers. The
song reminds us that by the last decade of the reign most of Elizabeth's principal favourites and ministers of her own generation,
such as Leicester, Hatton and Walsingham, were dead. She was a
living relic from a past age.

Spenser's examination of Cynthia's borderline position brings to
the fore the dark, unreliable, mortal side of the moon, and concludes by placing her firmly on the side of change. Mutabilitie
declares:

Euen you faire *Cynthia*, whom so much ye make
Ioues dearest darling, she was bred and nurst
On *Cynthus* hill, whence she her name did take:
Then is she mortall borne, how-so ye crake.

                                                    (VII.vii.50)

Unlike Spenser's earlier mythologisations of Elizabeth's conception
and birth as some form of divine and asexual insemination, the
stress here is on the earthliness of her origin. Nobody does 'crake';
no-one, at the assembly before Nature, refutes Mutabilitie's charge.
When Nature pronounces judgement, nothing is said about rein-
stating Cynthia on the throne from which Mutabilitie had dislodged
her. Instead, Nature pronounces that

... all things stedfastnes doe hate
And changed be: yet being rightly wayd
They are not changed from their first estate;
But by their change their being doe dilate:
And turning to themselues at length againe,
Doe worke their owne perfection so by fate.

                                                    (VII.vii.58)

Continuity is preserved by the replacement of the old with the new:
the solution to the dethronement of Cynthia is, presumably, to place
a new power on her throne. This is not a victory for Mutabilitie, in
that the body politic is preserved unimpaired; but neither is it a
victory for Cynthia, in her body natural, who must die to sustain
the cycle of renewal.

Spenser personifies the heavenly bodies as classical gods and
adopts a comical, burlesque tone, characterising them as human
and fallible.[111] This contributes to Mutabilitie's case: we see Jove
and the other gods as vulnerable and indecisive, preparing us for
the conclusion that the stellar region is as much in thrall to mutability as the sublunar world. The figures of Cynthia and Diana are
also subjected to this comic, deflationary treatment. Cynthia is em-
broiled in an undignified struggle with Mutabilitie over her throne;
Diana is humiliated by Faunus's laughter at 'some-what he did spy'
when he sees her bathing naked (VII.vi.46). She reacts angrily,

> Like as an huswife, that with busie care
> Thinks of her Dairie to make wondrous gaine,
> Finding where-as some wicked beast vnware
> That breakes into her Dayr'house, there doth draine
> Her creaming pannes, and frustrate all her paine.

(VII.vi.48)

This is a far cry from the stately pomp of Gloriana. It is also, in its ridicule of Diana's fuss over the exposure of her 'some-what', something of a satiric swipe at the central premise of the cult of the Virgin Queen.

If the gods can be shown as human, fallible, and faintly absurd, then, by implication, even the supposedly divine half of the Queen's dual nature is not immune to such infirmities. Just as Mutabilitie proves that the heavens and the earth are in fact identical in their subjection to change, so Spenser implies that both halves of the supposed dual nature of the Queen are identical. She is mortal in her whole being. The perfect universality embodied in paradox is now transferred away from Elizabeth to the figure of Nature; she appears hermaphroditic (VII.vii.5), and is:

> . . . euer young yet full of eld,
> Still moouing, yet vnmoued from her sted;
> Vnseene of any, yet of all beheld.

(VII.vii.13)

Elizabeth no longer embodies the ideal fusion of masculinity in femininity, divinity in humanity, immortality in mutability.[112] It is now merely femininity, humanity and mutability which cohere in her person; and after the departure of Diana from Ireland, Elizabeth disappears from the poem.

Some critics have seen a reappearance of Elizabeth in the 'God of Sabbaoth' of the closing lines, detecting a pun on 'Eli-zabeth'.[113] It seems that at least one Elizabethan was conscious of this pun; Laneham's Letter, which describes the festivities at Kenilworth in 1575, mentioned 'her Highnes' name Elizabeth, which I heer say oout of the Hebru signifieth (ammoong oother) the seaventh of my God'.[114] If there is a pun in Spenser, it could be read as a reconciliatory resolution: Elizabeth, Nature and God are united.[115] However,

I prefer to see the lines as turning away from Elizabeth to a higher, more certain power. Until this point, the main dynamic of *The Faerie Queene* was the desire to represent Elizabeth, a task which generated many different names for her many different aspects, while leaving always a sense that the true, essential Elizabeth existed outside the poem as a mystery beyond definition. The true naming of Elizabeth can be seen as the perpetually deferred, unfulfillable goal of the poem.[116] At this point, though, Spenser gives up the endeavour to name Elizabeth. Rather than praising her as image of God, he looks beyond her to God himself as the highest mystery and the ultimate fixed point of truth and certainty.

The celebratory tone of the earlier books of *The Faerie Queene* is gone. In Book II, Gloriana was 'th'Idole of her makers great magnificence' (II.ii.41).[117] In Book I, the Red Cross Knight's vision of the Heavenly Jerusalem may have been a deferred one, representing a goal not yet gained, but still to seek; nevertheless, Cleopolis, the capital of the Faerie Queene, was at least the closest image of that city which earth could achieve. There is no such vision linking heaven and earth as climax to the *Mutabilitie Cantos*; the 'Sabaoths sight' exists only in the next world.[118] The poem thus radically challenges, and in the end discards, representation of the Queen as immortal goddess, perfect icon, and image of God.

Despite the existence of some analogies between Elizabethan and Marian iconography in their shared use of lunar imagery, the predominant motivations and significances of representations of Elizabeth as Cynthia are quite the opposite of creation of a new Virgin Mary as an object of cult-worship.

7

Towards Death, and Beyond It

i. The extravagance of late panegyric

The questioning of the iconic perfection of the Queen by the writers
discussed in the previous chapter developed alongside the growth
of excess and hyperbole in panegyric. For one thing, it had become
as conventional to use religious and specifically Catholic terminology in royal panegyric as it had in courtly love poetry. In the 1591
entertainment at Elvetham, 'The Poet's speech to his Boy offering
him a cushion' urged, 'Now let us use no cushions, but faire hearts:
/ For now we kneel to more than usuall Saints'.[1] Thomas Churchyard, in 'A discourse of the ioy good subiects haue when they see
our Phenix abroad', 1593, described the Queen as 'like shrined Saint
in beaten gold'.[2] Sir John Davies, in the VIIIth of his *Hymnes of
Astraea*, 1599, 'To all the Princes of Europe', exhorted:

> Brave Princes of this civill age,
> Enter into this pilgrimage:
> This Saints tongue is an oracle,
> Her eye hath made a Prince a Page,
> And workes each day a Miracle.[3]

In Dekker's *Old Fortunatus*, 1599, Fortunatus describes the courts
he has visited:

> there to liue is rare, O tis diuine;
> There shall you see faces Angelicall,
> There shall you see troopes of chast Goddesses,
> Whose star-like eyes haue power, (might they still shine)
> To make night day, and day more christalline.
> Neere these you shall behold great *Heroes*,
> White headed Councellors and Iouiall spirites,

198

Standing like fierie Cherubins to gard
The Monarch, who in God-like glorie sits,
In midst of these, as if this deitie
Had with a looke created a new world;
The standers by, being the faire workemanshipp.[4]

Here the medieval appropriation of regal iconography to depict God or Christ as King of Heaven, surrounded by ranks of saints and angels, is reappropriated for secular power. The monarch as maker of men is depicted as a supreme creator, at the centre of a court which is an earthly facsimile of heaven.

Across a range of writings there was evidence of reduced anxiety about mentioning the Virgin and saints. In Robert Chester's *Loves Martyr*, 1601, King Arthur was said to bear on his shield 'The image of our *Ladie* with her *Sonne* / Held in her armes',[5] reviving a medieval tradition that Arthur was the champion of the Virgin.[6] In the 1590 *Faerie Queene*, by contrast, Spenser had erased this tradition in favour of a militantly Protestant iconography, giving Prince Arthur a shield which bore no image but was made of pure diamond; it dazzled opponents with holy light and thus defeated the forces of idolatry (I.vii.33–5, viii.19–21). There is evidence that Sir John Harington, Elizabeth's godson, had some sympathetic leanings towards Catholicism,[7] and in a religious poem entitled 'Fifteen several disticks on the fifteen divisions', he included scenes centring on the Virgin such as the Annunciation, the Nativity, the Assumption and the Glorification:

And after all theis things it is presumed,
the blessed virgin was to heaven assumed,
    God graunt me, when my life hath run the race,
    to say to her with saynts. *Haile full of grace.*[8]

The hyperbole of royal panegyric also included far more direct and blatant appropriations of Marian iconography than had occurred earlier in the reign. We have seen before how writers like Thomas Bentley in 1582 and Edward Hellwis in 1589 were beginning to move towards direct use of the Virgin herself as a source for typological comparison.[9] At the end of the reign we find the following poem apparently written for Christmas 1602, and possibly by Sir John Davies.

Verses of the Queene.

A virgin once a glorious starre did beare,
Like to the Sunne inclosd in globe of glasse;
A virgins hart is nowe the golden Sphere
Whence to this earth that influence doth passe.
He shynes on her, and she on him againe,
Reflecting Love all earthly starres doth staine.

He whylome tooke a stable for his Cell,
Thrise happie Cell in which a god hath ben,
But he will nowe in princes pallace dwell,
And wedds himselfe to rare *Eliza* queene.
Come wise men come, present your giftes devine,
Here standes the starr that makes your starr to shine.

This Sacred Nimphe, because noe mortall wight
Deserved to Lincke with her in chaines of Love,
Unto the god of soules her faith hath plight,
And vowde her selfe to him without remove.
Thus doth this brid tenn thowsand children breed,
And virgins milke the Church of god doth feed.

To see this birth did Angells sweetly singe,
Nowe singes that nest of nightingalls againe,
Joye, peace, goodwill [on earth] to men they bringe,
Of fortie five yeares thus tuninge they remaine.
Long maye they tune that sweete and pleasant songe,
And longe maye she our angell singe amonge.

For Syons sake preserve from death:
Our noble queene *Elizabeth*: Amen.[10]

According to this poet, Elizabeth's heart encloses Christ as did the
virgin's womb; his dwelling place of the stable has been replaced
by Elizabeth's palace; and, like the Virgin, Elizabeth is both bride of
Christ and mother of the Church. Of course these last two images
had biblical sources, in the Song of Songs and Isaiah, which were
not necessarily exclusively Marian. In this case, though, in the context of a typological reading of the Nativity, the vivid lines 'Thus
doth this brid tenn thowsand children breed, / And virgins milke

the Church of god doth feed' strongly evoke pre-Reformation iconography of the Virgin, as Mother of Mercy gathering a crowd of believers under her protective mantle,[11] and as suckling mother offering her milk-filled breast not only to her Son but to the whole Church.[12] In the final stanza, however, the iconography shifts away from Marian analogies to present Elizabeth at once as the messianic figure whose incarnation/accession the angels commemorate in song, and as one of the choir of angels hymning Christ.

It is important to note that the poem does not draw gratuitous and unprovoked parallels between Elizabeth and the Virgin, but is prompted by the specific occasion of Christmas. Various elements of the Nativity scene, including not only Mary as mother but also the newborn Christ and the choir of angels, are used as material for the witty and elegant drawing of comparisons with Elizabeth. Nevertheless, it exceeds earlier panegyric in its uninhibited, overt and extended use of the Virgin Mary as a typological source. This suggests not that she had dropped out of English culture and needed to be replaced with Elizabeth, but rather that, by this date, interest in the Virgin was enjoying some revival, and Marian iconography was being viewed with more relaxation as a source which panegyrists could openly use in their quest for inventive hyperbole. This was no doubt especially so on occasions like Christmas, when invocation of the Virgin had topicality.

When reading such hyperbolic panegyric, it is worth keeping in mind the examples of more negative writing about the Queen which I discussed in the last chapter. Recognition that extravagant praise coexisted with dissent and criticism can create an awareness that praise of Elizabeth as divine should not necessarily be read literally, and indeed can ring rather hollow. It is true that a German visitor to England in 1599, Thomas Platter, remarked of Elizabeth: 'For this is certain; the English esteem her, not only as their queen, but as their God.'[13] However, we perhaps need to be less literal-minded than he was, and to recognise that panegyric is less about expression of belief than about performative display by the poet in the hope of impressing potential patrons.

ii. William Perkins and 'civil worship'

In tracing the beginnings of panegyric of Elizabeth, I discussed attempts by early Elizabethan theologians to define the admissible and inadmissible use of images.[14] The writings of William Perkins

(1558–1602) provide one example of how the arguments had developed by the later years of the reign, after years of elevation and elaboration of Elizabeth as an icon. They also illustrate Puritan attitudes to such practices.

Perkins was a Cambridge don, a prolific and popular theological writer, and a staunch opponent of 'Romish' trappings of worship in the Church of England. In 1597 he published *A Reformed Catholike*, a significant contribution to the Puritan cause which was also well-received by anti-Puritans.[15] In a preface he explained that he had three intentions: to show that the Protestant and Catholic Churches could not be reconciled; to win over Catholics; and, 'that the common protestant might in some part see and conceiue the point of difference betvvene vs and the Church of Rome'.[16] This suggests that in the late 1590s there was a fear among Puritans that the Church of England was not making what they saw as necessary progress further away from the Church of Rome, and indeed might be slipping back towards it. Perhaps English worshippers were losing their grip on the original principles of the Reformation; perhaps they had not fully absorbed them in the first place.

In 1601 Perkins followed up *A Reformed Catholike* with *A Warning Against the Idolatrie of the last times*, in which he reiterated and elaborated upon many of the same arguments. In this case he declared his purpose as 'to informe the ignorant multitude touching the true worship of God. For the remainders of Poperie yet sticke in the mindes of many of them'.[17] He forbade the preservation of images that had formerly been worshipped (*WAI*, p.108), suggesting a worry, even in 1601, that icons from fifty years before were still being stored in private houses. He attempted to show:

> that we haue vpon good ground departed from the Church of Rome, and that we may not so much as dreame of any Vnion to be made, or Reconciliation of the two religions. It is not true, which many suppose, that we differ onely in matters of circumstance. Idolatrie is one speciall cause, that makes vs renounce the Romane religion.
>
> (*WAI*, pp.133–4)

However, in both books, Perkins concurred with earlier Elizabethan theologians in conceding that some images were acceptable:

> Wee acknowledge the ciuill vse of images as freely and truly as the Church of Rome doth. By *ciuill vse* I vnderstand, that vse

which is made of them in the common societies of men, out of the
appointed places of the solemne worshippe of God.

(*RC*, p.170)

Painting and 'grauing' (that is, carving, sculpting) were gifts from
God and therefore lawful, for several specified purposes: to adorn
civil buildings; to label coins; to commemorate the dead; to represent histories, including stories from the Bible (though not on church
walls); and even 'to testifie the presence or the effects of the maiestie
of God, . . . when God himselfe giues any speciall commandement
so to doe' (*RC*, pp.171–2; *WAI*, pp.106–7). Perkins cited scriptural
authorities for these uses of images, sustaining the Protestant emphasis on the textual over the pictorial, and indeed affirmed that
the Word of the gospel and its preaching was the 'most excellent
picture' of Christ (*RC*, p.173).

In *A Reformed Catholike*, Perkins attacked Catholics on the grounds
that they sustained a false distinction between idols and images
(*RC*, pp.174–6). He asserted, 'And the distinction they make that an
Image is the representation of true things, an Idol of things supposed, is false' (*RC*, pp.175–6). This runs contrary to the practice of
those numerous Protestant panegyrists who, as we have seen, presented glorious images of Elizabeth as a figure of divine truth, while
abhorring images of the Virgin and saints as false idols. In the
Warning, however, Perkins did distinguish between images and idols:
an idol is specifically 'such image as is erected to represent either
false or true God' (*WAI*, p.3). Even according to this definition,
though, presentations of Elizabeth as an image of God were presumably idols. He averred that, even though humanity was made
in the image of God, this did not make an image of a human personage an image of God:

Obiect[ion] *III*. Man is the image of God, but it is lawfull to paint
a man, and therefore to make an image of God. Ans[wer] A very
cavill: for first a man cannot be painted, as he is the image of
God, which standes in the spirituall gifts of righteousnes and
true holiness. Againe, the image of a man may be painted for
ciuil or historical vse, but to paint any man for this ende to represent God, or in the way of religion, that we may the better
remember and worship God, it is vnlawfull.

(*RC*, p.179)

However, Perkins also defined and accepted 'civil worship', which might be taken to include panegyric of Elizabeth. In place of the Catholic discrimination which he rejected between *latria*, the worship of God, and *dulia*, the worship of saints and angels (*RC*, p.247), he set up a Protestant distinction between civil and religious worship: 'it is lawfull for one man to worship another with ciuill worship, but to worship man with religious honour is vnlawfull' (*RC*, p.181; cf *WAI*, p.54). Kneeling or bowing to the chair of state in the absence of the monarch was lawful, because it was no more than a 'signe of ciuill reuerence' to show 'loyaltie and subiection', and had scriptural warrant. But it could not be used as an analogy to justify kneeling or bowing to a saint's image, which would constitute religious worship (*RC*, pp.182–3; cf *WAI*, pp.96–8). 'Religious worship . . . is due to God alone', whereas

> Ciuill worship is the honour done to men set aboue vs by God himselfe, either in respect of their excellent gifts, or in respect of their offices: and authoritie whereby they gouerne others. The right ende of this worship is to testifie and declare that we reuerence the giftes of God, and that power which he hath placed in those that be his instruments.
>
> (*RC*, p.248; cf. *WAI*, pp.118–19)

Yet Perkins warned:

> if any meere man shall be worshipped with any worship that is more then politicke or ciuill, he is made more then a man, & by this means he is transformed into an Idol . . . no more [should] be due to man but ciuill honour, though he be considered as the Image of God.
>
> (*WAI*, p. 93)

Civil adoration 'must be done as to a meere creature, though it be a prince. If it exceede . . . it inclines to religious worship'. (*WAI*, p.227).

Saints could not be the objects of civil adoration because they were not present to the worshipper (*RC*, pp.249–50). To adore them or to pray to them would be to accord them omniscience and omnipresence, which belong only to God (*RC*, pp.245–66). Perkins did not deny that the Virgin and saints were to be 'worshipped and honoured' (*RC*, p.245), but set down limitations: the proper forms of such worship were commemorating saints, giving thanks to God for them, and imitating their virtues (*RC*, pp.245–6). He cited: 'Epiphan. Let Marie be in honour; let the Father, Sonne, and holy Ghost be adored: let NONE ADORE MARIE' (*RC*, p.255); and he emphasised that there was no historical proof of the Assumption of the Virgin (*WAI*, pp.174–5).

In *A Reformed Catholike* Perkins described Catholics as turning the Virgin Mary into a 'detestable idol' and listed her many titles with contempt (*RC*, p. 343). In a similar passage in the *Warning* he wrote:

> The Romane false gods are two. The first is the Virgin Marie; whome the pretended Catholikes of this time of a Saint make a goddesse; for they call her the *queene of heauen*, the *queene of the world: our Ladie: the mother of grace and mercie.* Shee is esteemed as an vniuersall aduocate to the whole world, and ther be other mediatours vnto her, as to a queene.
>
> (*WAI*, p. 36)

Much of this seems highly ironic in the light of addresses by Perkins's contemporaries to Elizabeth in not dissimilar terms. Perkins also named as idolatrous practices 'sacrifices, oblations, lighting of ta-pers, burning incense, the erection of altars & temples, and pilgrim-ages' (*WAI*, p.111), many of which practices, as we have seen, had become conventional motifs in erotic poetry and in turn in royal panegyric.

In support of his distinctions between civil and religious wor-ship, Perkins often used monarchical metaphors and analogies. He implied that what was wrong with the Catholic use of religious images was precisely that it treated God as if he were merely a human monarch, and equally as representable. Images of God 'abol-ish and deface his Maiestie, . . . and doe as little beseeme his endles glorie as a picture of an Ape or of a foole, doth the excellency of an Emperour' (*WAI*, p.23; cf p.155). Idolaters ascribe to images '*propertie of representation,* wherby the Image stands in the stead, place, & room of god: not only as an Embassadour, but as a vice-roie or deputie is in the roome of the prince' (*WAI*, pp.102–3). To think of God as a king in these ways is to denigrate Him to an improperly human level.

Yet what Perkins sees as wrong with the cult of the Virgin is that it accords her the status of a queen, and that this is an excessively elevating metaphor, improperly aggrandising her above her Son:

'his Mother must be the Queene of heauen, and by the right of a mother commaund him there' (*RC*, dedication). The term 'king' is used elsewhere to describe the superlative pre-eminence of Christ and God: Christ is a king, as God is King over all things in heaven and earth, and as the redeemer of humankind, which makes him King over the Church (*RC*, p.286). In this sense, Perkins finds fault with the Catholic Church for not treating Christ sufficiently like a monarch: '[T]he . . . Catholike religion degrades [Christ] of his kingly office, by giuing to the Pope two royalties of the kingdom of Christ', to pardon sins and to make laws (*WAI*, p.12). Thus when Perkins seeks terms for the supreme power of God and Christ, he turns to the language of monarchy, inherently likening monarchy and divinity, and investing monarchy with high spiritual value.

In accordance with earlier reformists, Perkins's assault on papal authority entailed enhancement of secular authorities: 'we holde . . . that neither Peter nor any Bishop of Rome hath any supremacie ouer the Catholike Church: but that all supremacie vnder Christ, is pertaining to kings and princes within their dominions' (*RC*, pp.285 [numbered 225]–286). This in turn entailed a likening of kings to Christ:

> [A]s Christ is God . . . he hath his deputies on earth to gouerne the worlde; as namely kings & princes, who are therefore in scriptures called *gods*.
>
> (*RC*, p.286)

Priests are not Christ's 'deputies', but only his 'instruments' (*RC*, p.284). Catholics wrongfully give authority to the Pope 'to depose kings, to whome vnder Christ euery soule is to be subiect' (*RC*, p.341).

Although in these books Perkins never directly addresses the subject of praise of Elizabeth as icon, they contain much which suggests that he must have been disturbed by some of its more excessive manifestations. Yet at the same time, he leaves open possible justifications for veneration of the Queen which echo earlier Elizabethan theologians. Like them, he simultaneously separates and likens the sacred and secular spheres: praise of Elizabeth is only civil worship, not religious worship, and is therefore permissible; but at the same time Christ is a king, and monarchs are like Christ, and can therefore be addressed in similar terms.

iii. Controversy over Accession Day

In *A Warning*, Perkins contended that:

> Saints and Angels are made Idols, in that Temples, Altars,
> holidaies are consecrated to their honour & worship. For all these
> properly appertaine to the worshippe of God . . . Festivall daies:
> because God is the onely Lord of daies & times, and therefore
> they are onely to be dedicated to his honour. And though we
> retaine the names of Saints daies in the Church of England, yet
> are we altogether free from this Idolatrie, because we dedicate
> the daies themselues to the honour of God.
>
> (*WAI*, p.91)

Once again, one can infer that Perkins must have been troubled by
some of the excesses of the Accession Day celebrations; but that he
found arguments for tolerating the holiday, as in the final sentence
of this passage.

In the closing years of the reign, ministers of the Church of Eng-
land felt obliged to defend Accession Day against attacks by Catho-
lics; and to justify the celebration of Elizabeth's birthday, 7
September, which had also become a public holiday. In Edward
Rishton's continuation of Nicholas Sander's *Rise and Growth of the
Anglican Schism*, 1585, he had protested that:

> [Elizabeth's] birthday and . . . the day of her coronation [i.e. Ac-
> cession Day] . . . are kept with more solemnity throughout the
> kingdom than the festivals of Christ and of the saints . . . And to
> show the greater contempt for our Blessed Lady, they keep the
> birthday of queen Elizabeth in the most solemn way on the 7th
> day of September, which is the eve of the feast of the Mother of
> God, whose nativity they mark in their calendar in small and
> black letters, while that of Elizabeth is marked in letters both
> large and red. And, what is hardly credible, in the church of St.
> Paul, the chief church of London – whether elsewhere or not is
> more than I can tell – the praises of Elizabeth are said to be sung
> at the end of the public prayers, as the Antiphon of our Lady was
> sung in former days.[18]

Before we seize on this as evidence that Elizabeth was directly
substituted for the Virgin Mary, it is worth remembering that it was

very much in Rishton's polemical interests to claim that the English were shockingly worshipping Elizabeth when they ought to be venerating Mary. Another Catholic attack came in the form of *Calvino-Turcismus* by William Rainolds, 1597, which argued that Accession Day was a revival of pagan ritual.

Thomas Holland, a loyal servant of the Crown, replied point-by-point to the charges of Rainolds and Sander (including Rishton under this name), in the 'Apologie' for Accession Day which was published with his sermon of 17 November 1599.[19] In his case, attempts to execute the required sophisticated manoeuvres between the separation of secular and sacred and their likening are sometimes unconvincing. He maintained that 7 September and 17 November were not formal holy-days (sigs L2r, R1r–v); but this was contradicted by his own title-page, which announced a defence of 'observing the 17. of November yeerely in the forme of an Holyday'. He asserted that 17 November was a secular, not religious, celebration; but then justified it on the grounds that there was scriptural precedent for thanksgivings for virtuous rulers (sigs I2r–v, R3r–4r), whereas pre-Reformation feasts like the Nativity of the Virgin on 8 September or St Hugh's Day on 17 November had no scriptural authority (sigs K3r, L4r, N3r). He argued that the festivities were not idolatrous, because they did not worship Elizabeth, but thanked God for her peaceful rule (sigs H4v, Or–v); and yet his own sermon illustrates how hard this distinction was to maintain in practice:

> How rare a Phenix the *Queen* of England hath beene, & how bright a starre in these daies . . . For in the fruits of her peace she wil shine as a star in the Catalogue of her honorable predecessors, and for her learning and wisedome wil be as a Phenix renowned by many famous writers to the people of that age, which shal succeede her.
>
> (sig.A4v)

One foundation of Holland's argument that celebrations of Elizabeth's birthday and of Accession Day were not equivalent to saints' days was that they were not imposed by Church or State, but were outpourings of spontaneous joy, 'vsually and willingly exhibited by the people of our Land to expresse their vnfained loue to her Maiestie' (sigs H3r, N4r, O3r, R1r–v). However, this claim of universal popular support must be regarded with some scepticism in

view of the very fact that Holland, who was in effect a Crown
appointee, felt it necessary to preach and write a defence of these
holidays; and in the light of his own robust statement of his didactic and propagandist purpose, as that

> all faithful subiects of this Realme may behold as in a glasse the
> good fruites that due obedience vsually bringeth forth . . . & what
> offices of benevolence all true subiectes owe by the law of God
> and man, to their princes, superiours & governours, who beare
> the sword by Gods ordinaunce.
>
>   (sig.H1v)

Holland's 'Apologie' thus fails to dispel the evidence that Accession Day was primarily an example of State exploitation of religious authority to reinforce centralised power. Interestingly, though,
he remarks that the fact that the English celebrated the birth of
Elizabeth did not mean that they 'contemne to celebrate the Nativity of the *B. Virgine*' (sig.L2v). In writing of the Virgin Mary, he
sought to distance himself from

> my forefathers of our pretended reformation . . . whoe long agoe
> haue proclaimed open warre against Gods saintes, & especially
> against the *Blessed Virgine* . . . God forbid that I or any one that cal
> vpon the name of God, their God & ours, should speake
> dishonorably of the least member of Gods house, much lesse of
> them that walke with the lambe vpon mount Sion . . .
>
>   (sig.K4v)

He advised a middle course: 'some speake despitefully of the *B.
Virgine*, and that is impiety: some make her a God by deifying her,
and that is a madd fury' (sig.L1v). This seems to provide evidence
of some rapprochement towards Catholic positions by some ministers of the Church of England.

In 1602, John Howson (1557?–1632), a chaplain to Elizabeth and
newly elected Vice-Chancellor of Oxford University, preached an
Accession Day sermon in defence of the festivities, which was swiftly
published.[20] Howson was a staunch suppressor of Puritanism, and
in later life became Bishop of Oxford, Bishop of Durham, and a
supporter of Laudian policies.[21] Howson acknowledged in his dedication that the celebrations were not only opposed by 'Preistes and
Iesuites', but also 'haue their adversaries at home among vs'. The
festival 'hath found some maligners both at home and abroad'.

Howson consistently and carefully described the purpose of
Accession Day as 'to giue thanks to God for the happy raigne of our
Soveraigne Princess' (sig.A4r), and made much use of scriptural
authorities for such thanksgivings for secular rulers (sigs A1r, A4r).
Like Holland, for whom he expressed admiration (sigs C1v–2r), he
distanced himself from earlier reformers: 'Erasmus did . . . absurdly,
when he vilified feasts, and falsely when he said . . . No ancient
writer maketh mention of any feast' (sig.A3r). As his discussion
proceeded, he increasingly equated Accession Day with a saint's
day, affirming that, regarding feast days, there was

> nothing amisse, til the Calender being overcharged with false
> and counterfeite popish saints, we reduced it to the compasse of
> our most auncient and Christian festiuities.
>
> Al which festivities notwithstanding this reformation haue
> found their enemies, and oppugning arguments, as also this daie
> which now we celebrate.
>
> (sig.B3v)

This leads Howson into the following justification of Accession Day:

> If the particular Church of England had authority in Queene
> Maries daies to appoint two solemne & Anniversarie Masses to
> be yerely celebrated in St. Maries, the one on the 18. of Februarie
> beeing the Nativity of Queene Marie, & the other on the first of
> October, on which she was crowned . . . and moreover appointed
> two solemne processions vpon the same daies . . . I doubt not to
> affirme that the particular Church of England hath also auctority
> sufficient to institute, if it so please, the celebration of the Nativ-
> ity, and inauguration of her excellent Maiestie, with publike ser-
> mons, common praiers, & thankesgiving.
>
> (sig.C3r)

Puritan contemporaries like Holland must have found this extraordinary reasoning: whatever Catholics do is acceptable for Protestants to do too. For us, it provides more evidence of the continuity
of celebration of Elizabeth with the quasi-religious iconography and
ritual accorded to earlier queens.

In the end, Howson's main argument is simply a resounding
affirmation of the sacredness of monarchy: 'And surelie God is verie
iealous of the honour of Princes'. To maintain order and hierarchy,

'God honoreth Princes with his owne name, so that they are called *Gods*, and *Gods annointed*, and the *sonnes of the most high*: he calleth them by his owne name, and furnisheth them with divine and supernatural qualities'. These comprise the power of prophecy, depth of heart, miraculous healing, absolute power answerable only to God, authority to bless and curse, and the protection of a guard of angels. Howson gives scriptural authorities for all of these gifts, and proclaims that they are all manifested in Elizabeth. For instance, she has 'this gifte of prophecie, as I may call it, whereby shee hath foreseene, foretold, and, if I may so saie, forespoken that which an ordinarie wisdome could not imagine'; and she has performed 'the supernatural cures of weake diseased people, amounting to the number of three or four hundred a yeare' (sigs D1v–2v). The Royal Touch had itself been the subject of recent defences by William Tooker (1597) and William Clowes (1602).[22] Howson concludes with a rousing prayer for Elizabeth's immortality: 'O Lord send her salvation, O Lord send her prosperity: *Non moriatur sed vivat*, let her not die but liue, that shee may declare thy wonderous workes to many generations' (sig.D3r–v).

Holland and Howson can be compared with Perkins to give a sense of the diversity of opinion concerning the veneration of Elizabeth in the latter years of the reign. Perkins's definition of civil worship allows for the iconic celebration of Elizabeth, but places limits upon it; Holland steers an uneasy course between presenting Elizabeth as like and unlike a saint; Howson tends towards the unequivocal veneration of Elizabeth as close to divinity. Their works demonstrate that even in the last years of the reign, when we find some of the most hyperbolic celebrations of Elizabeth, belief in her sacredness was by no means uniform, and definitions of that sacredness varied. The ritual celebration of her rule was a contentious issue, and, consequently, such worship of her as was performed was far from unconscious.[23]

iv. An incident concerning the Queen's image, 1601

On 3 October 1601 William Waad, or Wade, Clerk of the Privy Council, wrote to Sir Robert Cecil, Elizabeth's chief minister. A chest belonging to a man called Harrison had been intercepted in shipment to France, and had been found to contain

a little box ... where I found her Majesty's picture in metal, and a kind of mercury sublimate which had eaten in the metal;

whereupon I sent the box by two of my folks unto Mr. Weymes, an apothecary, where it was found to be a very strong poison . . . I cannot conceive he can have a good meaning that will place the picture of her Majesty's sacred person with such a poison.[24]

Thomas Harrison was examined the next day by Launcelot Brown and 'W. Ward' – probably William Waad again. At first Harrison, who was no doubt quite nervous, said that the picture was 'of a woman, but of whom he doth not know'. When pressed, however, he admitted that he thought it was a picture of the Queen. He explained that it had been left over from Hilliard's work on models for the Great Seal some years before; Harrison was interested in alchemy, and had therefore asked Hilliard for a piece of the unusual metal, being 'mercury congealed with vinegar and verdigris'. He had placed it in the box with 'mercury crystallined or alcolisated' merely because they were the same substance.[25]

Harrison was also interrogated about a fine chalice which was found in his chest, and gave an explanation which can hardly have helped his case: that he had bought it as a gift for the Bishop of Boulogne, in whose house he had stayed in Paris in return for disclosing alchemical secrets. He must have looked like a suspicious customer to Waad and his colleagues. Waad was known as one of the most zealous persecutors of Catholics, and spent much of his time detecting treasonous plots and trailing and examining recusants. In James I's reign he acquired a reputation for falsely gaining signatures to confessions.[26] It is quite possible that Harrison's self-defence was true, and that Waad had enthusiastically pounced upon treasonous intent where none was present.

The contrast between Waad's suspicions and Harrison's explanation strikingly illustrates two widely variant interpretations of artefacts bearing the Queen's image. Waad invested the piece of metal with profound symbolic value, almost equating it with Elizabeth's physical presence; for him, placing her image in poison implied malice towards her. It seems that various enemies of her regime concurred in this attitude: other cases are recorded of the Queen's portrait being stabbed, stoned, burned, and hanged from gallows.[27] It is unclear how far these gestures were expressions simply of opposition, or of a superstitious belief that damage to the Queen's image could actually do harm to her person. On the other hand, Harrison's explanation, while (eventually, at least) acknowledging that the image represented the Queen, saw it primarily as a piece of mere metal, a certain kind of chemical substance to be categorised with other samples of such substance.

For Waad, the metal had been transformed by the imprint of the Queen's image into a sacred symbol to be handled and preserved with reverence. For Harrison, it was simply an artefact, a piece of matter which could bear other shapes just as readily as the picture of the Queen. Harrison's attitude bespeaks an indifference to images, whereas for Waad, ironically, the loyal Protestant government servant, the image was claimed to be so powerful and so closely identical to its subject that any affront to it constituted virtual sacrilege.

v. Elegies for Elizabeth

Just three months after the author of the 'Verses of the Queene' quoted above wrote 'For Syons sake preserve from death: / Our noble queene *Elizabeth*', the Queen died, on 24 March 1603, at the age of 69. In the wake of recent trends in panegyric, it is not surprising that elegies for her death included Marian iconography. It was from such elegies that Frances Yates selected most of her examples of the apparent substitution of the Virgin Queen for the Virgin Mary, in her highly influential account of the subject. After quoting *'Vivat Eliza!* for an *Ave Mari!'*, she noted that:

> There is an engraving of the queen, with her device of the Phoenix, below which is written 'This Maiden-Queen Elizabeth came into this world, the Eve of the Nativity of the blessed virgin Mary; and died on the Eve of the Annunciation of the virgin Mary, 1602 [old style]'. This statement is accompanied by the following couplet:
>
> > She was, She is (what can there more be said?)
> > In earth the first, in heaven the second Maid.[28]

Yates comments:

> This staggering remark seems to imply that the defunct Queen Elizabeth is now a second Blessed Virgin in heaven. What more can there be said indeed? Except to add that implications of this kind are not uncommon in Elizabethan literature.

For corroboration, though, Yates turns to more posthumous material, from two elegies by university poets:

> Lux ea quae divae festum natale Mariae
> Iuncta praeit, fuit illa dies natalis Elizae...[29]
>
> [The day which adjoined and preceded the feast day of the birth of holy Mary, was the birthday of Elizabeth...][30]

And:

> Virgo Maria fuit, fuit illa: beata Maria,
>   Inter foemineum[31] Beta (i.e. Elisabeta) beata genus.[32]
>
> [Mary was a virgin, she was a virgin: Mary was blessed, Beta was blessed among the race of women.]

Again, Yates comments:

> Here one of the names used of Elizabeth by her poets, namely 'Beta,' is assimilated to 'Beata Maria'. In the memorial poems the death of Elizabeth becomes a kind of Assumption of the Virgin, followed by a Coronation of the Virgin in heaven. She who was virgin queen and goddess on earth is invested with the glory of a Virgin Queen of Heaven.

Once more, she quotes from an elegy:

> Quae fuit in terris Dea, Virgo, Regia virgo
>   Nunc est in coelis Regia, Virgo, Dea.[33]
>
> [She who was on earth a Goddess, a Virgin and a Royal maiden is now in heaven Royal, a Virgin and a Goddess.][34]

As I have suggested, closer study of trends in panegyric through Elizabeth's reign reveals that such explicit Marian echoes are at once less typical of 'Elizabethan literature' as a whole than Yates suggests, and, in the light of developments in poetry and panegyric towards the end of the reign, perhaps less startling than Yates finds them. For instance, when Henry Petowe wrote in his elegy, 'She was, she is, and euermore shall bee, / the blessed Queene of sweet eternitie',[35] he was in part simply continuing the conventional late

Elizabethan conceit of celebrating the Queen's immortality, except that it was now clear that that immortality would be achieved only in terms of enduring fame, and in heaven. When he wrote, 'Diuine she is for whome my Muse doth morne',[36] he was claiming no more than countless other panegyrists before him. As Yates says, descriptions of Elizabeth's ascent to heaven and coronation there can appear to imitate the iconography of the Assumption and Coronation of the Virgin. There are numerous other examples of this besides those she quotes, such as:

> *Beta*, farewell, and let thy purest spirit
> (Where euer fled[)] the purest place inherite.
> Goe blessed soule, and vp to heauen climbe,
> Among the Angels seate thee there betime,
> Shine like an Angell with thy starrie crowne,
> And milke-white Robes descending fayrely downe,
> Wash't in the blood of the vnspotted Lambe,
> That slew the Beast, and made the Dragon tame.
> There let thy sacred life (most sacred Dame)
> Thy famous vertue, and thy vertuous Fame;
> Whereof so many Pens haue writ the Story
> Receiue the crowne of euerlasting glory.
> Feast euer there and feed on sweetest ioy,
> Without the tast of any sharpe anoy:
> Liue euer there, in that Coelestiall skie,
> Where (spight of death) thou nevermore shalt die;
> Raine euer there on that *Elyzian* greene:
> *Eliza*, well may be *Elyziums Queene*.[37]

However, the iconography of an ascent to heaven and subsequent coronation was by no means exclusive to the Virgin. The Bible promised all believers the reward of a heavenly crown and throne.[38] Saints, in particular, were thought of as being crowned in heaven; and having been conventionally addressed as a saint in life, naturally it was said of Elizabeth in death that 'From Men, with Sainctes she liues in high esteeme, / Seated in blisse, which best doth her esteeme'.[39] There was nothing outrageously idolising or distinctively Marian in, say, the line from John Fenton's elegy, 'Her body sunke her spotlesse soule aspir'd'.[40]

Other queens before Elizabeth, both Catholic and Protestant, had been represented at their death in a similar way. Alexander Ales, in describing Anne Boleyn to Elizabeth as a Protestant heroine, had told her that on the day of her death, '. . . the Archbishop then raised his eyes to heaven and said, "She who has been the Queen of England upon earth will to-day become a Queen in heaven"'.[41] Poems on the death of Mary Queen of Scots had represented her as a saint in heaven.[42] Protestant ideas of sainthood continued to encompass ascent to heaven and coronation there: twenty-eight years after Elizabeth's death, the Puritan Milton would write in his 'Epitaph on the Marchioness of Winchester', 'thou bright saint sit'st high in glory/ . . . No marchioness, but now a queen'.[43]

Another favourite figuration of Elizabeth in the elegies was that of bride of Christ:

> Whilst here shee liu'd, shee spent her virgin yeares
> In Royall pompe amongst her wiser Peeres:
> Nor mought shee daygne with earthly Prince to ioyne,
> To bring forth issue from her virgin loyne:
> She had espoused her selfe to th'Lord of life,
> So still shee liues, a maiden, and a wife.[44]

Another elegist wrote:

> Elizabeth our English Queene,
> The like to whome was neuer seene,
> Is gone from earth to Christ aboue
> To dwell with him her onely loue.[45]

And yet another declared:

> Shee kept her selfe a *Virgin* for the Lord,
> With whom she longed daily for to be,
> That onely he alwaies she did accord,
> Should haue the prime of her virginitie;
> Who hath aduanc'd her to his heau'nly throne,
> Where she enioyes the perfect vnion.[46]

Again, she was not the first or the last departed virgin to be eulogised as Christ's spouse. In the late-fourteenth-century poem *Pearl*, the dead girl-child describes to the dreamer how

> . . . my Lorde the Lombe, thurgh hys godhede,
> He toke myself to hys maryage,

Corounde me quene in blysse to brede
In length of dayes that ever schal wage.

(. . . my Lord the Lamb, through His godhead, took me
to be His bride, crowned me queen to flourish in bliss
for a length of days that ever shall endure.)[47]

In Donne's *Second Anniversary*, 1612, it is said of the late Elizabeth
Drury that she,

> . . . being solicited to any act,
> Still heard God pleading his safe precontract;
> Who by a faithful confidence, was here
> Betrothed to God, and now is married there.[48]

In both *Pearl* and the *Anniversary* the Virgin Mary was undoubtedly
being self-consciously alluded to as a model of virtuous femininity
and its rewards, and I would not wish to claim that these representations of Elizabeth as bride of Christ or a Queen in heaven were
devoid of Marian echoes. My point is that it is incorrect to suggest
that such iconography in elegies for Elizabeth was surprising, unprecedented, or exclusive, and constituted her elevation as a new
Virgin Mary.

Elizabeth was always the *second* maid; the pre-eminence of the
Virgin Mary was always maintained, and, if anything, emphasised.
The elegies could not be claimed to participate in the removal of the
Virgin Mary from the English religious consciousness; if anything,
they marked a movement in the opposite direction. At a time when
Marian iconography was undergoing some resurgence, when a
Queen who was also a virgin and symbolic mother of the nation
died and went to heaven, it was virtually inevitable that the obvious analogies between the two virgins should be made use of in
elegiac verses. This was less a way of creating a new Virgin Mary
to fill a psychological gap, than a way of constructing witty compliments and inventive rhetorical flourishes on an important public
occasion.

The identification of Elizabeth with the Virgin which Yates detects
in the elegies she quotes partly arises from their typological tenden-
cies. The 'Verses of the Queene' of 1602 were an example of how,
on a particularly Marian occasion like Christmas, Marian material
could be used typologically. Now, in the elegies, correspondences

between the Virgin and Elizabeth were catalogued, not to make Elizabeth into a replacement for the Virgin, but to endue her life and characteristics with momentous symbolic and spiritual import, as a figure of virtue and the advancement of faith. This all formed part of the sense of the recent history of Protestant England as an unfolding of God's purpose, whose design and meaning were slowly becoming apparent to human understanding.

There was particular interest in the fact that the dates of Elizabeth's birth and death were both eves of Marian feasts, the Nativity of the Virgin and the Annunciation respectively. This was used to invoke a sense of design behind Elizabeth's life, governed by divine Providence and destiny. One elegist declared,

> The blessed morne fore blessed Maries day,
>   On angels wings our Queene to heauen flieth;
> To sing a part of that celestiall lay
>   Which Alleluiah, Alleluiah crieth.
> In heauens chorus so at once are seene
> A virgin mother, and a maiden Queene.[49]

Again, these typological elegies suggest not so much that Elizabeth had supplanted the Virgin, as that there was some revival of interest in Mariology – even, ironically, such that correspondences to Marian feasts and attributes could be invoked as an signs of the divine purpose behind the progress of Protestant England.

Thomas Dekker's *The Wonderfull Yeare*, an account of the events of 1603, supplies what could be a piece of evidence that Elizabeth was thought of as a rival to the Virgin. He describes England at her death as 'a nation that was almost begotten and borne vnder her; that neuer shouted any other *Aue* than for her name'. However, his very next words are '. . . [that] neuer sawe the face of any Prince but her selfe'.[50] It is likely that he is referring to the acclamation of a ruler, 'Ave Caesar', rather than the Ave Maria. The point was that Elizabeth had ruled for so long that few of her subjects could recall a different monarch.

Some elegists self-consciously made play of the proximity of civil worship to idolatry. One suggested that the 'Day of our Queene's Death, and our King's Proclamation' should be made a holiday. However, it was the eve of the feast of the Annunciation, which was also the old New Year, and the writer was careful to present the religious festival as primary:

Be Holy Eue vnto our Holy day,
Wherein was told the comming of our Lord.
Begin the yeares with good hap both togither,
Weele keepe the one beginning as the other,
And as it falls, thou the Politicall
Serue sub-yeare to th'Ecclesiasticall.[51]

As in the defences of Accession Day, the proposed festivity both is
and is not presented as equivalent to a saint's day. Meanwhile,
Thomas Cecil addressed the dead Elizabeth:

O deare deare Saint, I could haue worshipt thee;
And still I would, but for idolatrie.
And yet I will i'the best place of my brest,
Build vp a chappell for thy sole behest.[52]

This begins like a confession of awareness that civil worship might
risk turning into idolatry, but ingeniously turns this into compliment: Cecil professes that he will willingly embrace the danger of
idolatry because he is so far in thrall to the Queen's memory. Again,
allusion to idolatry is deployed as a rhetorical flourish rather than
a statement of belief.

It is certainly true that the elegies for Elizabeth included more
overt applications of Marian iconography to the Queen than had
occurred earlier in the reign. However, this was only one highly-
coloured strand among many, as elegists reprised and elaborated
upon the whole compendium of personae from the course of the
reign. Indeed, E.C. Wilson heads his chapter on the elegies 'In
Memoriam – Judith, Deborah, Eliza, Elisa, Diana, Laura, Idea,
Cynthia, Gloriana, and Belphoebe – 1603' (Ch.IX). The extravagance
of the elegies should also be set against the evidence of continuing
disillusionment with the Queen, as fulsome expressions of grief coexisted with evidence of weariness of her rule.

The number of poets who wrote on Elizabeth's death was fewer
than for Sidney or, later, for Prince Henry; in fact, it was something
of a topos amongst the elegists of 1603 to complain that too few
colleagues were joining them in the task.[53] Glorification of Elizabeth
in the elegies was carefully balanced by celebrations of her successor. Poets attempted to poise dutiful and decorous expressions of
grief for the loss of the Queen against expressions of joy for the
arrival of James, using such titles as *Sorrowes Ioy*, or *Elizaes memoriall*.

King Iames his arriuall. In Thomas Byng's elegy, the English people's grief that God has 'reft away/The aged mother of these orphane lands' is quickly assuaged by God's gift of James:

> Your mother gon, he shall your father hight.
> The teares that earst rayned adown their cheeke,
> They lightly wipte.[54]

Thomas Cecil wrote: 'Eliza's dead: that rends my heart in twaine: /And Iames proclaimd: this makes me well againe.'[55] As one E.L. put it, 'Oh griefe, and ioy, so suddenly commixt, /Such sympathie was e're seene you betwixt?'[56]

A favourite conceit in these dual-purpose poems was to acclaim James as the sun rising after the moon. Henry Petowe wrote: '*Luna's* extinct, and now beholde the Sunne,/Whose beames soake vp the moysture of all teares.'[57] For Henry Campion, 'Phaebe gone, a Phaebus now doth shine'; and Edward Kellet consoled England, 'though thy moone decaies, thy sun doth rise'.[58] In cases like these, lunar imagery was deployed to evoke a waning, feminine power secondary to the masculine sun and outshone by its rising splendour.

A number of elegies also found a new appropriateness in the figure of the phoenix. This was already a favourite emblem for Elizabeth, not particularly because it had sometimes been used as symbol of the Virgin Mary, but rather because of its independent connotations of singularity, virginity, triumph over adversity, longevity, and miraculous asexual reproduction. This reproduction could now be deemed to have taken place, with the 'birth' of the new King from the dead Queen's ashes:

> . . . as Phoenix dies; Phoenix is dead,
> And so a Phoenix follows in her stead;
> Phaenix for Phoenix.[59]

John Lane gives another example:

> See how our *Phoenix* mounts aboue the skies,
> And from the neast another *Phoenix* flyes,
> How happily before the change did bring
> A Mayden-*Queene*, and now a manly *King*.[60]

Anthony Nixon perpetuated the application of messianic imagery to Elizabeth: '*Eliza* was our Iesus to withstand /Our enemies that sought to worke our woe'.[61] On the whole, though, the messianic mantle passed to James: he was a new shepherd for the nation, a King of Peace to replace the Queen of Peace.[62] This could also involve typology: John Savile used the fact that James had been proclaimed King on the day preceding the Annunciation to develop an extended similitude between his accession and the Incarnation. His 'Salutatorie Poeme' opened, 'Haile Mortall God, *Englands* true *Ioy*, great King'.[63] He related how the Virgin Mary's soul was possessed with immeasurable joy, and so were the souls of the English people longing for James to arrive; Mary blessed God in the Magnificat, and the English blessed James with acclamations. The angel's '*Ave*' heralded the reversal of the Fall; just so the English people hoped to reap incomparable fruit from James's accession. Gabriel greeted Mary, 'Haile full of Grace'; he should now 'bid God saue King *Iames* his Magestie' (sigs B4r–C1r). Strikingly, although he draws analogies between James and the newborn Christ, Savile at no point makes the identification which offers itself between the Virgin and Elizabeth; instead, the Virgin is identified with the English people.

One elegist not quoted by Yates avoided the usual formula of celebration of Elizabeth's heavenward ascent, and instead contrasted her quasi divinity in life with her humanity in death:

> Whome, least men, for hur pietye,
> Should Iudge, to haue bine a dietye,
> Heauen since by death did summon,
> To shew she was a woman.[64]

The elegies for Elizabeth cannot therefore be simplistically read as evidence that Elizabethans worshipped their Queen as a new Virgin Mary. They provide evidence of a wide range of attitudes to the dead Queen. Questions of sincerity are notoriously unfathomable, and no doubt the elegists included some fervent monarchists who regarded their dead ruler as a sainted heroine. However, it must be acknowledged that the elegies were the work of writers seeking attention and patronage, and were formal displays of patriotism and literary skill. Although many of them employ hyperbolic Marian iconography, they generally do so with a kind of typological wit, alongside puns on 'Eliza' and 'Elysium' and quips about the waning moon.

vi. Manningham's diary

John Manningham was a student at the Inns of Court who kept a diary for 1602–3.[65] The diary is a fascinating resource, not least because Manningham knew Dr Henry Parry, one of the Queen's chaplains, who was on duty in her chamber in her last sickness and told Manningham of her behaviour in her last days. In addition, Manningham wrote down observations on London life and witticisms and aphorisms made by his friends, giving a vivid sense of the atmosphere of the capital around the time of the Queen's demise.

The diary confirms that the days before her death were marked by tension and excitement. On 23 March 1603 Manningham went to the Court at Richmond to hear Parry preach, and 'to be assured whether the Queene were living or dead' (f.110r). Later the same day, he dined with Parry in the privy chamber, and heard reports of the Queen's demeanour from him and other eminent churchmen in attendance. They described her as melancholy and pensive, giving signs of faith and imminent ascent to heaven:

> She tooke great delight in hearing prayers, would often at the name of Iesus lift vp hir handes and eyes to heauen. Shee would not heare the Arch*bishop* speake of hope of hir longer lyfe, but when he prayed or spake of heauen, and those ioyes, shee would hug his hand, &c.
>
> (f.111r)

Before her death had even taken place, it was being turned into narrative and spectacle as an archetypal godly death, furnishing signs of her sanctity and election.[66]

Manningham recorded the Queen's death at about three in the morning on 24 March, expressing his confidence in her ascent to heaven in a manner which suggests conventional propriety rather than belief in her divinity: 'I doubt not but shee is amongst the royall saincts in heauen in eternall ioyes' (f.111v). Although James was formally proclaimed at ten o'clock, a hiatus ensued. Manningham conveys a powerful impression of bewilderment and suspended animation. The authority of many public officers was 'expired with the princes breath', and there was great fear of 'garboiles' (i.e. disturbances) (f.111v). Manningham also attributed the uncanny quiet to popular grief:

The proclamacion was heard with greate expectacion, and silent
ioye, noe great shouting: I thinke the sorrowe for hir majesties
departure was soe deepe in many hearts. They could not soe
suddenly showe anie great ioy, though it could not be lesse then
exceeding greate for the succession of soe worthy a King. And at
night they shewed it by bonefires, and ringing. Noe tumult, noe
contradicion, noe disorder in the city: every man went about his
busines as readylie, as peaceably, as securely, as though there
had bin noe change, nor any newes euer heard of competitors.
God be thanked, our king hath his right.

(f.112r)

It seems that if the calm and silence were indeed caused by general grief, this was only one among several factors, including fear
of civil disturbance, and numb shock as the city lived through a
momentous transition such as few could remember in their life-
times. In any case, this reflective pause was soon succeeded by a
hubbub of eager anticipation of James's new, masculine regime.

The people is full of expectacion, and great with hope of his
worthines, of our nations future greatnes: every one promises
himselfe a share in some famous action to be hereafter performed,
for his prince and country . . . all long to see our newe king.

(f.112r–v, 24 March)

After his proper utterances of mourning and respect for the old
Queen, Manningham quickly turns to finding material in her death
for gossip and banter: 'It is certaine the Queene was not embowelled,
but wrapt vp in cere cloth, and that verry il to, through the
couetousness of them that defrauded hir of the allowaunce of cloth
was giuen them for that purpose' (f.120r, 5 April); 'I heard the
Queene left behinde hir in mony plate and iewels: the value of:
120000001:, whereof in gold is said: 4000001:' (f.125r, 8 April). In
particular, he records conversations among his friends which often
prefigure some of the later, more formal literary and historical
memorials of Elizabeth, but which have a markedly less reverent
tone. For instance, years after her death, in 1617, the historian
Camden would record the fact that in her last sickness she:

commanded that Ring, wherewith shee had beene joyned as it
were in marriage to her Kingdome at her inauguration, and she

had never after taken off, to be filed off from her finger, for that it was so growne into the flesh, that it could not be drawne off. Which was taken as a sad presage, as if it portended that that marriage with her Kingdome contracted by the Ring, would be dissolved.[67]

Writing only a few days after her death, Manningham recounted:

> Dr Parry told me the Countes Kildare assured him that the Queene caused the ring wherewith shee was wedded to the Crowne, to be cutt from hir finger some 6: weekes before hir death, but wore a ring which the Earl of Essex gave hir, vnto the day of hir death.
>
> (f.119v, 3 April)

It would seem that Elizabeth's reported symbolic gesture was the talk of the town immediately after her death, but was narrated more scurrilously and irreverently than Camden's later use of it in his official history.

There is a similar variant use of the same material between Manningham and Dekker. In *The Wonderfull Yeare*, Dekker invested the dates of Elizabeth's birth and death with mystical significance, emulating the elegists in making typological use of the Marian feasts: 'Shee came in with the fall of the leafe, and went away in the Spring: her life (which was dedicated to Virginitie,) both beginning & closing vp a miraculous Mayden circle: for she was borne vpon a Lady Eue, and died vpon a Lady Eue'.[68] Dekker's formulation has poignancy and delicacy; but Manningham's diary indicates that he was using an observation which had been circulating among Inns of Court wags since the Queen's death, who had found in it material for wit rather than pious awe. In his entry for 29 March 1603 he records: 'Mr. Rous said, that the *Queen* began hir raigne in the fall, and ended in the spring of the leafe. Soe she did but turne ouer a leafe said B. Rudyerd' (f.117v). Dekker makes a further point also made earlier by Manningham, that 'a *Lee* was Lorde Maior when she came to the Crowne, and a *Lee* Lorde Maior when she departed from it.'[69] Other writers pointed out the fact that Thursday was evidently a fatal day for Tudor monarchs, since Henry VIII, Edward VI, Mary and now Elizabeth had all died on a Thursday.[70] The interest in the significances of Elizabeth's dates was evidently not exclusively to do with their Marian connections, but was only part of a general fascination with identifying intriguing coincidences surrounding her death. In some contexts these were treated as matters of high seriousness, but in others more as curious trivia.

Another feature of Manningham's diary was that he recorded at length sermons which he had attended. Roy Strong makes much of a passage from one of these, a sermon by Dr John King given at Whitehall three days after the Queen's death, on 27 March 1603.[71] Strong quotes the following passage:

> Soe there are two excellent women, One that bare Christ, and an other that blessed Christ: to these may wee ioyne a thrid, that bare and blessed him both. Shee bare him in hir heart as a wombe: she conceiued him in fayth, shee brought him forth in aboundaunce of good workes . . .
>
> (f.115v)[72]

Strong comments: 'Elizabeth is soberly hailed as a second Virgin giving birth to the Gospel of Christ. This alarming apotheosis was to be the keynote of the seventeenth-century cult of "Saint" Elizabeth.'[73]

However, King's words must be placed in context. Strong never explains who was meant by the woman who blessed Christ, and gives the impression that King mentioned the Virgin Mary because he was preaching on Elizabeth's death. In fact, he was preaching on Luke 11.14–29, a text which describes how Christ cast out a devil, then spoke of division in kingdoms, then was acclaimed by a woman in the company who 'lifted vp her voyce, & said vnto him, Blessed *is* the wombe that bare thee, and the pappes which thou haste sucked' (Luke 11.27).[74] King had not chosen this text for the occasion; 27 March 1603 was the third Sunday in Lent, and Luke 11.14–29 the gospel prescribed for that day.[75] As any preacher would, King made an effort to find topical relevance in his text, and he did this with every part of it, not just the reference to the Virgin. Thus he resembled Christ's casting out of the devil to Elizabeth's casting out of the devil of idolatry from the kingdom (f.115r); and he used Jesus's words about division in kingdoms to describe how, with the death its Queen, the state had sustained 'a diuision as of the body and soule, of the vine and the branches, of the hvsband and the wife, of the head, and the body' (f.115r–v). The comparison between Elizabeth and the 'two excellent women' thus comes in the middle of a long train of typological interpretation and figurative language, and is prompted by a prescribed gospel text; it is not, as

Strong's use of it implies, a gratuitous or outrageous supplantation of the Virgin with Elizabeth. The idea that Elizabeth was not only mother of the Church, but had specifically given birth to the true faith in England, was far from unprecedented, and can be traced back at least to Hellwis's *A Marvell Deciphered* in 1589.[76] The combination of text and occasion, and the existing convention of typological topical reading of Scripture, produced a situation where King could hardly have avoided speaking as he did.

Manningham recorded another remark made among his friends on Elizabeth's death: 'Wee worshipt noe Saints: but wee prayd to Ladyes in the *Queen's* tyme: [said] Mr. Curle. / This supersticion shall be abolished we hope in our kings raigne' (f.119r, 1 April). This may mean that he and his companions recognised that panegyric of the Queen had got out of hand, verging on idolatry; that they regarded this with some cynicism and jadedness, but hoped (erroneously, as it turned out) that with the accession of a male ruler lavish compliments would not be required as performances of loyalty. Alternatively, 'praying to ladies' may refer to the outpourings of Petrarchan poetry which had dominated the 1590s and were now passing out of fashion. Even in this case, the Inns of Court students were perceiving in the demise of the Queen the welcome end of an unduly feminised, extravagant culture.

Study of a private, informal source like Manningham's diary provides a different angle on what Elizabeth's subjects thought about her death. It suggests that, in at least one circle of Londoners, her departure inspired not only expressions of conventional dutiful respect, but also restless desire for the coming of her successor, and rather less deferential repartee and small-talk about her. Manningham appears simultaneously to have believed that the Queen was crowned in heaven, and that she was fair game for the disclosure of celebrity secrets. The diary is of course only a single, partial, circumstantial source, but it reinforces the fact that it is unwise to read the public, formal elegies as evidence of universal or deeply felt feelings or beliefs about the Queen.

vii. Full circle

Dekker's trope of Elizabeth's life and death as 'a miraculous Mayden circle' potently represented her life-cycle as a closed circle analogous to her perfectly enclosed virgin body. It might also serve as a figuration of the general way in which Elizabeth's death revived interest in her early life, representing her as having come full circle. Elegists re-invoked personae from the earlier years of the reign, like Deborah and Judith, and placed them alongside Cynthia and Gloriana. Elizabeth's coronation portrait was copied afresh, possibly for use in funeral or memorial ceremonies: presumably this signified the fact that she had ascended to a second coronation in heaven, and her long, loose hair, which in 1559 had symbolised marriage to the nation, now symbolised her marriage to Christ.[77] In ways like these the end of Elizabeth brought about an iconographic return to her beginnings.

Elizabeth's early life was reread for signs which prefigured and fell into a pattern with later historic events. At the same time, much of this posthumous material exceeded even the elegies in representing Elizabeth as sanctified. As she passed into history and fiction, she became an even more ethereal, mythical figure. Part 1 of Thomas Heywood's very popular play, *If you know not me, you know no bodie, or the troubles of Queene Elizabeth*, 1605 (performed 1604), dealt wholly with her life before she became Queen, ending with the coronation pageants.[78] The play was intensely hagiographical, continuing the tradition already established by Foxe and others of mythologising Elizabeth's early life,[79] but with added licence in depicting her as a saint now that she was regarded as having taken her place in heaven.

The play shows the Princess as a Patient-Griselda-like martyr on her sickbed, persecuted by her sister's henchmen (pp.200–1). The audience is constantly told that God is on her side (pp.204–5). When even hard-hearted servants are moved to tears by her plight, Elizabeth exhorts them,

> Weepe not, I pray;
> Rather, you should reioice. If I miscarry
> In this enterprise, and you aske why,
> A Virgin and a Martyr both I die.

> (p.205)

She steadfastly declares her faith:

> My God doth know,
> I can no note but truth; that with heauens King
> One day in quires of angels I shall sing.

> (p.207)

In a posthumous text, such statements are of course invested with the value of prophecy.

The Constable of the Tower, an evil Catholic, plots to inflict the kind of torments on Elizabeth which martyrs must endure:

> Cause she an alien is to vs Catholikes:
> Her bed should be all snakes, her rest despaire;
> Torture should make her curse her faithlesse prayer.

(p.217)

However, a dumbshow depicts how, when a gang of friars come to kill the Princess in her sleep, they are fought off by a guard of angels, who place an English Bible in her hand (p.228). The play is a Protestant saint's legend, reading back into Elizabeth's early life the posthumous certainty of the Queen's virginity and heavenly destiny.

Part 2 of the play (1632, first performed 1606?) deals with events of the reign itself, selecting for attention the opening of the Royal Exchange and the Armada victory. The presentation of the conflict with Spain is highly sexualised, continuing the identification of the nation with the Queen's body. Don Pedro, an evil Spaniard, mocks:

> I think we come too strong. What's our designe
> Against a petty island gouernd by a woman?
> I thinke, instead of military men,
> Garnish'd with armes and martiall discipline,
> She, with a feminine traine
> Of her bright ladies, beautifull'st and best,
> Will meet vs in their smocks, willing to pay
> Their maidenheads for ransome.

(pp.333–4)

Of course he is in for a shock, as Elizabeth enters 'compleatly armed', tells her soldiers that she has 'put on a masculine spirit', and vows that 'I'le paue their way with this my virgin brest' (p.337). This active warrior-woman is rather a different figure from the passively suffering martyr of Part 1. Even in this more aggressive mode, however, the Catholic threat is primarily another occasion for her to show her sanctified heroism: 'A march, lead on! we'le meet the

worst can fall; /A maiden Queene is now your generall' (p.342).
The victory is naturally acclaimed as 'by the hand of heauen, and
not our own' (p.343).

Much of the material in Part 1 of *If you know not me* was reused
by Heywood in a prose hagiography, *England's Elizabeth*, 1631. This
text repeats the observation that 'Lady *Elizabeth* [was] borne on the
Eue of the virgins Natiuity, and died on the Eue of the Virgins
Annuntiation 1603 . . . she is now in heauen with all these blessed
virgins that had oyle in their lampes.'[80] Again, Princess Elizabeth is
shown enduring the vicissitudes of her sister's reign with piety,
patience, and certainty of her heavenly destiny.

Shakespeare and Fletcher's *Henry VIII*, 1613, was another Jacobean text which retrospectively celebrated the 'miraculous Mayden
circle' of Elizabeth's life. The climax of the play is the christening of
the new-born Princess, at which Archbishop Cranmer is seized with
a prophetic impulse:

> She shall be, to the happiness of England
> An aged princess; many days shall see her,
> And yet no day without a deed to crown it.
> Would I had known no more! But she must die –
> She must, the saints must have her – yet a virgin;
> A most unspotted lily shall she pass
> To th'ground, and all the world shall mourn her.[81]

The dramatic rewriting of history includes King Henry's effusions
of joy at the child's birth and Cranmer's 'oracle of comfort' (1.66).

Another dramatic scene which may have been constructed after
Elizabeth's death is set at her first Parliament, in 1559. Parliament
had petitioned the Queen to marry; different versions of her reply
exist, of which I discussed the one which is probably closest to her
words.[82] Another much-quoted version, however, was given by
William Camden, writing in James I's reign, as follows:

> yea to satisfie you, I have already ioyned my selfe in marriage to
> an husband, namely, the Kingdome of *England*. And behold (said
> she, which I marvaile ye have forgotten,) the pledge of this my
> wedlocke and marriage with my Kingdome, (and therewith, she
> stretched forth her finger and shewed the ring of gold, wherwith
> at her Coronation she had in a set forme of words, solemnly
> given her selfe in marriage to her Kingdome.)[83]

All variant versions of the speech agree that Elizabeth expressed a personal preference for virginity, and ended with words approximating to the following: 'And to me it shall be a full satisfaction both for the memoriall of my name, and for my glory also, if when I shall let my last breath, it be ingraven upon my Marble Tombe, *Here lyeth ELIZABETH, which raigned a Virgin, and dyed a Virgin*'.[84] What is in doubt, though, is whether she made the dramatic gesture with her ring.[85] Even if she did speak and act as Camden reports, it was in a cameral reception of a parliamentary delegation, not in front of a whole sitting of Parliament, as some commentators have tended to assume.[86] Camden's emphasis on the ring assists him to present her life and death as a fulfilment of prophecy: as we have seen, he narrates how the gesture was ominously recalled on Elizabeth's deathbed, when she asked for the ring to be filed off, the first time it had been off her finger since her 'marriage' to the kingdom at her coronation, presaging the impending dissolution of that marriage.[87]

Some twentieth-century commentators have used Camden's account of the 1559 speech and other parts of his history as documentary evidence of Elizabeth's self-presentation, neglecting to take account of their Jacobean context, and of Camden's narrative artifice.[88] To do so can be to participate in the reading back of later hagiographical iconography into the early years of the reign. As I have tried to show, a phenomenon recognisable as a cult of Elizabeth developed gradually and was not well-established until the latter part of the reign, when even then it did not command universal support. Representations of the Queen in her early years as an iconic sanctified virgin may be back-formations, contributing to posthumous symbolic interpretations of her life.

viii. Beyond the grave

We see in such material that some of the loftiest apotheoses of Elizabeth date from after her death, when she could be uncontroversially thought of as a holy saint in heaven. Moreover, as James's reign proceeded, the enthusiastic welcome accorded him in the accessional verses dwindled away, and nostalgia for his predecessor grew. He was found wanting on a number of counts, including the perceived decadence of his court in comparison with that of the Virgin Queen; his lack of her gifts in public relations, showing himself to his subjects as little as possible; and his pro-Spanish foreign policy, conciliating England's traditional Catholic enemies.[89]

Celebratory commemoration of Elizabeth in texts like Fulke Greville's *Life of Sidney* and Camden's *Annals* operated as an implicit critique of Stuart rule, and images of the Queen as Protestant saint and champion functioned as rebukes to her heir. A version of Francis Delaram's engraving of Elizabeth as the Woman of the Apocalypse, crowned with stars and seated among billowing clouds (1617–19), was used as the frontispiece of the 1625 edition of the *Annals*, with these verses on the back:

> Here reade the dayes,
> > when Britann ground,
> VVith blessings all,
> > was compast round.[90]

In turn, in the reign of James's heir Charles, tributes to Elizabeth continued to be used as a means of voicing political dissent. The point was not so much to worship Elizabeth as to name specific policy areas, like foreign policy and relations with Parliament, which she was nostalgically recalled as having managed successfully and in which, by implication, her successors were failing. As Anne Barton puts it, Jacobean and Caroline writers were 'out to celebrate the memory, not of a Lylian Moon Goddess, but of a great, and politically astute Protestant queen ... Flattery of living monarchs is one thing. It is likely to seem both more disinterested and politically more purposeful when they are dead' (pp.713, 715).

In 1642 a pamphlet was published entitled *The Humble Petition of the Wretched, And most contemptible, the poore Commons of England, To the blessed ELIZABETH of famous memory. Also a most gratious Answer, with a Divine Admonition and Perpetuall Conclusion.*[91] It contained three poems, all of which had appeared earlier in a number of manuscripts. The first poem is called 'To the Blessed St Elizabeth of Famous Memory; The humble Petitions of the wretched and most contemtible, the poore Commonons [*sic*] of England', and had appeared in one manuscript which carries the dates 1619, 1621 and 1623.[92] The second poem is 'To the high and mightiest, most Just, and yet most mercifull, the great Chancellor of Heaven, and chiefest Judge of all the Earth', and can be dated on internal evidence to 1623 or '24.[93] The third poem is 'A most gracious answer, procured by the blessed Saint *Elizabeth*, with a divine admonition and

Propheticall conclusion', and is not datable;[94] but it appears that at least the first two poems, and possibly the third as well, were composed first as a complaint against James's rule, then reissued and reused in 1642 as a complaint against Charles.

In the first poem, the petition to Elizabeth, the Queen is uninhibitedly addressed as a saint and intercessor:

> If Saints in Heaven can eather see or heare
> Or helpe poore mortals, O then lend an eare;
> Looke doune blest Saint, O heare, O heare us now,
> Whose humble hearts, low as our knees doe bow.

> (p.1)

Elizabeth is asked to act as a mediatrix, to carry the Commons' complaints to

> the Barre,
> Where no corruption, no friend, no fraud, no bribe,
> No griping Lawyer, no avaricious Scribe,
> No favorite, no parrasite, no minnion
> Can either lead or alter the opinion.

> (p.1)

The satirical, political purpose of the verses is manifest. In fact, their whole form is not only imitative of petitions to saints, but of subjects' petitions to the monarch, which are now disregarded: their grievances include the fact that 'Thy once blest Subjects beene so often curst / For offering up petitions of this kinde' (p.2).

Elizabeth is promised, if she will 'daine to further this our poore Petition', that:

> we will make the name of blest *Eliza*,
> Equall the *Aves*, of the great *Maria* . . .
> The monument weele raise, shall make proud Rome
> On pilgrimage to come, and at thy shrine
> Offer thier gifts, as to a thing divine.
> And on an alter, fram'd of richest stones,
> Weele daily tender teares, and sighes, and groanes.

> (p.2)

In at least one manuscript (though not in the printed text) the petition is signed 'Thy perpetuall and faithfull Beadesmen / The distressed Commons of Englande'.[95]

In the third poem, Elizabeth descends from heaven to speak, and sternly reprehends the Commons that they have brought their sufferings on themselves through their sin and pride:

> had you still sat in vvealth,
> You never vvould have bovved your stubborne knee
> Either to God, to Saint in Heaven, nor me.

(p.10)

Yet although she lambasts the Commons in this fashion, and maintains that 'Princes are gods on earth, and subjects eyes / Upon their actions should not stand as spies' (p.11), Elizabeth is also made a mouthpiece for criticisms of current royal policies. She declares that princes should liberally share their wealth with their subjects, and laments the decline of the army and navy since her day, and the sale of Crown lands to favourites (pp.10–11).

After a burst of cryptic doom-laden prophecy (p. 12), Elizabeth informs the Commons that because they disdained both her and God, 'Bootlesse you shall lament, bootlesse complaine...' (p.13). Just before its close the poem rises to a crescendo, which differs between manuscript and printed text. At least one manuscript gives:

> *Harke Harke heauens Organs* summons me awaye
> My Comissions ended, I dare not staye
> The blessed Choristers of Heaven I heare
> Tuning there voices to our Soueraignes eare...[96]

The printed version in place of these four lines has merely 'Harke, harke, heavens trumpet summons me away, / Now my commission's ended, I must not stay' (p.13), cutting down on the Catholic paraphernalia; although more lines are added before the poem ends, driving home the need to prepare for the Day of Judgement. Again this may be the result of the poems' being used by different parties at different times, though with the shared purpose of expressing a grievance against a Stuart king.

The poems represent Elizabeth at her most sanctified, apotheosised, and pseudo-Marian; yet at the same time, she is endearingly robust and forthright. The context is all-important: the religious apparatus which surrounds the dead Queen is primarily motivated less by a desire to worship her than by a desire to castigate the living King. She is dead and gone, creating a freedom to mythologise her and deploy her as a fictional character, for whatever purpose the contemporary political climate creates.

The most important feature of the texts considered in this chapter is their diversity. Too often, writings from around the time of Elizabeth's death have been read superficially, out of context, as evidence that all her subjects worshipped her as a new Virgin Mary for all of her reign. Her death gave new impetus to representations of her as a heavenly saint; but even then, not everyone wrote of her as a quasi-divinity, and those who did, did so with different motivations and tones.

Epilogue:
Adulation or Anxiety?

It is worth considering why the idea that there was a cult of Elizabeth which replaced the cult of the Virgin Mary has taken such hold in twentieth-century scholarship. In the first place, many modern writers, both academic and popular, have been fascinated by the glamour of the figure of Elizabeth as they perceive her across history, and have themselves contributed to the enhancement and celebration of that glamour. It could justifiably be said that, whether or not there was a cult of Elizabeth in the Queen's own lifetime, there certainly has been one in the twentieth century. One of those chiefly responsible for this was the historian J.E. Neale, whose highly readable biography, *Queen Elizabeth*, 1934, is driven by the verve of a writer more than half in love with his subject, and conveys the same intoxication to the reader: he writes, 'It is difficult to convey a proper appreciation of this amazing Queen, so keenly intelligent, so effervescing, so intimate, so imperious and regal.'[1]

E.C. Wilson and Frances Yates wrote their studies of the cult of Elizabeth in 1939 and 1947 respectively, in the wake of this powerful version of Elizabeth. They also belonged to the same generation of scholars which produced, in literary criticism, T.S. Eliot's nostalgia for a time before the Civil War when a catastrophic 'dissociation of sensibility' had not yet set in, and E.M.W. Tillyard's *Elizabethan World Picture*, both visions of the sixteenth-century as an age of cultural unity, order and assurance.[2] Wilson's and Yates's depictions of the Elizabethan age as focused on a cult of the Queen reflect a similar idealisation of a more glorious and harmonious past. At the same time the evidence they gathered of sixteenth-century idolisation of Elizabeth seems to have disturbed them as sacrilegious. As I suggested in passing in my Introduction, this may be because they wrote out of early twentieth-century attitudes to monarchy. It seems likely that their simultaneously fascinated and appalled reaction to what they had identified as a cult of Elizabeth was grounded in divided feelings symptomatic of their own moment in history, including reaction to the abdication crisis of Edward VIII: on the one hand, nostalgia for an imagined time when monarchs were godlike and universally revered, and on the other a self-congratulatory sense that the modern age had achieved a more realistic and rational attitude to monarchs.

Roy Strong writes as an intellectual heir to Yates, and capitalises upon the glamorous aspects of Elizabethan culture in his lavishly produced and highly enjoyable books. His work provides more evidence of how the idea of a cult of Elizabeth allows the twentieth-century reader simultaneously to revel in the beauty and splendour of a lost past, and to feel a comfortable sense of modern superiority. As Strong wrote on the much-quoted couplet 'She was, She is (what can there more be said?) / In earth the first, in heaven the second Maid', closely echoing Yates, 'What more indeed can be said, than that this withered, vain old lady of seventy should now reign as a second queen of heaven!'[3]

New historicists such as Stephen Greenblatt, Louis Montrose and Leonard Tennenhouse have continued and intensified interest in the cult of Elizabeth because it provides support for their theories of the 'circulation of social energy'[4] between ruler and ruled. It can be understood as a reinforcement of centralised power which was neither solely imposed from above, nor produced by popular enthusiasm, but generated and perpetuated by some kind of dynamic exchange between authority and subject. It can be seen in terms of the staging of power, and can be analysed in terms of the psycho-analysis of culture, leading towards the anthropological method-ologies which new historicists favour.

Much of this thinking has proved very fruitful and has opened up fascinating new interpretations. Even so, it can be insensitive to topical detail, and to the Elizabethans' own sophistication and self-consciousness. In the present study, I have aimed to give some recognition of Elizabethan thinkers' own theorisations of their cultural practices, including definitions of legitimate 'civil worship', considerations of the moral justifications of panegyric, and explorations of the relationship between the Queen and her image.

As we have seen, these cultural practices changed over the course of the reign. In the early years, most praise of Elizabeth was tentative and provisional. It represented her as a virgin queen in the sense of being ripe for marriage; and it used scriptural typology to invoke divine approval for her rule, while scrupulously avoiding Catholic terminology. In the middle years, as Elizabeth passed beyond the possibility of childbearing, panegyric came to represent her as a static icon of perpetual virginity, which in turn encouraged representation of her as sanctified. She was also considered holy in the sense that she personified the English Protestant Church, regarded as the true Church. Typology which was more specifically Marian began to enter panegyric. However, representations of Elizabeth as divine should not necessarily be read literally: they drew on literary conventions of the metaphorical 'divinity' of classical goddesses and courtly-love mistresses; and in a number of significant writers they were produced by Protestant theories of panegyric as exemplary and didactic, outlining an ideal to be aspired to rather than one already fulfilled by the person being praised. In later years, increasingly hyperbolic and fantastic representations of Elizabeth, including assertions of her immortality, and the use of overtly Marian typology, coexisted with expressions of disillusionment and criticism.

As I have shown, Yates took most of her evidence for Elizabeth's supplantation of the Virgin from this late poetry and from elegies on the Queen's death. This creates an innaccurate impression of the reign as a whole; and in any case, these open allusions to the Virgin can be read in terms of a resurgence of Catholic themes in culture. In fact, the closest Elizabeth came to ousting and replacing the Virgin was in the middle period, when the typological identification of the Queen with figures previously identified with Mary, such as the bride of the Song of Songs and the Woman Clothed with the Sun, excluded any mention of or allusion to these figures' prior Marian associations, and thereby approached the deletion of the Virgin and the creation of a new immaculately conceived virgin-mother figure. Even so, the force of such panegyric was not to compensate for the psychological trauma of losing the Virgin as an object of worship, but to erect Elizabeth as a figurehead of militant nationalistic Protestantism.

Accounts of the cult of Elizabeth can neglect such changes over time, as well as other diversities in Elizabethan culture. Some of Elizabeth's subjects remained Catholic; Edward Rookwood and Henry Constable were two who attempted to reconcile their political and religious loyalties, but even they found their participation in displays of allegiance to the Queen obstructed by either public authorities or personal conscience. Even among the large number of panegyrists who were basically loyal, Protestant and nationalistic, motivations differed according to the social position of the writer and the genre of his work. For favoured courtiers such as Sir Christopher Hatton or Sir Walter Ralegh, the religious language of courtly love was a means of negotiating a difficult and unstable political and personal intimacy. For professional writers such as Thomas Churchyard or the authors of the university elegies, the composition of panegyric to mark royal occasions like civic visits or the Queen's death was a means of advertising their literary skills to potential patrons. Panegyric needs to be understood as rhetoric generated by various kinds of political and personal ambition and dependence, rather than as a sincere effusion of infatuation with Elizabeth's personality, or of attachment to a virgin-mother figure.

However, despite these diversities, all panegyrists of Elizabeth shared one common political motivation: the fact that celebration of their Queen as a sanctified icon constituted a statement of allegiance to England and the Protestant Church. In this sense, the tribal connotations of the term 'cult' are appropriate. Panegyric and ritual erected the Queen as the standard of a cause; participation in these cultural practices was a means of defining and announcing affiliation to a group identity. This elevation of Elizabeth as symbol of a collective identity was probably facilitated by the fact that she was female. I mentioned earlier that her gender may well have been a factor in the readiness of her subjects to identify her with the English Church and nation.[5] It is observable that, through many centuries of Western culture, allegorical representations of abstractions or collectivities have tended to be female figures.[6]

Elizabeth's gender was clearly an issue in the sixteenth century: as we have seen, she came to the throne in the midst of controversy about female rule, and in the later years of the reign, even after successes such as the Armada victory, dissent included a resurgence of misogyny. Not surprisingly, various societies, including Elizabethan England, whose normal structures were patriarchal, have regarded anomalously powerful women with suspicion, disquiet, and even revulsion.[7] At the same time, in counterpart to this, such situations have often produced intense fascination, awe and devotion towards the abnormally elevated female figure.[8] An example from recent history is Margaret Thatcher, who inspired extremes of adoration in her supporters and loathing in her opponents.

Both the adulation and the animosity can be understood as produced by the same basic misogyny. One way to accommodate a powerful woman, without disrupting a predominant cultural framework which regards women as inferiors and subordinates, is to represent her as a wonder and a miracle, an 'exceptional woman' whose marvellous gifts stand out in contrast to the general fallibility or even depravity of her sex. The Virgin Mary and Elizabeth as symbols are both examples of this syndrome; in these two cases, moreover, in Christian societies, the bestowal of marvellous powers on a mere woman could also be used as evidence of the power of God, choosing a weak vessel as his instrument the better to show his strength.[9]

Another observable phenomenon across different historical periods is the tendency to identify a powerful woman with other, prior, female figures. In Chapter 1 I described how the Virgin Mary accumulated attributes from classical goddesses, biblical heroines, courtly mistresses, and queens. Elizabeth in turn took on the attributes of earlier symbolic women, including many previously associated with the Virgin, and others besides. Spenser represented Elizabeth as the descendant of a dynasty of warrior-queens, 'bold *Bunduca*', 'stout *Guendolen*', 'Renowmed *Martia*', 'redoubted *Emmilen*', and 'Faire *Angela*' (*FQ* III.iii.54–6). All this can be understood as a means of 'normalising' the disturbing figure of an autonomous woman ruler. Identification of her with figures of female power which are already well known renders her more familiar and dilutes the sense that she is startlingly aberrant; the invention or rediscovery of powerful female ancestors for her has the same effect of placing her reassuringly in a tradition and continuity. Again, cultural responses to Margaret Thatcher present a modern example; in her heyday as Prime Minister she was widely compared, in newspaper articles, books and cartoons, with Britannia, Boadicea, and Elizabeth I.[10] Quoted in an article which marked her record as the longest-serving twentieth-century Prime Minister, Lord Hailsham said: 'You've got to put her in the same category as Bloody Mary, Elizabeth I, Queen Anne and Queen Victoria'.[11]

Thus there has long been a recognisable tendency to find precursors for powerful women with whom to conflate them. Recognition of this makes all the more striking the purposeful efforts of earlier Elizabethan panegyrists to avoid pseudo-Marian imagery, over riding the impulse to turn to a familiar and established iconography of femininity with the need to forge an iconography purified of Catholic associations. However, the tendency to conflate female figures may itself be an element in the desire by modern scholars to regard the cult of Elizabeth as merely a substitute for the cult of the Virgin Mary. Their urge to explain idealisations of Elizabeth as driven by a continuing need for a symbolic virgin-mother figure may itself merely reflect a tendency enduring into the twentieth century to reduce all powerful women to a single figure of Woman, and then to regard further explanation or analysis as unnecessary.

Indeed, the fascination of writers such as Neale with Elizabeth can be seen as resembling the sixteenth-century cult of Elizabeth in being adulation of an 'exceptional woman' which is grounded in a basic sexism, a disbelief that a woman should have achieved so much. Feminist writers have generally had a somewhat more ambivalent attitude to Elizabeth, often finding themselves initially drawn to her as an attractive figure of female autonomy, only to become disappointed as they find out not only how little she did personally for other women, but also how little the very fact of having a woman on the throne changed the status of women in general.[12]

It often seems to happen that a powerful woman gets turned into an archetypal figure of Woman. She then has to embody all supposedly feminine qualities, and acquires a multiplicity of representations; in Freudian terms, she becomes 'overdetermined'.[13] She is first isolated as an 'exceptional woman', then fragmented: masculine mythologisations of femininity as an enigma, a mystery whose essence continually provokes yet eludes definition, generate a plethora of different personae for her. Elizabeth's virginity further intensified her aura of being, in every sense, impenetrable.[14] As I have shown, her additional anomalousness as a virgin was turned to symbolic use as a way of enhancing her exceptionality, and as a way of representing the defiant impregnability of the English nation. Celebration of her virginity was less an attempt to replicate the cult of the Virgin than an effort to turn to nationalistic use enduring superstitions which associated the virgin female body with purity and the sexually active female body with pollution and mortality.

I would suggest, then, that the extremes of praise of Elizabeth can be seen as typical of the feverish adulation of figures of female power which patriarchal societies tend to produce, in reaction to repressed anxieties at the disruption of hierarchy and the physical otherness which a powerful woman represents. The remarks in Manningham's diary that 'wee prayd to Ladyes in the *Queen's* tyme', and that 'This super*s*ticion shall be abolished we hope in our kings raigne',[15] can be read as voicing a contemporary sense that professions of adoration of Elizabeth were produced by her gender, and that subjugation to a female ruler was an unsettling aberration. Such continuities as existed between the cult of the Virgin and the iconography of Elizabeth can therefore be seen as produced by entrenched sexual attitudes and by the perception of a female ruler as a problem.

The glorification of Elizabeth as the Virgin Queen was produced by far more complex and variable processes than just a desire to replace the Virgin Mary. For this reason, and for others I have outlined, the existence of a 'cult of Elizabeth' may, in certain senses, be questioned. The phrase is convenient and catchy shorthand to denote the combination of panegyric, ritual and portraiture which grew up around the Queen; but there is inaccuracy in its implications of universal and spontaneous worship. These in turn can produce a tendency to read panegyric at face value without allowance for rhetoric or irony. Closer analysis of representations of Elizabeth, looking beyond the term 'cult', might lead us towards a better understanding of both Elizabethan culture and feminine iconographies.

Notes

Introduction

A version of this Introduction appeared as 'Rediscovering shock: Elizabeth I and the cult of the Virgin Mary' in *Critical Quarterly* 35.3 (*Criticism after Theory*; Autumn 1993, pp.30–42). I am grateful to David Trotter for his editorial suggestions.

1. That is, 'it was boasted of'.
2. To decipher, detect, reveal; cf. George Gascoigne, *The Adventures of Master F.J.* (1573), in Paul Salzman, ed., *An Anthology of Elizabethan Prose Fiction* (Oxford: Oxford University Press, 1987), p.9.
3. Quoted from John Nichols, ed., *The Progresses and Public Processions of Queen Elizabeth*, 3 vols (London: J. Nichols for Soc. of Antiquaries, 1823), II, pp.215–19. See also Edmund Lodge, ed., *Illustrations of British History, Biography, and Manners, in the Reigns of Henry VIII, Edward VI, Mary, Elizabeth and James I*, 2nd edn, 3 vols (London: John Chidley, 1838), II, pp.119–25; Augustus Jessopp, *One Generation of a Norfolk House: A Contribution to Elizabethan History*, 3rd edn (London: T. Fisher Unwin, 1913), pp.94–7, 106–7 n.7; Paul Johnson, *Elizabeth I: A Study in Power and Intellect* (London: Weidenfeld, 1974), p.345; Dorothy Connell, *Sir Philip Sidney: The Maker's Mind* (Oxford: Oxford University Press, 1977), pp.56–7; Leah S. Marcus, *Puzzling Shakespeare: Local Reading and its Discontents* (Berkeley: University of California Press, 1988), pp.83–6.
4. Jessopp, p.106, n.7; Nichols, *Elizabeth*, II, p.216, n.1.
5. See Margaret Aston, *England's Iconoclasts, Vol.I: Laws against Images* (Oxford: Clarendon, 1988), p.318.
6. Lodge, II, p.120.
7. See Steven Mullaney, 'Strange things, gross terms, curious customs: the rehearsal of cultures in the late Renaissance', in *Representing the English Renaissance*, ed. Stephen Greenblatt (Berkeley: University of California Press, 1988), pp.65–92; Marcus, pp.85–6.
8. Aston, passim.
9. See Marina Warner, *Alone of All her Sex: The Myth and the Cult of the Virgin Mary* (1976; London: Pan-Picador, 1985), Ch.13.
10. For consistency, I use the term 'Marian' throughout this book to refer to the Virgin Mary, *not* to Mary I or her reign. I avoid the term Mariolatry because of its contentious implication that the Virgin Mary was given adoration (*latria*) on the same level as God, rather than simply being given high veneration (*hyperdulia*), as Catholic doctrine maintained. However, I will sometimes use the neutral theological term Mariology.
11. The Geneva Bible (1560), facs., introd. Lloyd E. Berry (Madison: University of Wisconsin Press, 1969). The Geneva Bible was the most

widely-used English Bible until 1611. It was a Calvinist translation, and included glosses printed alongside the scriptural text.

12. Ber- Gar[ter], *The Ioyfull Receyuing of the Queenes most excellent Maiestie into hir Highnesse Citie of Norwich* (London: Henry Bynneman, 1578?), sigs F3v–4r; Nichols, *Elizabeth*, II, p.171. The oration was not spoken, owing to a delay. For further discussion, see Ch.4.ii below.

13. See William Clowes, *A Short and Profitable Treatise touching the cure of the disease called Morbus Gallicus by Unctions* (London, 1579); Valerie Fildes, *Wet Nursing* (Oxford: Blackwell, 1988), p.72; Claude Quétel, *History of Syphilis* (1986; Cambridge: Polity, 1992), p.21. I am indebted to Margaret Healy for these references.

14. I am grateful to Henry Woudhuysen for this suggestion.

15. See Rev. William Benham, ed., *The Dictionary of Religion*, 2 vols (London: Cassell, 1887), II, p.638, 'Lord's Supper'; Alan Richardson and John Bowden, eds, *A New Dictionary of Christian Theology* (London: SCM Press, 1983), pp.187–90, 'Eucharistic Theology'.

16. Elkin Calhoun Wilson, *England's Eliza*, Harvard Studies in English vol.XX (1939; New York: Octagon, 1966); Frances A. Yates, 'Queen Elizabeth as Astraea', *Journal of the Warburg and Courtauld Institutes*, X (1947), pp.27–82; *Astraea: the imperial theme in the sixteenth century* (London: Routledge, 1975) (I am very grateful to Jacqui Gilliatt for the loan of this book); Roy Strong, *Portraits of Queen Elizabeth I* (Oxford: Clarendon, 1963); *The Cult of Elizabeth: Elizabethan Portraiture and Pageantry* (London: Thames & Hudson, 1977); *Gloriana: The Portraits of Queen Elizabeth I* (London: Thames & Hudson, 1987).

17. November 17th, the anniversary of Elizabeth's accession to the throne, was celebrated as a public holiday. The festivities may have begun in about 1570, but became official from 1576 with the institution of special church services. On the accession of James I the celebrations were moved to his Accession Day of 24 March, but after a few years Elizabeth's Accession Day was revived, and continued to be marked in some form for nearly two hundred years. See J.E. Neale, 'November 17th', *Essays in Elizabethan History* (London: Cape, 1958), pp.9–20; *Queen Elizabeth I* (1934; Harmondsworth: Penguin, 1960), pp.208–9; Strong, *Cult*, pp.117–63; Christopher Haigh, *Elizabeth I* (Harlow: Longman, 1988), pp.35, 146, 149, 157–8, 161, 166–7, 183.

Evidence of the endurance of the festivity includes some verses written in 1679 to celebrate Elizabeth's Accession Day, the 'birthday of the Gospel' (J.E. Neale, *Elizabeth I and her Parliaments*, 2 vols [London: Cape, 1953, 1957], I, p.418); and Anon., *A Protestant Memorial for the seventeenth of November, being the Inauguration Day of Queen Elizabeth* (London: 1713).

18. Yates, 'Astraea' (1947), p.75.

19. Connell, p.54.

20. Jean Wilson, *Entertainments for Elizabeth I* (Woodbridge: D.S. Brewer, 1980), p.21.

21. Stephen Greenblatt, *Renaissance Self-Fashioning from More to Shakespeare* (Chicago: University of Chicago Press, 1980), p.168. For further discussion of this speech, see Ch.2.iv, Ch.7.vii below.

22.   Lisa Jardine, *Still Harping on Daughters: Women and Drama in the Age of Shakespeare* (Hemel Hempstead: Harvester, 1983), pp.177–8. Cf. Richard Helgerson, 'The land speaks: cartography, chorography, and subversion in Renaissance England', in Greenblatt, *Representing*, p.336: 'the cult of Elizabeth had replaced the cult of the Virgin.'
23.   E.C. Wilson, p.200.
24.   E.C. Wilson, pp.207, 219, 226.
25.   Yates, 'Astraea' (1947), pp.74–5.
26.   John N. King, 'Queen Elizabeth I: Representations of the Virgin Queen', *Renaissance Quarterly* 43.1 (Spring 1990), pp.30–74; Peter McClure and Robin Headlam Wells, 'Elizabeth I as a Second Virgin Mary', *Renaissance Studies* 4.1 (March 1990), pp.38–70.
27.   Christopher Haigh, ed., *The English Reformation Revised* (Cambridge: Cambridge University Press, 1987), p.7 and passim.
28.   Aston, pp.173, 234, 342, 13, 236.
29.   Yates, 'Astraea' (1947), pp.74–5.
30.   Strong, *Portraits*, p.39; *Gloriana*, p.40.
31.   Strong, *Cult*, p.16.
32.   Louis Adrian Montrose, '"Shaping Fantasies": Figurations of Gender and Power in Elizabethan Culture', in Greenblatt, *Representing*, pp.31–64, especially p.33. Another version available as '*A Midsummer Night's Dream* and the shaping fantasies of Elizabethan culture: gender, power, form', in *Rewriting the Renaissance: the Discourses of Sexual Difference in Early Modern Europe*, eds Margaret W. Ferguson, Maureen Quilligan and Nancy J. Vickers (Chicago: University of Chicago Press, 1986), pp.65–87, especially p.66.
33.   Montrose, 'Shaping Fantasies' (1988), p.33.
34.   See McClure and Headlam Wells, pp.65–9.
35.   See Aston, p.17.

Chapter 1   Before Elizabeth

1.   For full accounts of this, see Warner, *Alone*; Geoffrey Ashe, *The Virgin* (London: Routledge, 1976).
2.   Ashe argues broadly along these lines.
3.   See, for instance, Nicole Loraux, 'What is a Goddess?', in *A History of Women in the West*, gen. eds George Duby and Michelle Perrot, *Vol.1: From Ancient Goddesses to Christian Saints*, ed. Pauline Schmitt Pantel, trans. Arthur Goldhammer, pp.11–44.
4.   For discussion of some of the continuities and discontinuities between the cult of the Virgin and previous goddess-cults, see Michael P. Carroll, *The Cult of the Virgin Mary: Psychological Origins* (Princeton: Princeton University Press, 1986), pp.5–10, 32–41, Chs 4 and 5.
5.   See for instance Carleton Brown, ed., *Religious Lyrics of the XVth Century* (Oxford: Clarendon, 1939), no.23, p.42, ll.19–20. Juno, Diana and Hecate were all associated with the persona of Lucina, goddess of childbirth. Maria Leach, ed., *Funk & Wagnall's Standard Dictionary of Folklore, Mythology and Legend* (London: New English Library, 1975), p.650. See below, Ch.6, iv.

6. Ashe, pp.192–3.
7. 'The Third Part of the Homily against Peril of Idolatry', John Griffiths, ed., *The Two Books of Homilies Appointed to be Read in Churches* (Oxford: Oxford University Press, 1859), pp.224–5. The Homilies were texts for sermons issued by the government for use in parish churches. This particular Homily was based on Bullinger's *De Origine Erroris in Divorum et Simulacrorum* (1528, enlarged 1539), and may have been written by John Jewel in about 1560 (Griffiths, pp.xxx–xxxii).
8. See Philippa Berry, *Of Chastity and Power: Elizabethan Literature and the Unmarried Queen* (London: Routledge, 1989), Ch.1.
9. The Song of Songs may itself contain ancient cultic songs of the pagan myth of Tammuz and Ishtar. *The New Catholic Encyclopedia* (New York: McGraw-Hill, 1967), III, pp.68–9.
10. Brown, pp.305–6.
11. All Latin texts from the Song of Songs quoted in this section are taken from 'Canticum Canticorum', *Biblia Sacra Iuxta Vulgatum Versionem*, 2 vols (Stuttgart: Württembergische Bibelanstatt, 1969), II. This edition hereafter referred to as Vulgate Bible.
12. John Kerrigan, ed., *Motives of Woe: Shakespeare and 'Female Complaint'* (Oxford: Clarendon, 1991), pp.90–3; R.T. Davies, ed., *Mediaeval English Lyrics: A Critical Anthology* (London: Faber, 1963), p.148; Warner, *Alone*, p.155.
13. The phrase 'veni coronaberis', so important for the iconography of the Assumption and Coronation of the Virgin, appears in the Vulgate, and is translated in the Rheims-Douai Old Testament, 1609–10, which was based on the Vulgate, as 'come: thou shalt be crowned' (*The Holy Bible* [Rheims 1582, Douai 1609; London: Burns, Oates & Washbourne, 1914]). However, it does not appear in verse 4.8. of the Song of Songs in English translations which went back to the original Hebrew, like the Geneva Bible and the Authorised Version.
14. Brown, p.65; BL Cotton MS Caligula A.ii, f.107v.
15. R.T. Davies, p.102.
16. There is no maid like you, so fair, so beautiful, so fresh, so radiant. Sweet Lady, pity me and have mercy on your knight. R.T. Davies, p.65. Davies's gloss.
17. See Roger Boase, *The Origin and Meaning of Courtly Love* (Manchester: Manchester University Press, 1977).
18. R.T. Davies, p.254.
19. Boase, p.86.
20. Ashe, p.216. For a fuller discussion of the interactions between the two traditions, see Warner, *Alone*, Chs 9 and 10.
21. See Simon Price, *Rituals and Power: The Roman Imperial Cult in Asia Minor* (Cambridge: Cambridge University Press, 1984).
22. See Price, p.247. For studies of monarchical cults in different societies, see the essays in David Cannadine and Simon Price, eds, *Rituals of Royalty: Power and Ceremonial in Traditional Societies* (Cambridge: Cambridge University Press, 1987).
23. See n.39 below.
24. Janet L. Nelson, 'The Lord's anointed and the people's choice: Carolingian royal ritual', in Cannadine and Price, pp.137–80; Marc

Bloch, *The Royal Touch: Sacred Monarchy and Scrofula in England and France* [*Les Rois Thaumaturges*], trans. J.E. Anderson (London: Routledge, 1973), pp.125, 268–9; Margaret Alice Murray, *The Divine King in England* (London: Faber, 1954), pp.165–85.

25. Bloch, pp.136–9; Murray, pp.179–80.
26. See Bloch, Ch.3, 'The sacred and miraculous aspects of royalty from the beginning of the touch for scrofula up to the Renaissance'.
27. Murray, pp.181–3. On her 1566 visit to Oxford, Elizabeth entered the cathedral under a canopy: see Katherine Duncan-Jones, *Sir Philip Sidney, Courtier Poet* (London: Hamish Hamilton, 1991), p.36. Elizabeth's persona of Mercilla in *The Faerie Queene* sits under a canopy (*FQ* V.ix.28–9). See Ch.6.iii below.
28. See John N. King, *Tudor Royal Iconography: Literature and Art in an Age of Religious Crisis* (Princeton: Princeton University Press, 1989), pp.36–7.
29. Bloch, pp.22–7, 103–7.
30. During the period 1141–47, Matilda, daughter of Henry I, had contested Stephen's claim to the throne, and for a brief period in 1141 she was triumphant and styled herself 'Queen of the English'. However, she was never crowned. *DNB* XXXVII, pp.54–8.
31. Bloch, pp.105, 189–90, 219, 256 n.7, 386 n.65, n.73, n.74; Raymond Crawfurd, *The King's Evil* (Oxford: Oxford University Press, 1911), pp.68–78.
32. Bloch, pp.130, 190–1.
33. Nichols, *Elizabeth*, I, pp.325–6.
34. *The first tome or volume of the Paraphrase of Erasmus upon the newe testamente* (London: 1548), quoted from Yates, 'Astraea' (1947), p.53.
35. Jean Calvin, *The Psalmes of Dauid and others, With M.Iohn Caluins Commentaries*, trans. Arthur Golding (London, 1571), Part 2, ff.29r–30v; Bloch, pp.187, 199.
36. Ernst H. Kantorowicz, *The King's Two Bodies: A Study in Mediaeval Political Theology* (Princeton: Princeton University Press, 1957), pp.193–232.
37. Edmund Plowden, *The Commentaries and Reports of Edmund Plowden, originally written in French, and now faithfully translated into English* (London, 1779), p.217, as quoted in Marie Axton, *The Queen's Two Bodies* (London: Royal Historical Society, 1977), p.17. See also Kantorowicz, p.7.
38. Axton, passim.
39. Price, p.203.
40. See, for instance, Matthew 5, 19.28, 25.31; 1 Corinthians 9.25; James 1.12; Revelation 2.10.
41. *NCE*, IX, p.386.
42. Warner, *Alone*, pp.65–6; *NCE*, IX, p.369.
43. Ashe, pp.185, 191. The temple of Artemis at Ephesus and its surrounding cult were thriving when St Paul visited the city in c.57 AD (Acts 19). The Goths destroyed both the city and the temple in 262, but the city revived and the cult of Artemis continued, though not in its former splendour. The temple probably finally closed at the same

time as all other pagan temples under the edicts of Theodosius, in c.390. It was then quarried for the construction of the cathedral of St John Theológos on a neighbouring hill. A large Byzantine building, possibly a church, arose on the central part of the temple site, but did not last long. *Encyclopedia Britannica*, 11th edn (Cambridge: Cambridge University Press, 1910), IX, pp.673–5; XXVI, p.771; *Encyclopedia Britannica* (London: William Benton, 1964), VIII, p.634.

44. Warner, *Alone*, Ch.7.
45. Yates, 'Astraea' (1947), pp.40–6; King, *Iconography*, Ch.3.
46. Warner, *Alone*, p.111.
47. Yates, 'Astraea' (1947), p.43.
48. Calvin, *Psalmes*, ff.29r, 30v.
49. Helgerson, pp.331, 336–7, 340.
50. McClure and Headlam Wells, pp.49–50.
51. King, *Iconography*, p.123.
52. See Strong, *Portraits*, pp.36, 41.
53. Strong, *Portraits*, p.31.
54. Richard Ormond, ed., *The National Portrait Gallery in Colour*, introd. John Hayes (London: Studio Vista-Cassell, 1979), pp.6, 22; Strong, *Gloriana*, pp.111, 164.
55. Nancy Mayberry, 'The controversy over the Immaculate Conception in mediaeval and Renaissance art, literature and society', *Journal of Mediaeval and Renaissance Studies* 21.2 (Fall 1991), pp.208, 209, 214–15; Christopher Harper-Bill, *The Pre-Reformation Church in England, 1400–1530* (London: Longman, 1989), pp.63, 70, 87, 88, 97.
56. St Augustine introduced the distinction between *latria* and *dulia* (C.G. Herbermann et al., eds, *The Catholic Encyclopedia*, 15 vols [New York: Robert Appleton, 1907], I, p.152, II, p.364, V, p.188). The term *hyperdulia* was used by St Bonaventure (c.1217–74) and was recognised by the Council of Trent (A. Vacant and E. Mangenot, *Dictionnaire de Théologie Catholique* [Paris: Letouzey and Avé, 1908], III, col.2407; *NCE*, XII, pp.962–3). The English Protestant polemicist William Perkins challenged the Catholic distinction between *latria* and *dulia* in *A Reformed Catholike* (Cambridge: John Legat, 1598), pp.247–8; see Ch.7.ii below.
57. John Jewel, *Apology of the Church of England*, trans. Anne Bacon (1564), ed. Rev. John Ayre (Cambridge: Cambridge University Press-Parker Society, 1849), p.65. From 1581 the *Apology* was bound with the catechism and articles of the Church of England, and endorsed as authoritative; subsequently, it was ordered to be placed in all churches. See *DNB* XXIX, pp.378–82.
58. R.T. Davies, p.204. For more late medieval poems which are catalogues of symbolic epithets of the Virgin see Mayberry, *passim*.
59. *Ritus Servandus In Solemni Expositione et Benedictione Sanctissimi Sacramenti* (London: Burns, Oates & Washbourne, 1928), pp.20–1. I am very grateful to Tony Hackett for the loan of this book.
60. Ashe, pp.217–18.
61. Sigmund Freud, *The Interpretation of Dreams*, trans. James Strachey, eds James Strachey, Alan Tyson and Angela Richards, Pelican Freud

Library IV (Harmondsworth: Penguin, 1976), pp.312–13n, 388–9, 399, 415–19, 444.
62. Warner, *Alone*, pp.55, 244.
63. Warner, *Alone*, pp.92–4; *NCE*, XIV, pp.1000–1; *The Encyclopedia of Religion*, ed.-in-chief Mircea Eliade (New York: Macmillan, 1987), IX, pp.249–52.
64. Vulgate Bible, 'Canticum Canticorum' 4.7.
65. Mayberry, passim.; *NCE*, VII, pp.378–82. In fact the Immaculate Conception did not become official dogma until 1854.
66. *NCE*, IX, p.354; Warner, *Alone*, Ch.4.
67. See Warner, *Alone*, Ch.5.
68. Anonymous, *The Oxford Dictionary of Quotations*, 3rd edn (Oxford: Oxford University Press, 1979), p.10 no.8. This line of the prayer derives from the Angel Gabriel's greeting to Mary in the Bible: 'have gratia plena' (Luke 1.28, Vulgate Bible). See Warner, *Alone*, p.306.
69. Thomas F. Simmons, ed., *The Lay Folks' Mass Book* (London: EETS, 1879), pp.183–4.
70. Warner, *Alone*, pp.113–14.
71. Mayberry, p.216.
72. King, *Iconography*, pp.196–7.
73. John Aylmer, *An Harborowe for Faithfull and Trewe Subiectes*, 1559, The English Experience 423 (Amsterdam: Theatrvm Orbis Terrarvm, 1972), sig.B4v; Alexander Ales to Elizabeth I, *Calendar of State Papers Foreign 1558–9*, ed. Rev. J. Stevenson (London, 1863), no.1303; E.W. Ives, *Anne Boleyn* (Oxford: Blackwell, 1986), pp.249, 272, 302–28, 414; Maria Dowling, 'Anne Boleyn and Reform', *Journal of Ecclesiastical History* 35.1 (Jan. 1984), pp.30–46.
74. John Leland and Nicholas Udall, *Versis and ditties made at the coronation of quene Anne*, BL MS Royal 18 A.lxiv; Anon., *The noble tryumphant coronacyon of quene Anne / Wyfe vnto the most noble kynge Henry the viij* (London: Wynkyn de Worde, 1533); F.J. Furnivall and W.R. Morfill, eds, *Ballads from Manuscripts*, 2 vols (London and Hertford: Ballad Society, 1868, 1873), I, pp.365–73; Sydney Anglo, *Spectacle, Pageantry, and Early Tudor Policy* (Oxford: Clarendon, 1969), pp.247–61; Ives, pp.283–4; King, *Iconography*, pp.50–3.
75. See comments by Cranmer in a letter written 18 days later. Furnivall and Morfill, I, p.386, n.4.
76. Leland and Udall, f.6v.
77. *Noble tryumphant coronacyon*, f.4r–v.
78. Anglo, p.253, n.2; Warner, *Alone*, p.23.
79. Leland and Udall, f.8v.
80. Leland and Udall, ff.8v–9v.
81. Leland and Udall, f.12v; Furnivall and Morfill, I, pp.394, 377.
82. Yates, 'Astraea' (1947), pp.30–4.
83. *Noble tryumphant coronacyon*, f.5r.
84. Leland and Udall, f.16r; Furnivall and Morfill, I, p.378, p.401 n.2.
85. Ives, pp.7–8; BL MS King's M59, ff.66v, 231r.
86. *OED*, 'kind', defn 6.

87. Immediately after Anne, Jane Seymour's coronation pageants again included the theme of the Coronation of the Virgin. Ives, p.281.
88. Ales, *CSPF 1558–9*, no.1303.
89. King, *Iconography*, p.182.
90. T. Park and W. Oldys, eds, *The Harleian Miscellany*, 10 vols (London: White & Cochrane, 1808–13), X, pp.253–4; Hyder E. Rollins, ed., *Old English Ballads 1553–1625, chiefly from manuscripts* (Cambridge: Cambridge University Press, 1920), pp.8–12; Louise Imogen Guiney, ed., *Recusant Poets I: St Thomas More to Ben Jonson* (London: Sheed & Ward, 1938), pp.149–50. Guiney notes that this ballad appeared as a broadside in 1553 and, intriguingly, was licensed for reprinting in 1569–70.
91. BL MS Harley 3444. Folio references will be given in parenthesis. Another version is *A Treatise declaring howe Christ by perverse preachyng was banished out of this realme: And howe it hath pleased God to bryng Christ home againe by Mary our moost gracious Quene*, 1554, Lambeth Palace Library press mark 30.4.18. See Guiney, pp.127–8; King, *Iconography*, p.127.
92. Sig.B2. The further lines of the prayer as known today were added by a bull of Pope Pius V in 1568: 'Sancta Maria, Mater Dei, ora pro nobis peccatoribus nunc et in hora mortis nostrae' (Holy Mary, Mother of God, pray for us sinners now and at the hour of our deaths). Simmons, pp.183–4; Warner, *Alone*, p.306.
93. By Leonard Stopes, from a unique broadside in the Society of Antiquaries. Rollins, *Old English Ballads*, pp.13–18.
94. This line of the prayer derives from Elizabeth's greeting to Mary in the Gospel, 'benedictus fructus ventris tui' (Luke 1.42, Vulgate Bible).
95. King, *Iconography*, p.218.
96. 'The Epitaphe vpon the Death of the Most Excellent and our late vertuous Quene, Marie, deceased, augmented by the first Author'. From a unique broadside in the Society of Antiquaries. Park and Oldys, X, pp.259–60; Rollins, *Old English Ballads*, pp.23–6.
97. For further examples of Mariological representations of Mary I, see King, *Iconography*, pp.197–9.
98. James Emerson Phillips, *Images of a Queen: Mary Stuart in Sixteenth-Century Literature* (Berkeley: University of California Press, 1964), p.165.

Chapter 2   A New Queen

1. John Knox, *The First Blast of the Trumpet against the Monstruous Regiment of Women* (1558), facs., The English Experience No.471 (Amsterdam: Theatrvm Orbis Terrarvm, 1972), f.24r. All further references will be to this edition.
2. Knox to Cecil, 10.4.1559; Knox to Elizabeth, 20.7.1559; *The Works of John Knox*, ed. David Laing (Edinburgh, 1864), VI, pp.19, 48.
3. *Letters of John Calvin, selected from the Bonnet Edition* (Edinburgh: Banner of Truth Trust, 1980), pp.211–12.

4. Knox, *Works*, VI, p.50.
5. Calvin, *Letters*, p.212. On Isaiah 49.23, see above, Introduction i.
6. McClure and Headlam Wells, p.68.
7. Axton, p.31.
8. Allison Heisch, 'Queen Elizabeth I: Parliamentary Rhetoric and the Exercise of Power', *Signs* 1.1 (Autumn 1975), p.33; Axton, p.38; Wallace MacCaffrey, *The Shaping of the Elizabethan Régime* (London: Cape, 1967), p.29.
9. Marina Warner takes the title of her book on the cult of the Virgin from Caelius Sedulius: 'She . . . had no peer / Either in our first mother or in all women / Who were to come. But alone of all her sex / She pleased the Lord' (Warner, *Alone*, p.xvii).
10. *The Quenes Maiesties Passage through the Citie of London to Westminster the Day before her Coronacion*, facs., ed. James M. Osborn, introd. Sir John Neale (New Haven: Yale University Press-Elizabethan Club, 1960). All further references will be to this edition.
11. David M. Bergeron, 'Elizabeth's Coronation Entry (1559): New Manuscript Evidence', *ELR* 8 (1978), p.4.
12. Anglo, pp.319–22.
13. Warner, *Alone*, pls 13, 24; McClure and Headlam Wells, pp.44–6. See King, *Iconography*, p.113 fig.31, pp.200–1, for other examples of Jesse trees in Elizabethan iconography.
14. Anglo, pp.177, 195, 284.
15. Anglo, p.346.
16. Richard Grafton, *Graftons Abridgement of the Chronicles of Englande* (London: Tottel, 1570), f.178v.
17. King, *Iconography*, pp.70–4, 229–30.
18. Anglo, pp.329–38.
19. David Bergeron compares the inventory of costumes for the pageant with the Venetian ambassador's description of Elizabeth's apparel on the occasion to speculate that Deborah and the Queen were dressed in very similar style. Bergeron, 'Coronation Entry', pp.6–7.
20. Grafton, f.179r.
21. Leland and Udall, f.4r.
22. Grafton, f.178r.
23. See David M. Bergeron, *English Civic Pageantry 1558–1642* (London: Arnold, 1971), pp.273–308.
24. Bergeron, 'Coronation Entry', pp.3–8.
25. Anglo, p.346.
26. Aylmer (see Ch.1, n.72 above), sig.G4v and passim. All further references will be to this edition.
27. I have corrected an obvious error in parenthesis in this passage.
28. Letter from Sir Thomas Pope to Queen Mary, 26.4.1558, Nichols, *Elizabeth*, I, pp.23–5; BL MSS Harl.444.7, Cotton Vitell.xii.16.8.
29. BL MS Lansdowne 94, no.14, f.29. A similar version of the speech is given in Grafton, ff.179v–80v. John King has convincingly argued that Camden's version of the speech in his *Annals* is unreliable and part of the posthumous mythologisation of Elizabeth (King, 'Queen Elizabeth'). See below, Ch.7.vii.

30. Damaged portion of MS text supplied from Grafton.
31. Letter by Cecil, 1561, Nichols, *Elizabeth*, I, pp.27–8; see also p.107. Cf. Thomas Wright, ed., *Queen Elizabeth and her Times: A series of Original Letters*, 2 vols (London: Colburn, 1838), I, pp.65–7, 79–80, 181–5; Neale, *Queen Elizabeth*, p.109.
32. See the quotations from Luther and Calvin in Julia O'Faolain and Lauro Martines, eds, *Not in God's Image: Women in History* (London: Virago, 1979), pp.208, 211–12; W. and M. Haller, 'The Puritan Art of Love', *Huntington Library Quarterly* V (1941–2), pp.235–72; C. and K. George, *The Protestant Mind of the English Reformation* (Princeton: Princeton University Press, 1961).
33. Thomas Becon, *Booke of Matrimony*, in *The workes of Thomas Becon*, 3 vols (1560–64), I, *The first part of the bokes, whiche Thomas Becon made and published in the name of Theodor Basille* (1560), ff.562r, 567r, 574r.
34. Becon, *Matrimony*, f.567r.
35. See Kathleen M. Davies, '"The sacred condition of equality": how original were Puritan doctrines of marriage?' *Social History* 5 (May 1977), pp.565, 573–4; Linda T. Fitz, '"What says the Married Woman?" Marriage theory and feminism in the English Renaissance', *Mosaic* 13.2 (Winter 1980), pp.7–8.
36. Thomas Becon, *A new Catechisme*, in *Workes*, I, f.327v.
37. Keith Thomas, *Religion and the Decline of Magic* (London: Weidenfeld, 1971), pp.38, 39, 215, 268.
38. John Milton, *A Masque presented at Ludlow Castle, 1634*, in *Complete Shorter Poems*, ed. John Carey (London: Longman, 1971), pp.168–229, ll.420, 435–6.
39. For further discussion of symbolic beliefs attaching to the virginal body, see Mary Douglas, *Purity and Danger: An analysis of concepts of pollution and taboo* (London: Routledge, 1966), pp.3–4, 7, 51–2, 114–26, 157–8; Mikhail Bakhtin on the 'classical' versus the 'grotesque' body, *Rabelais and his World*, 1965, trans. Helene Iswolsky (Cambridge, Mass.: MIT Press, 1968), pp.18–30, 315–25.
40. Warner, *Alone*, pp.48, 72.
41. Geneva Bible, Old Testament, f.280v. See Ch.4.iv below. The phrase 'Veni, coronaberis' ('Come, you shall be crowned') in Song of Songs 4.8 in the Vulgate does not appear in English Bible translations. The Geneva Bible also erases Marian interpretation from its commentary on what remains of the verse: 'Christ promiseth his Church to call his faithful from all the corners of the worlde' (f.281v).
42. Geneva Bible, New Testament, f.121v.
43. The 'Coronation' portrait has been assigned by tree-ring dating to 1600–10, but it is thought to be a copy of an earlier painting probably executed soon after Elizabeth's coronation. The date of the Hilliard miniature remains a subject of debate, but it does not appear to be the source for the larger portrait. See John Fletcher, 'The date of the portrait of Elizabeth I in her coronation robes', *Burlington Magazine* 120 (1978), p.753; Janet Arnold, 'The "Coronation" Portrait of Queen Elizabeth I', *Burlington Magazine* 120 (1978), pp.727–41; Strong, *Gloriana*, pp.163–4.

44. Murray, p.176; Ives, p.52; Furnivall and Morfill, I, p.368, p.383 n.3.
45. Berry, Ch.2.
46. Anglo, pp.319–25.
47. Anglo, p.328.
48. Kantorowicz, citing James I's self-description as the nation's husband, maintains that 'In mediaeval England, the marriage metaphor seems to have been all but non-existent' (p.223). It seems likely that James used it because it was so strongly identified with Elizabeth, as he sought to lay claim to her mythologised 'loving' relationship with her people.
49. Quoted from *The Penguin Book of Renaissance Verse 1509–1659*, selected and introd. David Norbrook, ed. H.R. Woudhuysen (London: Allen Lane-Penguin, 1992), pp.92–4. The ballad was entered in the Stationers' Register in 1558–9 and exists in a unique broadside of 1564 owned by the Society of Antiquaries. Also available in Park and Oldys, X, pp.260–2. Cf. E.C. Wilson, pp.4–6.
50. John Foxe, 'The miraculous preservation of the Lady Elizabeth, now Queen of England, from extreme calamity of danger and life; in the time of Queen Mary, her sister', *Fox's Book of Martyrs: The Acts and Monuments of the Church*, 1563, ed. Rev. John Cumming, 3 vols (London: George Virtue, 1844), III, pp.1070–86. Foxe's *Actes and Monuments*, popularly known as the *Book of Martyrs*, was first published in Latin in 1559, and in English in 1563, with further editions in 1570, 1576 and 1583. William Alabaster, *Elisaeis*, Bod. MS Rawl. D.293; *The Elisaeis of William Alabaster*, ed. and trans. Michael O'Connell, *Studies in Philology* 76 (1979), pp.1–77; Thomas Heywood, *If you know not me, you know no bodie, or the troubles of Queene Elizabeth* (London: N.Butter, 1605); Thomas Heywood, *England's Elizabeth, her Life and Troubles during her minoritie from the Cradle to the Crowne* (London: P. Waterhouse, 1631).
51. Neale, *Parliaments*, I, p.149. Cf. II, pp.321–2.
52. Griffiths, p.503.
53. Berry, p.67.
54. Johnson, p.428.
55. Anthony Munday, *A Watch-woord to Englande*, 1584, sig.A3, quoted in E.C. Wilson, p.218.
56. Berry, p.67.
57. R.T. Davies, pp.256–7.
58. William Wager, *The longer thou livest, the more foole thou art* (The Tudor Facsimile Texts, 1910), sig.A3r–v.
59. William Shakespeare, *King Lear*, ed. Kenneth Muir (London: Methuen [Arden Shakespeare], 1972), III.vi.25–8.
60. See, for example, Richard Crimsal, 'Constant, faire, and fine Betty', in William Chappell, ed., *The Roxburghe Ballads* (London: Ballad Society, 1869, 1899), I, pp.207–12; 'John's Earnest Request', in John Holloway, introd., *The Euing Collection of English Broadside Ballads* (Glasgow: University of Glasgow, 1971), p.242, no.154, a tale of seduction in dialogue form which begins 'Come open the Door sweet Betty'; and 'A proper new ballett, intituled Rowlands god sunne',

c.1584–5, Bod. MS Rawl. Poet. 185, ff.15v–19r, which is a dialogue between Besse, Ihon and her husband.
61. BL Huth 50 (28). Strong dates the woodcut which the verses accompany at c.1580–5 (Strong, *Gloriana*, frontispiece, p.111, pl.107), but E.C. Wilson identifies it with the 'pycture of quene Elyzabeth' entered on the books of the Stationers' Company in 1562–3 (E.C. Wilson, pp.9–10). The BL catalogue also dates it 1563.
62. Steven W. May, *The Elizabethan Courtier Poets: The Poems and Their Contexts* (Columbia, Missouri: University of Missouri Press, 1991), p.49.
63. Aston, p.278; Haigh, *Reformation Revised*, pp.16, 103, 178–9, 183.
64. W.P. Haugaard, *Elizabeth I and the English Reformation: the struggle for a stable settlement of religion* (Cambridge: Cambridge University Press, 1968), p.138.
65. Haugaard, *English Reformation*, pp.139–41; Aston, pp.298–302.
66. *The Book of Common Prayer* (Cambridge: Cambridge University Press, 1969?), *Articles of Religion*, no.22, 'Of Purgatory'.
67. Griffiths, p.247.
68. Aston, pp.320–4; Haugaard, *English Reformation*, p.275.
69. Aston, pp.295–8, 303–14, 336–7, 341; Haugaard, *English Reformation*, pp.148, 185–98, 220, 338.
70. Dowling, p.40.
71. For the view that the Book was written by Elizabeth herself and is therefore revealing evidence of her private faith, see Elizabeth I, *A Book of Devotions Composed by Her Majesty Elizabeth R.*, trans. Rev. A. Fox, foreword by Rev. Canon J.P. Hodges (Gerrards Cross: Colin Smythe, 1970); W.P. Haugaard, 'Elizabeth Tudor's Book of Devotions: A neglected clue to the Queen's life and character', *16th Century Journal* 12.2 (Summer 1981), pp.79–106. However, Henry Woudhuysen takes the view, expressed in conversation with me, that the book was a presentation copy prepared by a writing-master in pursuit of patronage.
72. *Letters of Stephen Gardiner*, ed. J.A. Muller (Cambridge: Cambridge University Press, 1933), pp.274–5.
73. Cannadine and Price, pp.2–3, 4, 6.
74. Aston, p.446. See James R. Siemon, *Shakespearean Iconoclasm* (Berkeley: University of California Press, 1985), p.34, for examples of Elizabethan anxiety that secular portraits might be idolatrous.
75. Aston, p.315.
76. Nicholas Sander, *The Rise and Growth of the Anglican Schism*, 1585, trans. and ed. David Lewis (London, 1877), p.172.
77. All references to Becon are to *Workes* I (see n.33 above).
78. Alexander Nowell, *A Catechisme or First Instruction and Learning of Christian Religion*, trans. Thomas Norton, 1570, facs., introd. Frank V. Occhiogrosso (Albany, NY: Delmar, Scholars' Facsimiles and Reprints, 1975). All references are to this edition.
79. *BCP* (1969?), 'Articles of Religion', no.25, 'Of the Sacraments'.
80. For further discussion of these issues, see Aston, pp.vii, 392–408; Siemon, pp.30–75; Kenneth Gross, *Spenserian Poetics: Idolatry,*

Iconoclasm, and Magic (Ithaca: Cornell University Press, 1985); Michael O'Connell, 'The Idolatrous Eye: Iconoclasm, Anti-theatricalism, and the Image of the Elizabethan Theater', *ELH* 52.2 (Summer 1985), pp.279–310; Mark Breitenberg, 'Reading Elizabethan Iconicity: *Gorboduc* and the Semiotics of Reform', *ELR* 18 (1988), pp.194–217; John N. King and Robin Smith, 'Recent Studies in Protestant Poetics', *ELR* 21.2 (Spring 1991), pp.283–307; Michael McKeon, *The Origins of the English Novel, 1600–1740* (Baltimore: Johns Hopkins University Press, 1987), pp.75–6; W. Haller, *Foxe's 'Book of Martyrs' and the Elect Nation* (London: Cape, 1963); Keith Thomas, 'From edification to entertainment: oral tradition and the printed word in early modern England', *Times Literary Supplement*, 23.8.91, p.5.

81. Jewel, p.58.
82. Griffiths, 'Sermon of Obedience', p.115; 'Sermon against Wilful Rebellion', p.567.
83. Linda Gregerson, 'Protestant Erotics: Idolatry and Interpretation in Spenser's *Faerie Queene*', *ELH* 58.1 (Spring 1991), pp.1–34.
84. Bernard McGinn, 'Revelation', in Robert Alter and Frank Kermode, eds, *The Literary Guide to the Bible* (London: Fontana, 1989), pp.529–35.
85. King, *Iconography*, pp.204–7.
86. Yates, 'Astraea' (1947), p.44, p.45, n.5.
87. Geneva Bible, 'Revelacion' 17.3–4.
88. Griffiths, pp.261–2.
89. John N. King, 'Patronage and Piety: the influence of Catherine Parr', *Silent But For the Word: Tudor women as patrons, translators and writers of religious works*, ed. Margaret P. Hannay (Kent, Ohio: Kent State University Press, 1985), pp.43–60; King, *Iconography*, pp.203–13, 249.

Chapter 3   1560–78: The Meanings of Virginity

1.   Neale, *Queen Elizabeth*, pp.82–8.
2.   Wright, I, pp.181–5.
3.   Janet Arnold, *Queen Elizabeth's Wardrobe Unlock'd* (Leeds: W.S. Maney, 1988), p.90.
4.   Neale, *Parliaments*, I, p.127. BL MS Lansdowne 94, no.15, f.30, gives 'so do I strive' for 'yet do I strive'.
5.   Neale, *Parliaments*, I, p.147.
6.   Victor von Klarwill, ed., *Queen Elizabeth and some Foreigners*, trans. T.H. Nash (London: Bodley Head, 1928), p.94.
7.   Neale, *Parliaments*, I, p.94.
8.   Neale, *Parliaments*, I, p.112.
9.   Heisch, 'Parliamentary Rhetoric', p.37, n.10.
10. Elizabeth I, *Letters of Queen Elizabeth I*, ed. G.B. Harrison (London: Cassell, 1968), p.105, letter dated 23.7.1572.
11. See J. Wilson, p.7.
12. Nichols, *Elizabeth*, I, p.197.
13. Nichols, *Elizabeth*, I, p.161; BL MS Harl.7037.109.

14. Neale, *Parliaments*, I, p.242.
15. Hatton to Elizabeth, 17.6.1573, in Sir Harris Nicolas, *Memoirs of the Life and Times of Sir Christopher Hatton* (London: Bentley, 1847), pp.26–7.
16. Neale, *Parliaments*, I, p.366.
17. Neale, *Queen Elizabeth*, pp.191–2.
18. W.C. Hazlitt, ed., *Fugitive Tracts*, 2 vols (London, 1875), First Series, *1493–1600*, no.XXII.
19. Wright, I, pp.457–9, 466–8; II, pp.37–41, pp.86–9.
20. Letter dated 2.3.1573, Wright, I, pp.466–8; BL MS Lans. 16,25.
21. Letter dated 6.7.1578, Wright, II, pp.97–8; BL MS Lans. 28, 32.
22. Aston, p.354.
23. Letter dated 12.4.1573, Wright, I, pp.475–7: BL MS Lans. 17, 27. Cf. Aylmer to Hatton, letter dated 29.4.1578, Nicolas pp.51–2, BL Add. MS 15891 f.54v; and Nicolas pp.55–6.
24. See Ch.2.ix above.
25. Neale, *Queen Elizabeth*, p.90.
26. For a detailed study of this, see Phillips.
27. Phillips, p.67.
28. Neale, *Parliaments*, I, p.289.
29. Neale, *Parliaments*, I, p.328.
30. King, *Iconography*, pp.204–9, 220.
31. Phillips, pp.85–117.
32. Nicolas, pp.14–15.
33. Among the numerous examples, see Nicolas pp.280–1, 243–7, 200–1; the 1563 Parliament, Neale, *Parliaments*, I, p.109; Gar[ter], sigs C1v, D1r, E4r, F1v; Richard Day, *A Booke of Christian Prayers*, London, 1578, facs., English Experience no.866 (Amsterdam: Theatrvm Orbis Terrarvm, 1977), sigs H1r, H4r, M2r, N1r; Elizabeth I, *Devotions*, pp.24–7.
34. See Ch.2.viii above.
35. Neale, *Parliaments*, I, p.156.
36. T.E. Hartley, *Proceedings in the Parliaments of Elizabeth I: vol.I: 1558–1581* (Leicester: Leicester University Press, 1981), p.138; Public Records Office State Papers Domestic, Eliz. 46/166, ff.3r–11v.
37. Neale, *Parliaments*, I, p.360.
38. Neale, *Parliaments*, I, p.423.
39. See May, pp.52–9.
40. Letter dated 5.6.1573, Nicolas, pp.25–6.
41. Letter of July/August 1573, Nicolas, pp.28–9.
42. Letter of 11.9.158[0?], Nicolas pp.155–6, BL MS Harl. 416, f.200.
43. Letter dated 19.8.1579, Wright, II, pp.99–100; Nicolas, pp.125–6; Eric St John Brooks, *Sir Christopher Hatton: Queen Elizabeth's Favourite* (London: Cape, 1946), p.158; BL Add. MS 15891, f.32.
44. See Ch.1.iii above.
45. Nicolas, pp.277–8, 141–3, 194–7, 301–4.
46. Letter dated 8.6.1578, Nicolas, pp.58–9, BL Add. MS 15891, f.38v.
47. Nichols, *Elizabeth*, I, pp.274–5 n.5.
48. Nichols, *Elizabeth*, I, p.410.

49. Neale, *Parliaments*, I, p.108.
50. King, *Iconography*, pp.154–6.
51. Letter dated 25.10.1582, Nicolas, pp.277–8, BL Add. MS 15891, f.97v.
52. The 'Phoenix' portrait is in the National Portrait Gallery, London; the 'Pelican' portrait is in the Walker Art Gallery, Liverpool. Strong, *Gloriana*, pls 64 and 65.
53. Psalm 102.6; Beryl Rowland, *Birds with human souls: a guide to bird symbolism* (Tennessee, 1978), p.119; Louis Reau, *Iconographie de l'art chrétien*, 3 vols (Paris, 1955–9), II, pp.2, 491–2; Strong, *Gloriana*, p.83; McClure and Headlam Wells, p.12, n.19.
54. For other examples of Elizabeth as pelican, see Strong, *Gloriana*, p.83.
55. McClure and Headlam Wells, p.44.
56. See, for instance, verses for the accession of Mary I, Guiney, pp.121–3.
57. Haigh, *Elizabeth* (1988), pp.3–5.
58. Neale, *Parliaments*, I, p.187.
59. For other examples of Elizabeth as phoenix, see McClure and Headlam Wells p.44; E.C. Wilson, pp.21, 23, 27 and passim; Strong, *Gloriana*, p.83.
60. See Ch.2.ix above.
61. Becon, *Workes*, I, f.561r.
62. Gar[ter], sig.A2r.
63. Letter dated 17.6.1573, Nicolas pp.26–7. For further examples of solar imagery, see May, p.118.
64. Gar[ter], sig.G2r.
65. Neale, *Parliaments*, I, p.364.
66. King, *Iconography*, p.114.
67. Day, sigs G3r, L4r.
68. Elizabeth I, *Devotions*, pp.32–3.
69. Elizabeth I, *Devotions*, pp.22–3.
70. Day, title-page, sigs B1r, C1v, F3v, G4r, M1v, H1v–I3v; King, *Iconography*, pp.112–15, 118–19.
71. Neale, 'November 17th', p.10; Strong, *Cult*, pp.117, 119.
72. King, *Iconography*, p.174; Strong, *Cult*, p.118.
73. *DNB*, XXVII, pp.158–9.
74. Thomas Holland, *A Sermon Preached at Pavls in London the 17. of November Ann. Dom. 1599 . . . Whervnto is adioyned an Apologeticall discourse . . .* (London, 1601), sig.N4r.
75. For more on Cooper's successful career under the patronage of Elizabeth and Leicester, and his later loyal defence of the Church establishment, see Eleanor Rosenberg, *Leicester, Patron of Letters* (New York: Columbia University Press, 1955), pp.124–8. For further discussion of Holland's defence of Accession Day, see below, Ch.7.iii.
76. Strong, *Cult*, pp.119–23; Edward Hake, *A commemoration of the most prosperous and peaceable raigne of our gratious and deere soueraigne lady Elizabeth, &c. Now newly set forth, this 17th day of November, being the first day of the eighteenth yeere of her majesties sayd raygne* (1575), Park and Oldys, X, catalogue, p.358, no.5.

77. *A fourme of Prayer, with thankes geuyng, to be vsed euery yeere, the .17. of Nouember, beyng the day of the Queenes Maiesties entrie to her raigne* (London: Richard Jugge, 1576).

78. The full text is not set out in the 1576 edition; therefore the version given here is from the 1578 edition, sigs B2v–3r. See next note.

79. *A fourme of prayer with thankes giuing, to be vsed of all the Queenes Maiesties louing subiectes euery yeere, the 17. of Nouember, being the day of her Highnes entrie to her kingdome* (London: Christopher Barker, 1578).

80. *Certaine prayers and other godly exercises, for the seuenteenth of Nouember: Wherein we solemnize the blessed reigne of our gracious Soueraigne Lady Elizabeth . . .* (London: Christopher Barker, 1585). All references are to this edition.

81. *A fourme of prayer*, 1578, sigs B4v, C2v.

82. *A fourme of prayer with thankesgiuing, to be vsed of all the Queenes Maiesties louing subiects euery yeere, the 17. of Nouember, being the day of her Highnesse entry to her kingdome* (London: Christopher Barker, 1590).

83. E.K. Chambers, *Sir Henry Lee: An Elizabethan Portrait* (Oxford: Clarendon, 1936), pp.37–8, 130, 133–5.

84. *Sir Philip Sidney*, ed. Katherine Duncan-Jones (Oxford: Oxford University Press – Oxford Authors, 1989), pp.2–4; 'AT 19', 'AT 21', *The Poems of Sir Philip Sidney*, ed. William A. Ringler Jr. (Oxford: Clarendon, 1962), pp.256–8. The songs are discussed in Duncan-Jones, *Courtier Poet*, pp.144–5; May, pp.73–5.

85. HMC, 8th report (1881), Appendix, p.27; Strong, *Cult*, pp.125–6.

86. Leland and Udall, ff.13r–14v.

87. Strong, *Gloriana*, pp.64–9. For other examples and precedents of the motif, see George Peele, *Life and Works*, gen. ed. Charles Tyler Prouty, 3 vols (New Haven: Yale University Press, 1952–70), III, *The Arraygnement of Paris* (1583/4), ed. R.Mark Benbow, Introduction, pp.13, 20.

88. Axton, pp.38–60.

89. Nichols, *Elizabeth*, I, p.506.

90. Nichols, *Elizabeth*, I, pp.514–15.

91. Axton, pp.63–4; Duncan-Jones, *Courtier Poet*, pp.13–14, 89–90.

92. Berry, p.87.

93. Verses written by 'M. Hunneys, Master of her Majesties Chappell', Nichols, *Elizabeth*, I, pp.486–7.

94. Nichols, *Elizabeth*, I, p.495.

95. Nichols, *Elizabeth*, I, p.582.

96. On the date of the masque, see May, p.70, n.3.

97. See for instance Louis Adrian Montrose, 'Celebration and Insinuation: Sir Philip Sidney and the Motives of Elizabethan Courtship', *Renaissance Drama* n.s. 8 (1977), pp.3–35.

98. 'Introduction' to *Lady of May*, in *Miscellaneous Prose of Sir Philip Sidney*, eds Katherine Duncan-Jones and Jan van Dorsten (Oxford: Oxford University Press, 1973), p.15; Duncan-Jones, *Courtier Poet*, pp.147–52; Catherine Bates, *The Rhetoric of Courtship in Elizabethan Language*

and Literature (Cambridge: Cambridge University Press, 1992), pp.61–9; May, pp.70–3.

99. Warner, Alone, pp.281–4; Boase, p.127.
100. Sidney, Miscellaneous Prose, p.31.
101. Letter dated 9.7.?, BL Add. MS 15891, f.53; Nicolas, pp.68–70.
102. Rosenberg, pp.184–229, Ch.6, 'Puritans and their works'; pp.230–77, Ch.7, 'Anti-Catholic propaganda'.

Chapter 4   1578–82: Into Perpetual Virginity

1. Until 1574 Francis de Valois was Duke of Alençon, while his elder brother Henry was Duke of Anjou. Each were proposed at different times as suitors for Elizabeth. In 1574 the elder brother became Henry III, and Francis became Duke of Anjou.
2. He was born on 18 March 1555.
3. BL Add. MS 15891; Lodge, II, pp.107ff; Nicolas pp.81–9.
4. Letter dated 9.10.1578, BL Add. MS 15891, f.44v; Nicolas, pp.93–4.
5. Aylmer to Hatton, 28.9.1579, BL Add. MS 15891, f.5; Nicolas, pp.132–4.
6. Neale, Queen Elizabeth, p.244.
7. Elizabeth I, Letters, pp.147–8.
8. Thomas Churchyard, A Discovrse of The Queenes Maiesties entertainement in Suffolk and Norfolk (London: Henry Bynneman, 1578); Gar[ter] (see above, Introduction, n.12. 'Ber- Gar-' is presumably the 'Maister Garter' named in Churchyard's text as one of the co-devisers of the pageants [sig.B4r]); Nichols, Elizabeth, II, pp.133–78, 179–213. All references will be to the 1578 editions.
9. See Introduction.i, above.
10. The only extant text of the poems is BL Cotton MS Vesp.E.viii ff.169–78. All references here will be to this manuscript. The heading of the poems describes them as 'a new yeares gifte' (f.169r), and the last poem refers to Elizabeth's accession 'twentye yeare agon' (f.177r), suggesting a date of New Year 1579. The author of the manuscript does not give his name, indeed states that he wishes to remain anonymous (f.169r). However, the author of the Arte of English Poesie (1589), generally supposed to be George Puttenham, includes extracts from the Partheniades (see George Puttenham, The Arte of English Poesie, eds Gladys Doidge Willcock and Alice Walker [Cambridge: Cambridge University Press, 1936], p.327). The term 'partheniad' could mean a song in praise of a virgin, but might also allude to the term 'partheneion', an ancient Greek lyric or hymn sung by a chorus of young women, in this case, the Muses, who are named in the margin as speakers of the different parts of the Partheniades. Furnivall and Morfill, II, pp.72–91; DNB, XXXXVII, pp.64–7; Norbrook and Woudhuysen, p.533 no.252, p.762 n.16, p.820 n.252.
11. This probably means Elizabeth's two French royal suitors, Anjou who was later Henry III, and Alençon who was later Anjou (see note 1 above). They were members of the ruling French house of Valois, who were descended from the Capetian dynasty.

12. That is 'Caesareans', members of the Imperial house? The two younger sons of the Emperor, the Archdukes Ferdinand and Charles, had both been proposed as matches for Elizabeth in the early years of the reign, and negotiations concerning Charles had continued through the 1560s. The third 'Caesarean' is perhaps Philip II of Spain, son of Emperor Charles V and nephew of his successor Emperor Ferdinand, who advanced his own suit in the months following Elizabeth's accession. Neale, *Queen Elizabeth*, pp.74–8, 81–2, 143–5, 148–9, 153–6.

13. King, 'Queen Elizabeth', pp.56–7.

14. Puttenham, *Arte*, pp.xxxiii–iv.

15. Puttenham, *Arte*, pp.4–5, 63, 181, 96–100, 237.

16. Edmund Spenser, *The Yale Edition of the Shorter Poems of Edmund Spenser*, eds William A. Oram et al. (New Haven and London: Yale University Press, 1989), pp.67–84. All further references to the 'Aprill' Eclogue will be to this edition. For illuminating readings of the Eclogue, see L. Staley Johnson, 'Elizabeth, Bride and Queen: A Study of Spenser's April Eclogue and the Metaphors of English Protestantism', *Spenser Studies* 2 (1981), pp.75–91; and see three articles by Louis Adrian Montrose: '"The perfecte paterne of a Poete": the Poetics of Courtship in *The Shepheardes Calender*', *Texas Studies in Literature and Language* 21.1 (Spring 1979), pp.34–67; '"Eliza, Queene of shepheardes", and the Pastoral of Power', *ELR* 10 (1980), pp.153–82; 'The Elizabethan Subject and the Spenserian Text', in *Literary Theory/ Renaissance Texts*, eds Patricia Parker and David Quint (Baltimore and London: Johns Hopkins University Press, 1986), pp.320–4.

17. See Ch.2.ii above.

18. See Ch.3.vi above.

19. BL MS Egerton 944, f.1v. See King, *Iconography*, p.259.

20. See Ch.1.vii above; Yates, 'Astraea' (1947), pp.30–3.

21. Nichols, *Elizabeth*, I, p.73.

22. E.H. Fellowes, ed., *English Madrigal Verse 1588–1632*, 3rd edn, eds F.W. Sternfeld and D. Greer (Oxford: Oxford University Press, 1967), pp.158–66, nos XI, XIII.

23. See Ch.2.ii above.

24. Geneva Bible, Old Testament, p.280.

25. John Lyly, *Euphues and his England* (1580), in *The Complete Works of John Lyly*, 3 vols, ed. R. Warwick Bond (Oxford: Clarendon, 1902), II, pp.191–217. All references will be to this edition.

26. By W.E., printed by Edward White, reproduced in Park and Oldys, X, pp.272–4.

27. Roman virgin goddess and custodian of the imperial flame.

28. Sir Philip Sidney, *The Countess of Pembroke's Arcadia*, ed. Maurice Evans (Harmondsworth: Penguin, 1977), Book 2, Ch.21, p.352.

29. Cf. the dedicatory epistles in Barnaby Rich, *Rich's Farewell to Military Profession* (1581), ed. Thomas M. Cranfill (Austin: University of Texas Press, 1959), pp.3–19; and cf. William Shakespeare, *King Richard III* (1592), ed. Antony Hammond (London: Methuen [Arden Shakespeare], 1981), I.i.1–31.

30. Gar[ter], sig.F4r.

31. Douglas, p.115.
32. Warner, *Alone*, pp.48, 72.
33. Cf. Ch.2.iii above, and Ch.5.iii below.
34. For other accounts of Elizabeth's body as symbol of the nation, see Peter Stallybrass, 'Patriarchal Territories: The Body Enclosed', in Ferguson et al., pp.123–42; Leonard Tennenhouse, *Power on Display; The Politics of Shakespeare's Genres* (New York: Methuen, 1986).
35. Thomas Blenerhasset, *A Revelation of the True Minerva* (1582), facs., introd. Josephine Waters Bennett (New York: Scholar's Facsimile, 1941), sig.C4ff, pp.x–xiii. All further references are to this edition.
36. Thomas Bentley, *The Monument of Matrones: conteining seuen seuerall Lamps of Virginitie*, 3 vols (London: 1582), I, dedication.
37. Bentley, I, dedication.
38. Bentley, I, sig.B2r.
39. Bentley, I, p.307, reproduced in E.C. Wilson, plate facing p.220.
40. See Ch.3.v. above.
41. Bentley, I, p.306, reproduced in E.C. Wilson, plate facing p.220.
42. E.C. Wilson, p.219.
43. McClure and Headlam Wells, p.44.
44. In 1579 Sidney wrote a public *Letter to Queen Elizabeth touching her marriage with Monsieur*, voicing the opposition of the Leicester-Walsingham circle to which he belonged. The aftermath of the controversy seems to have contributed to his withdrawal from court in 1579–80. Duncan-Jones, *Courtier Poet*, pp.162–7.
45. Sidney, *Arcadia*, p.352.
46. Duncan-Jones, *Courtier Poet*, p.232.
47. Sir Philip Sidney, *A Defence of Poetry*, in *Miscellaneous Prose*, p.78. All further references are to this edition.
48. Ben Jonson, 'An Epistle to Master John Selden', *The Complete Poems*, ed. George Parfitt (Harmondsworth: Penguin, 1988), p.148, ll.20–2.
49. Strong, *Portraits*, p.35. Axton makes a similar point: 'A flawless image of the Queen demanded that she should live up to it' (p.37).

Chapter 5   1583–93: Patronage, Prayers and Pilgrimages

1. See above, Ch.1.vii; and King, *Iconography*, p.196.
2. Carroll, pp.28–32.
3. See for examples, Nicolas, pp.149–54.
4. Letter of c. May 1580, Nicolas, pp.149–50; BL Add. MS 15891, f.72.
5. May, p.12.
6. Presumably [Sir] Christopher Yelverton (1535?–1612), at this time an MP and treasurer of the Inns of Court, later a judge and Speaker of the House of Commons. *DNB*, LXIII, p.315.
7. Letter dated 12.5.1582, Nicolas, p.248; BL Add. MS 15891, f.85v.
8. Letter dated 1.12.1579, Nicolas, pp.141–3; BL Add. MS 15891, f.25v.
9. Undated, Nicolas pp.353–5; BL Add. MS 15891 f.81.
10. King, *Iconography*, p.238.
11. Montrose, 'Shaping Fantasies' (1988), p.34.

12. Sander, pp.23–6.
13. In 1536 Anne's brother, Lord Rochford, had been one of the five men convicted of adultery with her.
14. Sander, pp.100–1.
15. Edward Rishton, *The Anglican Schism Renewed Under Elizabeth: The Continuation of the History*, in Sander, pp.287–8.
16. Sander, p.229.
17. Phillips, p.109.
18. Phillips, pp.110, 174, 129, 162–5.
19. Giacopo Brocardo, *The Revelation of S.Ihon reueled*, trans. James Sanford (London: Thomas Marshe, 1582). All further references are to this edition.
20. Hazlitt, 1st Series, no.XXIX.
21. Lyly, *Euphues and his England*, p.210. Cf. Aylmer, Ch.2.iii above.
22. Neale, *Parliaments*, II, p.170.
23. Cf. Ch.2.iii and Ch.4.v above.
24. 'A songe made by her ma*jes*tie and songe before her at her cominge from white hall to Powles throughe fleete streete in Anno *domini* 1588', National Maritime Museum MS SNG/4, reprinted in M.J. Rodríguez-Salgado et al., *Armada 1588–1988* (Harmondsworth: Penguin, 1988), p.274, item 16.3.
25. 'A proper new ballade wherin is plaine to be seene how god blesseth england for loue of our Queene: Soung to the tune of tarletons caroll', Bod. MS Rawl. Poet. 185, ff.13r–14r. See also Furnivall and Morfill, II, pp.92–5.
26. Edward Hellwis, *A Marvell Deciphered* (London, 1589), p.12. All further references are to this edition.
27. See Ch.2.iii above.
28. *The Poems of Henry Constable*, ed. Joan Grundy, 'Introduction', pp.21–6, 232 n. All subsequent references to Constable's works will be to this edition.
29. 1593. Constable, ed. Grundy, p.37 (ref. Hatfield House MSS XXXV, f.50); HMC Hatfield V, p.403. See also HMC Hatfield VII, p.86, letter from Harry Constable to the Earl of Essex from Paris, 1597.
30. All references to *The Faerie Queene* are to *FQ* (see 'Abbreviations' above).
31. See Ch.2.ix, Ch.3.iv, Ch.5.iii above.
32. See Ch.2.ix above.
33. Geneva Bible, 'Revelacion', 17.3–4.
34. *The Works of Edmund Spenser: A Variorum Edition*, eds E. Greenlaw, C.G. Osgood and F.M. Padelford (Baltimore: Johns Hopkins Press, 1932–57), III (1934), p.249; BCP (1969?), Psalm 110.
35. Thomas P. Roche, *The Kindly Flame: A Study of the Third and Fourth Books of Spenser's 'Faerie Queene'* (Princeton: Princeton University Press, 1964), p.105.
36. See above, Ch.2.ii, 4.iv, 4.viii.
37. Chambers, p.143.
38. E.C. Wilson, p.206.
39. Yates, 'Astraea' (1947), p.74.

40. Allison Heisch, 'Queen Elizabeth I and the Persistence of Patriarchy', *Feminist Review* 4 (1980), p.46.
41. Robin Headlam Wells, *Spenser's 'Faerie Queene' and the Cult of Elizabeth* (London: Croom Helm, 1983), p.18. See also Jardine, pp.177–8.
42. The song was also printed in Dowland's *First Book of Songs*. Peele and Dowland give the words in the third person, as 'His golden locks'. The song has been variously attributed to Peele or to Lee himself. Chambers, pp.138–9, 142; Fellowes, pp.464–5, 738; Strong, *Cult*, p.153; May, p.356.
43. Bod. MS Rawl. Poet. 148, f.75v. This version adds to 'Times eldest sonne', as a fourth stanza, the third stanza of 'His golden locks'.
44. Chambers, pp.138–9. See also Dowland, *1st Book of Songs*, no.XVIII, in Fellowes, pp.464–5.
45. Chambers, pp.142–3. See also John Dowland, *2nd Book of Songs*, nos VI–VIII, in Fellowes, p.469; May, pp.356–7.
46. See Ch.3.vii, viii above; Chambers, pp.86–7, 91.
47. Elizabeth I, *Letters*, p.207. When Elizabeth visited Theobalds in the early 1590s, a hermit-figure played a prominent part in the entertainments. Nichols, *Elizabeth*, III, pp.241–6; Berry, pp.103, 107.
48. HMC Hatfield, IV, p.136.
49. In placing and identifying the Latin phrases I have made use of F.P. Dutripon, *Concordantiae Bibliorum Sacrorum Vulgatae Editionis*, 2 vols (Paris: 1838); John Henry Blunt, *The Annotated Book of Common Prayer* (London: Longmans, 1903); *The Booke of Common Prayer, with the Psalter of Psalmes of David* (London: Christopher Barker, 1588).
50. See *BCP* (1588).
51. *BCP* (1588), sig.A2v. All quotations here from the Book of Common Prayer are from the 1588 edition. The version currently in use is substantially the same except for modern spelling.
52. *BCP* (1588), 'A Table for order of the Psalmes'.
53. *BCP* (1588), sig.A8v.
54. This psalm was used monthly at morning prayer, and at services of 'Commination against [i.e. denunciation of] sinners'. *BCP* (1588), 'Table', and sig.C1r.
55. *BCP* (1588), 'Table', and 'Propre Psalmes on certain dayes'.
56. *BCP* (1588), sig.A1r.
57. *BCP* (1588), 'Table'.
58. *BCP* (1588), 'Propre Psalmes' and 'Table'.
59. Elizabeth herself, for instance, told the 1563 Parliament, in a written reply read out by Nicholas Bacon: 'I hope I shall die in quiet with *nunc dimittis*'. Neale, *Parliaments*, I, p.127.
60. Chambers, p.19.
61. John Savile, 'A Salutatorie Poeme to the Magestie of King IAMES', *King Iames his entertainment at Theobalds: With his welcome to London, together with a salutatorie Poeme* (London, 1603), sig.R4v.
62. Chambers, pp.58–9, 61.
63. Chambers, p.137.
64. Chambers, pp.136–8.

65. See Ch.1.ii above.
66. See Berry, pp.81, 92–3, 100.
67. Chambers, pp.143–4; Robert Dowland, *A Musical Banquet* (1610),
     no.VIII, in Fellowes, pp.506–7.
68. *The Poems of Sir Arthur Gorges*, ed. Helen Estabrook Sandison (Ox-
     ford: Oxford University Press, 1953), p.67, no.65, l.4. For discussion
     of date, see pp.xxvii–xxxii; May, pp.103, 323.
69. *Fidessa, more chaste than kinde* (London, 1596), sig.D2v, sonnet XXXVI.
70. William Shakespeare, *Romeo and Juliet*, in *Complete Works*, ed. Peter
     Alexander (London: Collins, 1951), II.ii.113–14.
71. Barnabe Barnes, *Parthenophil and Parthenophe*, ed. Victor A. Doyno
     (Carbondale: Southern Illinois University Press, 1971), p.97.
72. 'Aprill' Eclogue, l.96.
73. In *Heliconia: Comprising A Selection of English Poetry of the Elizabethan
     Age*, ed. T. Park, 3 vols (London: 1815), II, p.6, sonnet 11; p.24, sonnet
     47; p.29, sonnet 57; pp.52–3, 'Hymne'.
74. Chambers, Appendix E, pp.276–97; J. Wilson, pp.136–41.
75. Chambers, p.147.
76. Chambers, p.282.
77. See 'Introduction' i, above.
78. *The Poems of Sir Walter Ralegh*, ed. Agnes M.C. Latham (London:
     Routledge, 1951), no.18, pp.18–19.
79. See above, Ch.1.v; Aston, p.234.
80. Bod. MS Rawl. Poet. 85 f.123r–v. Available in Norbrook and Woud-
     huysen, no.89, pp.247–8; Ralegh ed. Latham, no.21, pp.22–3. For loca-
     tions of other manuscript and early printed sources, see Francis
     Deaumont, *The Knight of the Burning Pestle*, ed. Cyrus Hoy, in *The Dra-
     matic Works in the Beaumont and Fletcher Canon*, gen. ed. Fredson Bowers
     (Cambridge: Cambridge University Press, 1966), vol.I, pp.90–1.
81. See Ch.6.vii below.
82. See Ralegh ed. Latham, p.120; William Chappell, *Popular Music of the
     Olden Time*, 2 vols (London: Chappell, 1855–7), pp.121–3.
83. From Thomas Ravenscroft, *Pammelia* (1609), in Fellowes, p.206.
84. For a list of references, see Beaumont, pp.90–1.
85. May, pp.119–20.
86. Andrew Clark, ed., *The Shirburn Ballads 1585–1616* (Oxford: Clarendon
     Press, 1907), pp.244–54; for date, see pp.1–2.
87. See Ch.2.vi above.
88. Hyder Edward Rollins, ed., *The Pepys Ballads*, 8 vols (Cambridge,
     Mass.: Harvard University Press, 1929), II, pp.22–8, no.50.
89. See Rollins, *Pepys Ballads*, II, p.22.
90. Chappell, *Popular Music*, pp.121–3. Chappell records that 'Walsing-
     ham' appears in a manuscript known as 'Queen Elizabeth's Virginal
     Book', but notes on p.xiv that this book is unlikely to have belonged
     to Elizabeth, since the scribe includes dates at various places of 1603,
     1605, and 1612.
91. Thomas Nashe, *Haue vvith you to Saffron vvalden, or, Gabriell Harueys
     Hunt is vp* (London: John Danter, 1596), sig.L1r.

92. Chappell, *Popular Music*, p.122; John W. Hales and Frederick J. Furnivall, eds, *Bishop Percy's Folio Manuscript*, 3 vols (London: N. Trübner, 1867–8), III, p.467.
93. William Shakespeare, *Hamlet* (1600), ed. Harold Jenkins (London: Methuen [Arden Shakespeare], 1982), IV.v.23–6.
94. Beaumont, II.464–7.
95. Norbrook and Woudhuysen, p.820, n.250.
96. Norbrook and Woudhuysen, no.250, pp.531–2.
97. Ralegh ed. Latham, no.12, p.12.
98. E.C. Wilson, p.221.
99. 'A Handful of Gladsome Verses, giuen to the Queenes Maiesty at Woodstocke this Prograce' (1592), Hazlitt, 1st Series, no.XXXI.

Chapter 6   The 1590s: The Literature of Disillusionment

1.   'Now we have present made', Walter Oakeshott, *The Queen and the Poet* (London: Faber, 1960), p.205.
2.   Thomas Dekker, *Old Fortunatus* (published 1600, performed 1599), in *The Dramatic Works of Thomas Dekker*, ed. Fredson Bowers, 4 vols (Cambridge: Cambridge University Press, 1953), vol.I, p.113.
3.   See Ch.1.i above.
4.   Winfried Schleiner has shown that the role of Amazon was regarded as disturbing and unnatural by Elizabeth's subjects, and was only directly applied to the Queen when circumstances like the Armada conflict rendered it particularly apt. '"Divina virago": Queen Elizabeth as an Amazon', *Studies in Philology* 75 (1978), pp.163–80.
5.   See above, Ch.3.vi.
6.   For example a song by Lodowick Lloyd (1579), E.C. Wilson, p.27; Prologue to Dekker, *Old Fortunatus*, p.113.
7.   Nichols, *Elizabeth*, II, pp.548, 549, 571.
8.   *FQ*, p.737.
9.   Bod. MS Rawl. Poet. 85, f.123r–v.
10. Pandora in Lyly's *The Woman in the Moone* (publ. 1597), who is by turns sullen, proud, warlike, amiable, wanton, false and mad, may represent a veiled critique of the Queen, and of the absurdity of the idea of her as all-gifted. See Helen Cobb, *Representations of Elizabeth I: Three sites of ambiguity and contradiction* (unpublished Oxford University D.Phil. thesis, 1989), pp.339–45.
11. Richard F. Hardin in *Civil Idolatry: Desacralizing and Monarchy in Spenser, Shakespeare, and Milton* (Newark: University of Delaware Press, 1992) traces opposition to monarchs who set themselves up as gods from figures like Herod in medieval drama, and from the political thought of Erasmus, through Book V of *The Faerie Queene* and Shakespeare's histories to Milton and the Civil War. His book contains much valuable material, but he somewhat underplays sixteenth-century views of monarchs as representatives of God in order to discover origins for seventeenth-century anti-monarchism.
12. For all dates of Greville's works, I follow Ronald A. Rebholz, *The*

Life of Fulke Greville, First Lord Brooke (Oxford: Clarendon, 1971),
Appendix 1.

13. *Poems and Dramas of Fulke Greville, 1st Lord Brooke*, ed. G. Bullough,
2 vols (Edinburgh: Oliver & Boyd, 1939), vol.II, pp.138–213, III.iii.
89–91.

14. *Mustapha* (c.1594–6), in Greville ed. Bullough, vol.II, pp.63–137,
V.iii.92–4.

15. 'The Excellencie of Monarchie Compared with Aristocratie and
Democratie Joyntlie', *A Treatise of Monarchy*, in *The Remains: Being
Poems of Monarchy and Religion*, ed. G.A. Wilkes (Oxford: Oxford
University Press, 1965), p.201, st.663.

16. 'Of Croune Revenue', Greville ed. Wilkes, p.145, st.439.

17. Rebholz dates *Caelica* 1–76 and 83 as composed 1577–87; *Caelica* 77–
81 as composed 1587–1603; *Caelica* 82 and 84–105 as composed 1604–
14; *Caelica* 106–9 as composed 1614–28 (Appendix 1).

18. All references to *Caelica* are to Greville ed. Bullough, I, pp.73–153.

19. The *Caelica* poems are variously addressed to Caelica, Cynthia or
Mira. It is not known whether these names represent a real mistress
or mistresses, but speculation has included suggestions that some
of the poems are addressed to Elizabeth. However, I concur with
Bullough's sense that no.81 is probably the only poem to Elizabeth.
See Greville ed. Bullough, p.42.

20. Fulke Greville, Lord Brooke, *A Dedication to Sir Philip Sidney, The
Prose Works of Fulke Greville, Lord Brooke*, ed. John Gouws (Oxford:
Clarendon, 1986), Ch.6, p.41.

21. See above, Ch.1.iii, Ch.3.iii.

22. See above, Ch.2.vi, Ch.4.v, Ch.5.i, Ch.5.iii.

23. Gar[ter], sigs D3v–4v.

24. Hazlitt, 1st Series, no.XXIX.

25. Bod. MS Rawl. Poet. 185, ff.13r–14r. See above, Ch.5.iii.

26. Nichols, *Elizabeth*, II, p.552.

27. See also Kenilworth, 1575 (Ch.3.vii above); and Norwich, 1578, where
Mars declared, 'oh Queene thou beest a Prince of peace' (Gar[ter],
sig.E2v).

28. See above, Ch.4.v.

29. Edmund Spenser, *A View of the Present State of Ireland*, in *Spenser
Variorum*, IX (1949), *Spenser's Prose Works*, ed. Rudolf Gottfried, p.148,
ll.1956, 2976–8.

30. Even so, the fact that Spenser's trial scene is symbolic and fictional
is indicated by divergences from fact, such as the presence of
Mercilla; Elizabeth was absent from Mary's trial, though an empty
chair symbolised her as presiding. See Helen Smailes & Duncan
Thomson, *The Queen's Image: A Celebration of Mary, Queen of Scots*
(Edinburgh: Scottish National Portrait Gallery, 1987), no.25, pp.
43–4.

31. Neale, *Parliaments*, II, p.96. For more likely reasons why Elizabeth
blocked the Bill, see Neale, *Parliaments*, II, pp.46–8.

32. Johnson, p.291; Neale, *Parliaments*, II, p.127.

33. Hazlitt, 1st Series, no.XXVIII.

34. See *FQ* p.593, notes on V.ix.27–9.
35. See Thomas H. Cain, *Praise in The Faerie Queene* (Lincoln, Nebraska: University of Nebraska Press, 1978), p.145: 'the point is . . . that the harmony of justice and mercy in the icon cannot be realised in political action.' Similarly, in a 'Brief Note of Ireland', Spenser praised Elizabeth as 'a glorious example of mercie and Clemencye' while voicing a fear 'leste your Majestes wonted mercifull minde should againe be wrought to your wonted milde courses' (Hardin, pp. 120–1).
36. For discussion of date, see Lyly ed. Bond, III, pp.10–13.
37. Warner, *Alone*, Ch.17.
38. Warner, *Alone*, pp.257–8.
39. *NCE*, IX, p.375; XIV, pp.1000–1.
40. Warner, *Alone*, pp.259–62. See above, Ch.1.i.
41. Oakeshott, p.26; Neale, *Queen Elizabeth*, p.217.
42. 'Letter to Ralegh', in *FQ*, pp.407–8.
43. Ormond, p.29.
44. Alexander, *MND* II.i.155–64.
45. Nichols, *Elizabeth*, III, p.111.
46. At the end of the *Epithalamion* Spenser invokes Cinthia as follows:

> . . . sith of wemens labours thou hast charge,
> And generation goodly dost enlarge,
> Encline thy will t'effect our wishfull vow,
> And the chast wombe informe with timely seed

(*Shorter Poems*, p.677, ll.383–6).

I find it highly unlikely that in this case Cinthia is intended to represent Elizabeth.
47. See, for instance, Richard Mulcaster, *Positions* (1581), (London: Longmans, 1888), p.173; Peele, *Arraygnement of Paris* (1583/4), Prouty, vol.III, ll.1227–36; Aske, *Elizabetha Triumphans* (1588), Nichols, *Elizabeth*, II, p.582; Barnes, *Parthenophil*, Canzon 2, l.45.
48. Nichols, *Elizabeth*, I, p.471.
49. *The Works of Thomas Kyd*, ed. F.S. Boas (Oxford: Oxford University Press, 1955), pp.161–230.
50. *The Riverside Shakespeare*, ed. G. Blakemore Evans (Boston: Houghton Mifflin, 1974), pp.1851–2.
51. Nichols, *Elizabeth*, III, p.243.
52. Strong, *Gloriana*, pp.146–51; *Portraits*, p.17; *Cult*, p.48; *The English Icon: Elizabethan and Jacobean Portraiture* (London: Routledge, 1969), p.29.
53. See above, Ch.4.ii, vi.
54. 'of the Q.', Gorges, pp.64–5, no.61.
55. Warner, *Alone*, p.xxiii, p.51, Ch.6.
56. See Warner, *Alone*, Ch.5.
57. *The Poems of George Chapman*, ed. Phyllis Brooks Bartlett (New York: MLA, 1941), 'Hymnus in Cynthiam' ll.16–18.

58. Dowland, *Third Book of Songs*, no.VII, in Fellowes, p.481.
59. Gorges, pp.131–2, no.109, ll.11–20.
60. Walter Bourchier Devereux, *Lives and Letters of the Devereux, Earls of Essex*, 2 vols (London: 1893), II, p.8; Nichols, *Elizabeth*, III, pp.513, 519, 578–9, 586, 595.
61. Von Klarwill, p.349; *Thomas Platter's Travels in England* (1599), trans. Clare Williams (London: Cape, 1937), p.192.
62. Elizabeth certainly wore wigs, not to cover baldness, but as a commonplace fashion accessory to cover grey hair. In 1578 the Countess of Essex gave her a New Year's gift of 'a yelo here, and another like black'. The royal accounts show that Roger Mountague supplied Elizabeth in 1592 with 'vij heads of haire to make attiers . . . and . . . Two periwigs of haire'; in 1595 with 'iiij perewigges of heaire'; and in 1601 with 'vj faire heddes of heire'. In 1602 Dorothy Speckard supplied 'six heades of haire', and the same again in 1603. Arnold, *Wardrobe*, pp.28, 206.
63. Eg. Paul Hentzner, *Travels in England During the Reign of Queen Elizabeth*, ed. H. Walpole, trans. R. Bentley, with *Fragmenta Regalia* by Sir Robert Naunton (London: Cassell, 1889), pp.47–8; André Hurault, Sieur de Maisse, *Journal*, trans and eds G.B. Harrison and R.A. Jones (London: Nonesuch, 1931), pp.25–6.
64. Neale, *Queen Elizabeth*, pp.391–2. However, John Manningham related in his diary a story that Elizabeth had nominated James on her deathbed (BL MS Harl.5353, f.133r, entry for 13 April 1603).
65. Chapman, 'Hymnus in Cynthiam', ll.31–9, 109.
66. Chapman, 'Hymnus in Cynthiam', ll.506–7.
67. See, for instance, the volumes of HMC Hatfield for these years.
68. Christopher Haigh, ed., *The Reign of Elizabeth I* (London: Macmillan, 1984), p.5.
69. Hurault, pp.11–12.
70. Quoted in Penry Williams, 'Court and Polity under Elizabeth I', *Bulletin of the John Rylands Library of Manchester* 65.2 (Spring 1983), p.270.
71. *Calendar of the Manuscripts of the Most Honourable the Marquess of Bath preserved at Longleat, Wiltshire*, 5 vols, V, *Talbot, Dudley and Devereux Papers 1533–1659*, ed. G. Dynfallt Owen, HMC 58 (London: HMSO 1980), p.266.
72. *The Letters and Epigrams of Sir John Harington*, ed. N.E. McClure (Philadelphia: University of Pennsylvania Press, 1930), p.123.
73. Chapman, 'Hymnus in Noctem', ll.392–403.
74. Hurault, p.115.
75. Devereux, I, pp.501–2.
76. Devereux, I, p.397.
77. See, for instance, Luther as quoted in Ian Maclean, *The Renaissance Notion of Woman* (Cambridge: Cambridge University Press, 1980), p.10.
78. Mulcaster, p.176. See also Berry, p.135.
79. See Cobb, pp.315–21.
80. May, pp.266–9.

81. II.ii.109–11, in Shakespeare ed. Alexander.
82. 'Tishe's Verses on the Order of the Garter', Furnivall and Morfill, II, pp.115–29, ll.277–84.
83. See John Lyly, *Endimion, The Man in the Moone*, in Bond, vol.III, pp.5–103; 'Introduction', pp.10–13. All subsequent references are to this edition.
84. See Lyly ed. Bond, vol.III, pp.89–91; Axton, p.72; Berry, p.129.
85. Hatfield House, Cecil Papers, 144, ff.240r–7r. Available in Norbrook and Woudhuysen, no.21, pp.102–16; Ralegh ed. Latham, no.18, pp.25–43.
   For summaries of different views of the date and context of the poem, see E.C. Wilson, pp.307–8, and Oakeshott, pp.133–8. Those who favour 1592 or soon after include E.C. Wilson (pp.306–8), Oakeshott (pp.54, 56, 136–8), Stephen J. Greenblatt (*Sir Walter Ralegh: The Renaissance Man and his Roles* [New Haven: Yale University Press, 1973], pp.78–9), and David G.E. Norbrook (*Panegyric of the Monarch and its Social Context under Elizabeth I and James I* [unpublished Oxford University D.Phil. thesis, 1978], pp.140–2; *Poetry and Politics in the English Renaissance* [London: Routledge, 1984], p.117). An example of the 1603 view is Katherine Duncan-Jones, 'The Date of Raleigh's "21th: And Last Booke of the Ocean to Scinthia"', *RES* 21 (1970), pp.143–58.
86. Norbrook and Woudhuysen, no.21, pp.102–16, ll.112–13. All further references are to this edition.
87. Heisch, 'Parliamentary Rhetoric', p.55.
88. 'Fantasy' at this date meant both caprice or changeful mood, and inclination or liking (*OED*, defns 6 and 7). 'Affection' could have its modern sense of fondness and loving attachment; or it could mean a malady or disease; or a temporary state; or an affectation (*OED*, defns 6a, 10, 11, 13).
89. Peele, *Arraygnement of Paris*, Prouty, vol. III, pp.1–131. See Louis Adrian Montrose, 'Gifts and Reasons: The Contexts of Peele's *Araygnement of Paris*', *ELH* 47 (1980), p.455.
90. Nichols, *Elizabeth*, I, p.512.
91. Dekker, *Old Fortunatus*, p.113, ll.25–7.
92. Ben Jonson, *Cynthia's Revels*, in *The Complete Plays of Ben Jonson*, ed. G.A. Wilkes, based on edn of C.H. Herford and Evelyn Simpson, 4 vols (Oxford: Clarendon, 1981–2), vol.II, V.viii.4–14.
93. See, for instance, Greenblatt, *Self-Fashioning*, pp.167–8. For a fascinating technical account of how Elizabeth's public image was manufactured through costume, see Arnold, *Wardrobe*, esp. Ch.1, pp.2–13, 'In the Eye of the Beholder'.
94. Neale, *Parliaments*, II, p.119.
95. See Ch.2.ii above; *Quenes Maiesties Passage*, sig.A2v.
96. See Ch.4.v above.
97. J. Wilson, p.44.
98. 'Cassandra', published with *Cynthia* (1595), in *The Poems of Richard Barnfield*, ed. Montague Summers (London: Fortune, 1936), p.79.
99. 'of the Q. Sonnet', Gorges, p.56, no.47, ll.13–14.

100. Sir John Davies, *Hymnes of Astraea*, in *Poems of Sir John Davies*, ed. Robert Krueger (Oxford: Clarendon, 1975), no.XXVI, 'To Envie'.
101. Spenser, *Shorter Poems*, p.290, ll.580–2.
102. Spenser, *Shorter Poems*, p.539, ll.344–55.
103. Spenser, *View*, p.147.
104. Spenser, *Shorter Poems*, p.543, l.453; p.550, ll.630–1, 640–7.
105. See *Spenser Variorum*, VI, pp.439–41, for Evelyn May Albright's view that the Cantos were among the earliest parts of *The Faerie Queene* to be composed. For the view that the Cantos were rejected material from earlier books of *The Faerie Queene*, see William Fenn De Moss, *Spenser Variorum*, VI, pp.436–7; and Alice Fox Blitch, 'The Mutabilitie Cantos: "In Meet Order Ranged"', *English Language Notes* 7 (1969–70), pp.179–86. However, the view of most critics is that they were a late or final composition. See F.J. Furnivall, *Spenser Variorum*, VI, p.315; F.M. Padelford, 'The *Cantos of Mutabilitie*: Further considerations bearing on the date', *Proceedings of the Modern Language Association* 45 (1930), pp.704–11; Edmund Spenser, *The Mutabilitie Cantos*, ed. S.P. Zitner (London: Nelson, 1968), p.3; Russell J. Meyer, '"Fixt in heauens hight": Spenser, Astronomy, and the date of the *Cantos of Mutabilitie*', *Spenser Studies* IV (1983), pp.115–29.
106. VIII.viii.1.6–7 can be read as 'An awareness of mutability [as destructive] makes me loathe this state of life so tickle and cast away love of things so vain.' This could represent a despairing rejection of Nature's consolation, or a calm resignation to mortality. For readings of the stanzas as rejecting consolation, see Douglas Bush, *Mythology and the Renaissance Tradition in English Poetry* (New York: Pageant, 1957), pp.121–2; Ricardo J. Quinones, *The Renaissance Discovery of Time* (Cambridge, Mass.: Harvard University Press, 1972), p.288; Lewis J. Owen, 'Mutable in eternity: Spenser's despair and the multiple forms of Mutabilitie', *Journal of Mediaeval and Renaissance Studies* 2 (1972), p.67; Thomas Hyde, 'Vision, Poetry and Authority in Spenser', *ELR* 13 (1983), pp.136, 144–5; Greenblatt, *Self-Fashioning*, p.179; Cain, pp.183–4; Gross, pp.251–2; Thomas M. Greene, *The Descent from Heaven: A Study in Epic Continuity* (New Haven: Yale University Press, 1963), p.323.

For readings of the stanzas as consolatory or resigned, see Spenser ed. Zitner, p.11; Michael Holahan, '*Iamque opus exegi*: Ovid's Changes and Spenser's Brief Epic of Mutability', *ELR* 6 (1976), p.267; Norbrook, *Poetry and Politics*, pp.154–5; William Blissett, 'Spenser's Mutabilitie', *Essays in English Literature from the Renaissance to the Victorian Age*, eds M. Maclure and F.W. Watt (Toronto: University of Toronto Press, 1964), p.42.

A further possible reading, which follows the syntax more closely, is: 'An awareness of mutability [as procreative] makes me loth [i.e. reluctant] to cast away this state of life so tickle and love of things so vain.' I am indebted to Isabella Wheater for alerting me to this reading. It has also been noted by Harry Berger Jr. (see note on these lines in *FQ*) and by Judith H. Anderson ('"A Gentle Knight was pricking on the plain": The Chaucerian Connection', *ELR* 15

[1985], p.173, n.20), who both also note the possibility that 'vaine' is an adverb.
107. Owen, pp.53–4, 64, 67–8.
108. Norbrook and Woudhuysen, no.18, p.100. Published in *The Phoenix Nest* (1593).
109. Jonson, *Cynthia's Revels*, V.xi.34.
110. E.C. Wilson, pp.317–18.
111. See Owen, pp.61, 64.
112. See Dennis Kay, ' "She was a Queen, and Therefore Beautiful": Sidney, his Mother, and Queen Elizabeth', *RES* XLIII.169 (Feb. 1992), pp.18–39, esp. pp.24–7.
113. See A.C. Hamilton, 'Our new poet: Spenser, "well of English undefyld" ', *A Theatre for Spenserians*, eds J.M. Kennedy and J.A. Reither (Manchester: Manchester University Press, 1973), p.110.
114. Nichols, *Elizabeth*, I, p.467.
115. This view is taken by David Quint, *Origin and Originality in Renaissance Literature: Versions of the Source* (New Haven: Yale University Press, 1983), p.165.
116. See Jonathan Goldberg, *Endlesse Worke: Spenser and the Structures of Discourse* (Baltimore: Johns Hopkins University Press, 1981); Elizabeth J. Bellamy, 'The Vocative and the Vocational: The Unreadability of Elizabeth in *The Faerie Queene*', *ELH* 54.1 (Spring 1987), pp.1–30.
117. See Ch.5.v above.
118. Cain comments that the *Mutabilitie Cantos* effect the 'separation of the real queen from her heavenly image' and 'the collapse of the claim that England partakes in Jerusalem' (p.184).

Chapter 7   Towards Death, and Beyond It

1. J. Wilson, p.104.
2. From *Churchyard's Challenge*, quoted in Robert Chester, *Loves Martyr*, ed. A.B. Grosart (London, 1878), p.xxx.
3. J. Davies ed. Krueger, p.75.
4. Dekker, *Old Fortunatus*, II.ii.178–89.
5. Chester, p.61/69.
6. J. Wilson, p.36, n.79.
7. May, p.151.
8. R.H. Miller, 'Unpublished Poems by Sir John Harington', *ELH* 14 (1984), pp.157–8. Miller's copy-text is Folger MS V.a.249; the poem also appears in BL Add. MS 12049. Steven May describes the BL MS as a collection of his epigrams which Harington prepared in 1602 for presentation to King James, which gives this poem a date sometime before that year. Cf. Peter Beal, comp., *Index of English Literary Manuscripts*, I, 1450–1625, Part 2, Douglas – Wyatt (London: Mansell, 1980), p.130, Hr20 and Hr21.
9. See Ch.4.vii, 5.iii above.
10. J. Davies ed. Krueger, p.307.
11. Warner, *Alone*, pl.VIII, pp.327–8.
12. Warner, *Alone*, Ch.13.

13. Platter, p.228.
14. See Ch.2.viii above.
15. See *DNB* XXXXV (1896).
16. William Perkins, *A Reformed Catholike*, 1597 (Cambridge: John Legat, 1598), 'The Avthor to the Christian Reader'. All further references are to this edition, referred to as *RC*.
17. William Perkins, *A Warning Against the Idolatrie of the last times* (Cambridge: John Legat, 1601), 'To the Reader'. All further references are to this edition, referred to as *WAI*.
18. Sander, pp.284–5.
19. See above, Ch.3.v. All references are to the edition of Holland cited above, Ch.3, n.73.
20. John Howson, *A Sermon Preached at St. Maries in Oxford the 17 Day of November, 1602, in defence of the Festivities of the Church of England, and namely that of her Maiesties Coronation* [i.e. Accession Day] (Oxford: 1602). All references are to this edition.
21. *DNB*, XXVIII (1891).
22. See above, Ch.1.iii.
23. For further diverse Elizabethan views of civil worship, see Hardin, pp.33–4.
24. HMC Hatfield XI (1906), p.404.
25. HMC Hatfield XI (1906), pp.405–6.
26. *DNB*, LVIII (1899), pp.401–4.
27. Strong, *Portraits*, p.40; *Gloriana*, pp.40–1.
28. Freeman M. O'Donoghue, *A Descriptive and Classified Catalogue of Portraits of Queen Elizabeth* (London: Bernard Quaritch, 1894), p.79, no.214. Yates has modernised the spelling. This engraving derives from the famous full-length engraving of Elizabeth by Crispin van de Passe after Isaac Oliver, c.1603 (see Strong, *Gloriana*, p.162, pl.180).
      Other sources for the couplet include 'Britain's Lachrimae', in Nichols, *Elizabeth*, III, p.652; and some verses in a Jackson MS at the University of Edinburgh, reprinted in Furnivall and Morfill, II, pp.286–7, ll.33–4, which appear without the couplet and with some other variations as 'On the Picture of Queene Elizabeth by Mr Iohn Vicars', Bod. MS Ash. 38, ff.24v–25r. The enduring currency of the couplet is evidenced by its appearance in Lewis Bayly, *The Practise of Pietie: Directing a Christian how to walke that he may please God*, 3rd edn (London: John Hodgets, 1613), pp.534–5; and by an echo of it in Thomas Fuller, *The Holy State* (Cambridge, 1642), p.318 ('Thus dyed Queen Elizabeth, whilest living, the first maid on earth, and when dead, the second in heaven').
29. Verses by R. Lake, *Oxonienses Academiae Funebre Officium in memoriam honoratissimam serenissimae et beatissimae Elizabethae, nvper Angliae, Franciae, & Hiberniae Reginae* (Oxford: 1603), p.145; cf. E.C. Wilson, p.381.
30. All translations mine.
31. Yates erroneously gives 'foeminum'.
32. Verses by Thomas Morton, *Oxoniensis Academiae*, p.116; cf. E.C. Wilson, p.382.

33. *Threno-thriambeuticon. Academiae Cantabrigiensis ob damnum lucrosum, & infaelicitatem foelicissimam, luctuosus triumphus* (Cambridge, 1603), p.25; cf. E.C. Wilson, p.383.
34. Yates, 'Astraea' (1947), pp.74–5.
35. Henry Petowe, 'The Induction', *Elizabetha quasi viuens, Eliza's Funerall, A fewe Aprill drops, showred on the Hearse of dead Eliza. OR The Funerall teares of a true hearted Subiect* (London: 1603), sig.A3v; cf. Nichols, *Elizabeth,* III, p.616.
36. Petowe, 'Eliza's Funerall', in *Elizabetha quasi viuens,* sig.B1r; cf. Nichols, *Elizabeth,* III, p.617.
37. John Lane, *An Elegie vpon the death of the high and renowned Princesse, our late Soueraigne Elizabeth,* quoted in E.C. Wilson, p.377; Hazlitt, 2nd Series, no.II.
38. See Ch.1.iv above.
39. *Aue Caesar . . . The ioyfull Ecchoes of loyall English hartes, entertayning his Maiesties late ariuall in England. With an Epitaph vpon the death of her Maiestie our late Queene,* quoted in E.C. Wilson, p.372. Cf. Hazlitt, 2nd series, no.IV.
40. John Fenton, 'A sorrowfull Epitaph on the death of Queene ELIZA-BETH', *King Iames his welcome to London. With Elizaes Tombe and Epitaph* (London: 1603), sig.B2v. Cf. E.C. Wilson, p.371.
41. See Ch.1.vii above.
42. Phillips, p.184.
43. Milton, ed. Carey, pp.126–9.
44. J. Jones, 'An Epitaph vpon the Death of our late gratious and dread Soveraigne *Elizabeth,* Queene of *England,* &c.', in Nichols, *Elizabeth,* III, pp.652–3.
45. L.G., 'A stay-griefe for English men, with a motion to the Pope, and *English Papists',* in *Sorrowes Ioy. Or, A Lamentation for our late deceased Soveraigne ELIZABETH, with a triumph for the prosperous succession of our gratious King, IAMES, &c.* (Cambridge: John Legat, 1603), pp.16–17. Cf. John Nichols, *The Progresses, Processions, and Magnificent Festivities, of King James the First,* 4 vols (London: 1828), I, p.12.
46. T.W., *The Lamentation of Melpomene, for the death of Belphoebe our late Queene* (1603), sigs A3v–B1v, quoted in E.C. Wilson, p.385. For another example of bridal imagery see Nichols, *Elizabeth,* III, p.620.
47. *Pearl, Cleanness, Patience, Sir Gawain and the Green Knight,* eds A.C. Cawley and J.J. Anderson (London: Dent, 1976), p.18.
48. John Donne, 'Of the Progress of the Soul: The Second Anniversary', in *The Complete English Poems,* ed. A.J. Smith (Harmondsworth: Penguin, 1971), p.299, ll.459–62.
49. I. Bowle, 'Singultientes Lusus', in *Sorrowes Ioy,* pp.19–21. Cf. Nichols, *James,* I, p.15; E.C. Wilson, p.379.
50. Thomas Dekker, *The VVonderfull Yeare. 1603,* ed. G.B. Harrison (London: Bodley Head, 1924), p.19.
51. R.B., 'Vpon the Day of our Queenes death and our Kings proclamation', *Sorrowes Ioy,* p.13. Cf. Nichols, *James,* I, p.10.
52. *Sorrowes Ioy,* pp.21–2. Cf. Nichols, *James,* I, p.16.
53. Dennis Kay, *Melodious Tears: The English Funeral Elegy from Spenser to Milton* (Oxford: Clarendon, 1990), pp.78–9, 85.

54. *Sorrowes Ioy,* pp.10–11.
55. *Sorrowes Ioy,* pp.21–2.
56. E.L., 'Nullo godimento senza dolore', in *Sorrowes Ioy,* pp.30–1.
57. Henry Petowe, 'Eliza's Funerall', in *Elizabetha quasi viuens,* sig.B3v. Cf. Kay, *Tears,* p.90; Nichols, *Elizabeth,* III, p.619.
58. *Sorrowes Ioy,* pp.14–16, 26–7. Cf Thomas Cecil, *Sorrowes Ioy* pp.21–2. Cf. Nichols, *James,* I, pp.4, 12, 16, 20. For another example of lunar imagery, see Robert Fletcher, *A briefe and familiar epistle shewing his maiesties title to all his kingdomes,* 1603, quoted in Kay, *Tears,* p.82.
59. *Sorrowes Ioy,* pp.21–2.
60. Lane, quoted in Hazlitt, 2nd Series, no.II.
61. Anthony Nixon, *Elizaes Memoriall. King Iames his arriuall. And Romes Downefall* (London: 1603), sig.B3v; cf. E.C. Wilson, pp.385–7.
62. Verses by Thomas Byng, I.G., *Sorrowes Ioy,* pp.10–11, 13–14. Cf. Nichols, *James,* I, pp.8, 10. Cf. E.C. Wilson, p.378.
63. Savile, sig.B4r. See Ch.5 n.61 above; all references are to this edition. Cf. Nichols, *James,* I, pp.140–4.
64. 'On Queene Elizabeth Queene of England', Bod. MS Ash. 38, f.167v. Cf. Furnivall and Morfill, II, p.101.
65. All references are to the manuscript of Manningham's diary (see Ch.6 n.64 above). It is also available as *Diary of John Manningham, 1602–1603,* ed. John Bruce (London: J.B. Nichols for Camden Society, 1868).
66. On the iconography of the godly death, see Jeri McIntosh, *English Funeral Sermons 1560–1640: The Relationship between Gender and Death, Dying and the Afterlife* (unpublished Oxford University M.Litt. thesis, 1990).
67. William Camden, *Annals, or, the Historie of the Most Renowned and Victorious Princesse ELIZABETH, Late Queen of England,* trans. R. N[orton] (London: 1635), p.584. I use the 1635 text for reasons given below, n.83; but cf. *Annales. The True and Royall History of the famous Empresse Elizabeth,* trans. Abraham Darcie, from French trans. by P.D.B. (London: 1625–9) pp.380–1; *The Historie of the Most Renowned and Victorious Princesse Elizabeth, Late Queene of England . . . Composed by Way of Annals,* trans. R. N[orton] (London: 1630), p.222. Cf. also King, 'Queen Elizabeth', pp.33–4. This passage occurs in the last part of the *Annals,* which was completed in 1617 but not published until after James I's death (see King, 'Queen Elizabeth', p.69).
68. Dekker, *VVonderfull Yeare,* p.25.
69. Dekker, *VVonderfull Yeare,* pp.25–6; Manningham, f.112v.
70. Stowe's Chronicle, ref. Manningham ed. Bruce, p.148, n.1.
71. King lived 1559?–1621, was a chaplain to Elizabeth, and was renowned for his preaching. He was later Dean of Christ Church and Bishop of London. *DNB,* XXXI (1892), pp.136–8.
72. Strong quotes from Manningham ed. Bruce, p.152.
73. Strong, *Portraits,* p.42; *Gloriana,* p.43.
74. Geneva Bible, New Testament, p.34. King would of course have been using the 1568 Bishop's Bible, but this text was unavailable to me.
75. See *BCP* (1588). The 'Almanacke' shows that in 1603, Easter Day was

24 April; 27 March was therefore the third Sunday in Lent. 'The Collectes' shows the prescribed texts for that day.

76. See Ch.5.iii above.

77. See Ch.2.v above.

78. For evidence of its popularity, see Thomas Heywood, *If You Know Not Me . . .*, in *The Dramatic Works of Thomas Heywood*, 6 vols (London: John Pearson, 1874), vol.I, p.191. All further references are to this edition.

79. See above, Ch.2.v.

80. Thomas Heywood, *England's Elizabeth* (1631), English Experience no.528 (Amsterdam: Theatrvm Orbis Terrarvm, 1973).

81. V.v.56–62, in Shakespeare ed. Alexander.

82. See Ch.2.iv above.

83. Camden, *Annals* (1635), p.16. I use the 1635 English text in preference to those of 1625 and 1630, for the following reasons. 1625 gives a similar version of the scene (p.28), but was itself translated from a French translation. 1630 was, like 1635, translated by R. Norton, but gives '(and therewith, she drew the Ring from her finger and shewed it . . .)' (pp.26–7). This is a mistranslation of the original Latin ('[simulque digito extento aureum ostendit annulum . . .]', *Annales Rervm Anglicarvm, et Hibernicarvm, Regnante Elizabetha, Ad Annum Salvtis M.D.LXXXIX* [London: 1615], p.34), which was corrected as shown in 1635, making 1635 the closest text to Camden's original.

84. Camden, *Annals* (1635), p.16.

85. King, 'Queen Elizabeth', pp.33–8.

86. Frances Teague, 'Queen Elizabeth in her Speeches', *Gloriana's Face: Women, Public and Private, in the English Renaissance*, eds S.P. Cerasano and Marion Wynne-Davies (Hemel Hempstead: Harvester, 1992), pp.72–4.

87. See Ch.7.vi above.

88. Eg. E.C. Wilson, p.6 n.2, p.61; Tennenhouse, p.22; Montrose, 'Elizabethan Subject', pp.309–10.

89. See J.P. Kenyon, *The Stuarts* (1958; Glasgow: Fontana/Collins, 1966), Ch.2.

90. Camden, *Annales* (1625), frontispiece. Cf. Strong, *Gloriana*, pp.162–5; King, 'Queen Elizabeth', pp.65–72; Anne Barton, 'Harking Back to Elizabeth: Ben Jonson and Caroline Nostalgia', *ELH* 48 (1981), pp.706–31.

91. *The Humble Petition of the Wretched, And most contemptible, the poore Commons of England, To the blessed ELIZABETH of famous memory. Also a most gratious Answer, with a Divine Admonition and Perpetuall Conclusion* (London, 1642), BL Thomason Tracts E108. All further references are to this edition unless otherwise stated.

92. Bod. MS Malone 23, p.32. See Margaret Crum, ed., *First Line Index of English Poetry 1500–1800 in Manuscripts of the Bodleian Library, Oxford*, 2 vols (Oxford: Clarendon, 1969), I, p.431, I937, for details of Bodleian manuscripts in which the poem appears.

93. It opens with the lament that:

> . . . thrice seaven sonnes have worne
> Their summer suits, since we began to mourne;

> *Egypts* ten plagues we have indur'd twice told,
> Since blest *Eliza* was with Saints inrould.

(p. 3)

In other words, it is twenty or twenty-one years since Elizabeth's death, making it 1623 or 24. The poem contains further references to the sufferings of 'these one and twentie yeares' and 'halfe fortie yeares' (p.7), and refers to the death of Prince Henry (p.5), which had happened in 1612.
    See Crum, I, p.419, I697, for details of Bodleian manuscripts in which the poem appears.

94. See Crum, II, p.1186, Y444, for details of Bodleian manuscripts in which the poem appears.
95. Bod. MS Ash. 36, 37, f.303v.
96. Bod. MS Rawl. D398 228v.

Epilogue Adulation or Anxiety?

1.   Neale, *Queen Elizabeth*, p.218.
2.   T.S. Eliot, 'The Metaphysical Poets', 1921, in *Selected Essays*, 3rd edn (London: Faber, 1951), pp.281–91; E.M.W. Tillyard, *The Elizabethan World Picture* (London: Chatto, 1943).
3.   Strong, *Cult*, p.15. Cf. Yates in Ch.7.v above.
4.   The phrase is Greenblatt's, in *Shakespearean Negotiations: The Circulation of Social Energy in Renaissance England* (Berkeley: University of California Press, 1988).
5.   See Ch.2.v above.
6.   Marina Warner, *Monuments and Maidens: The Allegory of the Female Form* (London: Weidenfeld, 1985).
7.   See Ch.6.i above, on negative attitudes to Elizabeth as female ruler, and some consequences for panegyric.
8.   For more discussion of this combination of extreme positive and negative attitudes to powerful women, see Antonia Fraser, *Boadicea's Chariot: The Warrior Queens* (London: Weidenfeld, 1988), esp. pp.6–7.
9.   See Ch.2.i above.
10. Fraser, plates between pp.304–5, pp.313–22; Warner, *Monuments*, pp.38–45, 51–60, pl.24.
11. Robert Harris, 'Prima Donna Inter Pares', *The Observer*, Sunday 3 January 1988, p.17.
12. See, for instance, Heisch, 'Persistence of Patriarchy'; Adrienne Rich, *On Lies, Secrets and Silence: Selected Prose 1966–78* (London: Virago, 1980), pp.10–11; Jardine, pp.169–79.
13. See Ch.1.v above.
14. See Berry, p.82.
15. See Ch.7.vi above.

Bibliography

Primary Sources

William Alabaster, *Elisaeis*, Bod. MS Rawl. D.293
——, *The Elisaeis of William Alabaster*, ed. and trans. Michael O'Connell, *Studies in Philology* 76 (1979)
Alexander Ales to Elizabeth I, *Calendar of State Papers Foreign 1558–9*, ed. Rev. J. Stevenson (London, 1863), no.1303
Anon., *A fourme of Prayer, with thankes geuyng, to be vsed euery yeere, the .17. of Nouember, beyng the day of the Queenes Maiesties entrie to her raigne* (London: Richard Jugge, 1576)
——, *A fourme of prayer with thankes giuing, to be vsed of all the Queenes Maiesties louing subiectes euery yeere, the 17. of Nouember, being the day of her Highnes entrie to her kingdome* (London: Christopher Barker, 1578).
——, *A fourme of prayer with thankesgiuing, to be vsed of all the Queenes Maiesties louing subiects euery yeere, the 17. of Nouember, being the day of her Highnesse entry to her kingdome* (London: Christopher Barker, 1590)
——, 'A gratious answere from that blessed Saint', Bod. MS Rawl. D398, ff.226r–8v
——, *The Humble Petition of the Wretched, And most contemptible, the poore Commons of England, To the blessed ELIZABETH of famous memory. Also a most gratious Answer, with a Divine Admonition and Perpetuall Conclusion* (London, 1642), BL Thomason Tracts E108
——, 'Loe here the pearle', BL Huth 50 (28) (1563)
——, *The noble tryumphant coronacyon of quene Anne / Wyfe vnto the most noble kynge Henry the viij* (London: Wynkyn de Worde, 1533)
——, 'On the Picture of Queene Eliz*abeth* by Mr Iohn Vicars', Bod. MS Ash. 38, ff.24v–25r.
——, 'On Queene Elizabeth Queene of England', Bod. MS Ash. 38, f.167v
——, 'A proper new ballett, intituled Rowlands god sunne' (c.1584–5), Bod. MS Rawl. Poet. 185, ff.15v–19r
——, 'A proper new ballade wherin is plaine to be seene how god blesseth england for loue of our Queene: Soung to the tune of tarletons caroll', Bod. MS Rawl. Poet. 185, ff.13r–14r
——, *A Protestant Memorial for the seventeenth of November, being the Inauguration Day of Queen Elizabeth* (London: 1713).
——, *The Quenes Maiesties Passage through the Citie of London to Westminster the Day before her Coronacion* (1559), facs., ed. James M. Osborn, introd. Sir John Neale (New Haven: Yale UP – Elizabethan Club, 1960)
——, 'To the blessed Sainct of famose memory Elizabeth', Bod. MS Ash. 36, 37, f.303r–v
John Aylmer, *An Harborowe for Faithfull and Trewe Subiectes* (1559), facs., The English Experience 423 (Amsterdam: Theatrvm Orbis Terrarvm, 1972)
Barnabe Barnes, *A Divine Centurie of Spirituall Sonnets* (1595), in *Heliconia:*

Comprising A Selection of English Poetry of the Elizabethan Age, ed. T. Park, 3 vols (London: 1815), II

——, *Parthenophil and Parthenophe*, ed. Victor A. Doyno (Carbondale: Southern Illinois University Press, 1971)

Richard Barnfield, *The Poems of Richard Barnfield*, ed. Montague Summers (London: Fortune, 1936)

Lewis Bayly, *The Practise of Pietie: Directing a Christian how to walke that he may please God*, 3rd edn (London: John Hodgets, 1613)

Francis Beaumont, *The Knight of the Burning Pestle*, ed. Cyrus Hoy, in *The Dramatic Works in the Beaumont and Fletcher Canon*, gen. ed. Fredson Bowers (Cambridge: Cambridge University Press, 1966), vol.I

Thomas Becon, *The workes of Thomas Becon*, 3 vols (1560–64), I, *The first part of the bokes, whiche Thomas Becon made and published in the name of Theodor Basille* (1560)

Thomas Bentley, *The Monument of Matrones: conteining seuen seuerall Lamps of Virginitie*, 3 vols (London: 1582)

Thomas Blenerhasset, *A Revelation of the True Minerva* (1582), facs., introd. Josephine Waters Bennett (New York: Scholar's Facsimile, 1941)

The Book of Common Prayer (Cambridge: Cambridge University Press, 1969?)

The Booke of Common Prayer, with the Psalter of Psalmes of David (London: Christopher Barker, 1588)

Giacopo Brocardo, *The Revelation of S.Ihon reueled*, trans. James Sanford (London: Thomas Marshe, 1582)

Cambridge University, *Threno-thriambeuticon. Academiae Cantabrigiensis ob damnum lucrosum, & infaelicitatem foelicissimam, luctuosus triumphus* (Cambridge, 1603)

Carleton Brown, ed., *Religious Lyrics of the XVth Century* (Oxford: Clarendon, 1939)

Edmund Bunny, *Certaine prayers and other godly exercises, for the seuenteenth of Nouember: Wherein we solemnize the blessed reigne of our gracious Soueraigne Lady Elizabeth* . . . (London: Christopher Barker, 1585)

Jean Calvin, *Letters of John Calvin, selected from the Bonnet Edition* (Edinburgh: Banner of Truth Trust, 1980)

——, *The Psalmes of Dauid and others, With M.Iohn Caluins Commentaries*, trans. Arthur Golding (London, 1571)

William Camden, *Annales Rervm Anglicarvm, et Hibernicarvm, Regnante Elizabetha, Ad Annum Salvtis M.D.LXXXIX* (London: 1615)

——, *Annales. The True and Royall History of the famous Empresse Elizabeth*, trans. Abraham Darcie, from French trans. by P.D.B. (London: 1625–9)

——, *Annals, or, the Historie of the Most Renowned and Victorious Princesse ELIZABETH, Late Queen of England*, trans. R. N[orton] (London: 1635)

——, *The Historie of the Most Renowned and Victorious Princesse Elizabeth, Late Queene of England* . . . *Composed by Way of Annals*, trans. R. N[orton] (London: 1630)

George Chapman, *The Poems of George Chapman*, ed. Phyllis Brooks Bartlett (New York: Modern Language Association, 1941)

Robert Chester, *Loves Martyr*, ed. A.B. Grosart (London, 1878)

Thomas Churchyard, *A Discovrse of The Queenes Maiesties entertainement in Suffolk and Norfolk* (London: Henry Bynneman, 1578)

Henry Constable, *The Poems of Henry Constable*, ed. Joan Grundy (Liverpool: Liverpool University Press, 1960)

Sir John Davies, *Poems of Sir John Davies*, ed. Robert Krueger (Oxford: Clarendon, 1975)

R.T. Davies, ed., *Mediaeval English Lyrics: A Critical Anthology* (London: Faber, 1963)

Richard Day, *A Booke of Christian Prayers* (London, 1578), facs., English Experience no.866 (Amsterdam: Theatrvm Orbis Terrarvm, 1977)

Thomas Dekker, *Old Fortunatus*, in *The Dramatic Works of Thomas Dekker*, ed. Fredson Bowers, 4 vols (Cambridge: Cambridge University Press, 1953), vol.I

Thomas Dekker, *The VVonderfull Yeare. 1603*, ed. G.B. Harrison (London: Bodley Head, 1924)

Walter Bourchier Devereux, *Lives and Letters of the Devereux, Earls of Essex*, 2 vols (London: 1893)

John Donne, *The Complete English Poems*, ed. A.J. Smith (Harmondsworth: Penguin, 1971)

Elizabeth I, *The Answere of the Quenes hyghnes to the peticion proposed vnto hir by the lower howse Concerning hir mariage* (1559), BL MS Lansdowne 94, no.14, f.29

——, *A Book of Devotions Composed by Her Majesty Elizabeth R.*, trans. Rev. A. Fox, foreword by Rev. Canon J.P. Hodges (Gerrards Cross: Colin Smythe, 1970)

——, *Letters of Queen Elizabeth I*, ed. G.B. Harrison (London: Cassell, 1968)

——, reply to parliamentary petition (1563), BL MS Lansdowne 94, no.15, f.30

The Euing Collection of English Broadside Ballads, introd. John Holloway, (Glasgow: University of Glasgow, 1971)

E.H. Fellowes, ed., *English Madrigal Verse 1588–1632*, 3rd edn, eds F.W. Sternfeld and D. Greer (Oxford: Oxford University Press, 1967)

John Fenton, 'A sorrowfull Epitaph on the death of Queene ELIZABETH', in *King Iames his welcome to London. With Elizaes Tombe and Epitaph* (London: 1603)

John Foxe, *Fox's Book of Martyrs: The Acts and Monuments of the Church*, 1563, ed. Rev. John Cumming, 3 vols (London: George Virtue, 1844)

Thomas Fuller, *The Holy State* (Cambridge, 1642)

F.J. Furnivall and W.R. Morfill, eds, *Ballads from Manuscripts*, 2 vols (London and Hertford: Ballad Society, 1868, 1873)

Stephen Gardiner, *Letters of Stephen Gardiner*, ed. J.A. Muller (Cambridge: Cambridge University Press, 1933)

Ber- Gar[ter], *The Ioyfull Receyuing of the Queenes most excellent Maiestie into hir Highnesse Citie of Norwich* (London: Henry Bynneman, 1578?)

George Gascoigne, *The Adventures of Master F.J* (1573), in Paul Salzman, ed., *An Anthology of Elizabethan Prose Fiction* (Oxford: Oxford University Press, 1987)

The Geneva Bible (1560), facs., introd. Lloyd E. Berry (Madison: University of Wisconsin Press, 1969)

The Poems of Sir Arthur Gorges, ed. Helen Estabrook Sandison (Oxford: Oxford University Press, 1953)

Richard Grafton, *Graftons Abridgement of the Chronicles of Englande* (London: Tottel, 1570)

Fulke Greville, Lord Brooke, *A Dedication to Sir Philip Sidney*, in *The Prose Works of Fulke Greville, Lord Brooke*, ed. John Gouws (Oxford: Clarendon, 1986), pp.3–135

——, *Poems and Dramas of Fulke Greville, 1st Lord Brooke*, ed. G. Bullough, 2 vols (Edinburgh: Oliver & Boyd, 1939)

——, *The Remains: Being Poems of Monarchy and Religion*, ed. G.A. Wilkes (Oxford: Oxford University Press, 1965)

B. Griffin, *Fidessa, more chaste than kinde* (London, 1596)

John Griffiths, ed., *The Two Books of Homilies Appointed to be Read in Churches* (Oxford: Oxford University Press, 1859)

Louise Imogen Guiney, ed., *Recusant Poets I: St. Thomas More to Ben Jonson* (London: Sheed & Ward, 1938)

Sir John Harington, *The Letters and Epigrams of Sir John Harington*, ed. N.E. McClure (Philadelphia: University of Pennsylvania Press, 1930), p.123.

——, 'Unpublished Poems by Sir John Harington', ed. R.H. Miller, *ELH* 14 (1984), pp.148–58

T.E. Hartley, *Proceedings in the Parliaments of Elizabeth I: vol.I: 1558–1581* (Leicester: Leicester University Press, 1981)

W.C. Hazlitt, ed., *Fugitive Tracts*, 2 vols (London, 1875)

Edward Hellwis, *A Marvell Deciphered* (London, 1589)

Paul Hentzner, *Travels in England During the Reign of Queen Elizabeth*, ed. H. Walpole, trans. R. Bentley, with *Fragmenta Regalia* by Sir Robert Naunton (London: Cassell, 1889)

Thomas Heywood, *England's Elizabeth, her Life and Troubles during her minoritie from the Crudle to the Crowne* (London: 1631), facs., English Experience no.528 (Amsterdam: Theatrvm Orbis Terrarvm, 1973)

——, *If you know not me, you know no bodie, or the troubles of Queene Elizabeth* (London: N.Butter, 1605)

——, *If You Know Not Me, You Know No Bodie; or, The troubles of Queene Elizabeth*, Parts 1 and 2, in *The Dramatic Works of Thomas Heywood*, 6 vols (London: John Pearson, 1874), I, pp.189–351

Miles Hogarde, 'Marie hath brought home, christe agayne', BL MS Harley 3444

Thomas Holland, *A Sermon Preached at Pavls in London the 17. of November Ann. Dom. 1599 . . . Whervnto is adioyned an Apologeticall discourse . . .* (London, 1601)

Henry Howard, Earl of Northampton, *Regina Fortunata* (c.1576–80), BL MS Egerton 944, f.1v.

John Howson, *A Sermon Preached at St. Maries in Oxford the 17 Day of November, 1602, in defence of the Festivities of the Church of England, and namely that of her Maiesties Coronation* (Oxford: 1602)

André Hurault, Sieur de Maisse, *Journal*, trans and eds G.B. Harrison and R.A. Jones (London: Nonesuch, 1931)

John Jewel, *Apology of the Church of England*, trans. Anne Bacon (1564), ed. Rev. John Ayre (Cambridge: Cambridge University Press – Parker Society, 1849)

Ben Jonson, *The Complete Poems*, ed. George Parfitt (London: Penguin, 1988)

Ben Jonson, *Cynthia's Revels*, in *The Complete Plays of Ben Jonson*, ed. G.A. Wilkes, based on edn of C.H. Herford and Evelyn Simpson, 4 vols (Oxford: Clarendon, 1981–2), II, pp.vii–117

John Knox, *The First Blast of the Trumpet against the Monstruous Regiment of Women* (1558), facs., The English Experience no.471 (Amsterdam: Theatrvm Orbis Terrarvm, 1972)

——, *The Works of John Knox*, ed. David Laing (Edinburgh, 1864), VI

Thomas Kyd, *The Works of Thomas Kyd*, ed. F.S. Boas (Oxford: Oxford University Press, 1955)

Sir Henry Lee, 'In yeeldinge vp his Tilt staff: sayd:', Bod. MS Rawl. Poet. 148, f.75v

John Leland and Nicholas Udall, *Versis and ditties made at the coronation of quene Anne*, BL MS Royal 18 A.lxiv

Edmund Lodge, ed., *Illustrations of British History, Biography, and Manners, in the Reigns of Henry VIII, Edward VI, Mary, Elizabeth and James I*, 2nd edn, 3 vols (London: John Chidley, 1838)

John Lyly, *Endimion, The Man in the Moone*, in *The Complete Works of John Lyly*, 3 vols, ed. R. Warwick Bond (Oxford: Clarendon, 1902), III, pp.5–103

——, *Euphues and his England* (1580), in *The Complete Works of John Lyly*, 3 vols, ed. R. Warwick Bond (Oxford: Clarendon, 1902), II, pp.191–217

John Manningham, Diary, BL MS Harl. 5353, f.133r

——, *Diary of John Manningham, 1602–1603*, ed. John Bruce (London: J.B. Nichols for Camden Society, 1868).

John Milton, *A Masque presented at Ludlow Castle, 1634*, in *Complete Shorter Poems*, ed. John Carey (London: Longman, 1971)

Richard Mulcaster, *Positions* (1581), (London: Longmans, 1888)

Thomas Nashe, *Haue vvith you to Saffron vvalden, or, Gabriell Harueys Hunt is vp* (London: John Danter, 1596)

John Nichols, ed., *The Progresses and Public Processions of Queen Elizabeth*, 3 vols (London: J. Nichols for Society of Antiquaries, 1823)

——, ed., *The Progresses, Processions, and Magnificent Festivities, of King James the First*, 4 vols (London: 1828)

Sir Harris Nicolas, *Memoirs of the Life and Times of Sir Christopher Hatton* (London: Bentley, 1847)

Anthony Nixon, *Elizaes Memoriall. King Iames his arriuall. And Romes Downefall* (London: 1603)

David Norbrook select. and introd., H.R. Woudhuysen ed., *The Penguin Book of Renaissance Verse 1509–1659* (London: Allen Lane – Penguin, 1992)

Alexander Nowell, *A Catechisme or First Instruction and Learning of Christian Religion*, trans. Thomas Norton (1570), facs., intro. Frank V. Occhiogrosso (Albany, NY: Delmar – Scholars' Facsimiles and Reprints, 1975)

Oxford University, *Oxonienses Academiae Funebre Officium in memoriam honoratissimam serenissimae et beatissimae Elizabethae, nvper Angliae, Franciae, & Hiberniae Reginae* (Oxford: 1603)

T. Park and W. Oldys, eds, *The Harleian Miscellany*, 10 vols (London: White & Cochrane, 1808–13), X

Pearl, Cleanness, Patience, Sir Gawain and the Green Knight, eds A.C. Cawley and J.J. Anderson (London: Dent, 1976)

George Peele, *Life and Works*, gen. ed. Charles Tyler Prouty, 3 vols (New Haven: Yale University Press, 1952–70)

The Pepys Ballads, ed. Hyder Edward Rollins, 8 vols (Cambridge, Mass.: Harvard University Press, 1929)

Bishop Percy's Folio Manuscript, eds John W. Hales and Frederick J. Furnivall, 3 vols (London: N. Trübner, 1867–8)

William Perkins, *A Reformed Catholike* (Cambridge: John Legat, 1598)

——, *A Warning Against the Idolatrie of the last times* (Cambridge: John Legat, 1601)

Henry Petowe, *Elizabetha quasi viuens, Eliza's Funerall, A fewe Aprill drops, showred on the Hearse of dead Eliza. OR The Funerall teares of a true hearted Subiect* (London: 1603)

Thomas Platter, *Thomas Platter's Travels in England* (1599), trans. Clare Williams (London: Cape, 1937)

George Puttenham, *The Arte of English Poesie*, eds Gladys Doidge Willcock and Alice Walker (Cambridge: Cambridge University Press, 1936)

——, *Partheniades*, BL MS Cotton Vesp.E.viii ff.169–78

Sir Walter Ralegh, 'As you came from the holy land', Bod. MS Rawl. Poet. 85 f.123r–v

——, *The Poems of Sir Walter Ralegh*, ed. Agnes M.C. Latham (London: Routledge, 1951)

Rheims-Douai Bible, *The Holy Bible* (Rheims 1582, Douai 1609), (London: Burns, Oates & Washbourne, 1914)

Barnaby Rich, *Rich's Farewell to Military Profession* (1581), ed. Thomas M. Cranfill (Austin: University of Texas Press, 1959)

Edward Rishton, *The Anglican Schism Renewed Under Elizabeth: The Continuation of the History, in Nicholas Sander, The Rise and Growth of the Anglican Schism*, 1585, trans. and ed. David Lewis (London, 1877)

Ritus Servandus In Solemni Expositione et Benedictione Sanctissimi Sacramenti (London: Burns, Oates & Washbourne, 1928)

Hyder E. Rollins, ed., *Old English Ballads 1553–1625, chiefly from manuscripts* (Cambridge: Cambridge University Press, 1920)

The Roxburghe Ballads, ed. William Chappell (London: Ballad Society, 1869, 1899)

Nicholas Sander, *The Rise and Growth of the Anglican Schism*, 1585, trans. and ed. David Lewis (London, 1877)

John Savile, 'A Salutatorie Poeme to the Magestie of King IAMES', *King Iames his entertainment at Theobalds: With his welcome to London, together with a salutatorie Poeme* (London, 1603)

William Shakespeare, *Complete Works*, ed. Peter Alexander (London: Collins, 1951)

——, *Hamlet*, ed. Harold Jenkins (London: Methuen [Arden Shakespeare], 1982)

——, *King Lear*, ed. Kenneth Muir (London: Methuen [Arden Shakespeare], 1972)

——, *King Richard III*, ed. Antony Hammond (London: Methuen [Arden Shakespeare], 1981)

——, *The Riverside Shakespeare*, ed. G. Blakemore Evans (Boston: Houghton Mifflin, 1974)

The Shirburn Ballads 1585–1616, ed. Andrew Clark (Oxford: Clarendon Press, 1907)

Sir Philip Sidney, *The Countess of Pembroke's Arcadia*, ed. Maurice Evans (Harmondsworth: Penguin, 1977)

——, *Miscellaneous Prose of Sir Philip Sidney*, eds Katherine Duncan-Jones and Jan van Dorsten (Oxford: Oxford University Press, 1973)

——, *The Poems of Sir Philip Sidney*, ed. William A. Ringler Jr. (Oxford: Clarendon, 1962)

——, *Sir Philip Sidney*, ed. Katherine Duncan-Jones (Oxford: Oxford University Press – Oxford Authors, 1989)

Thomas F. Simmons, ed., *The Lay Folks' Mass Book* (London: Early English Texts Society, 1879)

Sorrowes Ioy. Or, A Lamentation for our late deceased Soveraigne ELIZABETH, with a triumph for the prosperous succession of our gratious King, IAMES, &c. (Cambridge: John Legat, 1603)

Edmund Spenser, *The Mutabilitie Cantos*, ed. S.P. Zitner (London: Nelson, 1968)

——, *A View of the Present State of Ireland*, in *The Works of Edmund Spenser: A Variorum Edition*, eds E. Greenlaw, C.G. Osgood and F.M. Padelford (Baltimore: Johns Hopkins Press, 1932–57), IX (1949), *Spenser's Prose Works*, ed. Rudolf Gottfried, pp.39–231

——, *The Works of Edmund Spenser: A Variorum Edition*, eds E. Greenlaw, C.G. Osgood and F.M. Padelford (Baltimore: Johns Hopkins Press, 1932–57)

——, *The Yale Edition of the Shorter Poems of Edmund Spenser*, eds William A. Oram et al. (New Haven and London: Yale University Press, 1989)

Talbot, Dudley and Devereux Papers 1533–1659, Calendar of the Manuscripts of the Most Honourable the Marquess of Bath preserved at Longleat, Wiltshire, 5 vols, V, ed. G. Dynfallt Owen, HMC 58 (London: HMSO, 1980)

Victor von Klarwill, ed., *Queen Elizabeth and some Foreigners*, trans. T.H. Nash (London: Bodley Head, 1928)

William Wager, *The longer thou livest, the more foole thou art* (1569?) (The Tudor Facsimile Texts, 1910)

Thomas Wright, ed., *Queen Elizabeth and her Times: A series of Original Letters*, 2 vols (London: Colburn, 1838)

Vulgate Bible, *Biblia Sacra Iuxta Vulgatum Versionem*, 2 vols (Stuttgart: Württembergische Bibelanstatt, 1969)

Secondary Sources

Robert Alter and Frank Kermode, eds, *The Literary Guide to the Bible* (London: Fontana, 1989)

Judith H. Anderson '"A Gentle Knight was pricking on the plain": The Chaucerian Connection', *ELR* 15 (1985), pp.166–74

Sydney Anglo, *Spectacle, Pageantry, and Early Tudor Policy* (Oxford: Clarendon, 1969)

Janet Arnold, 'The "Coronation" Portrait of Queen Elizabeth I', *Burlington Magazine* 120 (1978), pp.727–41

——, *Queen Elizabeth's Wardrobe Unlock'd* (Leeds: W.S. Maney, 1988)

Geoffrey Ashe, *The Virgin* (London: Routledge, 1976).

Margaret Aston, *England's Iconoclasts, Vol.I: Laws against Images* (Oxford: Clarendon, 1988)

Marie Axton, *The Queen's Two Bodies* (London: Royal Historical Society, 1977)

Mikhail Bakhtin, *Rabelais and his World* (1965), trans. Helene Iswolsky (Cambridge, Mass.: MIT Press, 1968)

Anne Barton, 'Harking Back to Elizabeth: Ben Jonson and Caroline Nostalgia', *ELH* 48 (1981), pp.706–31

Catherine Bates, *The Rhetoric of Courtship in Elizabethan Language and Literature* (Cambridge: Cambridge University Press, 1992)

Peter Beal, comp., *Index of English Literary Manuscripts*, I, 1450–1625, Part 2, Douglas – Wyatt (London: Mansell, 1980)

Elizabeth J. Bellamy, 'The Vocative and the Vocational: The Unreadability of Elizabeth in *The Faerie Queene'*, *ELH* 54.1 (Spring 1987), pp.1–30

Rev. William Benham, ed., *The Dictionary of Religion*, 2 vols (London: Cassell, 1887)

David M. Bergeron, 'Elizabeth's Coronation Entry (1559): New Manuscript Evidence', *ELR* 8 (1978), pp.3–8

——, *English Civic Pageantry 1558–1642* (London: Arnold, 1971)

Philippa Berry, *Of Chastity and Power: Elizabethan Literature and the Unmarried Queen* (London: Routledge, 1989)

William Blissett, 'Spenser's Mutabilitie', *Essays in English Literature from the Renaissance to the Victorian Age*, eds M. Maclure and F.W. Watt (Toronto: University of Toronto Press, 1964), pp.26–42

Alice Fox Blitch, 'The Mutabilitie Cantos: "In Meet Order Ranged", *English Language Notes* 7 (1969–70), pp.179–86

Marc Bloch, *The Royal Touch: Sacred Monarchy and Scrofula in England and France* [*Les Rois Thaumaturges*], trans. J.E. Anderson (London: Routledge, 1973)

John Henry Blunt, *The Annotated Book of Common Prayer* (London: Longmans, 1903)

Roger Boase, *The Origin and Meaning of Courtly Love* (Manchester: Manchester University Press, 1977)

Mark Breitenberg, 'Reading Elizabethan Iconicity: *Gorboduc* and the Semiotics of Reform', *ELR* 18 (1988), pp.194–217

Eric St John Brooks, *Sir Christopher Hatton: Queen Elizabeth's Favourite* (London: Cape, 1946)

Douglas Bush, *Mythology and the Renaissance Tradition in English Poetry* (New York: Pageant, 1957)

Thomas H. Cain, *Praise in The Faerie Queene* (Lincoln, Nebraska: University of Nebraska Press, 1978)

David Cannadine and Simon Price, eds, *Rituals of Royalty: Power and Ceremonial in Traditional Societies* (Cambridge: Cambridge University Press, 1987)

Michael P. Carroll, *The Cult of the Virgin Mary: Psychological Origins* (Princeton: Princeton University Press, 1986)

E.K. Chambers, *Sir Henry Lee: An Elizabethan Portrait* (Oxford: Clarendon, 1936)

William Chappell, *Popular Music of the Olden Time*, 2 vols (London: Chappell, 1855–7)

Helen Cobb, *Representations of Elizabeth I: Three sites of ambiguity and contradiction* (unpublished Oxford University D.Phil. thesis, 1989)

Dorothy Connell, *Sir Philip Sidney: The Maker's Mind* (Oxford: Oxford University Press, 1977)

Raymond Crawfurd, *The King's Evil* (Oxford: Oxford University Press, 1911)

Margaret Crum, ed., *First Line Index of English Poetry 1500–1800 in Manuscripts of the Bodleian Library, Oxford*, 2 vols (Oxford: Clarendon, 1969)

Kathleen M. Davies, '"The sacred condition of equality": how original were Puritan doctrines of marriage?' *Social History* 5 (May 1977), pp.563–80

Mary Douglas, *Purity and Danger: An analysis of concepts of pollution and taboo* (London: Routledge, 1966)

Maria Dowling, 'Anne Boleyn and Reform', *Journal of Ecclesiastical History* 35.1 (Jan. 1984), pp.30–46

Katherine Duncan-Jones, 'The Date of Raleigh's "21th: And Last Booke of the Ocean to Scinthia"', *RES* 21 (1970), pp.143–58

——, *Sir Philip Sidney, Courtier Poet* (London: Hamish Hamilton, 1991)

F.P. Dutripon, *Concordantiae Bibliorum Sacrorum Vulgatae Editionis*, 2 vols (Paris: 1838)

Mircea Eliade, ed.-in-chief, *The Encyclopedia of Religion* (New York: Macmillan, 1987)

T.S. Eliot, 'The Metaphysical Poets', 1921, in *Selected Essays*, 3rd edn (London: Faber, 1951), pp.281–91

Encyclopedia Britannica, 11th edn (Cambridge: Cambridge University Press, 1910)

Encyclopedia Britannica (London: William Benton, 1964)

Linda T. Fitz, '"What says the Married Woman?" Marriage theory and feminism in the English Renaissance', *Mosaic* 13.2 (Winter 1980), pp.1–22

Margaret W. Ferguson, Maureen Quilligan and Nancy J. Vickers, eds, *Rewriting the Renaissance: the Discourses of Sexual Difference in Early Modern Europe* (Chicago: University of Chicago Press, 1986)

John Fletcher, 'The date of the portrait of Elizabeth I in her coronation robes', *Burlington Magazine* 120 (1978), p.753

Antonia Fraser, *Boadicea's Chariot: The Warrior Queens* (London: Weidenfeld, 1988)

Sigmund Freud, *The Interpretation of Dreams*, trans. James Strachey, eds James Strachey, Alan Tyson and Angela Richards, Pelican Freud Library IV (Harmondsworth: Penguin, 1976)

C. and K. George, *The Protestant Mind of the English Reformation* (Princeton: Princeton University Press, 1961)

Jonathan Goldberg, *Endlesse Worke: Spenser and the Structures of Discourse* (Baltimore: Johns Hopkins University Press, 1981)

Stephen Greenblatt, *Renaissance Self-Fashioning from More to Shakespeare* (Chicago: University of Chicago Press, 1980)

——, ed., *Representing the English Renaissance* (Berkeley: University of California Press, 1988)

——, *Shakespearean Negotiations: The Circulation of Social Energy in Renaissance England* (Berkeley: University of California Press, 1988)

——, *Sir Walter Ralegh: The Renaissance Man and his Roles* (New Haven: Yale University Press, 1973)

Thomas M. Greene, *The Descent from Heaven: A Study in Epic Continuity* (New Haven: Yale University Press, 1963)

Linda Gregerson, 'Protestant Erotics: Idolatry and Interpretation in Spenser's *Faerie Queene*', *ELH* 58.1 (Spring 1991), pp.1–34

Kenneth Gross, *Spenserian Poetics: Idolatry, Iconoclasm, and Magic* (Ithaca: Cornell University Press, 1985)

Christopher Haigh, *Elizabeth I* (Harlow: Longman, 1988)

——, ed., *The English Reformation Revised* (Cambridge: Cambridge University Press, 1987)

——, ed., *The Reign of Elizabeth I* (London: Macmillan, 1984)

W. Haller, *Foxe's 'Book of Martyrs' and the Elect Nation* (London: Cape, 1963)

W. and M. Haller, 'The Puritan Art of Love', *Huntington Library Quarterly* V (1941–2), pp.235–72

A.C. Hamilton, 'Our new poet: Spenser, "well of English undefyld"', in *A Theatre for Spenserians*, eds J.M. Kennedy and J.A. Reither (Manchester: Manchester University Press, 1973)

Richard F. Hardin, *Civil Idolatry: Desacralizing and Monarchy in Spenser, Shakespeare, and Milton* (Newark: University of Delaware Press, 1992)

Christopher Harper-Bill, *The Pre-Reformation Church in England, 1400–1530* (London: Longman, 1989)

Robert Harris, 'Prima Donna Inter Pares', *The Observer*, Sunday 3 January 1988, pp.17–18

W.P. Haugaard, *Elizabeth I and the English Reformation: the struggle for a stable settlement of religion* (Cambridge: Cambridge University Press, 1968)

——, 'Elizabeth Tudor's Book of Devotions: A neglected clue to the Queen's life and character', *16th Century Journal* 12.2 (Summer 1981), pp.79–106

Allison Heisch, 'Queen Elizabeth I: Parliamentary Rhetoric and the Exercise of Power', *Signs* 1.1 (Autumn 1975), pp.31–55

——, 'Queen Elizabeth I and the Persistence of Patriarchy', *Feminist Review* 4 (1980), pp.45–56

Richard Helgerson, 'The land speaks: cartography, chorography, and subversion in Renaissance England', in Stephen Greenblatt, ed., *Representing the English Renaissance*, (Berkeley: University of California Press, 1988), pp.327–61

C.G. Herbermann et al., eds, *The Catholic Encyclopedia*, 15 vols (New York: Robert Appleton, 1907)

Michael Holahan, '*Iamque opus exegi*: Ovid's Changes and Spenser's Brief Epic of Mutability', *ELR* 6 (1976), pp.244–70

Thomas Hyde, 'Vision, Poetry and Authority in Spenser', *ELR* 13 (1983), pp.127–45

E.W. Ives, *Anne Boleyn* (Oxford: Blackwell, 1986)

Lisa Jardine, *Still Harping on Daughters: Women and Drama in the Age of Shakespeare* (Hemel Hempstead: Harvester, 1983)

Augustus Jessopp, *One Generation of a Norfolk House: A Contribution to Elizabethan History*, 3rd edn (London: T. Fisher Unwin, 1913)

L. Staley Johnson, 'Elizabeth, Bride and Queen: A Study of Spenser's April Eclogue and the Metaphors of English Protestantism', *Spenser Studies* 2 (1981), pp.75–91

Paul Johnson, *Elizabeth I: A Study in Power and Intellect* (London: Weidenfeld, 1974)

Ernst H. Kantorowicz, *The King's Two Bodies: A Study in Mediaeval Political Theology* (Princeton: Princeton University Press, 1957)

Dennis Kay, *Melodious Tears: The English Funeral Elegy from Spenser to Milton* (Oxford: Clarendon, 1990)

——, ' "She was a Queen, and Therefore Beautiful": Sidney, his Mother, and Queen Elizabeth', *RES* XLIII.169 (Feb. 1992), pp.18–39

J.P. Kenyon, *The Stuarts* (1958; Glasgow: Fontana-Collins, 1966)

John Kerrigan, ed., *Motives of Woe: Shakespeare and 'Female Complaint'* (Oxford: Clarendon, 1991)

John N. King, 'Patronage and Piety: the influence of Catherine Parr', *Silent But For the Word: Tudor women as patrons, translators and writers of religious works*, ed. Margaret P. Hannay (Kent, Ohio: Kent State University Press, 1985), pp.43–60

——, 'Queen Elizabeth I: Representations of the Virgin Queen', *Renaissance Quarterly* 43.1 (Spring 1990), pp.30–74

——, *Tudor Royal Iconography: Literature and Art in an Age of Religious Crisis* (Princeton: Princeton University Press, 1989)

John N. King and Robin Smith, 'Recent Studies in Protestant Poetics', *ELR* 21.2 (Spring 1991), pp.283–307

Maria Leach, ed., *Funk & Wagnall's Standard Dictionary of Folklore, Mythology and Legend* (London: New English Library, 1975)

Nicole Loraux, 'What is a Goddess?', in *A History of Women in the West*, gen. eds George Duby and Michelle Perrot, *Vol.1: From Ancient Goddesses to Christian Saints*, ed. Pauline Schmitt Pantel, trans. Arthur Goldhammer, pp.11–44.

Wallace MacCaffrey, *The Shaping of the Elizabethan Régime* (London: Cape, 1967)

Peter McClure and Robin Headlam Wells, 'Elizabeth I as a Second Virgin Mary', *Renaissance Studies* 4.1 (March 1990), pp.38–70

Jeri McIntosh, *English Funeral Sermons 1560–1640: The Relationship between Gender and Death, Dying and the Afterlife* (unpublished Oxford University M.Litt. thesis, 1990)

Michael McKeon, *The Origins of the English Novel, 1600–1740* (Baltimore: Johns Hopkins University Press, 1987)

Ian Maclean, *The Renaissance Notion of Woman* (Cambridge: Cambridge University Press, 1980)

Leah S. Marcus, *Puzzling Shakespeare: Local Reading and its Discontents* (Berkeley: University of California Press, 1988)

Steven W. May, *The Elizabethan Courtier Poets: The Poems and Their Contexts* (Columbia, Missouri: University of Missouri Press, 1991)

Nancy Mayberry, 'The controversy over the Immaculate Conception in mediaeval and Renaissance art, literature and society', *Journal of Mediaeval and Renaissance Studies* 21.2 (Fall 1991), pp.207–24

Russell J. Meyer, ' "Fixt in heauens hight": Spenser, Astronomy, and the date of the *Cantos of Mutabilitie*', *Spenser Studies* IV (1983), pp.115–29

Louis Adrian Montrose, 'Celebration and Insinuation: Sir Philip Sidney and the Motives of Elizabethan Courtship', *Renaissance Drama* n.s. 8 (1977), pp.3–35

Louis Adrian Montrose, ' "Eliza, Queene of shepheardes", and the Pastoral of Power', *ELR* 10 (1980), pp.153–82

——, 'The Elizabethan Subject and the Spenserian Text', in *Literary Theory/ Renaissance Texts*, eds Patricia Parker and David Quint (Baltimore and London: Johns Hopkins University Press, 1986), pp.317–31

——, 'Gifts and Reasons: The Contexts of Peele's *Araygnement of Paris*', *ELH* 47 (1980), pp.433–61

——, '*A Midsummer Night's Dream* and the shaping fantasies of Elizabethan culture: gender, power, form', in *Rewriting the Renaissance: the Discourses of Sexual Difference in Early Modern Europe*, eds Margaret W. Ferguson, Maureen Quilligan and Nancy J. Vickers (Chicago: University of Chicago Press, 1986), pp.65–87

——, ' "The perfecte paterne of a Poete": the Poetics of Courtship in *The Shepheardes Calender*', *Texas Studies in Literature and Language* 21.1 (Spring 1979), pp.34–67

——, ' "Shaping Fantasies": Figurations of Gender and Power in Elizabethan Culture', in Stephen Greenblatt, ed., *Representing the English Renaissance*, (Berkeley: University of California Press, 1988), pp.31–64

Steven Mullaney, 'Strange things, gross terms, curious customs: the rehearsal of cultures in the late Renaissance', in *Representing the English Renaissance*, ed. Stephen Greenblatt (Berkeley: University of California Press, 1988), pp.65–92

Margaret Alice Murray, *The Divine King in England* (London: Faber, 1954)

Sir John E. Neale, *Elizabeth I and her Parliaments*, 2 vols (London: Cape, 1953, 1957)

——, *Essays in Elizabethan History* (London: Cape, 1958)

——, *Queen Elizabeth I* (1934; Harmondsworth: Penguin, 1960)

Janet L. Nelson, 'The Lord's anointed and the people's choice: Carolingian royal ritual', in David Cannadine and Simon Price, eds, *Rituals of Royalty: Power and Ceremonial in Traditional Societies* (Cambridge: Cambridge University Press, 1987), pp.137–80

The New Catholic Encyclopedia (New York: McGraw-Hill, 1967)

David G.E. Norbrook (*Panegyric of the Monarch and its Social Context under Elizabeth I and James I* (unpublished Oxford University D.Phil. thesis, 1978)

——, *Poetry and Politics in the English Renaissance* (London: Routledge, 1984)

Walter Oakeshott, *The Queen and the Poet* (London: Faber, 1960)

Michael O'Connell, 'The Idolatrous Eye: Iconoclasm, Anti-theatricalism, and the Image of the Elizabethan Theater', *ELH* 52.2 (Summer 1985), pp.279–310

Freeman M. O'Donoghue, *A Descriptive and Classified Catalogue of Portraits of Queen Elizabeth* (London: Bernard Quaritch, 1894)

Julia O'Faolain and Lauro Martines, eds, *Not in God's Image: Women in History* (London: Virago, 1979)

Richard Ormond, ed., *The National Portrait Gallery In Colour*, introd. John Hayes (London: Studio Vista – Cassell, 1979)

The Oxford Dictionary of Quotations, 3rd edn (Oxford: Oxford University Press, 1979)

Lewis J. Owen, 'Mutable in eternity: Spenser's despair and the multiple forms of Mutabilitie', *Journal of Mediaeval and Renaissance Studies* 2 (1972), pp.49–68

F.M. Padelford, 'The *Cantos of Mutabilitie*: Further considerations bearing on the date', *Proceedings of the Modern Language Association* 45 (1930), pp.704–11

James Emerson Phillips, *Images of a Queen: Mary Stuart in Sixteenth-Century Literature* (Berkeley: University of California Press, 1964)

Simon Price, *Rituals and Power: The Roman Imperial Cult in Asia Minor* (Cambridge: Cambridge University Press, 1984)

Ricardo J. Quinones, *The Renaissance Discovery of Time* (Cambridge, Mass.: Harvard University Press, 1972)

David Quint, *Origin and Originality in Renaissance Literature: Versions of the Source* (New Haven: Yale University Press, 1983)

Ronald A. Rebholz, *The Life of Fulke Greville, First Lord Brooke* (Oxford: Clarendon, 1971)

Adrienne Rich, *On Lies, Secrets and Silence: Selected Prose 1966–78* (London: Virago, 1980)

Alan Richardson and John Bowden, eds, *A New Dictionary of Christian Theology* (London: SCM Press, 1983)

Thomas P. Roche, *The Kindly Flame: A Study of the Third and Fourth Books of Spenser's 'Faerie Queene'* (Princeton: Princeton University Press, 1964)

M.J. Rodríguez-Salgado et al., *Armada 1588–1988* (Harmondsworth: Penguin, 1988)

Eleanor Rosenberg, *Leicester, Patron of Letters* (New York: Columbia University Press, 1955)

Winfried Schleiner, ' "Divina virago": Queen Elizabeth as an Amazon', *Studies in Philology* 75 (1978), pp.163–80

James R. Siemon, *Shakespearean Iconoclasm* (Berkeley: University of California Press, 1985)

Helen Smailes and Duncan Thomson, *The Queen's Image: A Celebration of Mary, Queen of Scots* (Edinburgh: Scottish National Portrait Gallery, 1987)

Peter Stallybrass, 'Patriarchal Territories: The Body Enclosed', in *Rewriting the Renaissance: the Discourses of Sexual Difference in Early Modern Europe*, eds Margaret W. Ferguson, Maureen Quilligan and Nancy J. Vickers (Chicago: University of Chicago Press, 1986), pp.123–42

Roy Strong, *The Cult of Elizabeth: Elizabethan Portraiture and Pageantry* (London: Thames & Hudson, 1977)

——, *The English Icon: Elizabethan and Jacobean Portraiture* (London: Routledge, 1969)

——, *Gloriana: The Portraits of Queen Elizabeth I* (London: Thames & Hudson, 1987).

——, *Portraits of Queen Elizabeth I* (Oxford: Clarendon, 1963)

Frances Teague, 'Queen Elizabeth in her Speeches', *Gloriana's Face: Women, Public and Private, in the English Renaissance*, eds S.P. Cerasano and Marion Wynne-Davies (Hemel Hempstead: Harvester, 1992), pp.63–78

Leonard Tennenhouse, *Power on Display; The Politics of Shakespeare's Genres* (New York: Methuen, 1986)

Keith Thomas, 'From edification to entertainment: oral tradition and the printed word in early modern England', *Times Literary Supplement*, 23.8.91, pp.5–6

Keith Thomas, *Religion and the Decline of Magic* (London: Weidenfeld, 1971)

E.M.W. Tillyard, *The Elizabethan World Picture* (London: Chatto, 1943)

A. Vacant and E. Mangenot, *Dictionnaire de Théologie Catholique* (Paris: Letouzey & Avé, 1908)

Marina Warner, *Alone of All her Sex: The Myth and the Cult of the Virgin Mary* (1976; London: Pan-Picador, 1985)

——, *Monuments and Maidens: The Allegory of the Female Form* (London: Weidenfeld, 1985)

Robin Headlam Wells, *Spenser's 'Faerie Queene' and the Cult of Elizabeth* (London: Croom Helm, 1983)

Penry Williams, 'Court and Polity under Elizabeth I', *Bulletin of the John Rylands Library of Manchester* 65.2 (Spring 1983), pp.259–86

Elkin Calhoun Wilson, *England's Eliza*, Harvard Studies in English vol.XX (1939; New York: Octagon, 1966)

Jean Wilson, *Entertainments for Elizabeth I* (Woodbridge: D.S. Brewer, 1980)

Frances A. Yates, *Astraea: the imperial theme in the sixteenth century* (London: Routledge, 1975)

——, 'Queen Elizabeth as Astraea', *Journal of the Warburg and Courtauld Institutes*, X (1947), pp.27–82

Index